THE
DIVINE
IMAGE

The Life of Devotion to Holy Laws and Virtues
Leading to the Divine-Image Consciousness

Jonathan Murro

ANN REE COLTON FOUNDATION
336 West Colorado Street
Post Office Box 2057
Glendale, California 91209

10/94

First Edition

ISBN: 0-917189-08-6

Library of Congress Catalog Card Number: 89-081537

For information regarding the writings and teachings
of Ann Ree Colton and Jonathan Murro,
write:

Ann Ree Colton Foundation
336 West Colorado Street
Post Office Box 2057
Glendale, California 91209-2057
Telephone: (818) 244-0113

Printed in the United States of America

DEDICATED

TO

ALL WHO BEHOLD

THE

IMAGE OF GOD

IN

THEIR FELLOW MAN

My gratitude to God for all
Teachers of Truth
anointed by His Spirit.
Gratitude for my Beloved Teacher,
Ann Ree Colton, for her love, wisdom,
patience and beauty of soul.

CONTENTS

PART I

vii

PART II

PART III

PART VI

PART I

And God said, Let us make man in our image, after our likeness.   —Genesis 1:26

For God created man incorruptible, and to the image of His own likeness He made him.   —Apocrypha

We moulded man into a most noble image.   —Koran

The syllable OM is verily thine image. Through this syllable thou mayest be attained.   —Upanishads

Establish the truth in your mind, for the truth is the image of the eternal; it portrays the immutable; it reveals the everlasting; the truth gives into mortals the boon of immortality.   —Buddha

But we all, with open face beholding as in a glass the glory of the Lord, are changed into the same image from glory to glory even as by the Spirit of the Lord.   —Saint Paul

Think of it! I gifted you with my image and likeness. And when you lost the life of grace through sin, to restore it to you I united with you, hiding it in your humanity. I had made you in my image; now I took your image by assuming a human form.   —Saint Catherine of Siena

An image seeks a living object, and a copy can only be formed from a model. Either man models himself on the god of his own invention, or the true and living God moulds the human form into His Image.   —Dietrich Bonhoeffer

We are made in His image, but we have somehow forgotten that truth. We have succumbed to the delusion that we are mortal beings, and we must sunder the veil of that delusion with the dagger of wisdom.

—Paramahansa Yogananda

Each one in the earth is eternal, swimming in universal love, a holy vehicle of light expressing the Image of God in him.   —Ann Ree Colton

THE IMAGE OF GOD

So God created man in his own image, in the image of God created He him; male and female created He them.

—Genesis 1:27

Wherever there is Life, there is God's Image and Grace.

—Ann Ree Colton

THE ULTIMATE REALITY

The Image of God is the most Beautiful Truth in the Universe.

The Image of God is the Ultimate Reality; it is the key to union with the Spirit of God within All Creation. To contemplate the Image of God is to contemplate the Cosmos with its myriad Stars and Galaxies. To contemplate the Image of God is to contemplate the Godhead in the core of man's being. These inspiring contemplations lead to the attaining of *the Divine-Image Consciousness.*

The Image of God within one's being is his link with the Spirit of God within all souls in the world, all Holy Presences in the Inner Kingdom, and all creations in the star-filled Universe. Unenlightened individuals absorbed with their own pleasures and desires are totally unaware of the Image of God within themselves and within others. The first signs of spiritual maturity and sensitivity are revealed through one's desire to reverence human life and to preserve the Word of God. This inspired attitude leads to the realization that life is holy, and that man, being imaged in the Likeness of God, is a sacred creation.

The Image of God is an *Eternal* Image. The immoral and barbaric attitudes of many persons in modern times reveal the absence of key virtues from their emotions and minds. Drug-addiction, abortion, child abuse, perversion, immorality, violence, war — all indicate that important virtues are missing from the consciousness minds and hearts of multitudes of individuals. In time, God will provide all virtues and soul-powers to each of His children. This will occur through His Eternal Image.

The Solar System in which mankind dwells requires that each person evolve from the darkness of unenlightenment to the light of Enlightenment. *Learning* is the purpose for each life one lives on earth; through the Principle of Trial and Error, he is gathering the fruits of wisdom. As one evolves from life to life, age to age, the knowledge gained is indelibly recorded in his soul's eternal memory.

For the teachable, God provides Teachers. For the unteachable, God provides repetitive lives until important lessons are learned. One who expresses a love for sacred truths evolves an inspired intuition, a discerning conscience and a sense of logic provided by the Image of God.

Self-love, prejudice and egotism are major obstacles to one's attaining a consciousness at one with all persons in the world. To think that one is superior to any other person or that his race and religion are superior to all other races and religions indicates that he has yet to unite with the *Omnipresence* of God Whose Image is in every living soul.

An enlightened individual *anointed* by the Spirit of God is one with all souls on earth and all creations in the Cosmos.

Through the Divine-Image Consciousness, he feels no separation from any living being on earth or in Heaven.

It is impossible to harm or destroy a human being after one attains the Divine-Image Consciousness. It is impossible for him to criticize or judge other persons because he knows that each individual is expressing a *degree* of Image-of-God development. From the Prodigal-Son states of consciousness to the Spiritually-Illumined states of consciousness, all persons breathing the breath of life are expressing various stages of Image-of-God evolution.

In the early stages of Image-of-God progression, one's senses are undisciplined — and he embraces the pleasure principle. If covetous, he will lie, cheat or kill in order to make his own life more comfortable. If a number of covetous souls are in a race or nation, they will feel justified in taking human life to further their own desires. Such persons are far from the Divine-Image Consciousness — however, they are expressing their particularized level of Image-of-God development through the budding forth of their senses, emotions and minds.

"The gift of God is eternal life." (Romans 6:28) The senses, emotions and mind represent degrees of energy provided by the Spirit of God. Each person is given the Gift of Eternal Life to learn how to work *with* God in the ethical and noble expression of all energy-processes.

As one evolves over the ages, his senses, emotions and mind become more disciplined. In this, his former obsession with *self* is replaced by humility, compassion and other beautiful virtues that inspire a loving concern for others.

Each virtue is an energy. The Image-of-God Consciousness consists of the radiating energies of holy virtues. When one approaches the Path of Virtue, he begins to identify with the enlightened teachings and attitudes of the Saints and the Great-Soul Teachers of the world. Those who strive to emulate the virtues of the Lord Jesus are following the example of One who expressed with perfection the Divine-Image Consciousness. *"I am the way, the truth and the life."* (St. John 14:6)

> *For God created man for immortality, And made him the image of His own eternity.*
>
> —Apocrypha

> *God in us is that Image Perfect. The Image of God seeks in His Spirit to create through us. Our true power in this earth is to create, to build and to bring this eternity system in which we live into perfection.*
>
> —Ann Ree Colton

NEWNESS OF LIFE

> *Ye have put off the old man with his deeds; And have put on the new man, which is renewed in knowledge after the image of him that created him.*
>
> —Colossians 3:10

When one sins, he sends shock waves to the Image of God in the core of his being. Sins registered upon the Image of God adversely affect the genes and the chromosomes. The penalties for the sins then are exacted through one or more energy-systems in the body. These include the immune system, the nervous system, the reproduction system, the lymph system, the hormone system, the glandular system, the respiratory system, the cellular system and other bodily processes.

A sin is a genetic curse. As long as sins remain unconfessed, their destructiveness is passed on to one's offspring through the genes and the chromosomes. This affects one or more energy-systems in the bodies, emotions and minds of his children "unto the third and fourth generation." (Exodus 20:5) The degrees of the weaknesses or afflictions and the capacity for learning are also affected by the unconfessed sins registered in the blood, the genes, the chromosomes, the soul's record and the Divine Image.

The widespread disobedience of the masses toward Scriptural Decrees is resulting in the many problems, ills and woes of the human spirit. However, mankind will not experience total destruction through the crushing weight of unconfessed sins from generation to generation because of *the Image of God*.

> *For I have not spoken of myself; but the Father which sent me, he gave me a commandment, what I should say, and what I should speak. And I know that his commandment is life everlasting: whatsoever I speak therefore, even as the Father said unto me, so I speak.*
> —St. John 12:49,50

It is inevitable that the Image of God will be fulfilled in the soul and life of each person, for this mighty Image works with the Laws governing *Life Everlasting*. Each Law of God, shaping and molding man in the Divine Image, has checks and balances that keep mankind at one with Cosmos Creation. Even though a person may destroy himself through his own sins, he will find endless opportunities for rectification through the Eternal Law of Reincarnation.

The Image of God works through the Law of Reincarnation to manifest its numerous facets and attributes. When a prodigal son turns to his Heavenly Father, he begins to activate the awesome energies of the Divine Image — and he is made *new*.

The Image-of-God energies are the most powerful energies in the Universe. Therefore, regardless of one's sins of omission and commission throughout many lifetimes, he can experience the newness of life and being through sincere repentance, honest confession, sacrificial penance, honorable

restitution, selfless service to others, and dedicated observance of all Scriptural Statutes.

> *And be renewed in the spirit of your mind; And*
> *that ye put on the new man, which after God is cre-*
> *ated in righteousness and true holiness.*
> —Ephesians 4:23,24

Jesus of Nazareth worked with Image-of-God energies.
While on earth, He manifested instantaneous healings, exorcisms and other miracles through His knowledge of the powerful transformation-energies of the Image of God within the
soul of *every* person. For a cripple or a leper to be restored to
perfect health in a moment of time through Jesus' Intercession testifies to the presence and power of the Image of God
and its restoration and normalization of all energy-systems
and bodily processes.

To work with the Lord Jesus through faith and love is to
come under the blessings of the Image of God, which makes
all things *new.* *"Therefore, if any man be in Christ, he is a*
new creature: old things are passed away; behold, all things
are become new." (2 Corinthians 5:17)

Through the sacred Gift of *Volition*, one can choose to remain in a state of unrestrained sinning. However, through
the Image of God in the core of his being, healing, mercy,
forgiveness and newness of life are *eternally* present through
the reverent use of volition.

Each day all persons are learning important lessons related
to volition. Through volition, one can walk the path of unrighteousness or the Path of Righteousness. The transformation of volition from unrighteousness to righteousness can
occur after thousands of lifetimes or in a moment of time.

Whereas sins produce poisons and toxins harmful to one's
health and well-being, the Image of God produces healing
essences and energies that prosper health and well-being.
The complex energy-systems in one's physical, emotional

and mental bodies are miraculously harmonized and synchronized through Divine-Image energies. This cardinal truth is at the heart of all miraculous healings and spiritual transformations.

As long as one misuses the Gift of Volition, he remains a victim of the unconfessed sins of his ancestors, parents and past lives. The moment he resolves to use the Gift of Volition in service to God and his fellow man, he begins to receive the newness-of-life healings, quickenings and enlightenments through the Light of the Christ and the Image of God.

> *As the earth spins, so does the soul vibrate and move, throwing off the old and taking on the new as creation.*
>
> —Ann Ree Colton

> *And he that sat upon the throne said, Behold, I make all things new.*
>
> —Revelation 21:5

UNIQUENESS

> *The soul works without ceasing to protect the very special uniqueness of each one.*
>
> —Ann Ree Colton

"Each star differeth from another star in glory." (1 Corinthians 15:41) Even as each star differs from another star in glory, so does each soul differ from another soul in uniqueness. The Glory of God in each soul differs from the Glory of God in other souls.

Through His Image, God blesses each of His children with rare and priceless gifts and graces that constitute sacred uniqueness. The more one unites with his soul and the Image of God, the more he expresses this uniqueness.

A Teacher of the higher life seeks to open each student to

the uniqueness that God has sealed into the student's soul through His Image. The joys of the higher life begin when this sacred uniqueness begins to manifest through sanctified virtues, creative-spiritual gifts, holy inspirations, and a soul-radiance reflecting the Beauty and Glory of God within His Image.

The uniqueness that God has sealed into each soul through His Image is indescribably beautiful, deeply profound, and richly rewarding. He who dares to unite with this dynamic uniqueness has tapped the Glory of God's Image in the core of his being.

The diverse miracles of Jesus testify to the uniqueness of the Image of God in Him and its freedom to manifest words of beauty and truth; healings of all manners of diseases and afflictions; exorcisms of all kinds of devils and demons; the raising of the dead; and the overcoming of death through His Resurrection and Ascension.

The Image-of-God uniqueness in Jesus was revealed through His words, works and life. So do all who follow His example learn of the Image-of-God uniqueness in their own beings and express it selflessly, reverently, joyfully in service to the Lord of Lords, the King of Kings.

Each race, nation and religion expresses a sacred uniqueness through the composite souls in the race, nation or religion. Each race, nation and religion is making its contribution toward the evolution of man in the Image of God. The closer a race, nation or religion is to God, the more its uniqueness is expressed through creative works, charitable acts and spiritual freedoms.

Uniqueness through the Divine Image is one's Spiritual Birthright. Those who earn this precious Birthright are in close communion with the Host of Heaven blessing the world from the Kingdom of God. *"But seek ye first the Kingdom of God, and his righteousness; and all these things shall be added unto you."* (St. Matthew 6:33)

All gifts of the soul are projected from the Image of God. These diverse gifts endow one with a spiritual individuality and creative versatility. As he applies devotional worship-procedures each day with love for God, the gifts of his soul flower forth.

The holy inspirations that flow into one's heart and mind through the Spirit of God are unique. Art, music, writing, teaching, healing, and all other spiritual-creative expressions of the soul contain the Image-of-God blessings of uniqueness.

Persons who seek to imitate their parents and ancestors have yet to unite with their spiritual-grace uniqueness through the soul and the Image of God. One who desires to emulate the Saints and the Lord Jesus experiences the Image-of-God quickenings that manifest his uniqueness through a spectrum of diverse skills.

When a devotee-initiate unites with the Living Christ through holy works and enlightened attitudes, the dimensional powers of his soul manifest as *apostolic gifts*. Apostolic gifts received through the soul and the Image of God express unique qualities and creative versatilities that signify oneness with God and Christ. The more one unites with the Kingdom of God, the more his soul and the Divine Image are free to bless the world through timely prophecies, realizations, revelations and pure creations.

Each Hierarch or Great Being in the Constellations of Cosmos has a vital uniqueness through the Image of God. The Hierarchs work together with love and harmony in the creation of Stars and Galaxies. When a devotee of the Lord emulates Jesus, his latent hierarchy nature* comes forth through Image-of-God quickenings — and he becomes a protégé of the Hierarchs blessing the world through Constellation energies. These starry energies stimulate and saturate his being

---

*Ann Ree Colton introduced the term *hierarchy nature* and many other terminologies contained in this volume.

with Cosmos revelations that contribute to the uniqueness of his works on earth as a servant of God.

When the Image-of-God energies within one's being fuse with the Image-of-God energies in the Cosmos, the Divine Marriage occurs—and the uniqueness of myriad blessings of Grace and Truth flows through his heart, mind and soul.

The very special uniqueness or signature of the master craftsman is supported by an invisible asset inherited from all craftsmen who have gone before him. The motives of a true craftsman are energized by a godly vitality.

When one creates something uniquely individualistic or brings forth a value hitherto unexperienced by man, he may be said to be beginning Self-Genesis.

—Ann Ree Colton

IMAGE-OF-GOD EVOLUTIONARY PROGRESSIONS

Is it not written in your law, I said, Ye are gods.
—St. John 10:34

Every living soul—from those expressing the prodigal-son nature on earth to the greatest Hierarchs in the far reaches of the Universe—represents a stage in the evolutionary progressions of the Image of God. The Hierarchs, serving the Creator throughout the Cosmos, are expressing the Divine Image on exalted levels of attainment on the Path of Eternal Life.

HIERARCHS
The Mighty Beings in the Universe working with
God in the Creation of Stars and Galaxies.

PROTÉGÉS OF THE HIERARCHS
Illumined Souls expressing high degrees of the
Image of the Creator.

SAINTS
Christlike attitudes and behavior.

PROTÉGÉS OF THE SAINTS
Devotion to God and His Commandments
through Vows. The beginning of the birth of
the divine nature.

PENITENTS
Turning one's face toward the Face of God through
repentance, confession, contrition, penance and
restitution.

PRODIGAL-SON STATES OF CONSCIOUSNESS
Lower Nature.

2

THE IMAGE OF CHRIST

And we know that all things work together for good to them that love God, to them who are the called according to his purpose. For whom he did foreknow, he also did predestinate to be conformed to the image of his Son, that he might be the firstborn among many brethren.

—Romans 8:28,29

PROTÉGÉS OF THE SAINTS

A clean conscience enables one to see the Image of God in all others and in all things. All Saints and Sages have attained the pure white stone and wear the garment of spirituality through the birth to conscience.

—Ann Ree Colton

A Saint is a Saint because of his or her ability to see each person as a sacred creation being imaged in God's Likeness. This holy attitude inspires patience, love, compassion, and other saintly virtues. Through virtues and conscience, a Saint remains in a high State of Grace untouched by the callousness, cruelties and persecutions directed against him by the unenlightened and the unrighteous.

14

An enlightened Teacher's task is to unite each responsive student with the reality of the Image of God as a Universal Truth. Students who respond to this sacred instruction become *protégés* of the Saints.

Saints and their protégés know that every sin-laden individual who has fallen from God's Grace may be forgiven, healed and redeemed through the Divine Image in the core of his being. The Image of God is an Eternal Door to freedom that begins to open with the first sincere prayer of repentance and the first honest confession.

Saints and their protégés with selfless hearts and compassionate minds are ever mindful of behaving like Jesus during times of trial, crisis and persecution. Such personages are committed to living and teaching the Commandments of Love and the Sermon-on-the-Mount Principles and Ethics. By serving their Lord as Teachers of Truth, they are heeding His directive: *"Feed my sheep."* (St. John 21:16)

> *Man need not be loveless, for he is loved; of all creatures under God, no one is so loved as man. Imaged by the Father, each one is a love-reflection center into which God would come to clarify His Image. The Angels devoted to man's rise love him with unwavering, upholding love. The Saints, knowing their own times in the earth in not feeling loved, love him; they seek to turn his heart toward all of the devoting, protecting sources of bounteous love, particularly toward the Lord of Love.*
>
> — Ann Ree Colton

". . . we shall be like Him." (1 John 3:2) A devotee who aspires to fulfill the Image of God must first fulfill the Image of Christ. He must become *like* Jesus through the expression of enlightened attitudes and holy virtues. His desire to heal others, teach them the Scriptural Word, and glorify the

Creator through words and works reveals that he is expressing a high degree of the Image of Christ.

The Image of Christ brings one to the knowledge and manifestation of the Image of God. *Union with the Image of Christ produces the Christ Consciousness. Union with the Image of God through the Christ Consciousness produces the Divine-Image Consciousness.*

The Christ Consciousness is the result of oneness with the Presence of Jesus within His Teachings and within the Sacrament of Communion. Armored with meekness, gentleness, selflessness, purity in motives, a love for righteousness and truth, a devoted follower of Jesus is fortified by the Christ Consciousness on his pilgrimage toward God-Realization.

When Jesus of Nazareth walked the earth, He sealed into the world the knowledge of the Commandments, Principles and Virtues that lead to the Kingdom of God. Through His flawless example, Jesus revealed the spiritual nobility of a soul totally committed to God through the expression of Image-of-God virtues.

> *The Son is the living, essential, and precisely similar Image of the invisible God, bearing the entire Father within Himself, equal to Him in all things, except that He is begotten by Him, the begetter. It is the Nature of the Father to cause; the Son is the effect. The Father does not proceed from the Son, but the Son from the Father. The Father who begets is what He is because of His Son, though not in a second place after Him.*
>
> —Saint John of Damascus

Individuals who desire to emulate the Lord Jesus have covenanted in their souls to fulfill the Image of Christ. The more their virtues and attitudes become Christlike, the more they are able to represent God and Jesus in the world as true ambassadors and apostles.

The Saints at one with Jesus through love are also one with God through love. Oneness with the Image of Christ brings oneness with the Image of God. *"I and my Father are one."* (St. John 10:30)

Jesus expressed a versatile range of supernatural gifts and miracle powers. As a devotee moves closer to God through humility, selflessness, compassion and love, he begins to express a creative-spiritual versatility; wisdom moves from his lips; and his prayers and ministering in Jesus' Name manifest miracles. These virtues and gifts are clear evidences that he is fulfilling the Image of Christ.

Through the Son of God, we come close to seeing our true Image of perfection.

— Ann Ree Colton

By being transformed into His Image, we are enabled to model our lives on His. How at last deeds are performed and life is lived in single minded discipleship in the Image of Christ and His words find unquestioning obedience. We pay no attention to our own lives or the new image which we bear, for then we should at once have forfeited it, since it is only to serve as a mirror for the Image of Christ on whom our gaze is fixed. The disciple looks solely at his Master. But when a man follows Jesus Christ and bears the image of the incarnate, crucified and risen Lord when he has become the Image of God we may at last say that he has been called to be the "imitator of God." The follower of Jesus is the imitator of God. "Be ye therefore imitators of God, as beloved children." (Ephesians 5:1)

— Dietrich Bonhoeffer*

---

*From *The Cost of Discipleship* by Dietrich Bonhoeffer. Copyright © 1959 by S C M Press, Ltd. Reprinted with permission of Macmillan Publishing Company.

THE EYE AND THE IMAGE

> *You must close the eyes and waken in yourself that other power of vision, the birthright of all, but which few turn to use.*
>
> — Plotinus

> *I am the Source of everything; from Me all creation emerges . . . Behold the unified worlds as My Cosmic Body . . . But thou canst not see Me with mortal eyes. Therefore, I give thee sight divine.*
>
> — Bhagavad Gita

Love is a mighty Commandment of Creation and Illumination.

Love enables a truth-seeker to transcend the Sea of Illusion and to establish a sacred oneness with God.

Love shepherds one to the Inner Cores of Divine Grace within his being.

Love cleanses the genes and the chromosomes through the supernatural energies of the Christ.

Love builds the spiritual insulation that protects a devotee from Satan's hypnotic seductions.

Love opens the eyes to the beauty and eternality of the Image of God.

Father, I pray to see Thy Image in each of thy children.

A devotee of the Lord progresses on the Spiritual Path only to the degree that he sees and loves the Image of God in every living soul. All persons in his life are providing numerous opportunities for him to evolve the ability to see and to love the Image of God in them. It is this love for the Image of God in others that produces the Divine-Image Consciousness.

"Love your enemies." (St. Matthew 5:44) To love one's enemies is to bless the Image of God in them. To love the

Image of God in one's enemies is to overcome any tendency to do bodily harm to another or to express feelings of anger, animosity, bitterness and unforgiveness. To apply the wisdom of Jesus' teachings of harmlessness, forgiveness, peacemaking and love is to hasten the day when the Divine-Image Consciousness will be worn as a Crown of Enlightenment.

If a husband and wife reverence the Image of God in each other, their marriage is blessed by the Peace and Providence of God. A father, mother and child who cherish one another as sacred creations being imaged in the Likeness of God experience the harmony, love and joy of a holy relationship.

When one serves the Image of God in others, he is never absent from Sacred Inspirations and Divine Guidance, and he always knows that he is loved.

To serve the Divine Image in one's fellow man is to fulfill the spirit of ministering as a dedicated servant of God. The spiritual life begins the moment a seeker after truth begins to see and to serve the Image of God in all souls.

When one sees the Image of God in every soul, he transcends the dark energies in the world that press heavily upon men. He experiences each day the exalted state of *Transcendence Grace*. Priceless rewards, gifts and inheritances illuminate his heart and mind with soul-beauty and Divine-Image beauty.

To see the Image of God in others as a way of life requires the supernatural help of God, the Christ, the Angels and the Saints. The ability to see the Image of God in all persons is necessary before one can attain the Transcendence Grace of the Divine-Image Consciousness.

We are imaged in God. We are imaged to be loving to one another, because God is Love. We are imaged in God to have a mind to create and to always be in the realm of new discoveries.
— Ann Ree Colton

"Blessed are the pure in heart: for they shall see God." (St. Matthew 5:8) Purity in heart denotes pure love and pure motives. This high degree of purity enables one to behold the Image of God in the souls of all persons.

The eye determines how one looks upon life. If the heart's love fills his being, his eyes are eyes of love and compassion, blessing all who come before his gaze. If the heart's love is impure, his eyes are filled with lust, anger, greed, possessiveness, covetousness and other negative seeing.

Through pure love, one who beholds the Divine Image in his fellow man knows him to be an Eternal Creation of the Living God. Through hate, one's eyes are blind to the Image of God in his fellow man. Possessive love causes a person to see his loved ones as possessions rather than as children of God to be loved and cherished.

Purity in heart comes from a cleansed subconsciousness, thereby enabling the eye to see true. A subconsciousness filled with guilts, fears and doubts contaminates the purity of the heart — and the eye becomes a faulty perceiver of reality.

The sight is directly linked with the subconsciousness and the consciousness. The more darkness is in the subconsciousness, the more the consciousness becomes a clouded instrument for perception. Through the cleansing and purging of the subconsciousness through spiritual disciplines, the consciousness mind makes a sacred linking with the heart's pure love — and the eye, in turn, becomes a blessed instrument for perception. The Image of God may then be seen clearly in its beauty and eternality.

God gives one divine eyes; and only then can one behold Him. God gave Arjuna divine eyes so that he might see His Universal Form.

— Ramakrishna

No physical eye can totally record and retain what is seen by the transcendental Divine Eye. Only the tran-

scendental eye of the soul can reveal itself for the Self
as it exists forevermore. The Self is an embodiment and
deathless particle of God.

The gift of inner sight holds and contains the promise
of infinite illumination.

The physical eyes are orifice portals for the third eye
when one is spiritually evolved. The two eyes act in dual
fashion to serve the third or inner eye situated within
the pineal gland.

Seership of the spiritual eye or divine eye is developed
over the ages. The portal of the divine eye is centered
between the eyebrows where the upper portion of the
nose joins the forehead.

— Ann Ree Colton

To see the Image of God as a Universal Constant in all
Stars, Galaxies and Souls requires a pure heart. To see the
Moon, the Sun and the Planets as manifestations of God's
Love creating Man in His Image and Likeness requires a
pure heart.

To see every man and woman as a child of God in the
process of being created in His Image requires a pure heart.
The desire to bless every individual on earth through the
heart's unconditional love is the desire of the eye at one with
the soul and the Divine Image.

The eyes are the most powerful instruments for
blessing or for cursing.

One's attitudes toward money and sex are based upon
either pure or impure motives. The heart and the eye may
conjoin to steal, cheat and covet; or they may become blended
instruments for charitable, selfless, healing works.

When a person is possessed by evil, impure and unclean
spirits, his eyes are not his own eyes — for the eyes of the dark
spirits are looking at others from the body they are possess-

ing. When one is exorcised of the demons and the devils of the Antichrist, his eyes are the first indicators of his releasement from a living hell. Clear, happy eyes denote the success of the exorcism through the Christ Light.

Furtive eyes cannot look directly into the eyes of others. A guilty conscience produces furtive eyes. The confession to God of one's sins is immediately reflected in the steadiness and peacefulness of his gaze.

When a devotee becomes one with God through love, his eye and the Eye of God become one. Peace with one's self and with God through a deep love for His Laws and Commandments radiates through the eyes. To love all Scriptural Statutes enables one to look into the Face of Jesus and the Face of God. Their Eyes become the eyes of the devotee, for he is looking at his fellow man through the divine virtues of compassion, love and the Image-of-God Consciousness.

> *The eye by which I see God is the same as the eye by which God sees me. My eye and God's eye are one and the same.*
>
> *The soul has two eyes—one looking inwards and the other outwards. It is the inner eye of the soul that looks into essence and takes being directly from God.*
>
> —Meister Eckhart

Persons who reject sacred instruction and the Love-Commandments perceive life through the eyes of the genes. They look upon their fellow man with the same prejudices, jealousies and rivalries as did unenlightened parents and ancestors.

The eye is the organ for casting hypnotic spells; or, through the spirit of blessing the Image of God in others, awakening them from hypnotic spells and inspiring them to become their true selves at one with the Father.

When a devotee sees God through purity in heart, he transcends the illusionary world of Maya* and earns a place at the Lord's Table, where he partakes of an unceasing Feast of Grace and Truth.

When sacramental meditation is based upon love for God and His Laws, love for one's fellow man and love for the Universe, the Christ opens his Divine-Eye clairvoyant perception. Extrasensory perception is a pure gift of the soul only when there is pure love in the heart. ESP, when used with impure motives, can be a harmful instrument for exploitation, cunning and destruction.

Love is the highest use of the Creation Principle. All anti-love energies are part of the Destroying Principle. The blessings sent forth from eyes of love add Creation-energies to the Universe. Eyes of anger send forth destructive energies damaging to others and to one's self. Thus, each moment of the day and the night the eyes may be contributing to Creation through love and compassion or to Destruction through anger and hate.

"The light of the body is the eye: if therefore thine eye be single, thy whole body shall be full of light. But if thine eye be evil thy whole body shall be full of darkness." (St. Matthew 6:23) One should pray to attain the eye single—the eye of love; for, in so doing, his entire body and being will be filled with the Immortal Light of the Soul, the Eternal Light of the Higher Self, the Supernatural Light of the Christ and the Transcendental Light of God.

> *There is an eye of the soul . . . which is more precious by far than 10,000 bodily eyes, for by it alone is truth seen.*
>
> —Plato

---

*Maya is a Sanskrit word meaning *illusion*.

God is Light, not such as these eyes see, but as the heart seeth, when thou hearest, 'He is Truth.'
      —Saint Augustine

He who is Christ is our Liberator. He is the Light and Liberator of this small planet. As a Magnet in the Eye of God, the Christ Spirit draws us into the Cosmic and the Cosmos virtue-expansions.
      —Ann Ree Colton

3

FROM DARKNESS TO LIGHT

Lead me from the unreal to the real!
Lead me from darkness to light!
Lead me from death to immortality!
— Upanishads

Allah is the Patron of the faithful. He leads them from darkness to light.
— Koran

Unto the upright there ariseth light in the darkness.
— Psalm 112:4

THE LADDER OF ETERNAL LIFE

And the earth was without form and void; and darkness was upon the face of the deep. And the spirit of God moved upon the face of the waters. And God said, Let there be light: and there was light.
— Genesis 1:2,3

God creates a void and then impregnates it with His Spirit. His impregnating Spirit contains all energies and elements necessary for a Star or a Galaxy to make the transition from darkness to light. From darkness to light is the theme of Creation throughout the Universe.

On the planet Earth, the soul of man has covenanted with God to experience the evolutionary energy-processes leading from darkness to light. All *anti-virtues* represent darkness; all *virtues* represent light. Man, in moving from darkness to light, is evolving from anti-virtues to virtues. Each step of progress leading from anti-virtue darkness to virtue-light is a rung on the Ladder of Eternal Life.

Darkness is a womblike state. From the darkness of the womb, a child is born to a world of light-energies. These light-energies increase in brightness as one learns to work with them. Ignorance is a womblike state of darkness; Illumination is a state of increasing light in heart, mind and soul.

Persons involved in the energy-process of darkness through anti-virtues are learning important lessons on their levels of expression and consciousness. As they evolve to higher rungs on the Ladder of Eternal Life, their consciousness minds begin to desire the expression of virtues. This desire is a monumental attainment in the soul's evolutionary quest for oneness with God through virtue-light.

Anti-virtues represent unprocessed energies. Through the Cycles of the Moon and the Sun over the ages, each individual on earth is learning how to process the darkness of anti-virtues into the light of virtues. When one desires to work with God in the transforming of anti-virtue darkness into virtue-light, he becomes a co-creator with Him; he has evolved from the prodigal-son states of consciousness to the higher states of consciousness. Each state of consciousness — from darkness to light, anti-virtue to virtue — moves one closer to the Lord Jesus as the Door to the Divine-Image Consciousness.

The Presence of the Christ Light in the world through the life and ministry of Jesus accelerated the learning-process through which one might evolve more quickly from the darkness of anti-virtues to the light of virtues. Those who are resisting the Christ Light are making a stronger commitment to evil, vice, immorality and unrighteousness; such persons are inviting stern reprovings through the Holy Laws of Karma and Reincarnation. Individuals who are accepting the Christ Light into their lives and beings are experiencing miraculous healings of the anti-virtue darkness in their natures and are making a commitment to express only virtues as their way of life.

The drama of life on earth will witness a widening division between persons committed to unrighteousness and those dedicated to righteousness. Individuals who are using the Gift of Volition to learn important lessons through the darkened energies of anti-virtues are equally important to the planet Earth as those who are using Volition to learn life's lessons through the lighted energies of virtues. The mathematics of God's Laws are always perfect in His Universal Energy-Drama of Creation involving darkness and light.

> *I am the light of the world: he that followeth me shall not walk in darkness, but shall have the light of life.*
>
> —St. John 8:12

TRANSENERGIZATION*

> *The spiritual life is to change negative energy into positive energy. You must replace every negation with positive elan of creation.*
> *The power of transenergizing is through the Christ.*
> —Ann Ree Colton

> *O Lord, come quickly and reign on thy throne, for now oft-times something rises up within me and tries*

Transenergization is a word introduced by Ann Ree Colton.

*to take possession of thy throne; pride, covetousness,
uncleanness and sloth want to be my kings; and then
evil-speaking, anger, hatred and the whole train of vices
join with me in warring against myself and try to reign
over me. I resist them, I cry out against them, and say,
"I have no other king but Christ!" O King of Peace,
come and reign in me, for I will have no king but thee.
Amen.*

—Saint Bernard

When an individual realizes that the Plan of God requires
that he evolve from darkness to light, he may perceive the
Creator's Wisdom in the Energy-Transformation Drama.
Spiritual Illumination occurs as one works with God and
Christ in the changing of the dark energies in his nature and
in the world into light energies.

While one is changing the dark energies of anti-virtues and
sins into light energies, the virtues within the Divine Image
come to birth through increasing quickenings. Each increase
of virtue received through Image-of-God quickenings expands his ability to work more closely with the Creator.

*The progressive stages and states of consciousness leading
to the Divine-Image Consciousness relate to the dual action
of virtues coming to birth through the Image of God and the
transformation of dark energies into energies of light.*

Each individual in the world may work with God and
Christ in the Energy-Transformation Process through which
the atoms in anti-virtues and sins are exploded into the light
of virtues, conscience, logic and love. When one *knowingly*
works with the Creator and His Son, he perceives each negative or dark energy in the world as *potential light*.

The Christ graces the selfless heart and the compassionate
mind with Hierarch-like powers through which darkness may
be transenergized into light. Through increasing love-sensitivities, a devotee gains a glimpse of the work of the Hierarchs
with God in the Creation of the Universe.

Even as man is changing the darkness of anti-virtues and sins into the light of virtues and grace, so are the Hierarchs changing the darkness of Cosmos Voids into the light of Stars and Galaxies. As the Image of God increases its quickening action over the ages, man will become a skillful craftsman in changing dark energies into light in ever-widening ranges of action and understanding.

Man is destined for hierarchy-power greatness through the Image of God in him. The Example and Mediation of Christ Jesus are accelerating the process through which he will become an illumined participant in the Energy-Transformation Drama occurring throughout the Universe.

> *Transenergizing is the Power Divine given to each soul that one may be with God as a builder, a mover of worlds.*
>
> *In the Undersoul, every dark mass of negativity has one penetrable point of energy. When the Esse light penetrates this point, the complete mass is transenergized. The great Masters, seers, healers and the angels use this technique of Holy-Spirit light-energized power with freedom and with knowing.*
>
> — Ann Ree Colton

Even as coal, uranium and plutonium can be processed into energies of light, so can each anti-virtue be transenergized into light. Man is earning increasing virtue-light throughout his numerous lifetimes on earth; the virtue-light gained through experience, struggle, trial and error is recorded in his soul's eternal record as an imperishable asset.

The soul, in its *Covenant* with God before each lifetime on earth, determines the paramount anti-virtue energies that will present themselves for transenergization into virtue-light. The soul's Covenent with God also determines the virtues that will come to birth through the Divine Image.

"Therefore I say unto you, What things soever ye desire, when ye pray, believe that ye receive them, and ye shall have

them." (St. Mark 11:24) When one desires to be healed of anti-virtues and negative attitudes, his *desires*, accompanied by prayer and faith, unite him with the miraculous Healing Power of the Great Physician.

Every anti-virtue, sin, irritation or other negative energy has an atom-core that responds to the explosive power of the Christ Light. This atom-core or point of energy is exploded by the Christ through one's honest confessions and desire to be healed. When a truth-seeker works directly with Jesus, all negative energies identified and confessed to God are immediately exploded into positive energies of light and grace. Even the smallest irritation, when identified by the consciousness mind and confessed to God, sets off a tremendous explosion of grace-energies through the Christ-Light penetration of the atom-core of the irritation.

When an anti-virtue, sin or irritation is identified through self-honesty and confessed to God, its transformed energy becomes an artery of grace to the Godhead. Through the Christ-Light explosions of the atoms in anti-virtues, sins and irritations, a penitent experiences miraculous healings, spiritual transformations of all energy-processes in his being, and draws closer to the Godhead Grace that produces increasing measures of the Divine-Image Consciousness.

Each increase of light in one's being through the Healing Power of the Christ increases the light in the world, the Solar System and the Universe.

> It is the nature of man, while living in the Maya state, to be dissatisfied with the partial. His soul desires, with the passion of the Holy Spirit, to be free within all of the potentials of the Image of God in him. There is a consciousness beyond Maya consciousness; it is a consciousness seated in God, inwardly directed by the Image of God which in its constancy varies not as to the intent of all men for this earth.
>
> —Ann Ree Colton

THE DIVINE NATURE

Grace and peace be multiplied unto you through the knowledge of God, and of Jesus our Lord. According as his divine power hath given unto us all things that pertain unto life and godliness, through the knowledge of him that hath called us to glory and virtue: Whereby are given unto us exceeding great and precious promises: that by these ye might be partakers of the divine nature.
                              —2 Peter 1:2-4

All holy virtues,
  God keep you,
  God, from whom you proceed and come.
                         —Saint Francis of Assisi

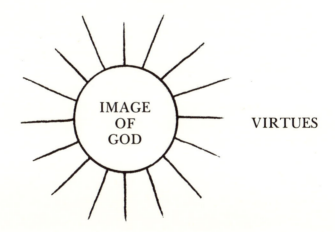

Virtues are rays of holy light proceeding from the Image of God.
Virtues are the blood of the Spirit.

Every aspirant comes to the Lord Jesus with a lower nature and a higher or divine nature. Through his divine nature, he recognizes the Sonship of Christ Jesus as the Messiah and Savior of the world. The overcoming of the lower nature and the increasing of the divine nature assure his progress as a servant of God.

Christlike virtues are one's only passport to the pristine purity of the Inner Kingdom. A God-sent Teacher encourages each student to express the holy virtues of his divine nature. Students who heed their Teacher's instruction come under the powerful blessings and direct guidance of Christ Jesus.

May the Peace of Christ abide in me.
May the Love of Christ abide in me.
May the Joy of Christ abide in me.

It requires superhuman effort and supernatural grace to remain on the Path of the Higher Life. The more the Christ Presence of Peace, Love and Joy abides in a devotee, the more the energies of his life are expressed through the divine nature. The divine nature aligns him with his Higher Self, the Soul's Grace-Record and the Redemption Power of Jesus.

Virtues are the Image of God in action. A person born with beautiful virtues is blessed with a soul's record of many past lives in which his virtues have been earned. Virtues are treasures one bequeaths to himself from life to life.

A devotee who dedicates to express the enlightened attitudes and holy virtues of Jesus comes under the manifold blessings of His miraculous ministrations. His union with the versatility of the Lord of Love is reflected in his versatile expressions of discipleship powers and apostolic gifts.

The Image of Christ is Pure Love.

The spiritual life is a commitment to constancy in love. It is only through the divine nature that one can be constant in love. As long as an aspirant wavers between his lower nature and higher nature, he has yet to attain the constancy in love required by the Commandments of Love: Love of God, Love of Neighbor, and Love of One Another. Through these beautiful Commandments and the virtues expressed in their fulfillment, a follower of Jesus becomes a true servant of God inspired and enlightened by His Holy Spirit.

A devotee becomes an heir of the *Inheritance* through the divine nature. The lower nature is the prodigal-son nature that keeps one from inheriting his Spiritual Birthright. The higher or divine nature receives increasing measures of Grace-Inheritance from the Kingdom of God.

The miraculous transformation from the prodigal or lower nature to the divine nature is experienced during the initiatory process of spiritual quickenings of virtues, conscience and soul-gifts. This wondrous occurrence can be experienced in one lifetime if a devotee applies the wise and powerful Principles of the Lord Jesus and works with his Living Teacher. *"He that receiveth you receiveth me, and he that receiveth me receiveth him that sent me."* (St. Matthew 10:40)

An enlightened Teacher is knowledgeable in the purification stages of the spiritual-birth process. He prepares earnest devotees to courageously meet the fiery trials and purgings that will release them from lower-nature reflexes and manifest the virtues of the divine or Christlike nature. *"Beloved, think it not strange concerning the fiery trial which is to try you, as though some strange thing happened unto you: But rejoice, inasmuch as ye are partakers of Christ's sufferings; that, when his glory shall be revealed, ye may be glad also with exceeding joy."* (1 Peter 4:12,13)

During accelerated initiation, one opens the truth-gaskets of his conscience. In these fiery periods, he literally walks through the furnace of death to old practices and habits of the physical, emotional and mental life. He dies to the lower will and mind through this purging.
— Ann Ree Colton

The lower nature contests the divine nature. This contesting, described in all Sacred Scriptures, is *the Holy War* experienced within one's own being until he is liberated through virtues and love.

> *Where love is not, Satan abides.*
> *Where love is, Christ abides.*

Satan works through the lower nature of man; Christ works through the higher nature. Sins committed through the lower nature cause one to move out of timing with Universal Creation. The dedication to observe the Ethics and Principles of Jesus brings one into perfect timing with Universal Creation.

Satan, *the blocking spirit*, tries to block the birth of virtues and conscience; block faith in God; block the memory of Scriptural Edicts and Ethics; and block the flow of Grace-prosperings through the Spiritual-Birthright Inheritance. The Christ frees a penitent soul from the influences and enticements of the blocking spirit.

The lower nature is easily angered and unforgiving. The divine nature expresses holy equanimity, kindness and forgiveness. The lower nature is ungrateful, egotistical, prideful. The divine nature expresses gratitude, self-honesty and humility. The lower nature is nonreceptive to spiritual gifts. The divine nature expresses spiritual gifts with naturalness in service to God.

"Verily, verily, I say unto thee, Except a man be born again, he cannot see the kingdom of God." (St. Matthew 3:3) To be "born again" is to be born to the divine nature. As long as an aspirant expresses lust, anger, greed, pride, covetousness, procrastination, prejudice or other negative traits, he has not died to his lower nature. As a devotee on the Path dies to his lower nature, he is born to the radiant virtues of the divine nature.

The Christ has the power to change the prodigal-son nature instantly, miraculously, when one proves sincerely ready to apply His "sound doctrine." (2 Timothy 4:3) Those who receive Him are transformed and enlightened in their present lifetimes. Laggard individuals who delight in their egotism and prodigal-son resistances to the Will of God may require numerous lifetimes, ages and eternities before they receive Him.

To embrace the Redeeming and Illuminating Grace of the Christ is to accept God's Gift of Pardon through which the lower nature is miraculously transformed into the divine nature.

The divine nature and the Divine Image are one.

ANTI-VIRTUE ENERGIES OF
THE LOWER NATURE

Adultery
Aggressive, Overly
Agnosticism
Ambivalence
Amorality
Anger
Antisocial
Arrogance
Atheism
Attachment
Avariciousness
Belligerence
Bigotry
Bitterness
Boastfulness
Brutality
Cheating
Competitive, Overly
Constant Complaining
Contemptuousness
Contrariness
Covetousness
Critical-mindedness
Cunning
Cupidity
Cynicism
Deceitfulness
Depression
Despair
Despondence
Disagreeableness
Dishonesty
Disobedience
Disrespect
Egotism
Envy
Evil
Faultfinding
Fear
Fecklessness
Fickleness

Forcefulness
Furtiveness
Gluttony
Gossip
Greed
Harmful Habits
Hate
Haughtiness
Hostility
Hypocrisy
Impatience
Impracticality
Inconsideration
Infidelity
Ingratitude
Insincerity
Intolerance
Irresponsibility
Irreverence
Irritability
Jealousy
Judging of others
Laziness
Lethargy
Licentiousness
Lust
Lying
Malice
Meanness
Mercenariness
Miserliness
Murder
Nagging Nature
Narrow-
　　mindedness
Non-reverence
Parasiticalness
Parsimony
Perversion
Pettiness
Petulance

Possessiveness
Prejudice
Pride
Procrastination
Rage
Rapaciousness
Resentfulness
Retaliation
Revengefulness
Rudeness
Ruthlessness
Scandal-spreading
Self-delusion
Self-deprecation
Selfishness
Self-love
Self-pity
Sensuality
Sloth
Spitefulness
Stealing
Sullenness
Surliness
Uncharitableness
Unchaste Speaking
Uncleanness
Uncontrolled Tongue
Undisciplined
Unfaithfulness
Unforgiveness
Unjustness
Unlovingness
Unmercifulness
Unthoughtfulness
Untrustworthiness
Vanity
Vindictiveness
Vulgarity
Wickedness
Willfulness
Wrathfulness

VIRTUE ENERGIES OF
THE DIVINE NATURE

Adaptability
Amiability
Appreciativeness
Benevolence
Carefulness
Character
Charitableness
Chaste Speaking
Chastity
Childlikeness
Cleanliness
Compassion
Congeniality
Conscientiousness
Considerateness
Contentment
Cordiality
Courage
Courteousness
Craftsmanship
Decency
Dedication
Dependability
Detachment
Devotion
Dignity
Diligence
Discernment of the
   True and the False
Dispassion
Earnestness
Equanimity
Ethicalness
Faith
Felicity
Fidelity
Flexibility

Forbearance
Forgiveness
Fortitude
Friendliness
Generosity
Gentleness
Giving
Godliness
Good Cheer
Goodness
Graciousness
Gratitude
Guilelessness
Harmlessness
Holy Concern
Holy Enthusiasm
Holy Poverty
Honesty
Honorableness
Hope
Hospitality
Humaneness
Humility
Integrity
Just
Keeping One's Word
Kindness
Love of Study
Love of Work
Loyalty
Magnanimity
Meekness
Mercy
Mindfulness
Moderation
Modesty
Morality

Neatness
Obedience
Optimism
Patience
Perseverance
Persistence
Philosophical
Politeness
Prudence
Punctuality
Purity
Reliability
Renunciation
Reverence
Righteousness
Sacrifice
Self-Control
Self-Denial
Selflessness
Sense of
   Responsibility
Serenity
Simplicity
Sincerity
Stewardship
Tact
Teachableness
Temperance
Tenderness
Tranquility
Trust in God
Trustworthiness
Truthfulness
Veracity
Vigilance
Wholesome Sense
   of Humor

4

THE FOUR INNER CORES

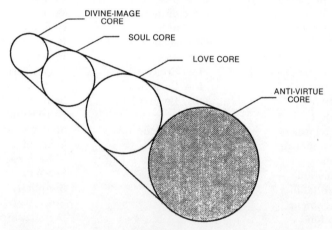

The Path of Devotion leads a devotee from the Anti-Virtue Core to the Love Core. From the Love Core, he progresses to the Soul Core and, eventually, the Divine-Image Core.

One who travels the Path of Devotion with love experiences freedom from the tumultuous energies of anti-virtues. As long as a probationer on the Path expresses lust, anger, greed, pride, prejudice, covetousness or any other anti-virtue, he will think, feel and act through the Anti-Virtue Core.

Anti-virtues represent the Prodigal-Son Consciousness. When one works with the Christ to change the dark energies of anti-virtues into the lighted energies of love and virtues, he begins to unite with the Love Core within his being. Centered in the Commandments of Love and the Sermon-on-the-Mount Principles of Jesus, the devotee begins his union with the Soul Core.

The spiritual gifts that move forth from the Soul Core are dimensional gifts beyond Time and Space, for the soul is eternal and omnidimensional. Union with the Soul Core produces *Soul-Knowing* and *Soul-Radiance*.

The Soul Core prepares a devotee-initiate for union with the Image of God within the Godhead. The Divine-Image-Core energies provide the *Fulness Grace* through which an anointed servant of God presents to the world an ever-flowing stream of wisdom and knowledge.

The Divine-Image Core is the Godhead Core.

The Love Core relates to the First Heaven; the Soul Core, to the Second Heaven; and the Divine-Image Core, to the Third Heaven. As one breaks free from his bondages to anti-virtues, the Christ lifts him ever closer to the Glory and Wisdom of God within the Three Heavens.

One who unites with the Love Core attains *Self-Realization*. Union with the Soul Core produces *Soul-Realization*. Oneness with the Divine-Image Core results in *God-Realization*.

The Divine-Image Consciousness is the natural result of freedom from the Anti-Virtue Core and oneness with the Spirit of God within the Love Core, the Soul Core and the Divine-Image Core.

> *Think through the Image;*
> *Love through the Image;*
> *Create through the Image;*
> *Rejoice through the Image—*
> *for the Image of God is the Creator's Gift to each*
> *of His children through which they are eternally*
> *linked to His Mighty Will and Plan.*

SPIRITUAL GIFTS AND THE LOVE CORE

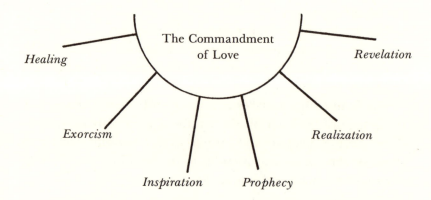

The Commandment of Love Ye One Another
gives instant union with the Image of God.

When one fulfills the Commandment of Love, he unites
with the Love Core within his being. The Commandment of
Love and the Love Core are one, for God has *sealed* the
Love-Commandment and all other Commandments in the
Core of each of His children.

The Love Core contains the light of many beautiful virtues. Union with the Love Core is a major stride on the Path
of Eternal Life.

After a devotee unites with the Love Core through wor-
ship-disciplines, enlightened virtues, holy vows and unwavering faith, he is graced with spiritual gifts. All spiritual gifts
are manifestations of God's Spirit radiating from the Commandment of Love and the Divine Image.

The Love Core is the door to the Kingdom of God. It is
only through love and virtue that one can enter into the
greater degrees of Light, Grace and Truth within the Inner
Kingdom.

Probationers in bondage to pride, egotism, jealousy, unforgiveness and other deadly anti-virtues are far from the Love Core. Such persons are constantly *offending* the Commandment of Love and the Divine Image. Union with the Love Core produces a sweetness of soul that radiates throughout all of one's words and works.

Before one can become a spiritual leader endowed with soul-gifts, he must be centered in the Love Core through the fulfillment of the Commandment of Love. The soul's ageless wisdom moves from the Love Core into his heart and mind, enabling him to serve God with a love-filled wisdom.

The Creator continues to send Great Teachers and Saints to the world as examples of pure love, devotion, humility and compassion. As one evolves the ability to perceive the wisdom in their words, he begins his liberation from the hypnotic hold of the Anti-Virtue Core.

Individuals expressing the dark energies within the Anti-Virtue Core are the persecutors and the tormentors of the Saints, the Anointed Prophets and the Great-Soul Teachers.

Persons who persist in expressing anti-virtues as a way of life may attract "evil spirits" (St. Luke 7:21) or other satanic demons and devils. These unholy spirits create problems and conditions that hasten the learning process within the Anti-Virtue Core. In His Way and Timing, God mercifully frees each of His rebellious children who falls into Satan's traps and pitfalls. The Learning Process is slow but thorough over the lifetimes, the ages and the eternities.

> *Love is the living essence within the core of all the virtues.*
>
> — Ann Ree Colton

The Love Core radiates through all virtues expressed in service to God and one's fellow man. Through love expressed over many existences, a devotee begins to unite with the Soul Core; in this, the gifts of the soul come to birth with increasing purity, vibrancy and versatility.

The *Ethics* in the use of spiritual gifts and soul-powers are learned over many lifetimes of serving God's Image in one's fellow man. Through a constancy in love, virtues and ethics, a devotee begins to unite with the Divine-Image Core and its Illumination-Treasures of Supernal Grace and Dimensional Truth.

To be constant in love is to be one with the Constant of God's Love. In this, one attains transcendence above the anti-virtue energies in the world. Anti-virtue energies are heavy energies that keep one trapped in karmic enclosures. Virtues, being of God's Holy Image, have a buoyant, uplifting energy that draws one ever upward toward Heaven's Light and Grace.

The transcendental state is known by all Great Souls and Saintly personages. The world of oneness with God is a world beyond the duality world of opposing forces. The Christ makes possible one's being lifted above the duality cross-currents into an Energy-World stabilized by God's Love and Grace—the World of the Constant. *"For I am the Lord, I change not."* (Malachi 3:6)

> *God is the Constant. He is unvarying in man's variabilities. The Image Matrix in the Higher Self contains the Constant of God. All must seek to remain united with their Constant; through the Constant, God is realized.*
>
> *Jesus, as co-atom to our Father, makes His homeplace within our Constant, where dwells the Father's Image within us.*
>
> —Ann Ree Colton

Transcendence through love brings total freedom through God and Christ. Daily worship and Sabbath-Day worship are necessary keys to attaining transcendence through love. The worship of God leads to the gifts of the soul that enable a truth-seeker to experience and to explore the Dimensional Worlds of Divine Love.

Emotional stability is the first requirement for spiritual leadership. Emotional stability is of utmost importance in those chosen to represent God in the world and to make the decisions that will preserve the priceless Scriptural Principles of the East and the West. Emotional immaturity expressed through childish attitudes, pettiness, ego-pride sensitivities, tantrums, irritations and impatience are serious offenses against the Commandment of Love and the Divine Image.

To express *any* anti-virtue is to transgress the Commandment of Love. Each anti-virtue is a snare of the Antichrist. Virtues keep one centered in the Protection and Grace of the Heavenly Father. To turn the other cheek, to forgive instantly, and to minister at all times as a steadfast follower of Jesus requires an unwavering dedication to the Commandment of Love.

The *Beauty* of God's Love radiates through the Love Core. Thus, those who have attained union with the Love Core express works and words of exquisite Beauty.

The Love of God is creating every Star and Galaxy in the Universe. When one becomes centered in the Love Core through the Commandment of Love, he is in perfect harmony with the Creation of the Universe.

To betray the Commandment of Love is to betray Life, the Image of God and the Universe. To betray love is to betray Jesus, the Lord of Love. To be faithful to the Commandment of Love reveals spiritual maturity, constancy in virtue, a love for morality and truth. He who walks the Eternal Way of Love and Devotion is a steadfast servant of God united with His Holy Spirit.

True propitiation, supplication and prayer with the most choice and precious offering—the self for God—are acceptable on His Altar. By giving what one is, one fulfills the Image of God within. All energies turned toward God with selflessness in

heart and mind empower the Presence of God
within to act as Love, as Light, as Life, as Will.
—Ann Ree Colton

SWEETNESS OF SOUL

For we are unto God a sweet savour of Christ.
—2 Corinthians 2:15

Union with the Love Core produces sweetness of soul. The sweetness of soul expressed by enlightened individuals and saintly personages is, in reality, an extension of the Sweet Love of God *within* their souls. *Sweet souls are filled with the Sweet Love of God.*

Sweetness of soul comes through union with the *Presence* of Jesus within the Commandment of Love Ye One Another and the Sacrament of Communion.

One's progress on the Spiritual Path is revealed by his sweetness of soul. When his emotions and mind are welded together through an unwavering commitment to his Vows to God, his soul is free to radiate increasing degrees of its innate sweetness, purity and splendor. The versatility of creative-spiritual gifts comes through a soul-radiating sweetness.

A true servant of God or saintly personage combines a sweetness of soul with an indomitable spirit.

The proof that one is in the Saints' stream is
character-sweetness during the time of persecution.
—Ann Ree Colton

During the initiatory tests of a devotee's temperament, he or she will either reveal a sweetness of soul or a meanness of spirit. A devotee who expresses a sweetness of soul during harmonious times and a mean spirit during times of stress and crisis is in bondage to the spirit of ambivalence. Such persons have not evolved the *constancy in love* that prospers communion with God and Christ.

A devotee with an ambivalent spirit expresses love-hate actions in marriage, love-hate feelings with co-disciples, or love-hate attitudes toward his Living Teacher. Such persons should pray to unite with the *Constant* of God's Love — and the spirit of ambivalence will be replaced by the sweetness of soul as a Holy Constant.

Jesus, while on the Cross, epitomized sweetness of soul when He said: *"Father, forgive them, for they know not what they do."* (St. Luke 23:24) Saint Stephen, while being stoned to death, revealed his sweetness of soul when he said to his Lord: *"Lay not this sin to their charge."* (Acts 7:60) The test of a true sweetness of soul is when one is being persecuted or put to death — and feels nothing but love and compassion for his tormentors and murderers.

Sweetness of soul is always accompanied by compassion, kindness, politeness and consideration for others. The Agape spirit of ministering to others and offering them a cup of cold water in Jesus' Name denotes a sweetness of soul that cares about the welfare of others more than one's self.

There are numerous *Sweetness-of-Soul Initiations* on the Path of the Higher Life. These Initiations are seeking to exorcise *all* negative spirits from one's being and to bless him with the *Mary-Magdalene Experience.* Jesus exorcised Mary Magdalene of "seven devils" (St. Luke 8:2); thereafter, she became His devoted disciple, expressing the sweetness of soul of a liberated and illumined spirit.

"Beware of false prophets, which come to you in sheep's clothing, but inwardly they are ravening wolves." (St. Matthew 7:15) Many students come to a spiritual teaching as wolves in sheep's clothing. These students give the appearance of being sincere disciples (sheep) of Jesus. However, they also have *a mean spirit* that they hide from others as long as possible. In time, the Christ Light will inevitably expose each wolf in sheep's clothing; each mean-spirited individual and each sincere devotee will be known to others.

A wolf or mean-spirited student may be brilliant, articulate and charismatic; however, the mean spirit in him will sooner or later *lash out* at his mate, his co-disciple or his Teacher. He will call them *mean* names or do *mean* things to them because of the ferocious nature of the wolf or mean spirit within him. One mean-spirit word or act is as a bullet directed against one's mate, co-disciple or Teacher—and his finger pulling the trigger is accompanied by the fingers of every mean-spirited ancestor who has ever offended the Commandment of Love.

If the wolflike student *desires* to be healed by the Christ, he must ask to be exorcised of the spirit of meanness and all other evil, wicked and foul spirits. If he is receptive to the Christ Light, he will invite a total Mary-Magdalene Experience; and the dark energies within the possessing spirits will be transenergized into the sweetness-of-soul energies of a sincere penitent. Thereafter, he will become a true disciple of Christ Jesus.

A *sheep in wolf's clothing* is a student heavy laden with negative ancestral traits until his genes and chromosomes are healed by the Christ. With the healing, the wolf's clothing is removed and the innate gentle or sheep nature of the devotee is free to be expressed in selfless service to God.

Saul of Tarsus was a sheep in wolf's clothing before his experience with Jesus on the road to Damascus. After shedding his wolf's clothing, he became a devoted sheep of his Shepherd-Lord. Many students follow the example of Saint Paul in their transformation from ancestral wolflike traits of anger and hostility to the gentleness and harmlessness of the obedient sheep of the Lord Jesus.

> *And the mean man shall be brought down.*
> —Isaiah 5:15

The spirit of meanness under the Antichrist is producing hordes of mean men and women in the world.

Mean-spirited, conscienceless drug-dealers are using cheap

chemicals to make young children, adolescents and adults into lifelong drug addicts.

Mean-spirited married persons are committing acts of adultery. Mate-abuse and child-abuse are at the hands of mean-spirited men and women.

Incest is a mean act, for it places emotional and psychological burdens on young children.

Rapists, arsonists, murderers, robbers, kidnappers, torturers, terrorists and many other criminal types are driven by a mean spirit.

Persons whose deliberate lies in a court of law place innocent people in jail are mean-spirited.

Parents who do not teach their children about God and His Laws are expressing a mean spirit; also, permissive parents who do not discipline their children. To deprive a child of the knowledge of God and Scriptural Commandments is an act of meanness, for their child will not be fortified for the challenges of life.

Men who delight in causing young, unmarried girls to lose their virginity are mean-spirited.

Persons with sexually-transmitted diseases who do not inform their lovers about their afflictions are mean-spirited.

To lie, slander, cheat, embezzle, and to inflict emotional, mental or physical pain on another — all indicate the presence of a mean spirit.

Any student on the Path who commits one act of meanness or speaks one word of meanness is a protégé of Judas, not a disciple of Jesus. A mean act, word, thought or emotion is a *betrayal* of the Commandment of Love Ye One Another and its Author.

One mean-spirited word, act, thought or emotion of a student on the Path *shatters* his integrity and credibility as a disciple of Jesus; it also shatters the Ethic in the student-Teacher association — an Ethic more delicate than the finest glass. Such persons also desecrate the grave of every saint and martyr dedicated to the Cause of Christ.

The same mean spirit that possessed Judas is finding more and more persons to possess in the world.

Until a student is constant in love, he will be exposed to the *Ancestral-Sin Core* with its vile and vicious energies. The Ancestral Sin-Core is within the Anti-Virtue Core. Constancy in love reveals union with the Love Core. Oneness with the Love Core produces a sweetness of soul throughout all of one's words and works.

"Truly the light is sweet." (Ecclesiastes 11:7) To become a lighted soul through the Redemption Power of Jesus is to be healed of all shadows of meanness and to radiate a sweetness of soul blessed by the Holy Spirit.

Thank Thee, Father, for all who are expressing a sweetness of soul in service unto Thee.

BLACK HOLES IN THE SPIRITUAL LIFE:
REVERSE TRANSENERGIZATION

But ye are a chosen generation, a royal priesthood, an holy nation, a peculiar people; that ye should shew forth the praises of him who hath called you out of darkness into his marvellous light.

—1 Peter 2:9

Countless Stars radiate light throughout the Cosmos. In various areas of the Universe, black holes suck in the Starlight—and the light disappears. Even entire Stars are believed to be sucked in by the larger black holes; such Stars disappear forever from the family of radiating Stars.

In the spiritual life, anti-virtues act the same as black holes in the Universe. Virtues represent the starlike light of the soul. An anti-virtue black hole literally sucks up the light of virtues and *increases* its destructive power through the added energy.

Even as there are large and small black holes in the Universe, so do the lesser and greater degrees of anti-virtues in one's nature determine the magnitude of their influences upon his life. The lesser and greater degrees of his virtues are priceless treasures of soul-light.

Each person in the world is either increasing in virtues or in anti-virtues — or both. This is due to the *Principle of Increase* through which God is creating the Universe. Man, as a creation of God within one of the multitudinous Solar Systems in Space, is subject to the mighty Cosmos Principle of Increase related to dark and light.

Probationers on the Path who continue to be plagued by temperament problems endanger the Cause of Christ, for they are unstable and undependable. Until an aspirant resolves to work with the Christ in the Transenergization Process, he will continue to express negative thoughts, emotions, words and actions. Rather than changing darkness into light, such persons are changing light into darkness. This *reverse transenergization* increases their negativity in thought, emotion, word and action.

Each time one meditates, prays, fasts and makes penance, he is blessed by the Spirit of God. This God-sent *blessing* is an *increase* of light as energy. However, if a devotee is not vigilant in his thoughts or constant in love and self-control, he will receive the *energy* of God's blessing and use it to increase the most prominent anti-virtues in his nature. This is the reason why many aspirants on the Path *increase* in negative thoughts, feelings, words and actions.

Through reverse transenergization, a selfish and unloving probationer becomes more selfish and unloving after each prayer, meditation, fast or penance. A selfless devotee with great love becomes more selfless and loving after each reverent act of worship, for he is receiving and expressing each increase of God's Spirit as Light. The Light of God's Spirit is Pure Virtue. The Virtue of God's Holy Spirit adds its Light to all virtues being expressed by a faithful devotee in service to Him.

> *Every anti-virtue is a wolf endangering the Lord's sheep.*

The reverse-transenergization process continues until an aspirant realizes through self-honesty that the anti-virtues he is expressing are undesirable and self-defeating traits. However, if certain anti-virtues are ingrained from repetitive use in one's present life and past lives — and he has no desire to repent and make restitution — he will not respond to Scriptural directives or his Teacher's instruction. Such students must await coming lives before they evolve the virtue of self-honesty that will enable them to discern the difference between right and wrong, good and evil.

The more the dark energies within negative thoughts and emotions are changed into the lighted energies of holy thoughts and peaceful emotions, the more the Light of the Christ abides in one. The *"mind of Christ"* (1 Corinthians 2:16) is a mind of Light earned through many transenergizations of darkness into light.

Jesus, as the Light of the world, becomes the Light in one's being through self-honesty, compassion, humility, self-denial, renunciation, self-control and all other virtues that constitute the spiritual life.

Many persons think that they are worshipping God and serving Him; however, their *increasing* negativities in thoughts, feelings, words and actions reveal that they are, in reality, changing the energy-blessings of God into the dark energies of hypersensitivity, the critical mind, anger, pettiness, egotism, stubbornness and other anti-virtues. Rather than serving the Christ through virtues, they are serving the Antichrist through anti-virtues.

Many probationers on the Path are not aware of the great power they generate through their negative thoughts and emotions. This power is destructive. Every judgmental, critical-minded thought and each angry, revengeful emotion is highly destructive. Such persons are the unwitting senders of curses rather than blessings.

The Sun's light provides energy for life on earth. An evil person utilizes the Sun's life-giving energies to perform evil, malicious and destructive acts. A good person uses the Sun's light as energy to do good works.

Evil creates a powerful gravity-suction action. Judas became the pivotal point of anti-virtue black-hole suction that led to the Crucifixion of Jesus. So powerful was the satanic evil working through Judas' anti-virtues that it was able to snuff out the physical life of Jesus and to scatter His Disciples.

Evil persons fulfill the black-hole principle of the Universe when they draw others into their dark schemes, acts, addictions, hates, murders, stealings, wars.

Evil increases, even as good increases. The increase of good or evil is dependent upon the virtues or anti-virtues expressed by the individual.

A disciple of Jesus in any age and time who continues to express anti-virtues is betraying his Lord in numerous ways. Such persons are capable of great destruction through telepathy or through words, emotions and actions.

Love is a *Commandment*. To offend the Commandment of Love in any degree is to add to the anti-virtue black holes that draw one into depressions, guilts, animosities, retaliations, and other negative behavior. The spiritual life begins only when one commits himself to the fulfilling of the Commandment of Love Ye One Another, applying its wisdom and grace in any and all circumstances, situations and associations.

When a devotee works with God and the Christ through self-honesty, compassion, humility and love, the blessings received through the virtue-energy of God's Spirit increase from prayer to prayer, meditation to meditation, fast to fast.

Each vigilant, sincere and devoted follower of Jesus experiences steady increases of Grace and Truth until he qualifies to receive the Fulness-Anointing of the Holy Ghost.

Many newcomers on the Path who eagerly begin the daily practice of prayer and meditation immediately become more negative, critical-minded, hypersensitive and anger-filled. Such persons are walking black holes that change the energy-light of God's blessings into anti-virtue energies.

Individuals and nations being drawn deeper and deeper into financial debt are permitting anti-virtue traits to act similar to black-hole energies. Immorality also acts in a manner similar to a black hole, drawing persons into greater and deeper sin-darkness through perversion, unfaithfulness and lust.

When the followers of a religious or spiritual teaching retain anti-virtues rather than repent and confess to God, they become the victims of their own self-deception and negativity—for their anti-virtues flourish. If such unwary aspirants desire possessions before they have earned them, they will be drawn increasingly into deeper indebtedness; if lustful, they will become more immoral than before; if critical-minded and petty, they will increase in critical-mindedness and pettiness. These are the negative results of the black-hole nature of anti-virtue energies.

Each anti-virtue black hole becomes as a dragon that gorges its insatiable appetite for light-energy—and destroys one's efforts to unite with God.

Many persons on the Path have a number of virtues and several major anti-virtues. Until the anti-virtues are identified through self-honesty, they will remain destroyers of light and will increase in intensity, adversely influencing one's feelings, thoughts and actions.

Any lingering hatred or sense of retaliation and
revenge must be examined and weighed. Malice, an-

ger and hatred must die and be reborn as forgive-
ness, compassion, acceptance and understanding.
Everything that is negative conceals a great spir-
itual current.

— Ann Ree Colton

When a devotee identifies one or more anti-virtues in his
nature, and works diligently with God and Christ Jesus to be
healed, the powerful sucking-action of the anti-virtue black
holes will decrease until the aspirant is completely healed—
and all of the dark energy-masses within each confessed anti-
virtue will be miraculously changed into powerful energies of
light. The light changed to darkness by the Antichrist will be
changed back to light through the Christ! This mighty transformation from darkness to light heralds the birth of the
divine nature through the Holy Ghost. *"Receive ye the Holy
Ghost."* (St. John 20:22)

The *timing* of one's spiritual transformation by the Christ
through the Holy Ghost is dependent upon his degree of self-
honesty, sincerity and fervent desire to serve God in the
world. One becomes a true servant of God only after the anti-
virtue black holes in his nature are healed and their powerful energies transformed into light through the Christ.

All black holes in the Universe and in the individual fulfill necessary functions of absorbing light until they are exploded *in God's timing* into mighty surges of light and
creation. The individual who experiences this paramount
Principle of Universal Creation becomes a co-creator with
God and Christ through the *Illumination* that occurs when
all anti-virtue black holes in his nature are exploded into
light. This indescribable blaze of Illumination is experienced
by one who receives the Divine-Marriage Anointing. Thereafter, he walks in the world as a *light-bringer*, showing others
the way to Salvation and Enlightenment through the Eternal
Love of God and the Redeeming Grace of Christ Jesus.

One cannot attain total harmony in his own being as long as he is subject to the anti-virtue black-hole devourings of the virtue-light attained through his devotional practices. An aspirant on the Path cannot identify an anti-virtue until his conscience is awakened in his consciousness mind. The conscience, as an energy of the soul, enables him to experience the healings, quickenings and transformations that lead to the Divine-Image Consciousness.

Priests and ministers who have the anti-virtues of prejudice, pettiness or an obsessive ambition to attain positions of prominence, authority, wealth or fame become victims of the black-hole principle that changes the virtue-energy of God's blessings into the dark energies of increasing prejudice, pettiness, pride and other anti-virtues. Love, compassion and humility protect a servant of God from falling into Satan's black-hole traps.

Satan is always seeking to block a devotee of the Lord from attaining his Spiritual-Birthright Inheritance. An aspirant who increases in negative emotions, moods, thoughts and actions *after* he steps foot on the Spiritual Path is playing into Satan's hands. A sincere repentance, honest confession to God and application of Jesus' teachings produce harmony and polarization in one's life and being. Such persons are experiencing the Scriptural promises and prophecies regarding the *redeemed*, the *chosen*, the *enlightened*.

Blessed be the Lord for His Mighty Plan of Universal Creation in which Darkness is changed into Light. Man, being created in the Image of God, is in the process of learning the Principles of Universal Creation through which he will become a *lighted being* at one with all Lighted Beings in the Kingdom of God and in the Galaxies of Cosmos.

While ye have light, believe in the light, that ye may be the children of light.

—St. John 12:36

5

GODHEAD-ENERGIES

*For the invisible things of Him from the creation
of the world are clearly seen, being understood by
the things that are made, even His eternal power
and Godhead.*

—Romans 1:20

*We worship with reverent silence the unutterable
Truths and, with the unfathomable and holy vene-
ration of our mind, approach that Mystery of Godhead which exceeds all Mind and Being.*

—Saint Dionysius

ARCHETYPAL SPLENDOR

*Since it (the human nature) was fashioned to rule over
others, it was created as a living image, to be in communion with the name and dignity of its archetype.*

—Saint Gregory of Nyssa

*Man is a prototypal, God-Imaged vehicle expressing
the Archetypal Light or Mind of God in his soul and
within his consciousness. A prototype is a man-being
projected and imaged by the Will of God. A prototype
is a Divine seed-form or zodiacal mold-pattern vehicle
expressing an individualized Archetypal Idea or Image
reflecting the Cosmos Mind of God.*

*One's own Archetypal Image is the Image of God
within himself. Each life is given to one that he may
reclaim the virtues gained in former lives and use them*

55

to bring forth latent virtues which are potential within
the Archetype or Image of God within him.

—Ann Ree Colton

The Mind of God has conceived all creations in all worlds,
and the Spirit of God gives them life. Man, uniquely created
in the Image of God, is endowed with attributes and potentials unlike any other creation of God.

Jesus came to link man on Earth with all other Image-of-
God creations in the Universe. A thrilling new era awaits man
as the teachings of Jesus unlock for him the Cosmic and
Cosmos treasure chests of Divine-Image knowledge relating
to the Universe.

Through the Image of God in his soul, man has the *capac-*
ity to comprehend the Plan of God for all Stars and Galaxies.
Through the Christ, this sacred capacity will be an increasing reality over the centuries and the ages.

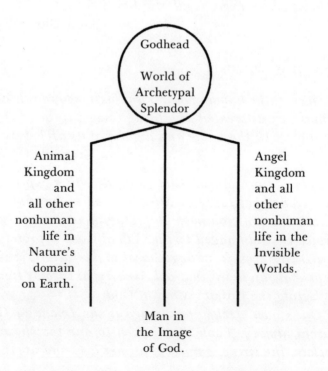

Godhead

World of
Archetypal
Splendor

Animal
Kingdom
and
all other
nonhuman
life in
Nature's
domain
on Earth.

Angel
Kingdom
and all
other
nonhuman
life in the
Invisible
Worlds.

Man in
the Image
of God.

The Godhead is a World of Archetypal Splendor. The Original Archetypes or *Blueprints* for all Galaxies, Stars, Kingdoms, and for all visible and invisible forms of life are within the Godhead.

Man is under the *direct* Archetypal Image-of-God expression. All nonhuman forms of life in Heaven and on Earth have their own Archetypal expressions as projections of Godhead-energy.

Animals, insects, plants, trees and all other nonhuman forms of life on the planet Earth; and the Angels, Archangels and all other nonhuman forms of life in the Invisible Worlds, are making vital contributions to the creation of Man in the Image of God.

"God is a Spirit." (St. John 4:24) The Spirit of God is in all atoms of Creation in the Universe. The Spirit of God within these atoms is differentiated through the various Archetypal expressions. The *Image-of-God Atoms* within His Spirit sound tones in the creation of Man that differ from the atom-tones of all other forms of nonhuman life in Nature and in the Heaven Worlds.

Jesus of Nazareth came into the physical world to shepherd the human spirit toward its Archetypal Destiny as a majestic creation in the Image of God. The magnificence of Godhead Light moved brightly through the Wisdom and Miracles of Jesus. Man, in emulating the virtues of Jesus, will attain new levels of comprehension of the Image of God, the Godhead, and the unanimity of all Archetypes in their manifested glory throughout the Universe.

An illuminative knowledge of the Image of God is opening to mankind through the Mediation of Jesus. This knowledge holds the key to man's understanding his present evolutionary progressions on Earth and his future expressions as an enlightened utilizer of his Image-of-God potentials on a Cosmos level. *"Verily, verily, I say unto you, He that believeth on me, the works that I do shall he do also; and greater works than these shall he do; because I go unto my Father."* (St. John 14:12)

A wise man lives after the image of God and is not guided by the ways of the world. And he who imitates the images of God will conquer the stars.
— Paracelsus

I already possess all that is granted to me in eternity. For God in the fullness of His Godhead dwells eternally in His Image.
— Meister Eckhart

THE SUN AND THE GODHEAD

Forasmuch then as we are the offspring of God, we ought not to think that the Godhead is like unto gold, or silver, or stone, graven by art and man's device.
— Acts 17:29

Stars
and
Galaxies

Sun

Energy-Atoms
for Life on Earth.
Man being created in
the Image of God.

Godhead
Energy-Field:
The Universe.

All Stars and Galaxies in the Universe are radiating energies received from the Godhead. The *core* of each Star and Galaxy and the *core* of each individual Soul derive their energy from the *same* Godhead. The Spirit of God is animating every Celestial Creation in the Universe and every Soul on Earth.

All Image-of-God energies radiate from the Godhead. Man cannot escape the Image-of-God energies. In life and in death, in this Solar System and in future Solar Systems, he is destined to be created in the Image of God.

Man's resistances to God are part of the evolutionary process. Each resistance represents an unborn virtue. The *total* acceptance of the Will of God is destined to occur for each individual at some point in Time and Space. God's Patience is an Eternal Patience; His Plan is an Eternal Plan.

The Sun receives Godhead-energy from the celestial bodies in the Cosmos and contributes its own Godhead-energy from its core.

The Sun is the distributor of Godhead-energy in the Solar System. All atoms of energy derived from the Sun and utilized for the life of man are *sacred* because the core of the Sun is fired by the Godhead energy-light.

The energies in one's thoughts, emotions and physical body are atom-energies from the Sun and the Godhead. When one uses these precious energies with love and virtue, he is in harmony with all other Godhead-energies blessing the Universe through the Stars and the Galaxies. Enlightened Teachers present knowledge of the Scriptural Laws, Commandments, Principles, Ethics and Virtues through which *all* atom-energies used by the heart, mind and body are in accordance with God's Will. A devotee on the Path of Devotion becomes a co-creator with God through his oneness with the mighty Laws and Principles governing the Creation of the Universe.

The discovery of the atom as a source of energy introduced man to a new world of power and responsibility. The atomic-energy potential for creation and destruction is requiring that mankind evolve a world-system of values related to ethics and morality. As man learns to reverence atomic energy as a gift from God, new and greater energy resources will open to him.

The *integrity* of Universal and Eternal Creation sealed into the Image of God in each soul will always prove victorious. The use of volition to destroy will be changed over the ages to the use of volition to create, to bless, to heal, to reach to the Stars and the Kingdom of God for wisdom and understanding. Through the Divine Image, each living soul is destined to attain Spiritual Enlightenment through the sacred use of volition.

The Path to Enlightenment begins with the noble, ethical and moral use of all energies entrusted to the individual by the Creator. The joy of life and the joy of creation increase through the honorable, lawful use of life's energies provided by the Godhead through the Sun.

The Sun is a Sentinel of Godhead Light. Man is being bathed in Godhead Light through the energies of the Sun. These energies in their pristine essences are utilized as God-given energies by the spiritually-enlightened personages in the world. The unenlightened receive these same energies; however, the energies are *changed* through the selfish, immoral, unlawful or corrupt use of volition. The results are various forms of destruction of one's self, his loved ones, and his fellow man.

The destruction of health, the destruction of harmony, the destruction of prospering, the destruction of happiness, the destruction of human life—all are caused by the unenlightened use of life's energies and volition.

To use the power of volition with love is a milestone achievement in the soul's record of Eternal Life. To love is to be one with God. To love is to free the Glory and Beauty of God within His Holy Image.

Reverence for life on Earth leads to reverence for all

energy-creations within the Cosmos. Every atom of life, breath and creation on Earth and in the Universe is charged with Spirit-of-God energies. There is no separateness where there is reverence for Earth Life and Celestial Life.

The Image of God is the Unifying Constant throughout all Star Systems and Galaxy Clusters. This unification or oneness of all creations in the Cosmos is occurring through the Spirit of God within His Image.

The advent of the Atomic Age in the 20th Century began for mankind a scientific awareness of the unanimity of all Celestial Creations in the Universe. This awareness will increase as man learns to reverence every atom of energy. In time, he will know that the Spirit of God in the core of the atom is seeking to reveal mighty truths regarding the sacred purposes of Life Everlasting for Souls and for Stars.

Enlightenment begins with the *right* use of volition. Enlightenment increases through the *inspired* use of volition. Enlightenment becomes the *illumined* use of volition through reverence for the Image of God as an Eternal Constant in self, mankind and the Universe.

Man is an entitized particle sustained by Universal Cause, corrected by Equation. Billions of years have been required to develop him to his present state. Billions of years are yet necessary to perfect him as he is Imaged in Eternality.

The soul of man cannot be unpoised nor separated from his eternality. Sealed into each soul is a resounding spiritual tone directing him. Spiritual reality keeps the soul of man intact, though man often seems to offend Cosmic Law. Despite his striving and his unknowing, he rests in a suspended Universal Cradle harmonized by Universal order, peace.

— Ann Ree Colton

THE SOUL AND THE LAW: SCRIPTURAL STANDARDS

Each of us possesses a soul, but we do not prize our souls as creatures made in God's image deserve, and so we do not understand the great secrets which they contain.

— Saint Teresa of Avila

The soul is supernatural energy overdirected by the Presence and Image of God.

— Ann Ree Colton

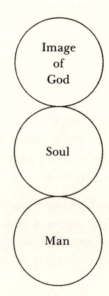

The soul is the mediator between man and God. Spiritual Illumination occurs when the heart and the mind are receptive to the soul's radiance and the Image-of-God versatilities.

The soul may be likened to a vast library with books describing the Inner Kingdom and the Outer Universe and their relationship to the Image of God. The library of the soul contains the records of all lives one has lived throughout Eternal Life. The memory-essences of the soul, when opened by the Hand of God, become part of the Divine-Image Consciousness. The key to one's uniting with the library of the soul is love — a love inspiring a reverent devotion to the Laws and Commandments of God.

> *Each Holy Law, Commandment, Principle, Ethic and Virtue known to man has its origin in the Godhead.*

The spiritual life begins when one evolves the *Commandments Consciousness.* Until one thinks through Holy Law, he is yet an outlaw, a prodigal son. The Commandments Consciousness makes fertile the heart and the mind, and the Spirit of God communes freely through the open door of the soul.

Law plus love equals Enlightenment. Law plus bigotry equals spiritual pride. Narrow-mindedness, prejudice and pride nullify the Enlightenment Process, thereby causing many religiously-inclined individuals to remain shut away from the Illumination-Treasures of their souls. A true love for God and for all souls being created in His Image keeps open the door to the soul's treasure chest of eternal memory, sacred truths and holy inspirations.

A *State of Grace* begins with the Commandments Consciousness at one with God through love. A mind expressing bigotry and separateness is closed to Heaven's Light and

Grace. A spiritually-enlightened mind knows nothing of religious barriers and separateness. The Divine-Image Consciousness is ever receptive to the beauty and wisdom of the soul flowing in increasing measures of Holy Grace.

In religions where *"the blind lead the blind"* (St. Matthew 15:14), the uninspired lead the uninspired. In religions blessed by the Spirit of God, holy inspirations abound. If any religious individual is not receiving an abundance of holy inspirations through the Spirit of God, he is failing in one or more ways to fulfill the basic Scriptural Commandments.

To love God is to love His Image. To love God is to love every person being created in His Image. It is this love that prospers union with God through the Commandments Consciousness. In time, the Commandments Consciousness becomes the Christ Consciousness through the application of the Sermon-on-the-Mount Principles and Ethics of Jesus.

"If ye love me, keep my commandments." (St. John 14:15) The meekness, gentleness, kindness, forgiveness, love and other virtues inspired by the Sermon on the Mount lead a devotee from the Christ Consciousness to the Divine-Image Consciousness. Thereafter, he may serve God through the realizations, prophecies and revelations proceeding from His Kingdom in Holy Flows and Fulnesses of Grace. *"And of his fulness have all we received, and grace for grace."* (St. John 1:16)

> *To know the Eternal Law is Enlightenment.*
> *And to not know the Eternal Law*
> *Is to court disaster.*
>
> — Lao Tsu

SCRIPTURAL STATUTES

The tenth shall be holy unto the Lord.

—Leviticus 27:32

Thou shalt have no other gods before me.

Thou shalt not make unto thee any graven image.

Thou shalt not take the name of the LORD thy God in vain.

Remember the sabbath day, to keep it holy.

Honour thy father and thy mother.

Thou shalt not kill.

Thou shalt not commit adultery.

Thou shalt not steal.

Thou shalt not bear false witness.

Thou shalt not covet.

—Exodus 20:3–17

Thou shalt love thy Lord thy God with all thy heart, and with all thy soul, and with all thy mind.
Thou shalt love thy neighbor as thyself.

—St. Matthew 22:37–39

A new commandment I give unto you, That ye love one another; as I have loved you, that ye also love one another.

—St. John 13:34

Each Law and Commandment of God represents a standard established by the Creator for His children. To ignore or mock the basic Scriptural standards reveals prodigal-son attitudes. Each Commandment of God fulfilled with reverence, love and devotion requires that one have a wholesome conscience. The closer one is to his soul, the more his conscience relates to each Scriptural Law and Commandment.

The Divine Image is centered in the Godhead, which projects its energies into the soul. The soul, in turn, gradates the powerful Godhead-energies into one's life and being through the conscience and the consciousness.

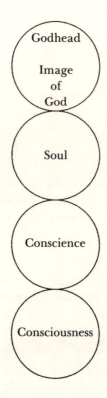

The consciousness remains the Prodigal-Son Consciousness as long as the dark veil of selfishness and irreverence exists between the mind and the soul's energy-rays of conscience.

The conscience may come to birth in the consciousness in gradual stages over many lifetimes or it may appear suddenly as a bright sun hidden behind a dark cloud. The birth of conscience heralds the beginning of the Commandments Consciousness and a closer communion with God through faith, love and law.

> *Sins offend the purity and holiness of the Image of God. Sins are telepathic; they build a dark-energy mass in the world. Sins are recorded in the soul's record. Sins affect the genes and the chromosomes.*

Many persons have yet to understand the destructive nature of sins. The individual with the Prodigal-Son Consciousness is especially unaware of the relationship between sin and pain, sin and suffering.

The high standards of the Lord Jesus protect His followers from invoking the distressing results of sins. When the high standards of the Great Shepherd are ignored or compromised, His sheep remove themselves from His protection and expose themselves to numerous problems and pitfalls.

Many individuals in the religions of the world fall far short of the Old-Testament standards represented by the Ten Commandments and the Law of Tithing. To offend the Morality Commandments, the Sabbath-Day Commandment and the Law of Tithing is not true religion; it is unlawful behavior.

The high standards of Jesus are the only way to attain Spiritual Illumination. A seeker after truth must prove faithful to the Old-Testament standards before he can begin to understand the high standards of Jesus.

Religions that do not teach the logic of Reincarnation are rendering a disservice to their flocks, for they are blocking the Spirit of God from revealing many illuminative insights and understandings. An honorable servant of the Living God knows that he is responsible for all of his actions, feelings and thoughts in his previous lives as well as in his present life and that his soul's record will determine his future lives.

"Moreover I call God for a record upon my soul." (2 Corinthians 1:23) Everything one thinks, feels, speaks and does is recorded in his soul's record. If he falls short of the Old-Testament standards, he will experience coming lives that will seek to manifest the virtues necessary to fulfill these standards. For many persons in modern times, the evolution of virtues will require numerous lifetimes before they begin to relate to the high standards of Jesus in the New Testament.

The widespread disregard of *all* Scriptural standards is taking an enormous toll on the health and happiness of persons. The repetitive sins affecting the genes and the chromosomes are condemning one's self and his offspring to conditions of unhappiness through health problems, financial difficulties and loss of freedoms.

To stray from the Scriptural standards is to move farther away from the Godhead. The refusal of many persons to accept the wisdom and guidance of the Scriptures is adding volumes of sin-energy to the world. Sin-energy short-circuits the Grace-electricities of the soul and the Divine Image. The results of these wilful offenses against God-given Ordinances are the tragic problems besetting the human spirit.

Individuals who are answering the call of their souls to turn to the Scriptural standards are the only hope for the world. As they prove faithful to the Old-Testament standards, they will find that their reverent efforts and serene steadfastness will prepare them for the New-Testament standards.

The New Testament is the door to the Christ-Mind Cosmos Revelations, the Soul's Covenant-Treasures and the Image-of-God Illuminations. Through the New-Testament moral and ethical standards, Jesus becomes one's Shepherd. To follow the Great Shepherd is to receive the powerful **Divine-Marriage Anointing.**

The high standards of Jesus will remain throughout the

ages as rungs on the ladder leading to the Divine-Marriage Anointing. The Path of Initiation relating to Scriptural Laws, virtues and conscience prepares one for this powerful Anointing and Benediction.

It is extremely rare to be graced with a Teacher anointed by God's Holy Spirit. An Anointed Teacher is not welcome in traditional religions because the Spirit of God is always revealing *new* truths and *new* revelations about His secrets and mysteries. True Enlightenment attracts persecutions from religious authorities when it threatens their rigid doctrines. The Holy Spirit in Jesus caused Him to be persecuted and martyred by the priesthood. The Holy Spirit in the Apostles of Jesus led to their persecution, exile or martyrdom.

The Holy Spirit in a modern-day Apostle of Jesus introduces new truths that many religious leaders are not prepared to comprehend. The Holy Spirit *always* offends the rigid, the complacent, the compromised.

To be filled with the Holy Spirit is to be an anointed prophet. Prophets come to open new avenues of thought and action for the human spirit. Each new thought that meets with the world's resistance germinates over the centuries and the ages, for it is inspired by the Spirit of God.

The Gift of Archetypal Prophecy inspired by the Holy Spirit denotes that one has united his consciousness mind with the conscience, the soul and the Divine Image.

The soul and the Image of God contain dimensional energies beyond Time and Space. As these immortal and eternal energies fill the heart and the mind, one begins to comprehend the Scriptural promises of the Prophets, the Saints and the Lord Jesus. These promises relate to the gifts, powers and joys that come to those who love God and embrace His mighty Laws and Commandments.

He who receiveth a prophet in the name of a prophet shall receive a prophet's reward.
—St. Matthew 10:41

PART II

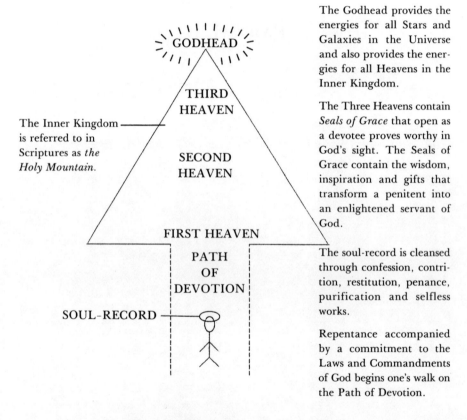

The Godhead provides the energies for all Stars and Galaxies in the Universe and also provides the energies for all Heavens in the Inner Kingdom.

The Three Heavens contain *Seals of Grace* that open as a devotee proves worthy in God's sight. The Seals of Grace contain the wisdom, inspiration and gifts that transform a penitent into an enlightened servant of God.

The soul-record is cleansed through confession, contrition, restitution, penance, purification and selfless works.

Repentance accompanied by a commitment to the Laws and Commandments of God begins one's walk on the Path of Devotion.

THE PATH OF DEVOTION

6

THE PATH OF DEVOTION

Every devoted thing is most holy unto the Lord.
—Leviticus 27:28

Devotion is a necessity in the spiritual life. A philosophy absent from devotion produces intellectual speculation.
—Ann Ree Colton

THE THREE HEAVENS

I knew a man in Christ above fourteen years ago, (whether in the body, I cannot tell; or whether out of the body, I cannot tell: God knoweth;) such an one caught up to the third heaven.
—2 Corinthians 12:2

In thy power is all this world and even the third most sacred heaven.
—Upanishads

"*Behold, the kingdom of God is within you.*" (St. Luke 17:21) When one heeds the guidance of Jesus to seek the Kingdom of God within, he progresses toward the Holy Energies of the Godhead. His progress on the Path of Devotion prepares him for union with the First Heaven, the Second

73

Heaven and the Third Heaven. The Three Heavens contain
pristine Godhead Power and Light.

The Image of God is centered in the protection of the Godhead. To seek to draw closer to the Three-Heavens degrees
of the Godhead requires pure motives and selfless love. *"Who
shall ascend into the hill of the Lord? or who shall stand in
his holy place? He that hath clean hands, and a pure heart,
who hath not lifted up his soul unto vanity, nor sworn deceit-
fully."* (Psalm 24:3,4)

A Teacher's task is to shepherd each student to the Lord
Jesus; thereafter, Jesus works to guide the devotee to God-
Realization. God-Realization is the result of communion with
the Image of God sealed in the Godhead within the core of
his being.

Meditation is a journey to the Godhead. However, before
one can begin to commune with the Inner Kingdom, he must
first prove to God the sincerity of his repentance and contrition; he must also prove his loyalty, devotion and love
throughout many testings and trials.

The Godhead, or *Jewel in the Lotus*, is the key to union
with the Cosmos. Through one's expression of virtues, the
Path of Devotion becomes the Way to oneness with the *Omnipresence* of God creating the Universe. To unite with the
Universal Omnipresence of the Creator and His Son is to attain Fulness and Fulfillment. In this, the soul and the Image
of God are free to manifest their Treasures of Illumination.

The Image of God is a Universal Constant. Union with the
Three Heavens provides increasing knowledge of numerous
Universal Constants and their contributions toward the crea-
tion of the Solar System and the Cosmos.

A new world of comprehension related to Time and Space
is beckoning to mankind. Reverent individuals traveling the
Path of Devotion toward the Timeless Dimensions of the
Godhead will contribute increasingly to this knowledge.

The Christ has come to enlighten the human spirit regarding the synchronized creations of the mighty Universe. Those who respond to His tutelage will become the forerunners of new levels of understanding related to the Moon, the Sun, the Planets, the Stars and the Galaxies. The Path of Devotion is the only way sincere devotees can experience their ordained potentials as heirs of God's Universe, Image and Kingdom. *"Unto you it is given to know the mystery of the kingdom of God."* (St. Mark 4:11)

In the modern age, an enlightened Teacher teaches the Scriptural requirements for a safe and joyful walk on the Path of Devotion; he also teaches the Universal Principles, Constants and Cycles that constitute the Path of Cosmos Knowledge.

> *Love and Light build all arts and all gifts in expression. And Love alone bringeth these to the height of creation of which men shall ultimately share in the Fountainhead and Godhead.*
> — Ann Ree Colton

FLOWS OF GRACE

Heavenly Father, I pray to unite with Thy Holy Flow of Law, Providence and Creation Grace. In Jesus' Name. Amen.

The Plan of God manifests through *flows*. Each Star and Galaxy is *flowing* through the Universe. Each Planet and Moon in a Solar System is also flowing through the Cosmos in accordance with the mathematics of God's Ordained Cycles.

The *Grace* of God's Spirit is omnipresent within all starry bodies and within all invisible Kingdoms. Grace fulfills the Law of Flows in Heaven and on Earth. Each soul experiencing Life Eternal must learn about the various Grace-Flows. When a penitent steps foot on the Path of Devotion, his love for God immediately unites him with the Flow of *Inspiration Grace* from the First Heaven. This beautiful Grace-Flow is accelerated through diligence, vigilance and gratitude.

Aspirants who respond to the cleansings and quickenings by the Lord Christ unite with the greater Grace-Flows from the Inner Kingdom. An enlightened Teacher has the Gift of *opening* sincere devotees to these progressive Flows of Grace so that worthy students may become knowledgeable servants of God at one with the Three Heavens.

The First-Heaven Flow of Grace produces *Devotional Illuminations*. The Second-Heaven Flow of Grace produces *Realization Illuminations*. The Third-Heaven Flow of Grace produces *Archetypal Illuminations*.

The initiatory process requires constant vigilance through each testing of one's sincerity, loyalty, purity in motives and love for the Truth. As a devotee approaches the Inner Kingdom, the initiations become intensified. Only courageous, conscientious and persistent truth-seekers can move through the fiery veils protecting each of the Three Heavens.

In ages past, the enlightened sages, saints, teachers, gurus, prophets and other sacred personages of the East and the West united with the First Heaven and the Second Heaven; and, in rare instances, the Third Heaven. Since the coming of the Christ, all earnest aspirants on the Path of Devotion are given the opportunity to unite with the *Archetypal Seals* within the Third Heaven. To attain this high degree of union with God, a devotee must be centered in the Love-Commandments and the Sermon-on-the-Mount Principles; he must also utilize the supernatural power within the *Name* of Jesus. *"And whatsoever ye shall ask in my name, that will I do, that the Father may be glorified in the Son. If ye shall ask anything in my name, I will do it."* (St. John 14:13,14)

"I will put my law in their inward parts." (Jeremiah 31:33) Each Holy Law, Commandment, Virtue, Principle, Ethic and Living Truth has its First-Heaven, Second-Heaven and

Third-Heaven degrees of Light. *Enlightenment* is a progressive communion with the Power of Godhead Light and Love within the Three Heavens. *"The commandment of the Lord is pure, enlightening the eyes."* (Psalm 19:8)

The Path of Devotion requires a pure and wholehearted love for God before the Door will open to the resplendent Beauty of the Godhead. To love any one or any thing more than God is to remain shut away from the Kingdom-of-God blessings and anointings.

The Creator tests the love of each devotee who desires union with Him. Every test on the Path of Devotion is a test of love for God and His Truth. If the love for self, family, nation, race, religion, or for any other person or institution is greater than one's love for God, he is failing the test of love.

The Path of Devotion is one of renunciation, sacrifice and self-denial. God provides for the needs of His faithful servants, thereby enabling them to serve Him with peace and plenty.

> *He who offers to me with devotion only a leaf, or a flower, or a fruit, or even a little water, this I accept from that yearning soul, because with a pure heart it was offered with love.*
> — Bhagavad Gita

> *When faith is whole through devotion, will is in a state of perfection.*
> — Ann Ree Colton

THE PATH AND THE TIMES

> *True devotion . . . presupposes love of God; rather, it is nothing else than true love of God.*
> — Saint Francis of Sales

> *There is no devotion without virtue.*
> — Nanak

The Path of Devotion beckons to all men. In the East and the West, many devoted worshippers are walking the Path in service to God.

Devotion to God consists of many virtues. If any one of these essential virtues is missing, the aspirant is not expressing a true and whole devotion. To be lacking in any cardinal virtue will hinder his efforts to unite with the Almighty.

Many persons who believe they are walking the Path of Devotion are, in reality, walking the Path of the Critical Mind or the Path of Hypersensitivity leading to retreatism. In such instances, key virtues are absent from their natures. As long as a truth-seeker is fulfilling all Scriptural Statutes with reverent constancy and selfless love, he is traveling the Path of Devotion.

In recent generations, permissiveness has become a way of life for millions of persons. Where there is permissiveness, there is no allegiance to morality, no conscience when the Commandments of God are offended.

When permissive individuals begin their walk on the Path of Devotion, their immature attitudes become obstacles to spiritual progress. A permissive student rejects the disciplines represented by the Laws of God and is offended by reprovings received from his Teacher. A student who perceives the importance of Scriptural Decrees and gratefully responds to his Teacher's admonitions makes rapid progress on the Path of Devotion.

A parent who is permissive with his children will expect his spiritual Teacher to be permissive with him. Permissiveness in homes and in churches has produced generations of aspirants on the Path who are incapable of any serious commitment to God and Christ.

Permissiveness by religious leaders results in compromise — and compromise negates the effectiveness of God's Word. The masses of people in organized religions who have not received *one* creative thought or holy inspiration testify to the compromise of many religious leaders and their own unenlightenment through permissiveness. The same is true of gurus and other teachers of the East and the West who do not have the ability to unite their chelas or students with the First-Heaven Flow of Inspiration Grace.

The Spirit of God is alive, vital, creative, revelatory.

An enlightened Teacher has the Grace of God with him — and he passes this Grace onto his charges. Responsive students immediately begin their union with the First-Heaven Flow of Inspiration Grace, thereby making the environment of an Anointed Teacher a beehive of enthusiastic and inspired devotees experiencing the honey of God's Spirit.

Union with the First Heaven is a great attainment in the soul's quest for Spiritual Illumination. Many devotees are content to remain on this level of Grace on the Path of Devotion. Thinking they have reached the pinnacle of illumination, they bask in the radiant blessings of First-Heaven Grace. However, an Anointed Teacher will urge his students to accept the disciplines and make the vows that will elevate them to the higher levels of Grace within the Second Heaven and, eventually, the Third Heaven.

Any aspirant who remains unreceptive to the Flow of Holy Inspiration has yet to taste the sweet elixirs of Divine Grace. Such persons should search their hearts and purify their attitudes toward the basic Commandments of God.

Many students remain uninspired and unenlightened because of incorrect attitudes toward their God-sent Teacher. Disrespectfulness, laziness, procrastination and other negative traits erect barriers between a probationer and the Flows of Grace from the Inner Kingdom.

As a devotee comes closer to the Christ through love and devotion, the Great Shepherd works directly through his vows and dedications. In this, the Path of Devotion becomes the Path of Increasing Freedoms through the Christ.

Through the Image of God, it is the destiny of every living soul to turn toward the Path of Devotion at some time in Eternal Life. Self-will, irreverence and immorality are temporary avenues of expression. Through Reincarnation Cycles, one experiences the Image-of-God quickenings that will place his feet firmly on the Path of Devotion.

The Divine Image manifests through *Clusters* of Virtues. When devotion, reverence, simplicity, faith and other holy virtues within the *Devotional Cluster* are quickened within one's being, he is able to minister to others in the world as a faithful servant of God. These beautiful virtues, when accompanied by the other Virtue Clusters, enable a devotee to remain true to his vows to God; receive inspired flows of thought from the Three Heavens; and minister to others in Jesus' Name with no thought of self, reward or claim for fame.

> *That man attains peace who, abandoning all desires, moves about without attachment and longing, without the sense of "I" and "mine."*
> — Bhagavad Gita

> *A valiant disciple of valiant works dares to manifest the Image lying nigh unto his soul. He dares to bring forth new ideas to man—ideas which correlate to God.*
> — Ann Ree Colton

A servant of the Almighty cannot walk the Path of Devotion and the Path of Compromise at the same time. To compromise Scriptural Laws and Commandments is to sell one's spiritual birthright. A compromised priest or minister falls far short of the integrity, daring and devotion of the first Apostles of Jesus and all other courageous saints and martyrs.

Prejudice, bigotry, separateness, narrow-mindedness and self-righteousness are stumbling blocks on the Path of Devotion. Prejudice toward any race, religion, nation, sex or individual is a major offense against the Commandment of Love and the Image of God. To believe oneself to be religious or spiritual while harboring prejudices, hates or bigotry is self-deception.

The hope for the world is in true devotees who are dedicated to the Path of Devotion with its reverent disciplines, dramatic miracles and joyful blessings. The Path of Devotion is the only Path leading to the Kingdom of God.

It is your Father's good pleasure to give you the kingdom.

—St. Luke 12:32

A pilgrim for the Christ is thousands of miles ahead of the creedbound. He is jet-propelled by a non-personal zeal to move forward with the Flow of God and to unite with God-minded souls.

The Flow will not work through a person who is not reverent.

— Ann Ree Colton

HOLY-INSPIRATION GRACE

But there is a spirit in man: and the inspiration of the Almighty giveth them understanding.

—Job 32:8

No man was ever great without some portion of divine inspiration.

— Cicero

Inspiration is a Gift of Grace from God. The more the Spirit of God abides in one's heart, mind and soul, the more he expresses pure and holy inspirations.

During the first stages of union with God, the devotee gains knowledge of the diverse kinds of divine inspirations. Each sacred inspiration is a nugget of spiritual gold leading him to the Mother Lode of All Grace—the Godhead.

In ministries blessed by the Holy Spirit of Almighty God, divine inspirations abound. In ministries uninspired by the Holy Spirit, priests, ministers and their congregations depend upon rigid dogma and repetitive statements that foster bigotry and separateness.

Divine inspiration is the leaven in the bread of the spiritual life. The Spirit of God and divine inspiration are one.

"Then was Jesus led up of the spirit into the wilderness to be tempted of the devil." (St. Matthew 4:1) The *attitudes* of Jesus regarding His Power of Miracles were tested by Satan before Jesus began His ministry in the world. So is each servant of God in every age and time tested in his attitudes before he may progress to the higher Flows of Grace.

During the first years on the Path, a sincere aspirant learns of the attitudes, wisdom and examples of Jesus and the Saints. The entire probationary period of the spiritual life relates to one's correcting his incorrect attitudes. In this, he has the Holy Bible and his Teacher's instruction to assist him in his daily efforts to attain correct attitudes.

One's attitudes are his own personal Jerusalem where live friends and foes alike. Until the foes or incorrect attitudes are converted into friends or correct attitudes, his own personal Jerusalem will remain a city of unrest; the dark and the light within his heart and mind will experience constant struggle.

The attitudes of a probationer on the Path may be likened to the keys of a piano. Each attitude receives repeated testings and adjustments until it sounds a right and true tone for God. Only when a devotee's attitudes are sounding pure and holy tones may the Hand of God play His beautiful melodies and symphonies of Grace and Truth.

Enlightened attitudes are the results of *Virtue-Cluster quickenings* by the Christ. Each virtue undergoes many testings until it becomes a permanent light and tone in the heart and the mind. The more virtues one utilizes in service to God, the more the Divine Image may manifest its sacred essences and energies.

"And I appoint unto you a kingdom, as my Father hath appointed unto me; that ye may eat and drink at my table in my kingdom." (St. Luke 22:29,30) A devotee who corrects his attitudes through Virtue-Cluster quickenings is invited by the Christ to sit at the Lord's Table. The Lord's Table consists of a sumptuous feast of spiritual nourishment manifesting as gifts and graces of many kinds.

Some probationers blessed with Holy-Inspiration Grace earned in previous lives are lacking in practicality. Through the Quickening Power of Christ Jesus, these devotees receive the virtues that inspire practicality.

To be a good steward of the manifold Grace of God, one must be practical as well as mystical. The blending of the practical with the mystical enables a truth-seeker to function in the world of man while receiving Holy-Inspiration Grace and Guidance through the Spirit of God.

To be born with a mystical, devotional nature denotes lives past on the Path of Devotion. However, before one can qualify to become a responsible steward of the mysteries of God and a trustworthy Teacher of others, he must attain the balance of the practical and the mystical.

Many students who are practical are not open to Holy-Inspiration Grace due to an absence of faith, reverence, devotion and other key virtues. When such students respond to the Christ-quickenings of their missing virtues, their practicalness and mysticalness come into balance and harmony.

When the practical is without the mystical, an aspirant remains materialistic. When the mystical is without the practical, a probationer tends to express hermit-like or escapist desires. The Lord Christ seeks to place mysticalness in one's practicalness and practicalness in his mysticalness.

The mastery of Earth-energies and the mastery of Heaven-energies represent a high State of Grace that comes through the Virtue-Clusters quickened and synchronized by Christ Jesus.

Whatever a poet writes with enthusiasm and a divine inspiration is very fine.

—Democritus

In telepathic communion through faith in God, one receives uninterrupted inspiration and guidance.

—Ann Ree Colton

IN HIS NAME JOURNAL

I pray to flow with the Love of God in His Creation of the Universe and in His Creation of Man in His Image and Likeness.

An enlightened Teacher is sent by God into the lives of students to liberate them from their bondages and to open them to Heaven's Light. A student can assist his Teacher in this freeing process by keeping a *journal* of inspired thoughts that come during meditation and at other times of the day and the night.

Any thought that contains *holy inspiration* has been given to the devotee as a gift from the Spirit of God. Each inspired thought contains within it the Light of Heaven. When a devotee of the Lord records the inspired thought in his journal, he has sealed the Light of Heaven into the Earth. In this way, he is working with God to establish His Kingdom in the world of matter.

Whatever one does in the Name of Jesus will be blessed and prospered. If a conscientious devotee keeps a journal *in Jesus' Name*, the Inspiration Grace of the First Heaven will flow increasingly into his heart and mind.

Holy Inspiration manifests in different forms of creation. The devotee should be alert to new ideas, new insights, new songs and any other manifestation of Holy Inspiration. *It is extremely important that the student express gratitude to God for each Holy Inspiration received through His Mercy and Love.* This may be accomplished by a prayer of gratitude on the knees. If one is meditating in a seated position when he receives a holy-inspiration blessing, he should always speak words of gratitude such as, "Thank Thee, Father. Blessed art Thou, O Lord." Similar words of gratitude should also be spoken within one's thoughts if he is in a public place while receiving Holy-Inspiration Grace.

> *What we write, we never forget. That is why it is so important to always keep a journal.*
> — Ann Ree Colton

When a devotee records his inspired thoughts in his I.H.N. (In His Name) Journal, he should know that he is *experiencing* the Process of Illumination. Holy Inspiration through the Spirit of God is the *first step* toward a State of Grace. Many other doors of Grace will open if one faithfully records each Holy Inspiration. He should also realize that whatever God sends him is a Grace-gift to be shared with others. A new song, a poem, a parable, a wisdom-sentence, or any other Holy Inspiration received by the devotee is a sacred gift, which, in a timing determined by the Creator, will bless and inspire others.

The failure to record Holy-Inspiration thoughts or other spiritual-creative blessings will short-circuit the Grace Flow. Laziness, procrastination, indifference, ingratitude, and other foes of the spiritual life will keep the aspirant from ascending the Ladder of Divine Grace.

Any Holy Inspiration received by a devotee is not for self-glorification; it is for the Glory of God. If one is a good steward of Holy-Inspiration Grace from the First Heaven, the Expanding Grace of God will reward him with other priceless treasures from His Kingdom.

So he drove out the man; and he placed at the east of the garden of Eden Cherubims, and a flaming sword which turned every way, to keep the way of the tree of life.

—Genesis 3:24

The Angels work closely with dedicated devotees of the Lord who aspire to become Teachers of Truth. Even as the Cherubim Angels were placed by God to protect the Garden of Eden, so do they welcome and bless all souls who turn toward Heaven in their hearts and minds. The Cherubim Angels become the first initiators in the devotee's union with the Flow of Inspiration Grace from the First Heaven. Their work is to prepare the student for union with other Holy Mediators in the Kingdom of Heaven.

An Angel kiss is a wisdom-sentence.

Before one can unite directly with the Christ-Mind State of Grace, he must first be prepared by the Angels, the Saints and other Spiritual Beings and Presences working in the First Heaven. In time, as he proves faithful, obedient and selfless, he will begin to unite with the Illuminati, the Great Immortals or Masters, Mary and the Most High Saints working with Her in the Second Heaven. In this, the Flow of Holy Inspiration will increase in great measure in the devotee's heart and mind.

Until you develop the Bhakti* heart and know the Love of God, and God as Love, go through the door of Mary to God. Through her Bhakti Heart you will bring forth the flowers of Bhakti within your own heart, which you will offer to God as devotion.

—Ann Ree Colton

---

*Bhakti is a Sanskrit word meaning devotion, love.

Inspiration Grace will expand into Realization Grace through the Mediation of the Great Beings working in the Second Heaven. The next State of Grace is the Christ-Mind Dimensional Gifts that open through the Beings and Presences in the Third Heaven. Initiates and Teachers who have united with Third-Heaven degrees of Revelation Grace are receptive to the Archetypes of God, and therefore serve the Creator as revelator-prophets. Anointed Teachers at one with the *Archetypal Flow* of the Third Heaven utilize the Gifts of the Holy Ghost and the Christ Mind to reveal beautiful new truths to the world.

O Angels and Saints, bless me.

O Illuminati and Great Immortals, inspire me.

O Mary and Disciples of Jesus, heal me.

O Lord Jesus, Heavenly Father and Divine Mother, consecrate me.

O Hierarchs, Archangels and Lord Christ, sanctify and illumine me.

Almighty God, anoint me, that I may glorify Thee and create eternally within Thy Holy Flow of Divine Love and Unceasing Grace.

7

SACRED SEALS

And I saw in the right hand of him that sat on the throne a book written within and on the backside, sealed with seven seals. And I saw a strong angel proclaiming with a loud voice, Who is worthy to open the book, and to loose the seals thereof?
— Revelation 5:1, 2

SEALS OF GRACE

GODHEAD
Image of God

THIRD HEAVEN:
Archetypal Seals
Revelation Seals
Prophetic Seals

SECOND HEAVEN:
Realization Seals

FIRST HEAVEN:
Holy-Inspiration Seals

The Godhead contains the Pure Bliss of God's Holy Spirit. The Seals of Grace in the Third Heaven contain the Bliss-Essences of Godhead Grace. The Seals of Grace in the Second Heaven are filled with the Ecstasy degrees of the Divine Presence. The Seals of Grace in the First Heaven produce Holy-Joy inspirations and creations. Multitudinous Seals contain various combinations of Bliss-Ecstasy, Bliss-Joy and Ecstasy-Joy.

"And of his fulness have all we received, and grace for grace." (St. John 1:16) A State of *Fulness Grace* is attained when a servant of God experiences the continuous opening of the lesser and the greater Seals in the Three Heavens. Each Seal releases the Grace-energies for pure creations into one's heart, mind and soul. These beautiful creations add their light to the world through music, art, writing, teaching, healing and other spiritual-creative expressions.

> *The opening of the Seals of Grace makes of one a co-creator with God.*

All things in the Higher Worlds are *sealed.* Only the Hand of God, working through the Host of Heaven, can open a Seal of Grace. When one's motives and dedications are pleasing in God's sight, he experiences the progressive openings of increasingly beautiful Seals. The opening of these precious Seals determines his rate of progress toward the Divine-Image Consciousness.

An aspirant on the Path begins his communion with the Seals of Grace through humility and a sincere repentance for all sins committed. In certain instances, a halfhearted probationer may experience the opening of various Seals due to grace earned in previous lives; however, if he refuses to progress toward a wholehearted repentance and humility, he will eventually lose touch with the Sacred Seals.

"God giveth grace to the humble." (James 4:6) Humility sustains one's receptivity to the Seals of Grace as they bless,

enrich and prosper his life on all levels of spiritual activity and creative expression. As long as he sounds the *tone* of a true repentance, he will transcend the dark sin-clouds in the world and commune with the Sacred Seals in the Heaven Worlds.

After the Cherubim Angels begin to open the Seals of Grace in the First Heaven, a devotee becomes increasingly qualified to serve God with understanding and inspiration. In time, the Sacred-Realization Seals in the Second Heaven and the Divine-Revelation Seals in the Third Heaven will begin to reveal their wisdom-truths. To be initiated in the receiving of the different Seals of Grace is to become knowledgeable in the diverse manifestations of the *Presence* of God.

> *The world is imprisoned in its own activity, except when actions are performed as worship of God. Therefore you must perform every action sacramentally, and be free from all attachments to results.*
>
> —Bhagavad Gita

> *Anything having sacramental action is the beginning of the opening of the Sacred Seals. The Seals are actual whirling masses of neutralized energies keeping under control and sealing away great ideas from man until he is ready to receive them.*
>
> *The Cherubim Angels work with the lesser Seals, and also seal away from the profane or manipulative the great truths and ideas. The Archangels release the Great Seals and work with the Holy Spirit that man may receive them in timing.*
>
> —Ann Ree Colton

"*O sing unto the Lord a new song.*" (Psalm 96:1) The new songs that come to Teachers and their students on the Path denote the opening of Holy-Inspiration Seals. When one receives a beautiful new song, he *knows* the words and the melody, for God has *sealed* this knowing into him. The *essences* of God's Spirit within a Holy-Inspiration Seal move into one's heart, mind and being—and he is blessed with a new song or some other holy-inspiration creation.

A Seal of Grace is as a music box that wafts its creation-essences into one's being. Music, tones, color and light are within each Grace Seal. A devotee's soul-gifts determine when and how he receives and expresses each Grace Seal.

The versatile creations of an enlightened Teacher testify to his or her union with the Spirit of God manifesting through a diversity of Grace Seals. Dedicated students of an enlightened Teacher who are receiving the Grace of God through Holy-Inspiration Seals are being prepared by the Spirit of God for the time when they will experience and express the *Versatility Illuminations* of the Divine-Image Consciousness.

An Anointed Teacher is under the Flow of the Archetypal Seals in the Third Heaven. As these majestic Seals open, the Teacher passes their wisdom-essences to his receptive students. Eventually, sincere students will begin to personally experience the opening of Inspiration Seals and Realization Seals correlating to the Archetypal-Seals knowledge and wisdom pouring upon their Teacher through the Holy Spirit.

The Divine-Revelation Seals and Archetypal Seals in the Third Heaven are one's link with the Godhead Energy-Flows from the Inner Kingdom and the Outer Universe.

Jesus sealed men of the earth into the Greater Christed Son-of-God Archetypes when He was on the Cross. He could do this only when He was in the state of victory over death. Had he lived an ordinary life like any other, He could not have sealed men in, that they become Eternal and Universal in consciousness.

The Archetypal Seals are masses of vibrational energy-particles which are constantly being reinforced by the

Archangels, the Cherubim and the Devas, who seal away
the Greater Truths from the unprepared. Under Christ,
the Hierarchy, the Archangels and the Greater Devas
open the Archetypal Seals when men are prepared.
— Ann Ree Colton

Seals of Grace may open at any time of the day and the
night. Certain dream symbols release Grace-Seal energies
that inspire beautiful creations during the day. As long as one
remains constant in love, observes Scriptural Statutes, serves
his Lord with humility and meekness, and expresses reverence
and gratitude, he will receive the continuous opening of the
Seals of Grace—and his life will be blessed.

Each *anointing* a devotee-initiate receives through the
Spirit of God *seals* into his being the seeds of priceless gifts
and blessings. As these seeds are quickened by the Christ, one
experiences the manifold rewards and cyclic inheritances of
broader and deeper ranges of Grace Seals.

Now he which stablisheth us with you in Christ,
and hath anointed us, is God; Who hath also sealed
us, and given the earnest of the Spirit in our hearts.
— 2 Corinthians 1:21,22

REVERENCE AND GRATITUDE

To open a Seal on the plane of consciousness through
initiation, one must have the key to the sacred Word of
Creation. Only those having access to the great Arche-
typal Tones of the Holy Spirit can do this.

Sacred mantras are sealed into the consciousness by
the Holy-Ghost Archetones; and thus the true initiates
having access to the great mantras and mantrams can
activate these Seals. One has to penetrate the Sound
Current or the Word holding together all creation—in-

finite and finite—sealing away from man knowledge he is yet unready to receive.

—Ann Ree Colton

A pure tone of reverence is expressed by the pure in heart. Reverence for life is to behold the Image of God in all persons. Reverence for energy makes of one a good steward of the energies of the body, the mind, the emotions, the soul. Reverence for the elements inspires the sacramental use of fire, earth, air and water. Reverence in sex invites the blessings of the Heavenly Father and the Divine Mother upon one's marriage and family. Reverence in one's attitudes toward the earning and spending of money keeps him centered in the Providence of God. Reverence for vows made to God strengthens one's spiritual insulation, thereby qualifying him to receive the more powerful voltages of God's Spirit within the Greater Seals of Grace.

The key of Reverence opens the Grace of God and establishes a communion with His Love-Presence. Gratitude keeps the Grace of God flowing in increasing measures in one's life and being. Each manifestation of God's Grace represents the opening of one or more Grace Seals.

Gratitude and reverence work hand in hand. Reverence *attracts* God's blessings; gratitude *keeps* the blessings flowing. The greater the reverence, the greater the blessings; the greater the gratitude, the closer the Love-Presence of God.

Reverence for the simple things of life reveals God's Bliss-Presence within simple things. Reverence is the key to union with God's Bliss-Presence within all that *Is*. Every atom of life, every element, every soul is God's Creation. His Bliss-Presence is within *all* things, all souls, all Stars.

Reverence is sacramental seeing of God's Presence in all. Reverence is sacramental knowing, serving and rejoicing.

"Thou wilt keep him in perfect peace, whose mind is stayed on thee: because he trusted in thee." (Isaiah 26:3)

Reverence sanctifies the thought energies and keeps one's mind *"stayed"* on God. Reverence sanctifies the emotional energies and suffuses them with Holy Peace.

To reverence the Laws and Commandments of God produces righteousness, prospering and understanding. Gratitude for each Scriptural Law and Commandment assures one's receiving the first fruits of God's blessings through the opening of the Grace Seals.

Through God's Laws, the Universe is being created. To be one with the Creator through reverence for His Laws is to know a sweet oneness with His Universe.

Reverence for the Star-filled Cosmos manifests the Galaxy Consciousness through the mighty Christ-quickenings of the mind and the heart. Gratitude for each atom of life, each cell, each soul and each Star expands the chalice of one's being so that Divine Bliss may reveal its Treasures of Universal Principles and Constants.

Reverence for God's Gift of *Time* unites a devotee with the Presence of God within Time. Reverence for Time produces punctuality, orderliness, harmony, fulfillment. When the Hand of God removes the *Time-Seals* on His Holy Laws and Commandments, His servant becomes an enlightened prophet and revelator.

The Presence of God abides in the Body Temple when reverence is present within the thoughts and the emotions. A sincere devotee of the Lord reverences the Body Temple at all times. Addictions and cravings pollute the Body Temple. The Presence of God abides only in a purified Body Temple.

Reverence for the Body Temple of one's mate, children, co-disciples and others reveals a high degree of reverence through which God may reveal cardinal truths related to the soul and the Divine Image. Reverence for the Body Temples of others is the key to the receiving of healing powers through the Holy Spirit.

"Ye shall keep my sabbaths, and reverence my sanctuary." (Leviticus 19:30) To observe each Sabbath Day in the sanctuary of the Lord reveals a beautiful expression of reverence, devotion and love. The Spirit of God is Omnipresent throughout the Sanctuary of the Universe. To reverence His sanctuary on Earth in the Sabbath-Day Cycle of seven days is to prepare oneself to receive the Seals of Grace that contain wisdom and knowledge regarding other Sacred Cycles of the Solar System and the Galaxy.

Each Celestial Cycle of the Moon, the Sun and the Planets is contributing to the creation of Man in the Image of God. The Sabbath-Day Cycle holds the key to enlightenment regarding the sacredness and sanctity of Cycles. To be constant in reverence toward all Sabbath Cycles and Celestial Cycles is to be receptive to the secrets of Creation revealed through the Seals of Grace.

Gratitude for the Body Temple and the Image of God; gratitude for the Gift of Eternal Life; gratitude for the Sabbath-Day Commandment and all other Scriptural Laws and Sacred Cycles open the devotee to the Flow of the Grace Seals through which God reveals the beauty, harmony and perfection of His Plan.

"In everything give thanks." (1 Thessalonians 5:18) For each test, give thanks. For each lesson, give thanks. For each stumbling, give thanks. For each purification, give thanks. For each purging, give thanks. For each inspiration, give thanks. To give thanks for the painful lessons as well as the joyful blessings is to remain centered in Holy Gratitude—and therefore a State of Grace.

Reverence and gratitude keep a truth-seeker united with God and His unceasing blessings, rewards and Grace-Inheritances. Reverence and gratitude combined with love remove every obstacle to the Treasures of the Soul and the Bliss Seals of the Godhead.

> *Let Jesus be the door. Let the Great Sages and*
> *Gurus of the Path echo or reflect His words, that*
> *one may enter into the true life, light, love and will*
> *instruction, safely reaching God-Bliss and Heaven.*
> *Such Bliss is the Way, the Truth and the Life.*
> — Ann Ree Colton

WISDOM SEALS

> *And whatsoever we ask, we receive of him, be-*
> *cause we keep his commandments, and do those*
> *things that are pleasing in his sight.*
> — 1 John 3:22

> *Wisdom is the principal thing.*
> — Proverbs 4:7

"If any of you lack wisdom, let him ask of God, that giveth to all men liberally, and upbraideth not; and it shall be given him." (James 1:5) When one asks God for wisdom, he receives it *liberally* from several sources: the Wisdom of the Eternals sealed within his Higher Self; the Wisdom recorded in his soul's record; the Wisdom of the Scriptures and other sacred writings; the Wisdom of his Teacher; and the Wisdom blessing him through the Seals of Grace.

The Wisdom of the Eternals is his heritage and birthright earned during countless lifetimes, ages and eternities throughout Everlasting Life. The Wisdom of the Eternals sealed within his Higher Self begins to come forth when he is ready to receive it in his present life.

The numerous lives one has lived have built a tremendous reservoir of wisdom in the soul's record. The Hand of God may open the soul's treasure chest of wisdom at any time and make it available to the devotee. This monumental blessing may occur in gradual stages or instantly, depending upon the aspirant's sincerity, dedication and love-motives.

The miraculous transformation of a sinner into a reverent devotee of the Lord occurs through the opening of the wisdom-treasures in the soul's record and in his Higher Self.

> *The Higher Self awaits to instruct and to channel the greater wisdom of the real and true to man.*
> *Bliss-wisdoms are the Selfless Self's way of revealing that the True Self is beyond ego.*
> *The nature of the Higher Self is love, peace and harmony. Thus, if you live through the nature of the Higher Self, you have peace within your self; you have harmony in your environment; and you are a love-vehicle for God.*
>
> — Ann Ree Colton

The Wisdom of God manifesting through an enlightened Teacher is a continuous source of revelatory wisdom for a sincere devotee. The Teacher is constantly seeking to unite his students with the Wisdom Seals in the Heaven Worlds, with the wisdom recorded in their souls' records and Higher Selves, and with the wisdom in the Holy Bible and other sacred writings.

"Be ye doers of the Word." (James 1:22) The wisdom in the Holy Bible and other Sacred Scriptures becomes part of one's life and being only through study and application. As one reverences this God-given wisdom, the Creator quickens the Gift of Understanding; for in reverencing the Scriptures of the world, he is reverencing all Sages, Saints and Great-Soul Teachers anointed by God's Holy Spirit.

"Ask, and it shall be given you." (St. Matthew 7:7) When one asks God for wisdom, his attitudes toward Scriptural Laws and Commandments determine whether or not the Wisdom Seals and other Grace Seals will open or remain closed. If his attitudes and motives prove worthy in God's sight, the Wisdom Seals, Inspiration Seals and other priceless Seals open to him and fill him with various *Knowings*.

His ear becomes attuned to the Wisdom Seals that God is opening to his Living Teacher; also, the Timeless Wisdom of the Saints and the Great-Soul Teachers is absorbed into his heart and mind through his study of the Sacred Scriptures of the East and the West.

Thus, after asking God for wisdom, one is literally bathed inwardly and outwardly with the Wisdom-essences of God's Spirit blessing him through Wisdom Seals in the Heaven Worlds, his Soul's and Higher Self's *eternal* record of wisdom earned in countless past lives and eternities, the wisdom of his Living Teacher, and the wisdom contained in the Holy Bible and other sacred writings.

When a devotee *knows* that he is being blessed, healed, transformed and enlightened through the Spirit of God and the Mediation of Christ Jesus, his progress on the Path of Devotion is one of joy, happiness and fulfillment. The opening of the Wisdom Seals, Inspiration Seals and other Sacred Seals *is* the glorious State of Grace experienced by all devoted servants of God.

> *When reverence is present in the student, wisdom is free in the Teacher.*
>
> — Ann Ree Colton

When one qualifies for the opening of the *Greater* Seals of Grace, the Wisdom pouring forth from these powerful Seals anoints him with prophetic vision and revelatory perception. The Wisdom of God within the Cycles of the Moon, the Sun and the Planets determines the *timings* when the lesser and Greater Seals of Grace are opened for each individual on the Path of Devotion.

The opening of each Wisdom Seal increases one's *knowing*. To *know* is to grow in Grace and Truth. To *know* is to become an enlightened servant of God at one with His Presence and its multitudinous manifestations of Love and Wisdom.

All Gifts of the Soul are sealed. When the Creator removes the Seals from the Soul, each Gift comes forth in perfect timing to one's need to increase his capacity for serving the Altar and Word of God. The opening of the Wisdom Seals in the Heaven Worlds coincides with the opening of the Seals on the Soul's Gifts, for God desires that His faithful servants use with wisdom each Holy Gift of the Soul.

To trust in God is to trust in His wise and perfect Plan for each of His children. Trust in God provides a solid foundation of faith through which each sincere devotee may experience the progressive stages of union with the Seals of Grace.

The Image of God is sealed. When the Wisdom Seals related to the Image of God open, the Creator reveals to His servant many secrets and mysteries regarding His Eternal and Universal Plan. This sacred knowledge is the basis for the Greater Illuminations that manifest through the Divine-Image Consciousness.

> *But we speak the wisdom of God in mystery, even the hidden wisdom, which God ordained before the world unto our glory.*
> — 1 Corinthians 2:7

MEDITATION AND THE MASTER BLUEPRINT

> *The Spirit of God is in the smallest atom and in the greatest Galaxy. The Spirit of God permeates All Creation. The Spirit of God is in all Heavens. The Spirit of God Is.*

The Master Blueprint for the creation of all Stars and Galaxies is *sealed* in the Image of God in the Godhead Core of every living soul. Each person has the knowledge of this mighty Blueprint stored eternally in the core of his being.

Enlightened Sages, Saints and Teachers direct their hearts'

love toward the *Inner* Kingdom of God through sacramental meditation, thereby communing with the Master Blueprint within the Divine Image. The resultant realizations, revelations and prophecies regarding the Plan of God for the Solar System and the Universe are based upon their communion with the Image-of-God Seals in the Third Heaven.

God desires that each of His children become a knower and a doer of His Will. The Image of God in the core of one's being is ever-ready to reveal the Master Plan for souls, Stars, Galaxies.

Jesus, the Perfect Prototype and Example of the Image of God on earth, directed His disciples to *"Seek ye first the Kingdom of God, and His righteousness . . ."* (St. Matthew 6:33) Priceless treasures of truth regarding the Image of God and the Master Plan of Cosmos Creation come forth during one's quest to reach the Inner Kingdom through sacramental meditation. *"The kingdom of God is within you."* (St. Luke 17:21)

The knowledge of the *Cosmos* Commandments, Constants, Principles, Virtues and Ethics will increase for the human spirit through the new-era meditators at one with God and His Image.

Every time one meditates with love, faith, reverence, gratitude, humility and compassion, he adds something of the superconscious energies of the soul to his consciousness mind. These powerful energies of the soul continue their increase until the consciousness mind becomes one with the Kingdom of God through the Divine-Image Consciousness.

> *My meditation of him shall be sweet.*
> —Psalm 104:34

> *To the mind that is still, the universe surrenders.*
> —Chinese Saying

PROVIDENTIAL-GRACE SEALS

> *Beloved, I wish above all things that thou mayest prosper and be in health, even as thy soul prospereth.*
>
> —3 John 2

> *Thou art the source of all happiness and of all prosperity. Thou art the refuge of those who surrender themselves to thee.*
>
> —Upanishads

To the Divine-Image Consciousness, God's Love-Presence is an *abiding* Presence opening priceless Seals of Grace of diverse kinds and also providing for all of one's needs. True prosperity on the physical, emotional, mental and spiritual levels of life manifests when the Living God removes the Seals on His Providence. When this occurs, Providential Grace flows forth from the bosom of God's Love in exact timing to one's needs.

Providential-Grace Seals open in accordance with the Energy-Laws of the Moon's Cycles. When a devotee is in timing with the New Moon and Full Moon Cycles, he remains receptive to the blessings of Providential Grace relating to financial provision, holy inspirations and love-associations. *"The Father knoweth what things ye have need of."* (St. Matthew 6:8)

To offend the Energy Laws governing money energies, sexual energies and other energy-processes of the body, heart, mind and soul attracts impoverishment and other hardships in one's present life or in coming lives. Widespread poverty in the world occurs when the continuous sinning of multitudes of persons blocks their communion with the Providential-Grace Seals.

God is bountiful with His Providential-Grace blessings

when one remains faithful to the Tithe Law and the other Scriptural Statutes throughout all tests and trials.

All blessings received from God flow from His Providence. Gratitude for each blessing and using each blessing to serve and to glorify the Creator keep one united with the ever-increasing opening of the Providential-Grace Seals.

> *The borrower is servant to the lender.*
> — Proverbs 22:7

> *Think what you do when you run into debt; you give to another power over your liberty.*
> — Benjamin Franklin

When a devotee earns the flowing blessings of God's Providential Grace, he remains debt-free and in a state of holy prospering. Debts denote bondage. Providential Grace represents freedom. The freedom to serve God and to minister to the needs of His children is a freedom blessed and prospered by the Creator through His Providential-Grace Seals.

Trust in God and His Providence rewards His servants with the joys of prospering and with the *effortless effort* to accomplish their dedications of serving and creating through the unceasing opening of the Sacred Seals.

> *Let them shout for joy, and be glad, that favour my righteous cause: yea, let them say continually, Let the Lord be magnified, which hath pleasure in the prosperity of his servant.*
> — Psalm 35:27

PROPHETIC SEALS

> *Desire spiritual gifts, but rather that ye may prophesy.*
> — 1 Corinthians 14:1

A conscientious devotee who applies sacred instruction will eventually qualify for the opening of the *Prophetic Seals*. Every Scriptural Truth, Law and Commandment contains priceless Seals of Wisdom, Knowledge and Prophecy. Each Ethic and Principle of Jesus is pregnant with Prophetic Seals and other beautiful Seals of Grace.

An enlightened prophet of God is blessed with the opening of the Prophetic Seals within the Scriptural Laws and Commandments and other sacred truths. As these mighty Seals are opened by the Hand of God, the long-range purposes of each Holy Law and Commandment are revealed to him.

The Laws and Commandments of God creating the Solar System and creating Man in His Image are part of the Universal Whole. Thus, the Commandments revealed to Moses and Jesus are filled with Cosmos knowledge through the Prophetic Seals. The eye of the anointed prophet perceives the sacred purposes of each Scriptural Commandment through a dimensional and timeless sight made possible through the opening of the Prophetic Seals.

The past, the present and the future of the planet Earth and the human spirit are enscrolled in the Prophetic Seals within each Scriptural Law and Commandment.

The Holy Law of Tithing is a mighty Law of Creation through which mankind remains receptive to the Providential Grace of God. The opening of the Prophetic Seals within the Tithe Law reveals to the prophet the sacred purposes of this Divine Edict as a fashioner of man in the Image of God.

Each of the Ten Commandments and the Commandments of Love contains Prophetic Seals that open to enlightened seers in God's perfect timing. These Seals unite one with Soul Grace and Godhead Grace beyond Time and Space. This close communion with the *Eternal* Spirit of the Living God places upon his shoulders the mantle of the Prophet-Teacher.

Dimensions beyond Time and Space are known and experienced by enlightened personages receptive to the Prophetic Seals. Over the centuries, numerous Prophetic Seals have revealed their holy splendors to receptive servants of God.

Many persons believe that an individual lives only one life on earth. The Holy Law of Reincarnation inspires a truth-seeker to perceive each person as an on-going creation of God throughout the ages of the planet Earth and the endless eternities of the Universe. The consciousness mind that reverences the Law of Reincarnation is in a position to receive the opening of the Sacred Seals on this mighty Law of Eternal Creation.

"My sheep hear my voice, and I know them, and they follow me: And I give unto them eternal life." (St. John 10:27, 28) The evolution of the Prodigal-Son Consciousness to the *Eternal-Life Consciousness* is the work of the soul and the Image of God. Man is destined for dimensionality in thinking and knowing. Through reincarnation and the Commandment of Life Everlasting, each living soul will bring forth in God's timing the radiant facets and eternal attributes of His Holy Image.

Many religious leaders hinder the spiritual progress of their followers by ignoring, mocking or condemning the ages-old knowledge of the Law of Reincarnation. This sacred Law holds an important key to the attaining of the Prophetic Gifts and Illumination Graces of the Divine-Image Consciousness.

> *The peace beyond the Maya-stimulated and controlled world is a Kingdom of bliss-joy and creative illumination.*
>
> — Ann Ree Colton

"Ye shall receive the reward of the inheritance: for ye serve the Lord Christ." (Colossians 3:24) The opening of the various Seals of Grace is the beginning of one's receiving the *In-*

heritance of his Spiritual Birthright as a son of God. The Wisdom Seals, Inspiration Seals, Realization Seals, Revelation Seals, Prophetic Seals and all other Sacred Seals that open to illumined servants of God testify to the reality of the Inheritance.

To love God and to reverence all energies of Life and Creation lift one above the mundane toward the Timeless and Spaceless Dimensions of the soul and the Divine Image. The Seals of Grace in the First, Second and Third Heavens open to the degree that one's adoration of God and reverent observance of His Commandments remain constant over the years.

Man stands on the threshold of receiving the blessings of God through the opening of key Seals by modern-day prophets and revelators that will be his first communion with the Cosmos. These Seals will reveal the relationship between all Scriptural Statutes and the Image of God as a Universal Constant. Even as the removal of certain Seals on the Laws of Nature introduced man to the Age of Atomic Energies, so will the removal of mighty Seals on the Scriptural Laws, Commandments and Principles be his first glimpse of his destiny as an eternal son of God through the Cosmos energies of the Divine Image.

Worship God: for the testimony of Jesus is the spirit of prophecy.

—Revelation 19:10

PURGING

I am the true vine, and my Father is the husbandman. Every branch in me that beareth not fruit he taketh away: and every branch that beareth fruit, he purgeth it, that it may bring forth more fruit.

—St. John 15:1,2

Each Seal of Grace represents a Blessing from God that manifests as Purging and Quickening.

The releasing of Holy-Spirit energy through a Seal of Grace manifests the dual action of Purging and Quickening. The Light and Truth of God's Spirit within the Grace Seal seek to purge darkness from the soul's record and to add more virtue and grace to one's life and being.

To be purged by the Spirit of God is a blessing and to be quickened by His Spirit is a blessing. However, if a devotee refuses to work honestly and humbly with the purging process accompanying the opening of the Sacred Seals, he will endanger his remaining on the Path.

Many egotistical, prideful and self-deceived probationers refuse to accept purging as a necessary cleansing action through which the Spirit of God seeks to remove darkness from the soul's record. As long as darkness remains, one will continue to express negative traits and attitudes that will hinder his spiritual progress.

> *For whom the Lord loveth he chasteneth, and scourgeth every son whom he receiveth. If ye endure chastening, God dealeth with you as with sons; for what son is he whom the father chasteneth not?*
> —Hebrews 12:6,7

The unconfessed sins recorded in the soul's record create crystallized-energy deposits in the subconsciousness. One's success on the Spiritual Path is determined by his ability to work with the Christ in the dissolving of the sin-sediment in the depths of the subconscious mind.

Sincere repentance and honest confessions to God provide an entry way for the laser-like Light of the Christ to penetrate to the depths of the subconscious and to break up the crystallized sin-energies. The purging of the subconscious mind by the Christ is directly related to the opening of the Grace-Seals: the stronger and deeper the purgings, the greater the Seals of Grace that release their pristine essences of Pure Creation.

The closer a devotee moves toward the Godhead, the more intensive becomes the purging of the darkness from his soul's record. If he works with God, the Christ and his Living Teacher during these inevitable purging times, he will qualify for the opening of the Greater Seals of Grace. The cleansing of the soul's record through purgings results in increasing freedoms, spiritual quickenings, and union with the more powerful voltages of God's Spirit.

It requires great courage, self-honesty and humility to expose one's self to the chastening action of Pure Truth. The Wisdom of God is within every chastening, purging and purification through which one attains the higher rungs on the ladder leading to the Divine-Image Consciousness.

There are minor and major Golgothas in one's life when he walks the Path of the Lord Jesus. These are the times when Satan's forces launch the lesser and greater attacks against a servant of God. Each satanic attack is a time of testing, an opportunity for experiencing spiritual growth and soul-gift quickening.

Each Golgotha or Crucifixion time brings one closer to God and Christ through the fiery purging or cleansing of the soul's record. Thereafter, the faithful devotee experiences Resurrection Grace through which come the birth and expansion of the supernatural gifts of the soul and the dimensional capabilities of the Divine Image. Following each purging, a sincere truth-seeker experiences an increased capacity to receive and to express the Grace of God within His Sacred Seals.

Help us, O God of our salvation, for the glory of thy name: and deliver us, and purge away our sins, for thy name's sake.

—Psalm 79:9

8

THE CREATIVE IMAGINATION

In the center of the forehead resides a spiritual portal called the imaging portal. The higher imagination is active in this portal.

— Ann Ree Colton

The Body-Temple Energy-Field

What? know ye not that your body is the temple of the Holy Ghost which is in you, which ye have of God, and ye are not your own?

— 1 Corinthians 6:19

Every person in the world is an Eternal Creation through the Image of God in the core of his being. He is an energy-universe at one with all energies creating the Cosmos.

Three important attributes the Creator bestows upon each of His children through His Image are *Will, Imagination* and *Memory*. The will, imagination and memory determine one's use of the energies of his senses, emotions and mind. These and all other energies utilized by the individual constitute a creative energy-vortex of action called *the Body-Temple Energy-Field*.

109

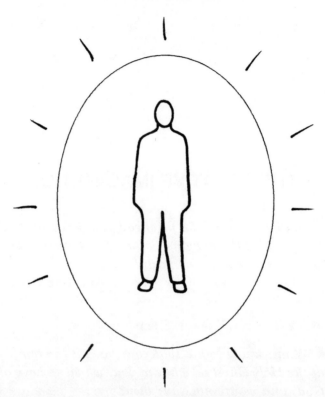

Within the Body-Temple Energy-Field are negative energies and positive energies. All negative energies are potential
positive energies.

Negative energies in the Body-Temple Energy-Field include the misuse of will, imagination and memory; the unconfessed sins of one's present life and past lives; the sins of
parents and ancestors; anti-virtues, vices, harmful habits and
selfish attitudes. These negative energies pollute the Body-
Temple Energy-Field and create dark barriers between the
consciousness mind and the soul.

Positive energies within the Body-Temple Energy-Field relate to the grace earned in the present life and in previous
lives; talents, skills, aptitudes; parental and ancestral grace;
conscience, virtues, logic, love, soul-gifts and other benefic
energies.

Through the purgings and purifications of the spiritual life, a devotee experiences the decrease of negative energies and the increase of positive energies in the Body-Temple Energy-Field. Over the years, loyalty to his vows to God adds increasing measures of Soul-energies, Christ-Light energies, Kingdom-of-Heaven energies, Universal-energies and Image-of-God energies.

> Let us put on the armour of light.
> —Romans 13:12

> Put on the whole armour of God, that ye may be able to stand against the wiles of the devil.
> —Ephesians 6:11

The contest between the negative energies and the positive energies within the Body-Temple Energy-Field continues until all dark energies are vanquished by the Light of God and Christ. When this occurs, the Body-Temple Energy-Field becomes *the armour of light, the whole armour of God.* The attaining of Spiritual Insulation offers protection against the subtle influences of the Antichrist and enables one to remain in an *increasing* State of Grace.

All energy-processes in the Universe fulfill three stages: (1) *Tamasic* * or Dormant Energy; (2) *Rajasic* or Fiery Energy; and (3) *Sattvic* or Harmonious Energy. As a Star prepares for birth, its energies are first dormant; next, it experiences a period of fiery chaos; and, finally, it becomes a radiating light in the Universe. The creation of man in the Image of God fulfills these same three stages. *Tamasic* individuals are inert, apathetic and complacent. *Rajasic* persons are forceful, impulsive and aggressive. *Sattvic* individuals are peaceful, orderly and harmonious.

The energies of the senses, feelings, emotions, thoughts, words and actions may be disciplined or undisciplined. The

---

Tamasic, Rajasic and *Sattvic* are Sanskrit words.

degree of one's self-discipline in all energy processes determines whether he is tamasic, rajasic or sattvic.

The Power of Imaging is a God-given Gift that will become a powerful instrument for man's future work as a co-creator with God. Presently, individuals who are learning how to change the dark energies in their lower natures into lighted energies are beginning their work as protégés of the Saints. The more one expresses the Power of Imaging in service to God, the more he works *knowingly* to change dark energies into energies of light within the Body-Temple Energy-Field.

The Body-Temple Energy-Field of an enlightened servant of God is an *Atmosphere* of Love, Peace and Wisdom; for, with the receiving of the Holy Ghost, his will, imagination and memory become charged with Image-of-God energies.

Thank Thee, Father, for all Thou art revealing of the Splendor of Thy Universe and the Glory of Thy Image.

Man is destined for greatness through the Divine Image. As a co-creator with God, he will experience the joys and raptures of working directly with the Will of God with wisdom and understanding. Through the inspired use of his will, imagination and memory, he will express a beautiful spectrum of virtues and conscience; moral and ethical behavior in all relationships; an unceasing communion with the Three Heavens; and a cognizant awareness of the importance of the planet Earth in its placement in the Milky Way Galaxy and in the Universe.

Imaging is a power of God in you.

Inspiration and the power of spiritual imaging may be attained only through the love of God, the love of life, the love of one's fellow man.

Man is using the power of thought, that it may become the power of imaging through thought. If man fulfills his potential on earth, he will produce creative works and skills of Cosmos proportion. The power of imaging within his mental logos will unite him with the mighty Builders—the Hosts or Hierarchs of the Universe.

—Ann Ree Colton

IMAGE-OF-GOD QUICKENINGS

O Lord, quicken in me those virtues that are yet weak or missing. Quicken in me the conscience, the logic and the love that will enable me to serve Thee and to Glorify Thy Name. May the Grace of Thy Image be free in me, that I may create within the joy of Thy Love. In Jesus' Name. Amen.

In marriage, a husband may try to make his wife and children into *his* image, or a woman may try to make her mate and offspring into *her* image. In a nation, a tyrant or dictator may try to make the citizens into his image. There are many instances in life where individuals consider themselves to be the perfect image that others should imitate.

In many households, the Image of God is never mentioned. Masses of persons throughout the world have accepted political leaders or entertainment personalities as their idols and follow their examples.

The knowledge of the difference between right and wrong, good and evil, is the product of virtue-quickenings and conscience-quickenings through the Image of God. When the holy energies of virtues and conscience are quickened spiritually, one discerns the difference between false images and the Divine Image.

The *will* of man devoid of virtues and conscience becomes a destructive energy in his own life and in the lives of others.

A wilful person may live many lifetimes of self-caused agony and unhappiness before he desires to make God's Will his way of life.

> *Quicken me, O Lord, according to thy loving kindness.*
>
> —Psalm 119:159

"Ask, and it shall be given you." (St. Matthew 7:7) Priceless Image-of-God quickenings can be experienced in one's present life simply by *asking* for them. Each person has the gift of free-will to ask or not to ask for this monumental blessing. One's asking to be spiritually quickened is his first direct working with the deeper and broader ranges of his Divine-Image potential within his will, memory and imagination.

> *As self-creators, men use a mighty function given to them by God. This is the hierarchy-nature will. Men literally are creating themselves with this God-Omnipresence power. It is their heritage.*
>
> —Ann Ree Colton

"I give thee charge in the sight of God, who quickeneth all things." (1 Timothy 6:13) The miraculous transformation from sinner to enlightened Saint in one lifetime testifies to the Power of God's Quickening Spirit. This mighty drama of transformation and illumination occurs in the Body-Temple Energy-Field.

"The Son quickeneth whom he will." (St. John 5:21) One who receives progressive Christ-Light quickenings lives, meditates and prays in an exalted State of Grace—and his soul is free to sing the song of its Eternal Covenant with God.

"The meek shall inherit the earth." (St. Matthew 5:5) Meekness is one of the major virtues that awakens man to his innate potential as a protégé of the Hierarchs. Through Image-of-God quickenings and Christ-Light quickenings,

meekness, harmlessness and love produce the illuminative expressions of the will, the memory and the imagination.

> *And so it is written, the first man Adam was made a living soul; the last Adam was made a quickening spirit.*
>
> —1 Corinthians 15:45

THE CREATIVE AND THE DESTRUCTIVE IMAGINATION

> *And God saw that the wickedness of man was great in the earth, and that every imagination of the thoughts of his heart was only evil continually.*
>
> —Genesis 6:5

> *When one seeks to overcome the trespass laws protecting thought, his mind will become a vessel of peaceful imaging in thought. When one fulfills the ethic correlating to the ethic within all forms and all images, he will become a unifier for all planes, all spheres, all kingdoms.*
>
> —Ann Ree Colton

Man becomes a co-creator with God through the creative imagination. When the imagination is fed by the creation-energies of the Divine Image, one creates immortal works inspired by the Spirit of God.

Where there is sense-domination of the heart and the mind, the creation-energies of the soul and the Image of God cannot be expressed in their purity, originality and uniqueness. The purification of the senses, emotions and thoughts enables the soul and the Divine Image to send their radiant energies into the heart and the mind. The creative imagination then becomes the norm in one's thinking, feeling and serving as an enlightened servant of God.

The imagination is an energy through which God may reveal new ideas, new truths. To be in a State of Grace is to create for and with God through the Divine-Image Consciousness. The Divine-Image Consciousness makes of the imagination a sanctified energy-field of lighted thoughts and holy knowings.

When the imagination is a fertile field for the receiving of the seeds of soul-wisdom, spiritual gifts are activated, and the Presence of God is free to bless and enlighten in increasing measure. The Gift of Prophecy and other sacred gifts of the soul and the Divine Image become natural ways of thinking, seeing, knowing and creating.

> *The wicked in his pride doth persecute the poor:*
> *let them be taken in the devices that they have*
> *imagined.*
>
> —Psalm 10:2

> *He hath shewed strength with his arm; he hath*
> *scattered the proud in the imagination of their*
> *hearts.*
>
> —St. Luke 1:51

The imagination may be a powerful instrument for destruction. The unholy use of the senses creates distorted images, producing destructive energies in the emotions, thoughts and actions.

Man, as an imager, can create distorted images through selfish motives, impure thoughts and immature emotions, or he can create works of soul-beauty through oneness with the Image of God.

Every person is continuously imaging his future path in life. His imaging may be dark images of pessimism, gloom and cynicism, or his imaging may be optimistic, hopeful and cheerful. One's future lives are the direct results of his present-life use of the power and gift of Imaging.

The Holy Law of Reincarnation works with the Solar-

System Cycles to create man in the Image of God. When one desires to work with God in his present life and in all future lives, he has begun to transcend self-made dark images that act as curses upon his present life and coming lives. The dismal lives of masses of poverty-ridden, spiritually-ignorant persons throughout the world testify to the destructive power of dark images. These dark images are past-lives' self-made curses that enclose persons in the prisons of misery, poverty and despair in their present lives.

Dejection, depression and all other negativities of life are the results of dark images created by the destructive imagination.

If one uses the Imaging Principle to create hate-images and violence-images, he will attract hate and violence in coming lives. The imaging of good for others will attract good in one's future lives; his imaging of pure love will attract pure love. *He who expresses good and love in service to God and his fellow man is working with the creative power of Imaging.*

Imaging or visualizing health for others, peace for the nations, and enlightenment for *all* children of God indicates that one is beginning to work with the power of the creative imagination. The purity of the images in one's thoughts keeps him receptive to the Pure Grace of the Soul, the Pure Light of the Christ and the Pure Energies of the Image of God. In this, he works with his hierarchy nature within the Body-Temple Energy-Field.

All negative expressions of the imagination must be healed before the Image of God may utilize the imagination on spiritual, creative levels.

The tendency to dark imaginings can be inherited through the ancestral genes if one's parents and ancestors were pessimistic; always thinking the worst about their children; discouraging rather than encouraging the creative and spiritual desires of their offspring.

The fantasized imagination; the weird imagination; worry,

in which one imagines an unhappy future; projected images based upon the fear of failure; judging, critical-minded, cursing thoughts that image misery, pain and suffering in the lives of one's enemies — all are expressions of the negative or destructive imagination.

The expression of a negative imagination can be destructive for an individual or for masses of persons.

> *To discipline an imprudent imagination, refrain from condemnation, judgment. Envision the soul-grace and pure prototypal presence of each person; and look for the angel standing nigh each one.*
>
> — Ann Ree Colton

The creative imagination receives holy ideas, inspirations and wisdoms from the soul and Heaven's Light. The destructive imagination produces the grotesque, the violent, the antagonistic. When Satan feeds lies into the destructive imagination, one imagines that he has no self-worth, is unloved, and he imagines unreal fantasies that often lead to jealousies and estrangements.

The destructive imagination imagines the false to be true; it blows out of proportion trivial matters, expanding them into major crises.

The creative imagination is a gift from God, providing hope, optimism, inspiration, joy. The destructive imagination is a tool of Satan used to drive the gullible into chronic depressions; separations from loved ones; feelings of unworthiness leading to suicide.

It is just as easy for God to forgive *all* of one's sins as it is for Him to forgive *one* sin. Many devotees on the Path cannot *imagine* that God can be so forgiving; thus, they place mental barriers to their experiencing the Full Forgiveness of God and the Redemption Power of Jesus.

The creative imagination works with the Image of God. The destructive imagination, working with unholy energies from the subconscious levels, builds barricades between man and his divine nature as a child of God.

> *One may create a self-image based upon feelings of unworthiness and self-pity, or he can create a self-image based upon his closeness to the Lord Jesus and his faith in God.*

NEPTUNE

> *The tone of Neptune is an initiator for the imagination, and enables the adept to relate himself to the powers of Universal Imaging.*
>
> *The Neptunian energy-rays play upon the pineal gland and the imaginative processes of the mind. The lunar initiate failing to understand the power of imaging through the process of imagination is a receiver of images rather than a sender of images. A solar psychic initiate using Neptunian planetary power receives his images from the Greater Archetypes and sends them through the power of his own imaging, knowing and creating. All great mystics having sending and receiving telepathic powers have access to the Neptunian fiery crown in the gleaming brain.*
>
> *The highest aspect of clairvoyance is produced through Neptune's osorius or highest pranic atmosphere, that is, wavelengths of revelation superior to mortal sense.*
>
> — Ann Ree Colton

The planet Neptune's higher energies provide the imagination with holy-creation ideas, insights and inspirations. Neptune, the Planet of Divinity, blesses, inspires and enlightens the humble heart and the reverent mind.

The materialistic mind and immoral emotions express wrong imaginings through the lower energies of Neptune. The weird, the unbeautiful, the violence and the sexual fantasies being portrayed in the theater arts, motion pictures and television come from imaginations inspired by the lower energies of Neptune.

Man escapes the Maya-Sea energies through love, virtue and selfless service to God. In this, the mind and emotions become telepathic receivers of the higher energies of Neptune and the other Planets, the Sun and the Moon. Thus begins one's communion with God through the higher or creative energies of the Celestial Bodies in the Solar System.

The creative imagination perceives the prophetic purposes of the Scriptural Commandments, Ethics and Principles. The creative imagination envisions the good for man through the eternal perspective of reincarnation and the Image of God.

The Christ Mind is the creative imagination at one with the soul and the Image of God.

> **Heavenly Father, I pray to think only those thoughts that are pleasing in Thy sight. I pray to express only those emotions that are pleasing in Thy sight. In Jesus' Name. Amen.**

Dark Imaginings

Image in man is perfect. All sickness is distortion of Image. Distortion of Image in man is sense and sentient information based upon duality. The sattvic or hierarchy-nature healer does not ignore all of the functionings which have produced obsession and therefore distortion of Image.

Sattvic and hierarchy are of the divine three or third existing in all forms by and through which man is made perfect in the Image of God, in the atmosphere of perfect good, as realized by the Father for man and as sealed into him in the beginning of this eternity system.

Myopic sense revelation is biased toward disease. The vibration of Ahimsa moves one out of sense-related Im-

age interpretation. Therefore, to be healed, the healer must teach the sufferer to rearrange his heart as a vessel of harmlessness, whereby healing moves beyond mercy of the bearing of suffering into total healing and return to perfect Image as given of God.

—Ann Ree Colton

Many persons are never happy because of dark imaginings. They use the gift of imagination to imagine the negative rather than the positive.

Dark spirits inspire dark imaginings. As long as the mind is receptive to seeds of negative thoughts planted by Satan's agents, one will continue to imagine the worst about everything.

Fearful thoughts that paralyze the body are dark imaginings that destroy the energy processes.

Hypochondriacs are the victims of dark imaginings. Such persons live in a state of fear rather than in a state of grace.

The joy of life is impossible if one is susceptible to the dark side of imagination. The light of the soul fills the heart and mind with thoughts of optimism, good cheer, encouragement; in this, the light of the soul becomes the light in the imagination. A lighted imagination in the Body-Temple Energy-Field produces a continuity of holy, creative thoughts that bring hope and joy to others.

Many persons in the religious and spiritual life are dark imaginers who remain unenlightened because of their unwarranted fears and unreasoning jealousies. Such persons do not bring joy to their mates, families and ministries; they cast shadows of doubt, fear, despondency, depression, gloom, black moods and other negativities fed by dark imaginings.

The Christ heals dark imaginings when they are confessed to God. The healing of dark imaginings unites one with the creative imagination through which God manifests beautiful, inspiring thoughts, words and actions.

One cannot become a disciple, apostle or minister under

Christ if he is serving Satan through dark imaginings. The
true servant of God is recognized by his joy and enthusiasm
in the knowledge of the Father's Mercy, Forgiveness, Compassion and Bountifulness.

**Heavenly Father, I pray to be healed of wrong
imaginings, that I may serve Thee and Thy Beloved Son through a Creative Imagination inspired by Thy Love. In Jesus' Name. Amen.**

Inspired composers, artists, authors and other craftsmen
in the arts and sciences are blessed with a creative imagination at one with the Inspiration-Grace Seals in the Heaven
Worlds. This Grace has been earned by them in previous lives
and returns to bless their present lives.

The true beauty is the beauty of the soul. Through the
creative imagination, one's inspired creations are filled with
soul-beauty; therefore, his works live from decade to decade,
century to century. Soul-beauty in art, music and literature
contains the *eternal* essences of the soul and is recognized by
the souls of others in successive generations. Soul-beauty in
creative works has lasting appeal because of the Eternal Spirit
of God that abides in Holy Inspirations.

Some devotees on the Path are born with high degrees of
Inspiration Grace; however, if they do not have a sense of
practicality to balance their creative imagination, their impracticality will attract major lessons regarding stewardship.
When one has earned in past lives the grace of a fertile, creative imagination, a love for God, and a sense of practicality,
he will live a balanced life of inspired works, faith and good
stewardship.

Probationers who squander or misuse creative-imagination
grace will lose touch with the Sacred Seals in the Heaven
Worlds. When one knows in his heart, mind and soul that he
should use all artistic and spiritual gifts for the glory of God,
he will experience Divine Providence in all areas of his life

and being—and the Seals of Grace will increase their flow through his consciousness mind and creative imagination.

> . . . *whatsoever ye do, do all to the glory of God.*
> —1 Corinthians 10:31

ENTHUSIASM: GOD WITHIN

> *And whatsoever ye do, do it heartily, as to the Lord, and not unto men; Knowing that of the Lord ye shall receive the reward of the inheritance; for ye serve the Lord Christ.*
> —Colossians 3:23,24

> *If anything is worth doing, do it with all your heart. A half-hearted ascetic covers himself with more and more dust.*
> —Buddha

> *We must have joy and enthusiasm to our last breath.*
> —Ann Ree Colton

The word "enthusiasm" comes from a Greek word meaning *God within*. The more the Spirit of God abides in one's heart, mind and soul, the more he expresses a holy enthusiasm. Individuals filled with the Spirit of God's Love and Wisdom express with naturalness a joyful enthusiasm in their service to the Creator and their fellow man.

By serving God and loving His Image in all souls, one remains in constant communion with Him. A creative imagination fired by holy enthusiasm qualifies him to receive the reward of the Inheritance.

Zealousness is not the same as enthusiasm. Zealousness burns itself out; holy enthusiasm is as a steady flame of joy-filled love for God and one's fellow man that inspires him to continue from day to day in his spiritual disciplines and dedications.

The creative imagination thrives in an atmosphere of holy enthusiasm. Over the years, a true student of the higher life increases in holy enthusiasm and creative imagination, for he personally experiences the Redeeming Power of Jesus and the rewards of the Inheritance.

> *In order to do great things, one must be enthusiastic.*
>
> —Saint Simon

> *Everyone must do his work to the fullest. He must give all of himself. He must have ardor in what he is doing. He must enjoy it. He must have enthusiasm. And he must always be a spirit of happiness in the presence of evil.*
>
> —Ann Ree Colton

Progress on the Spiritual Path is measured by the degree of constancy in love. One who proves his love for God over the years of fiery trials, purgings and purifications is a worthy candidate for the Divine-Marriage Anointing.

Enthusiasm is a requisite for an aspirant who would earn the Divine Marriage with his beloved Lord.

A devotee who covenants with his soul to undergo Job's Trials will experience major initiations regarding his health, money, honor and family. Each trial is a test of his integrity to see if he will blame God for his difficulties or if he will continue to love God with an enthusiastic love. When he affirms and re-affirms his love for God during each initiatory trial and testing, he will strengthen the fabric of his dedication, thereby qualifying to receive increasing measures of his Spiritual-Birthright Inheritance. "*. . . till I die I will not remove mine integrity from me.*" (Job 27:5)

A decrease in an aspirant's enthusiasm indicates that the Antichrist, rather than Christ, is influencing his emotions and thoughts. Satan, the Great Thief, is always trying to steal a person's enthusiasm and to block him from receiving the Inheritance. A devotee on the Spiritual Path must be eternally vigilant or else he will permit Satan to influence his emotions and thoughts. A sure sign that one is being victimized by the Antichrist is when he no longer feels any enthusiasm in his attitudes toward God, Life or Truth.

Probationers who succumb to "the wiles of the devil" (Ephesians 6:11) fail to worship God on the Sabbath Day, or worship as a duty rather than as a sacred privilege. They either decrease their giving to God or cease placing their tithes and offerings on His Altar. They also discontinue their daily worship-periods of prayer, meditation and study, and disregard the instruction of their Teacher.

> *Enthusiasm is the genius of sincerity, and truth accomplishes no victories without it.*
> —Bulwer-Lytton

> *Nothing great was ever achieved without enthusiasm.*
> —Ralph Waldo Emerson

Enthusiasm inspires the hopeful expectation of receiving blessings and quickenings through God's Holy Spirit from Sabbath to Sabbath, New Moon to New Moon.

As long as one has breath in his body, he can experience the blessing of God's Spirit which will manifest as increasing enthusiasm. Thereafter, the Creator can use his life and ministry in miraculous and beautiful ways.

In ministries in which the Spirit of God is withdrawing, there is less and less joy, less and less enthusiasm for life, for worship of God, for serving others. A Holy-Spirit Ministry is a study in enthusiasm, for the Spirit of God is ever-present, providing new songs, new inspirations and new realizations.

Enthusiasm charged with God's Spirit is filled with hope, good cheer, optimism. When this joyous enthusiasm is used in service to God and Christ Jesus, one becomes a true Apostolic Ambassador for the Lord of Love. The healings, reconciliations and miracles of the spiritual life add surge after surge of God's Spirit to one's ministering, creating and serving in Jesus' Name.

A Teacher anointed by the Spirit of God and appointed by the Christ has proved worthy because of a childlike faith and an enthusiastic willingness to do humble tasks.

> *The hierarchy-nature imaging power is most successful when one is optimistic. When one is depressed and negative, fearful and unbelieving, he is united with the Destroying Archetypes. One who is continually in a state of depression assures himself of a life of limitation and of failure. All healers are enthusiastic and joyful transcribers of their Archetypal Imaging Power.*
>
> — Ann Ree Colton

There is a real enthusiasm and a synthetic enthusiasm. One cannot fool God. The Creator knows who has an enthusiastic love for Him and His Laws — and He rewards them bountifully.

God loves each of His children enthusiastically. When one experiences the enthusiastic love of God for him, his joys multiply rapidly. *"These things have I spoken unto you, that my joy might remain in you and that your joy might be full."* (St. John 15:11)

An enthusiastic love for the Image of God within one's mate, loved ones, friends, co-disciples and his fellow man provides him with the insulation necessary for the attaining of Spiritual Enlightenment.,

A married couple may have an enthusiastic love in the beginning of their marriage; however, if they are not vigilant, Satan will strip away their enthusiasm until their marriage becomes an exercise in boredom, mediocrity and, in many instances, disrespect, discouragement and depression. Such marriages often lead to separation and divorce.

When God's Spirit blesses a husband and wife for their dedication and devotion to Him, His energies of Divine Love enfold the marriage and family. There are effervescent joys; creativity abounds; and love increases, giving rise to greater enthusiasm. Where there are increasing joy and love, the Spirit of God is blessing and energizing the marriage.

An enthusiastic father and mother are good examples to their children. Such parents are planting seeds of grace in receptive children. Children feel warmed and protected when they observe their parents' enthusiastic love for one another and will emulate their parents' examples in their own lives and marriages.

A marriage without love and enthusiasm is a dull, boring, *tamasic* marriage. In a *rajasic* eye-for-an-eye marriage, husband and wife are easily offended, irritated and angered—and try to hurt each other by retaliating through words, actions, emotions and thoughts. An enthusiastic love heals and exorcises the spirit of lethargy in tamasic marriages and the retaliative eye-for-an-eye attitudes in rajasic marriages.

In a *Love-Ye-One-Another Marriage*, the husband and the wife love each other with a holy constancy. Peace, harmony, creativity and worship-of-God make of the marriage a *sattvic* marriage. The Spirit of God abides in such marriages, and both the husband and the wife are receptive to the opening of the Seals of Grace in the Heaven Worlds. In such marriages, there are sweet joys, spiritual growth, prospering and the creative imagination.

God tests one's enthusiasm in work, marriage and in his spiritual life.

Before a devotee may sit at the Lord's Table, he must have in his hand the key to the Inner Kingdom—the key of enthusiasm. The key of enthusiasm provides him with the Illumination-Treasures of his Spiritual Birthright that come in increasing measure.

> *Two inches below the navel of the physical body dwells a vital secondary chakra which is a repository of white light, virility and vitality. This vitality is a derivative of pure Akash—the substance used in all imaging, forming and shaping. This white pranic kundalini-light seated two inches below the navel regenerates the life-force in all chakras and nadis, making vigorous the vital aspects of life. To consciously utilize this intermediary chakra and the reinvigorating white fire below the solar-plexus chakra is to receive extended length of life, ultra vitality to the brain, resiliency to the nervous system, bubbling enthusiasm and perpetual joy.*
>
> *When one draws this white light to the heart chakra and meditates on the sacred atom within the center of the heart chakra, clockwise action is assured within the three lower chakras. The chakras below then become his servants, his intuitive revealers, and his volitional energizers.*
>
> —Ann Ree Colton

When a student proves diligent in his study and conscientious in working with his Living Teacher, he experiences the clockwise action of the three lower chakras. In this, the kundalini and chakras send forth vital energies to be used in service to God and his fellow man. Enthusiasm reveals that all chakras are working in clockwise harmony with the Will of God. Such persons are at peace with themselves and channel the Joy of God and Christ to the world.

Enlightened virtues and a cleansed conscience produce good cheer, a happy spirit and wholesome, stabilized attitudes unwaveringly at one with God. Through enlightened virtues, a cleansed conscience and clockwise chakras, one receives the continuous opening of the Seals of Grace. In this, his creative imagination remains a fertile field at one with the Eternal Wellspring of God's Love and Wisdom.

My works now become joyous with holy enthusiasm; and, if it is the Will, I would partake of the Saintly communion accompanying works of worthiness.

—Ann Ree Colton

9

THE BLISS CONSCIOUSNESS

When man contains the full spectrum of virtues, this is total happiness and bliss consciousness, blessing all. Only the bliss consciousness can give the eternal blessing.

— Ann Ree Colton

BLISS, ECSTASY AND JOY

Rouse thyself! do not be idle! Follow the law of virtue! The virtuous rest in bliss in this world and in the next.

— Buddha

Bliss, ecstasy and joy play important roles in God's Plan of Creation, Procreation, Initiation and Illumination. The classic Path leading toward union with God contains many stages, degrees and dimensions of bliss, ecstasy and joy.

The Bliss Consciousness is a reality. It is a state of attainment on the Spiritual Path through the Image of God.

Many modern-day religious pray-ers and meditators seek spiritual ecstasies and divine bliss rather than serving others and liberating souls in bondage to Satan. Jesus had the Bliss Consciousness; however, He never stopped serving His fellow man and contesting the evil in the world. To seek bliss or ecstasy for its own sake is to disconnect oneself from the teaching of Jesus to minister to others and to endure the rigors of active Apostleship in His Name.

The Bliss Consciousness must be earned. It is earned through the disciplines, dedications, virtues and vows of the spiritual life.

Many persons enter into a physical marriage only to discover that their mates are disloyal, lazy, petty, and lack self-control. God protects against this happening in the Divine Marriage by requiring that each sincere devotee experience a thorough and continuous screening of his attitudes, virtues and motives during the probationary period. Aspirants who qualify for the receiving of the Divine-Marriage *Bliss-Anointing* become the appointed servants of the Living God. The Bliss Anointing that begins the Divine Marriage is indescribable in its beauty and profound in its dimensionality.

> *The Lord thy God is a consuming fire. In truth the fire which is God consumes, to be sure, but it does not destroy. It burns sweetly. It leaves one desolate unto bliss.*
>
> — Saint Bernard

> *When you are truly baptized by the Holy Spirit, you drop everything and you stand naked before God.*
> *Anointing does not always come with ecstatic joy. To one who must serve his God, anointing must come through the rain of fire. When the smoke and stench of self-consummation have been fulfilled, the cool logic of Seraphim is at hand. One is then ready for the scepter or wand of Mediation and Peace.*
>
> — Ann Ree Colton

As God's Spirit approaches a worthy devotee, the *Pure Truth* within His Spirit seeks to purge out all wrong attitudes; to cleanse the soul's record of sin-debts; and to replace negative traits with holy virtues. Thus, for those who retain sin-shadows in their souls, the Bliss Anointing of Pure Truth is an Agony and Ecstasy experience, for Pure Truth exposes and magnifies one's faults as well as reveals the secrets and mysteries of God. As one's faults are confessed and corrected, the bliss-ecstasy of Pure Truth may be experienced without the agony of dying to lower-nature traits.

God speaks through pain; He speaks through bliss. Important lessons are learned through pain and bliss. Pain gives birth to Truth; bliss gives birth to Truth. Pain gives birth to Conscience; bliss gives birth to Conscience. Pain gives birth to Virtue; bliss gives birth to Virtue. Pain gives birth to Soul-Powers; bliss gives birth to Soul-Powers. God as Omnipresence is present within all lessons learned and all processes through which they are learned. Blessed is he who listens to the Voice of God speaking through pain and through bliss.

"Receive ye the Holy Ghost." (St. John 20:22) The disciples of Jesus at Pentecost experienced the Holy Ghost and were accused by observers of being drunk from the effects of "new wine." The Presence of the Holy Ghost produced a spiritual intoxication that the uninitiated could not understand.

To experience the Dimensional Bliss and Ecstasies of the Divine-Marriage Anointing transforms a devotee into an enlightened Teacher of Truth. An Anointed Teacher holds sacred and holy the times of bliss and ecstasy experienced in the Divine Marriage. The fruits of each bliss and ecstasy visitation by God's Holy Spirit become manifested works of Pure Creation, Archetypal Knowledge and Universal Wisdom.

> *Eternal Spirit is that One called God. Holy Spirit or Esse is an Intelligible attribute of Eternal Spirit or God acting as sound, movement, ecstasy, revelation, bliss, peace, power.*
>
> *Through love the Anointing and the Blessing come. From Blessing comes Bliss. Bliss is the highest state of Grace! There is no limit to the Bliss Principle.*
>
> —Ann Ree Colton

When two people meet and fall in love, they experience many new joys; there is bliss and ecstasy in each touch and embrace. It is only *after* they speak their Marriage Vows that they are lawfully and spiritually permitted to experience the bliss-ecstasies of love-making involving the procreation energies.

When a devotee first turns toward God, there are holy joys received through various healings, inspirations, coincidings, and prayers answered. He experiences ecstasy and bliss when reading the beautiful Scriptural passages charged with God's Holy Spirit, and also when receiving sacred instruction from an enlightened Teacher. However, there are *deeper* levels and dimensions of bliss and ecstasy that open when the devotee is impregnated by God's Holy Spirit through the Divine-Marriage Anointing. With impregnation comes Fulness of Grace. Fulness of Grace is the Bliss Consciousness.

The student must become as a babe at the breast of instruction, taking of the milk of truth with perfect trust in his Teacher. In this, he receives knowledge into his own truth-core of being and experiences the elevated bliss of the mind illumined.
— Ann Ree Colton

God places an enlightened Teacher in one's life so that the student can be prepared for the Divine Marriage. Conscientious students work with their Teacher heart to heart, mind to mind, soul to soul.

Through daily devotions, self-denial, self-honesty, humility, compassion, righteousness and the other great virtues of the soul and the Image of God, one weaves his wedding garment for the Divine Marriage. His wedding garment of holy virtues protects him from the wiles of Satan and enables him to channel the greater voltages of God's Holy Spirit.

Through procreation-bliss, a child is conceived; through the Bliss of God's Anointing Spirit, Soul-Gifts are conceived.

Even as the birth of a new child means added responsibility, so does the birth of Spiritual Gifts mean new and greater responsibilities. God knows the exact moment a devotee is ready to honorably meet the new responsibilities accompanying Soul-Gift births and blesses him accordingly. All aspirants on the Path should prove to God each day their ability to fulfill their responsibilities in all areas of stewardship. As their honorableness in stewardship increases, so will their Gifts and Graces increase along with their responsibilities.

Each virtue, being a facet of the Divine Image, contains Heaven's Light within it. The light in a virtue may be expressed on the level of the First Heaven, the Second Heaven or the Third Heaven. When one meditates with his virtues expressing the First-Heaven degrees of God's Grace, he has attained the Nirvana levels of the Bliss Consciousness. *Nirvana* means the extinction of the lower self with its many attachments to the Pleasure Principle. The death of the lower nature precedes the birth of the higher nature.

Through the initiatory process, a servant of God is prepared for virtue-quickenings that lift him to the Second-Heaven degrees of God's Grace. If he earns the next stage of virtue-quickenings, he will express the Third-Heaven degrees of God's Grace, which is Revelation Grace through the Divine-Image Consciousness. The Revelation Bliss experienced by an anointed servant of God is filled with priceless understandings and insights of Cosmic and Cosmos proportions.

The Divine-Image Consciousness and the Bliss Consciousness are one.

PURE LOVE

The joy of the Lord is your strength.
—Nehemiah 8:10

The heart center is the mediator. With love in the heart for all, holding hatred for none, uniting

*with the divine, the bliss of eternality comes to rest
in the diamond medallion of the soul.*
—Ann Ree Colton

To qualify for the Bliss Anointing of the Divine Marriage,
one's only thoughts should be love for God, love for His Image,
love for His Cosmos Plan, love for His Beloved Son, and
love for His children. Love is the only way a devotee can unite
with the Presence of God and its infinite degrees and dimensions
of bliss, ecstasy and joy.

When a husband and wife have *pure love* for each other,
it is sheer ecstasy being together. When a devotee of the Lord
has pure love for God and his fellow man, he enjoys an ecstatic
communion with the Love of God's Image sealed within
his fellow man.

Pure love for a mate is bliss and ecstasy. Pure love for God
is bliss and ecstasy. As long as one expresses *pure love*, he will
experience the ecstasy of communion with God and with a
beloved mate.

Pure love for the Image of God in all souls results in the
joy and ecstasy of miracles and grace-manifestations.

Persons who love flowers become ecstatically happy each
time they look at a flower with its delicate beauty in color and
design. The more spiritually-minded they are, the closer they
feel to God when contemplating His creation of flowers in
their combinations of colors, fragrances and graceful responses
to the wind.

Lovers of music become blissfully ecstatic when hearing an
inspired composition. Persons who do not have the sensitivity
of the music lover or the flower lover do not experience
the same bliss-ecstasies and joys. Music means nothing to
them and flowers are taken for granted.

The *spiritualized sensitivity* of an anointed servant of God
inspires him to delight in *all* of God's creations in Nature, in
color, in music, in the human spirit. His love for God is translated
into a love for *all* that God has created. In this, he re-

mains in a state of bliss-ecstasy, joyfully united with the Presence of God within all that Is.

A Truth-lover is in a state of ecstasy whenever he hears the Truth or reads the Truth. God's *Spirit* in the Truth inspires ecstatic responses and joyful inspirations in devotees who love God as the Pure and Absolute Truth.

When a self-infatuated person hears or reads the Truth, he is unresponsive. When a faithful devotee of the Lord hears or reads the Truth, he is made ecstatically happy by the Spirit of God within the Truth.

The Bliss-Presence of God abides in the core of every number, letter and symbol. Dynamic realizations occur through union with the Presence of God within a number, letter or symbol.

One's love for people brings the joy of life.

To love the Image of God is to experience a bliss-communion with God in all souls. Through this inspired love, one knows that the Eternal Image of God contains the seeds for man's attaining Godlike powers and that each life is a step toward these powers. He does not see man as hopelessly bound to sin, for he knows that all men will become like the Illumined Jesus in some age or eternity.

Eternal life is in the soul of man. This provides him with eternal powers, bringing peace, bliss and joy into his life.

— Ann Ree Colton

An unenlightened individual will look on the faces of persons and see nothing unusual and experience nothing spiritual. An enlightened servant of God will look on the faces of persons and experience a bliss-ecstasy communion with the Image of God within them. Only God can open this bliss-ecstasy knowing of His Image. To experience even a brief glimpse of the innate divinity of man through the Image of God is a memorable encounter with a powerful truth.

Whatever blessing of joy, ecstasy or bliss one receives from God should be returned to Him in the spirit of Holy Poverty. This keeps the devotee receptive to the expanding flow of blessings through the Holy Increase of God.

The Sacrament of Communion cleanses and purges as it redeems and enlightens. To recognize the Christ Light as it affects every area of one's life and being is to work with His Light. Joy and ecstasy result when a devotee is freed from ancestral-sin bondages and past-lives' sin-debts through the Redeeming Grace of Christ Jesus within the Sacrament.

The Bliss Consciousness denotes the marriage between the love-emotions and the compassionate mind. When this blending occurs, all energies of the emotions and the mind are in harmonious accord with the soul and the Image of God.

When the emotions are married to God, one is in the state of holy ecstasy or divine intoxication.
— Ann Ree Colton

And I make it my business only to persevere in His holy presence, wherein I keep myself by a simple attention, and a general fond regard to God, which I may call an actual presence of God; or, to speak better, an habitual, silent, and secret conversation of the soul with God, which often causes me joys and raptures inwardly, and sometimes also outwardly, so great that I am forced to use means to moderate them and prevent their appearance to others.
— Brother Lawrence

THE LAWFUL AND THE UNLAWFUL

It is difficult for a man laden with riches to climb the steep path that leadeth unto bliss.
— Muhammad

In the duality of the world, the taste of pleasure is both bitter and sweet. In expression of good, the taste of divine rightness within the perfect and fulfilling Law of Truth is bliss-happiness and bliss-joy.

— Ann Ree Colton

There are *lawful* and *unlawful* joys, ecstasies and bliss.

Bliss may be on the sensual levels of the lower nature or on the spiritually exalted levels of the divine nature. Lower-nature bliss is karma-laden. Divine-nature bliss comes through the Image of God in the Bliss-Dimensions of the Godhead. Divine Bliss unites one with the Godhead-energies through which the Creator is creating the Universe.

Sexual ecstasies experienced by unmarried persons are unlawful. Lust expressed by unmarried or married persons offends the Holy Laws governing ecstasy and bliss, exacting painful penalties. There also are heavy penalties for ecstasies and bliss attained through the taking of drugs.

God's Plan is one of order based upon Laws of Creation in which joy, ecstasy and bliss fulfill important functions. However, Satan tries to entice persons into experiencing joys, ecstasies and bliss *before* they have been earned through Morality, Righteousness, Virtue and Love.

Many persons are falling into Satan's snares through unlawful ecstasies and bliss. Promiscuous sex, fornication, premarital sex, perversion and adultery are unlawful ecstasies used by Satan to drag persons farther away from their Divine-Image natures and locking them in the prisons of karmic bondage. Such persons attract pain equal to their unlawful pleasures.

A pure sexual life must be supported by reverence, sacrifice and right giving.

When the act of sex is consummated as a sacramental action, the consciousness rises into the greatest of all powers: pure will and true imaging. Thus, it is important that one aspire to become a

cleansed instrument for God. A pure, passionless instrument transposes passion as ecstasy into the higher superconscious state of grace. Intense feeling, when selfless, is holy ecstasy.
—Ann Ree Colton

The bliss-ecstasy of the procreative act is connected with the bliss-ecstasy of the Godhead. Even as the energies of the Godhead perpetuate the creation of Stars and Galaxies in the Universe, so do the energies of procreation perpetuate human life on earth.

The sexual function fulfills God's Will when observed with love, reverence and an awareness of the Divine Image in one's mate. The children born through the bliss-ecstasy energies of procreation are offered the sacred opportunities of life to discover their Divine-Image potentials.

Sexual energies are sacred; however, they can be desecrated. Money as energy is sacred; it, too, can be desecrated. Any energy given to man by God is sacred, but it can be desecrated. When *all* energies provided by the Creator are used reverently, sacramentally, they retain the sacred essences of God's Pure Spirit. Thus, through reverent and sacramental living, a Saintly soul remains in close communion with God through the basic energies of life, which to him are *holy*. The unenlightened receive the same God-given energies—and desecrate them.

Cigarette-smoking, intoxication through alcohol, drug-related highs through marijuana, heroin, cocaine, and other addictive drugs—all are offenses against the Body Temple, the Soul and the Image of God. Millions of persons die each year from the effects of cigarette smoking, alcohol and drugs. Millions more suffer destruction of the brain cells, the memory, the nervous system, the immune system and other energy processes. Satan claims many prisoners through unlawful ecstasies. The price paid for unlawful bliss and ecstasy may require payment extending over many coming lives.

"Deliver us from evil." (St. Luke 11:4) To be delivered from the spirit of addiction, the spirit of immorality, the spirit of perversion and other evil spirits is the beginning of a new and transformed life through the Christ. The sacred joys, ecstasies and bliss experienced through God's Holy Spirit and the Christ Light are healing energies that prosper one's life, ennoble his being, and contribute to his enlightenment.

"There is joy in the presence of the angels of God over one sinner that repenteth." (St. Luke 15:10) Holy joy begins with sincere repentance. The joy of the Angels flows into the life, heart, mind and soul of the penitent. Thus begins his walk on the Path of the Higher Life as a devotee of the Lord of Unceasing Grace.

Sincere repentance *unlocks* the prison of karma; confession to God *opens* the prison door; and penance and restitution keep one *free* so that he may begin to experience the *lawful* pleasures, joys, ecstasies and bliss of the Holy Spirit! God is magnanimous with diversities of gifts and bountiful blessings for those who love Him and keep His Commandments.

"It is your Father's good pleasure to give you the kingdom." (St. Luke 12:32) The Father's good pleasure is the *Higher Pleasure Principle*. Even as there is a spectrum of lower pleasure-principle joys through the sensual nature, so is there a spectrum of Higher Pleasure-Principle joys that follow repentance.

> *Joy has two relatings in the mind of man: sensual joy and spiritualized joy. Sensual joy feeds the lower mind of man. Sensual joy is rooted in man's desire nature to experience pleasure at any cost. Sensual joy obscures and obliterates the conscience. Spiritualized joy stems from the true bliss-nature founded upon rightness or righteousness within the will or hierarchy nature of the Higher Self. One must choose between the two joys.*
>
> *As man develops more and more definitive quali-*

*ties in his intellect, he is likely to crave sensual joy
through wrong sentiment attitudes. Through excessive pride, he draws upon the lower pleasure principle to obtain indulgences in every form of action.*

*When one enters into bliss, he is in the Most
High Pleasure Principle.*

— Ann Ree Colton

SAINTLY SOULS AND THE SUPERCONSCIOUSNESS

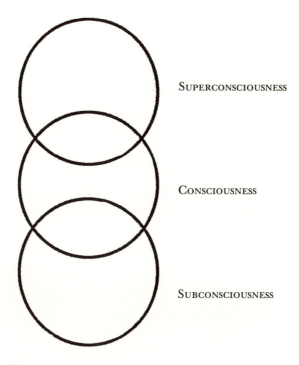

SUPERCONSCIOUSNESS

CONSCIOUSNESS

SUBCONSCIOUSNESS

*O martyr's blood
    that did fall,
    forgive us all.
O martyr's pain,
    help us to refrain
    from persecuting the righteous and the pure.*

O martyr's soul,
*   your life and death were not in vain.*
*   For your testimony doth remain*
*   in the bosom of the earth forevermore.*

While many persons in modern-day religions do little or nothing in service to God, the history of the world is filled with the heroic examples of Saints and Martyrs who have laid down their lives for righteousness' sake. God rewards with abundant gifts and graces all who suffer persecution and martyrdom for His Name's sake.

The soul-joys, sacred ecstasies and bliss-visitations of the Holy Spirit experienced by Saintly souls are among the many rewards earned through their sacrifices and their loyalty to God over many lifetimes. The Creator anoints these courageous ones from life to life with the priceless blessings of inspiration, wisdom and spiritual gifts.

"Blessed are they which are persecuted for righteousness sake: for theirs is the kingdom of heaven." (St. Matthew 5:10) To walk the Path of the Martyred Jesus is to represent righteousness and truth in a world filled with violence, immorality, greed and unrighteousness. To serve the Cause of Christ from life to life is to receive priceless blessings and Inheritances of Grace whether one is in Heaven or on earth.

> *The Joy is in serving the Cause of Christ. Regardless of the punishing blows by the Antichrist-forces in the world, the servant of God remains at one with the Joy of serving the Cause of Christ. This is true Bliss; this is true Ecstasy.*

Righteous souls who attain Sainthood have reached high degrees of Image-of-God expression in their hearts, minds and lives. The virtues of a true Saint represent major accomplishments on the Path of Eternal Life. Through virtues and conscience sanctified by the Holy Spirit, a Saint is able to think through the *superconscious* mind.

A consciousness mind at one with the superconsciousness receives thoughts of inspiration, joy, gladness and holy enthusiasm inspired by the soul and the Spirit of God. Thus, a Saintly soul is optimistic at all times, expressing hope and good cheer even under the most adverse conditions, persecutions and martyrdoms.

The Divine-Image Consciousness is a mind filled with superconscious energies.

There are countless combinations of expressions in the consciousness. Many of these may be fed by the subconsciousness, which is a world of fantasies, fears, dark energies, buried guilts, obsessions, depressions, and numerous other negative compulsions. A consciousness mind devoted to thoughts of lust, anger, greed, pride, egotism, prejudice or covetousness is receiving these unwholesome attitudes from the subconsciousness.

A materialistic consciousness absorbed with worldly pleasures and possessions blocks the superconsciousness from dissolving one's fixations, wilfulness and selfishness. Atheism and agnosticism denote a deficiency of superconscious soul-light in the consciousness mind.

A penitent walking the Path of the Saints and the Lord Jesus is given many sacred tools with which to protect himself from the Pandora's Box of the subconsciousness and to prepare his consciousness mind to receive the Spirit of God as superconscious energy. As the residue of unconfessed sins in the subconsciousness is cleansed, the superconsciousness becomes an increasing presence in the consciousness mind.

The Bliss Consciousness represents a cleansed subconsciousness. The cleansing of the subconsciousness brings peace and joy through freedom from guilt, depression, fears and doubts. In this, the soul's radiance is free to shine through the chakras or soul-gates relating to all energy-processes of the physical body, the emotions and the mind.

> *Each one in the earth is eternal, swimming in universal love, a holy vehicle of light expressing the Image of God in him. When one desires to throw off the weight of his karma, he is seeking to come to quiet, hungering for union with God, the Eternal One. When one desires with a holy intensity to know the Will of God for him, Kundalini joyously breaks out of her prison cell at the base of the spine, moving upward rather than outward.*
>
> *By taking hold of one's karma, by being teachable, by knowing oneself to be Eternal, the rise of Kundalini is joy, bliss-peace and happiness.*
>
> — Ann Ree Colton

Repentance, confession, penance and restitution transform one's mental and emotional energies into beautiful expressions of Soul Grace and Divine Grace. These powerful practices activate the creative and prophetic influences of the superconsciousness in dreams and in the waking state.

The superconscious mind expresses the dimensional and transcendental powers of the soul. When the light of the superconsciousness fills the chalice of the consciousness mind, a truth-seeker has an *enlightened* consciousness — a spiritual-creative consciousness blessed by God and Christ.

The superconsciousness, as a bright light, blesses the consciousness mind with wisdom, grace and peace. One may perceive and fulfill the Will of God only through the supernatural qualities of the superconsciousness.

Jesus was able to perform His miracles through His superconsciousness mind blessing the Image of God in those whom He healed, raised from the dead, and sanctified with the Holy-Ghost Baptism.

All Saints and their protégés hold before man the Image of that which he will become when his soul graces him with the superconscious energies of the Bliss Consciousness.

> *In the present time, the Saints in Heaven come to revive the fervency within worship. The down-pouring of Saintly-ecstasy is rolling in as ocean waves into the congregations, that the congregations may press forth to the Altars, demanding the charge of the Holy Spirit; demanding the virtue to return to the Altars.*
>
> *He who steps into the radiant light of a Saint is blessed. Transmission bliss-power is inevitable when one lives near and by a Saint. There is no Being having had human form more aware of human need than a Saint with bliss consciousness.*
>
> — Ann Ree Colton

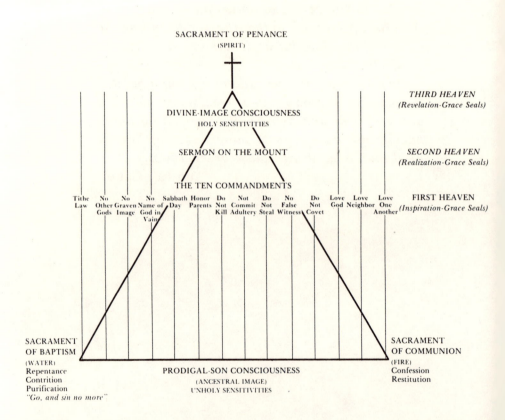

SACRAMENT OF PENANCE
(SPIRIT)

DIVINE-IMAGE CONSCIOUSNESS
HOLY SENSITIVITIES

SERMON ON THE MOUNT

THE TEN COMMANDMENTS

THIRD HEAVEN
(Revelation-Grace Seals)

SECOND HEAVEN
(Realization-Grace Seals)

FIRST HEAVEN
(Inspiration-Grace Seals)

Tithe Law	No Other Gods	No Graven Image	No Name of God in Vain	Sabbath Day	Honor Parents	Do Not Kill	Not Commit Adultery	Do Not Steal	No False Witness	Do Not Covet	Love God	Love Neighbor	Love One Another

SACRAMENT
OF BAPTISM
(WATER)
Repentance
Contrition
Purification
"Go, and sin no more"

PRODIGAL-SON CONSCIOUSNESS
(ANCESTRAL IMAGE)
UNHOLY SENSITIVITIES

SACRAMENT
OF COMMUNION
(FIRE)
Confession
Restitution

10

REDEMPTION: PROGRESSIVE
STATES OF GRACE

Giving thanks unto the Father, which hath made us meet to be partakers of the inheritance of the saints in light: Who hath delivered us from the power of darkness, and hath translated us into the kingdom of his dear Son: In whom we have redemption through his blood, even the forgiveness of sins: Who is the image of the invisible God, the firstborn of every creature.

—Colossians 1:12–15

DIMENSIONAL REDEMPTION

There is a soul-contract between God and the contrite and repentant heart. Grace remains in one's life only if he ceases to do that thing for which he asks to be forgiven. To be in a State of Grace is to be karma-free, unblemished, pure.

All avatars before Jesus brought soul-expansion containing something of Grace. Jesus brought man to the place where he can recognize and receive Grace in its fulness. He revealed to man how he could become a vessel to channel Grace.

147

He who walks this earth in a State of Grace in one life must return to the earth as a vehicle of Grace, that others may be benefited by the supernatural and divine operations within Grace.

— Ann Ree Colton

The spiritual life is a life of Grace. He who is in a State of Grace is reaping the rewards and inheritances of a life devoted to God.

"And of his fulness have all we received, and grace for grace. For the law was given by Moses, but grace and truth came by Jesus Christ." (St. John 1:16,17) The Path of Redemption through the Christ takes one through progressive States of Grace. These include the Probationer State-of-Grace, the Devotee State-of-Grace, the Initiate State-of-Grace, and the Teacher State-of-Grace. Each State of Grace represents many lessons learned and blessings earned.

The closer you come to the Divine Image, the more you are filled with Grace and Truth.

Redemption is God's Gift to man through Christ. Every person being created in the Image of God may receive the Cup of Redemption at any time; all he needs to do is reach forth his hand through Repentance — and the Cup of Redemption is his.

To the Anointed is given the sacred task of presenting the Cup of Redemption to others. He who receives this Cup with gratitude and presses it to his lips with reverence begins to walk the Golden Pathway. With the Lord of Love to shepherd him, he becomes one of the redeemed. Resurrected, he works with the Lord Christ as His apostle; anointed, he works with God as His son.

The Cup of Redemption offered by the Christ is filled with the Love and Mercy of God. Forgiveness comes and healings manifest through the Cup of Redemption. Redemption begins with the *Remission* of sins and eventually produces the *Absolution* of sins.

Heavenly Father, I pray to have a right repentance, that I may know a true Redemption through Christ, my Lord.

"For all have sinned, and come short of the glory of God; Being justified freely by his grace through the redemption that is in Christ Jesus." (Romans 3:23,24) The Redemption Power of Jesus not only redeems the individual who repents and turns toward God, but the *Grace* forfeited through sinning in the present life and in past lives is also redeemed! Through the miraculous Redemption Power of Jesus, a sincere penitent experiences the progressive States of Grace occurring through the reconciliation and synchronization of the Redeemed Grace of the present life with the Redeemed Grace of previous lives.

As one proves devoted to the Laws and Commandments of God and the Sermon-on-the-Mount Principles of Jesus, he becomes more centered on the Path of Devotion. In cyclic timings, he is given the opportunity to make restitution for sin-debts incurred *before* he stepped foot on the Path. As long as a devotee remains humble, contrite, self-honest and honorable, he will meet each debt as it is presented. In this, he unites with the *Dimensional Degrees* of the Redemption Power of Jesus that produce the higher States of Grace.

Everything is redeemable through Christ. Every mistake one has ever made in this life or in past lives; every sin he has committed, either wittingly or unwittingly; every failure to keep vows in marriage or in his spiritual life — all are forgiven, healed, resolved and rectified through his working with the Dimensional, Supernatural Powers of the Great Redeemer, Christ Jesus. Thereafter, he may stand in the freedom-light of his soul, resplendently adorned in the radiance of the Divine Image with its diamond-like versatilities of gifts and graces.

Through Christ, all of the *Blessings* and *Inheritances* of God forfeited through sinning in former lives can be redeemed in one's present life! As an aspirant establishes his sincerity, integrity and honorableness in God's sight, he experiences the miraculous transformations in body, heart, mind and soul that occur through the Dimensional Redemption Power of Christ Jesus.

Each progressive State of Grace gives one a clearer picture of the Image of God. The more a devotee reverences the Image of God within his own being and within his fellow man, the more he is blessed with sacred realizations about the Divine Image and its relationship to the planet Earth, the outer Cosmos and the Inner Kingdom.

The judgmental, critical mind closes the Door of Grace. The compassionate, charitable mind opens the Door of Grace. When a devotee on the Path of Devotion lives each day in the spirit of penance and restitution for his own sins and the sins of the world, he is careful to express charitable thoughts, feelings and actions. As long as this compassionate attitude of charitableness is accompanied by works of righteousness and selfless creation, he will experience the progressive States of Grace under the blessings of the Mediation Host in Heaven.

> *Charity shall cover the multitude of sins.*
> —1 Peter 4:8

> *Charity is, indeed, a great thing, and a gift of God, and when it is rightly ordered, likens us to God Himself, as far as that is possible; for it is charity which makes the man.*
> —Saint John Crysostom

GRACE AND THE SACRAMENTS

> *The Blessed Flow*
> *Doth let me Know*
> *God is nigh.*

Baptism, Communion and Penance form a mighty Triad of Sacraments that bless all other Sacraments in the spiritual life.

The Grace-Flow of God's Holy Spirit begins to open through the Sacrament of Baptism or Christening. The Sacrament of Communion received with reverence, gratitude and love prospers the Flow of Grace in one's life and being. The Sacrament of Penance unites him with the Resurrection Grace of the Lord Jesus earned through His suffering on the Cross.

All Sacraments in the spiritual life are powerful activators of Redemption Grace when a devotee proves his love for God and His Commandments. The selfless desire to serve others in the Name of the Lord Jesus promotes the Flow of Soul Grace and Divine Grace.

The Grace of Redemption begins with *Remission-of-Sins Grace*. The Grace earned through works of penance and restitution leads to *Absolution Grace*. Through Absolution, one experiences a new beginning on the Path of Eternal Life. The Grace of a Full Pardon produces the freedom and the soul-gifts that enable one to serve God as a full-fledged Apostle of Christ Jesus.

> *God is Grace.*
> *Christ is Grace.*

"As every man hath received the gift, even so minister the same one to another, as good stewards of the manifold grace of God." (1 Peter 4:10) The key to union with the Manifold Grace of God is the *desire* to make penance and restitution for *all* Scriptural Laws and Commandments not fulfilled in

one's present life and former lives. To remain unrepentant for offending any Scriptural Commandment is to negate the Flow of Holy Grace. Even as a probationer can increase the Flow of God's Grace through reverence and love, so can he decrease the Flow of Grace through carelessness and transgressions.

Ingratitude for God's Mercy and Forgiveness nullifies Grace; gratitude to God keeps the Flow of Grace in a state of Holy Increase.

Through the Redemption Power of Christ Jesus, a devotee unites with previous lives in which he studied the Sacred Scriptures and applied their principles. This redeemed *Scripture Grace* is accompanied by the wisdom, knowledge and skills earned in past lives of living according to Holy Writ.

The redemption of past-lives' Grace unites one with the *Soul's Memory* of the importance of prayer, meditation, fasting and almsgiving. When these devotional practices observed in former lives are observed in the present life, the Grace earned in previous lives of worship and devotion to God moves into one's heart, mind and soul—and he is spiritually transformed. This miracle is made possible through the Redemption Power of Christ Jesus manifesting through the Sacraments.

"The simplicity that is in Christ." (2 Corinthians 11:3) Through simplicity comes effortless effort. To serve God with effortless effort is the result of *Grace* synchronized and sanctified by Christ Jesus.

> *To do all things sacramentally through Vows to God is to prosper in Grace Unceasing, Timeless, Abundant.*

THE SACRAMENT OF COMMUNION

> *This do in remembrance of me.*
> —St. Luke 22:19

Abide in me, and I in you. As the branch can-
not bear fruit of itself, except it abide in the vine;
no more can ye, except ye abide in me.
                                          —St. John 15:4

The Image of God is within all Souls, all Universes, all Kingdoms. The Sacrament of Communion, containing the Presence of the Lord of Redemption, Christ Jesus, is filled with Divine-Image energies. As these powerful energies begin their restoration, healing and quickening action through the Sacrament, a sincere aspirant on the Path becomes healed, redeemed, quickened, and enlightened in Cosmic and Cosmos understanding.

In the Sacrament is the concealed miracle of the
Christ.
                                          —Ann Ree Colton

The noblest sacrament, consequently, is that
wherein His Body is really present. The Eucharist
crowns all the other sacraments.
                                          —Saint Thomas Aquinas

"This is my blood of the new testament, which is shed for
many for the remission of sins." (St. Matthew 26:28) For the contrite sinner, the Sacrament of Communion means the remission of his sins. For the penitent, the Sacrament cleanses and purges the darkness in his soul's record, preparing him for the time when he will receive the Spirit of God in the Divine Marriage.

For the faithful devotee, the Sacrament of Communion is a mighty quickener of virtues, conscience, wisdom, logic, love, inspiration and other priceless blessings. For the Anointed Teacher, the Sacrament of Communion is a powerful revelator of Cosmos Truths and Kingdom-of-God Prophecies and Revelations.

Wherefore whosoever shall eat this bread, and drink this cup of the Lord, unworthily, shall be guilty of the body and blood of the Lord. But let a man examine himself, and so let him eat of that bread, and drink of that cup. For he that eateth and drinketh unworthily, eateth and drinketh damnation to himself, not discerning the Lord's body.
　　　　　　　　　　　　　— 1 Corinthians 11:27-29

To serve the Bread and Wine worthily should be the prayer of those who administer the Sacrament. To receive the Eucharist worthily should be the prayer of all recipients of this Holy Blessing.

For the unrepentant, the unrighteous and the unlawful, the Sacrament is a stern reprover and admonisher. Woe unto him who receives the Sacrament of Communion and continues to sin.

For the repentant, the righteous and the lawful, the Sacrament produces New Life, Greater Love and Manifold Grace.

Many persons taking the Sacrament are not fulfilling the Ten Commandments or the Law of Tithing. Still others are expressing lust, anger, greed, pettiness, prejudice, covetousness and other lower-nature traits. Self-love, self-pity, guilt, doubt, pride, egotism, vanity — all represent different expressions of the lower nature. Through the lower nature, one who receives the Bread and the Wine is in danger of becoming an agent for Satan. Through the divine-nature expressions of love, self-denial and other beautiful virtues, the recipient of the Sacrament becomes an inspired ambassador for the Christ, for the Presence of the Lord abides in him.

In this Cup is Redemption.
In this Cup is Eternal Life.

MANIFESTATIONS OF GRACE

> *Blessed art Thou, O Lord,*
> *and Thy Spirit of Grace*
> *in the Soul of Man,*
> *in the Soul of Nature,*
> *in the Soul of Heaven.*

The Redemption Power of Jesus opens many degrees and dimensions of Grace as a devotee is ready to receive them. These progressive States of Grace are earned through his daily efforts to see and to serve the Image of God within his fellow man.

The Spirit of God is within all First-Heaven, Second-Heaven and Third-Heaven degrees of Grace. The purity and clarity of the inspiration, wisdom, logic and love within one's thoughts reveal his level of union with the Grace of God.

Devotional Illuminations manifest through union with the Grace of God within the virtues of reverence, devotion, dedication, harmlessness, obedience and other cardinal virtues. Certain degrees of *Devotional-Illumination Grace* do not require that a devotee understand the reality of Reincarnation. However, the greater degrees of *Spiritual-Illumination Grace* may be attained only when a dedicated servant of the Lord knows that Reincarnation is a Just Law of God.

Devotional Illuminations, Logic Illuminations, Realization Illuminations and *Revelatory Illuminations* occur through union with God's Grace within various Virtue Clusters. The Illuminations one experiences on the Path of the Higher Life are determined by the Virtue Clusters anointed and quickened by the Spirit of God. The Virtue Clusters relate to Morality, Devotion, Worship, Study, Giving, Compassion, Stewardship, and other sacred dedications.

Teacher Grace is the Grace of having an instructor knowledgeable in the Process of Initiation leading to God-Realization. To come into timing with the Grace-Cycles of one's Teacher is to be lifted above the heavy or gross cycles of the Maya planes.

The Cycles of the Solstices and the Equinoxes and the Cycles of the Moon, the Sun and the Planets work with the Energy-Flows of the Christ Light. These powerful Cycles coincide with the Holy-Day Cycles and their profound Increases of Grace.

All Holy-Day, Seasonal and Solar-System Cycles are *Christ-Cycles* that contribute to the creation of man in the Image of God. It is the Teacher's task to inspire his students to fulfill these powerful Cycles with reverence and understanding, that they may experience the higher states of Redemption Grace.

Prototypal Grace is earned through a pure love for the Spirit of God within mankind. Each sign of the zodiac represents a Countenance of God. When one has made his peace with the Presence of God within all twelve Zodiacal Prototypes, he earns Grace related to the persons born in the signs of Aries, Taurus, Gemini, Cancer, Leo, Virgo, Libra, Scorpio, Sagittarius, Capricorn, Aquarius and Pisces. Prototypal Grace results in Prototypal Illuminations; *Archetypal Grace* produces Archetypal Illuminations. Through the Synchronization Power of Christ Jesus, the Process of Initiation reveals its treasures of Grace through progressive Prototypal and Archetypal Illuminations.

Sabbath-Day Grace is the key to all levels and degrees of Soul Grace and Divine Grace. The Sabbath Cycle activates the Grace within all other Commandment Cycles.

Dream Grace is a beautiful Gift of God through which the Angels of the soul's record may reveal knowledge and wisdom relating to the past, the present and the future. The interpretation of the symbols and nuances in visions and dreams is a special Grace received through the Spirit of God.

> *To master the grotesque level in dreams, one must have perfect faith in the Father and His Image for man.*
> — Ann Ree Colton

Elements Grace relates to the blessings of life that come through Fire, Earth, Air and Water. Through the sacramental use of the four elements, a devotee unites with the Glory of God within each element. The Bread and the Wine of the Sacrament of Communion reveal to receptive hearts and minds secrets of Elements Grace regarding the Earth and the Cosmos.

Heavenly Father, thank Thee for Thy Gift of Fire, Earth, Air and Water. May all Elements be used sacramentally in service to Thee and for Thy Glory. In Jesus' Name. Amen.

"And all things are of God, who hath reconciled us to himself by Jesus Christ, and hath given to us the ministry of reconciliation." (2 Corinthians 5:18) *Reconciliation Grace* is experienced when one is reconciled to God through the Mediation of Jesus. Reconciliation with Ancestral Grace, Past-Lives' Grace, Soul Grace, Divine-Image Grace and all other degrees and dimensions of Grace occurs through the mighty powers under command of Christ Jesus. To serve and minister in Jesus' Name is to be a reconciler of individuals with God and with one another; a reconciler of marriages and families; a reconciler of devotees with their Souls' Covenants and Spiritual Gifts.

Remission-of-Sins Grace through the Sacrament of Communion awakens one from the hypnotic spells of Maya and the Antichrist working through ancestral-gene negative traits and past-lives' sin-tendencies; in this, a seeker after truth may begin to express his spiritual individuality through soul-freedom and Divine-Image quickenings. The Grace received through the Presence of Jesus within the Sacrament prospers only when one is sincerely repentant and devoted to Scriptural Laws and Commandments.

Absolution Grace occurs through a selfless life devoted to serving others in the spirit of penance and restitution. Sacrifice, renunciation, holy poverty, humility, honorableness and other cardinal virtues expressed in service to God accelerate the cleansing of the soul's record so that the devotee may experience the joys, miracles and inheritances of Absolution Grace.

The *Providential Grace* of God provides for all physical, emotional, mental and spiritual needs of His faithful servants. One remains free from the stress of monetary debts through dedication to the Owe-No-Man Principle (Romans 13:8) and other Scriptural Principles and Stewardship-Ethics that prosper union with Divine Providence.

Tithing Grace keeps one united with the Bountifulness and Magnanimity of God in his present life and in future lives.

As a devotee proves to be a good steward of *Money Grace*, he receives steady increases of other levels of Grace from the soul. Stewardship of Money Grace prepares an aspirant on the Path to become a good steward of *all energies* entrusted to him by the Spirit of God. One must prove to be honorable and ethical in his stewardship of money and other energies before he is given the responsibilities regarding the stewardship of Souls. A spiritual leader is a steward of the Souls placed in his charge by the Living God. This high-calling stewardship is earned after years of faithful ministering as an apprentice of an Anointed Teacher.

Marriage Grace blesses a husband and wife with a happy, creative, spiritual marriage based upon their mutual love for God. Faithfulness in their vows to God and to one another produces dramatic increases of Marriage Grace from year to year.

Sex Grace comes to married couples who love purely and reverence the Image of God in each other.

Children Grace is a God-given Grace that blesses a family with intelligent, healthy and obedient children.

In-Laws Grace is a love and respect shared between a married couple and their parents.

Religion Grace blesses a worshipper with peace, happiness and contentment in his spiritual home.

National Grace provides freedoms, opportunities and prosperity.

Education Grace grants the freedom to select one's own life-path through the schools of his choice.

Employment Grace blesses one with harmony, creativity and prospering in his work environment.

House Grace enables single or married householders to enjoy a home blessed with the Love-Presence of God. The Family Altar is a sacred polarity in the home where the worship of God is rewarded with His choicest blessings.

Ancestral Grace is received from ancestors who worshipped God and obeyed His Commandments. Ancestors who led lives of morality, righteousness, courage and love bless their offspring through the genes and the chromosomes. These ancestral blessings provide priceless strengths, talents and providences from generation to generation.

Parental Grace manifests as wholesome attitudes, aptitudes and a strong immune system. The memory of a reverent and honorable father and mother inspires one's efforts to reach toward God and to live a life of worthiness.

Past-Lives' Grace is bequeathed to oneself from former incarnations. Previous lives of virtue, faith and illumination bless his present life through the Cycles of the Moon, the Sun and the Planets.

Genius Grace expressed in previous lives returns to one's present life to be used in service to God. As long as he uses past-lives' Genius Grace with modesty, humility and for the Glory of God, he avoids the pitfalls of pride, egotism and vanity.

Physical-Body Grace relates to the health and graceful movements of the body. The body as a temple houses the Spirit of God through dedications, covenants, vows.

Emotional-Body Grace produces disciplined, peaceful and loving emotions. Before one can serve God with equanimity, poise and self-control, his emotional-body energy-currents must be synchronized with the soul and the Divine Image. In this, he becomes a peacemaker, a healer, a mediator at one with the Lord of Love.

Mental-Body Grace blesses one with a teachable, open mind free from prejudice and critical-mindedness. The mind at one with God remains telepathically receptive to the Flow of Divine Inspiration, Realization, Prophecy and Revelation from the Three Heavens.

Virtue Grace provides necessary supports for one's efforts to qualify for the Divine-Marriage Anointing. Each of the 108 Virtues proceeding from the Image of God is a World of Grace. Virtue-insights lead to Virtue-Illuminations. The Path of Virtue is the one and only Path to the Godhead. All Teachers and Teachings emphasizing the importance of Virtue and Law are true representatives of the Dharma.

Vows Grace unites one's present-life dedications to God with Vows Grace earned in previous lives. Through Vows kept, a devotee unites with the joys, rewards and illuminations earned in past lives of faithful service to God. The monumental receiving of the Holy Ghost in God's Timing is a testimony of one's keeping Holy Vows in his present life and in past lives.

Yang Grace relates to the Masculine Principle and Polarity; *Yin Grace*, to the Feminine Principle and Polarity. Many initiations on the Path of Devotion pertain to the Yin and Yang Polarities within one's being and in his associations with all male and female persons in his life. The blending of the Yin and Yang Polarities in the life and being of a devoted servant of God produces the Divine Marriage.

Timing Grace enables one to live in harmony with the rhythmic Cycles of the Soul and the Ordained Cycles of the Moon, the Sun, the Planets, the Stars and the Galaxies. God as Omnipresence blesses the devotee-initiate with numerous coincidings, confirmations and provings that confirm his being in timing with His Will and Plan.

Christ Jesus, the Lord of the Solar System, utilizes the Cycles of the Moon, the Sun and the Planets to bless each faithful servant of God with priceless Inheritances of Grace.

Man is being prepared to experience *Christ-Mind Illumination Grace*. In this, he will comprehend the Mighty Cycles of the Solar System, the Stars and the Galaxies. Through the Synchronization Power of Christ Jesus, the Plan of God for the Cosmos will be made understandable to the minds of men. When a devotee reverences the starry heavens as the handiwork of God, he is opening his heart and mind to the secrets and mysteries of the Universe.

Godhead Grace denotes that the devotee has reached the Jewel in the Lotus in the core of his being. In this, he becomes an anointed servant of God blessed with the Galaxy Consciousness. The Great Shepherd guides His obedient sheep to the splendor of the Bliss-Presence of the Creator within the Godhead.

To know the Fulness-of-Grace Blessings of God through the Synchronization Power of His Beloved Son is to attain oneness with the myriad Stars and Galaxies in the Universe; oneness with the Three Heavens of the Solar System; and oneness with the Spirit of God creating the human spirit in His Image and Likeness.

Sensitivities Grace manifests through union with the healing energies within the Commandment of Love-Ye-One-Another. As these powerful love-energies bathe and clothe one's emotions and nervous system, he evolves the holy sensitivities that prosper oneness with the Divine Omnipresence. The Antichrist keeps a tight control on his victims through their insensitivities and hypersensitivities. The escape from Satan's destructive influences into the Peace and Redemption Power of the Christ is made possible when one's unholy sensitivities are sanctified and transformed into holy sensitivities. Holy sensitivities keep one united with the Spirit and Grace of God within the Three Heavens.

Eternal Grace occurs through union with the Higher Self,

which is one's true identity as a child of God. The Higher or True Self contains all the Wisdom and Grace one has earned throughout Life Everlasting.

Archetypal Grace is the receiving of revelatory knowledge through communion with the Archetypes or Blueprints of God in the Third Heaven.

Logos Grace is the ability to speak of God and His Plan with clarity, inspiration and love. One who articulates Archetypal Knowledge is expressing a high degree of Logos Grace.

Revelation Grace, Exorcism Grace, Healing Grace, Prophecy Grace and other manifestations of Grace received through the Holy Spirit transform a devotee into an enlightened Apostle of the Lord Jesus.

Resurrection Grace is a perpetual Gift of God through which one can be resurrected from a life of sin and self-indulgence to a life of morality and self-denial through which comes Spiritual Illumination. Resurrection Grace is present in all initiations that lead to the receiving of Sacred Inheritances within the Increase of God. *"Blessed be the God and the Father of our Lord Jesus Christ, which according to his abundant mercy hath begotten us again unto a lively hope by the resurrection of Jesus Christ from the dead, to an inheritance incorruptible, and undefiled, and that fadeth not away, reserved in heaven for you."* (1 Peter 1:3,4)

> *To accept the Jesus Resurrection polarizes us into the wholeness of self which can know no death, defeat or failure. To all who believe and seek fulfillment in wholeness, Jesus comes to consecrate the marriage of spirit and soul, of mind and body, of heart and desire.*
>
> —Ann Ree Colton

PART III

11

PENANCE AND RESTITUTION

Repent ye therefore, and be converted, that your sins may be blotted out, when the times of refreshing shall come from the presence of the Lord; and he shall send Jesus Christ, which before was preached unto you: Whom the heaven must receive until the times of restitution of all things, which God hath spoken by the mouth of all his holy prophets since the world began.

—Acts 3:19-21

Before God created the world, he created Penitence and said to him: "I am going to create a man in the world, on condition that every time he turns to you, you are ready to forgive him his sins."

—Zohar (c. 1290)

REPENTANCE AND CONFESSION: CREDIBILITY

A person who truly stands for Repentance on the Spiritual Path is making Penance for all mankind.

—Ann Ree Colton

"Repent: for the kingdom of heaven is at hand." (St. Matthew 4:17) A wholehearted repentance opens the Flow of Grace from the Heaven Worlds. The Flow of Grace continues to increase as long as the penitent heeds Jesus' directive: *"Go, and sin no more."* (St. John 8:11)

165

The Remission-of-Sins Grace of Jesus through the Sacrament of Communion protects one only when he is sincerely repentant and sins no more. The more one yields to negative actions, feelings and thoughts, the more he removes himself from the protection of Jesus through the Sacrament. Such persons become more entrenched in karmic enclosures, reportraying their ancestrally-inherited tendencies to sin. The tendency to commit adultery; the tendency to express anger and tantrums; the tendency to lie, cheat and steal; the tendency to be prejudiced and unforgiving; the tendency toward procrastination and unpunctuality; and all other tendencies to sin passed on through the genes claim nonvigilant aspirants on the Path who have yet to express a wholehearted repentance.

The *desire* to be healed is a necessary key to the healing of negative ancestral-gene traits and reflexes. Unfortunately, many persons do not desire to be healed of their negative, sinful and selfish ways. The moment one desires to be healed and *asks* for the supernatural helps of God and Christ, he has begun the process of Redemption. His sincere repentance will open the door to Heaven's Light and Grace, and his days will be filled with the rewards and inheritances received through the Sacrament.

"The just man walketh in his integrity: his children are blessed after him." (Proverbs 20:7) A true and wholehearted repentance establishes one's *integrity* in the sight of God. It is extremely important that one prove his integrity to God, his Teacher and his co-disciples so that he can be trusted as a worker in the Vineyard of the Christ.

Until one expresses a sincere repentance, he will continue to remain prodigal toward one or more Scriptural Laws and Cardinal Virtues. Many persons in the religions of the world remain unenlightened because of their lower-nature expressions that thwart a sincere and wholehearted repentance. One progresses spiritually only to the degree that he proves his integrity in the sight of God.

If we say that we have no sin, we deceive our-
selves, and the truth is not in us. If we confess our
sins, he is faithful and just to forgive us our sins,
and to cleanse us from all unrighteousness.
                                            —1 John 1:8,9

"For it is written, As I live saith the Lord, every knee shall
bow to me, and every tongue shall confess to God." (Romans
14:11) Confession is a gift from God so that His children can
be redeemed and restored to their rightful inheritances as
heirs of His Kingdom.

God forgives sins *after* He thoroughly tests the sincerity of
one's repentance, the honesty of his confession and his commitment to sin no more. As long as one retains any desire to
sin, he forfeits the Grace of God's Full Forgiveness and remains in bondage to his unforgiven debts.

The Mercy of God is ever-ready to forgive *all* sins of the
present life and previous lives as soon as one is sincerely repentant and confesses them with contrition and humility.
However, the consciousness mind of a person will repent and
confess according to its own comprehension of sin, which may
be very limited in its understanding. In such instances, lingering attitudes of permissiveness, compromise and self-justification will block one's receiving the rewards of a wholehearted repentance.

Confession should be explicit and specific, for one must
prove to God that he knows the difference between right and
wrong, good and evil, virtue and vice. The future of each
aspirant on the Path is determined by his prayers of confession as a daily spiritual practice. Honest confession opens
one's heart to God, and the Creator reciprocates with priceless measures of Grace.

Confession enables the Christ to transenergize sin-darkness
into light; therefore, the more a devotee confesses to God, the
more the Christ can enlighten his heart, mind and soul. Confession is always followed by blessings of Grace. This is a Law

of God's Mercy manifesting through the Healing and Redeeming Power of His Beloved Son.

> **Heavenly Father, I confess my sins against the Ten Commandments, the Law of Tithing, the Commandment of Love Ye One Another and the Sermon-on-the-Mount Principles. I pray, with Thy Help, to make penance and restitution for these offenses and all other sins of omission and commission committed in the present life and in past lives. May all scales of the soul come into balance and harmony with Thy Perfect Plan of Universal Creation. In Jesus' Name. Amen.**

There are several different levels of Redemption Grace that can manifest in a penitent's life after he turns toward God. If he repents of any sin and confesses it to God, he receives the Grace that comes through repentance and confession; however, if he also makes restitution for the same sin, he receives the Grace that comes through restitution. A deeper degree of Grace manifests through the making of penance for the sin. A more profound degree of Grace is also attained when one teaches others to fulfill the Scriptural Laws and Ethics that he has offended.

God's Grace multiplies in increasing measures when one teaches in public the importance of Scriptural Wisdom. To inspire others to turn toward the Altar of God produces the greatest Flows of Divine Grace. Jesus directed His Disciples to go into the world and give testimony to the Truth. Their messages of love and devotion, their lives of sacrifice and renunciation, and their awareness of the Redemption Power of the Living Christ remain as eternal testimonies to bless each new generation of Altar-servers.

> *The magnificent restitution is* Teaching.
> *Restitution is the transforming power in the soul.*

From the Restitution compulsion comes a willingness to serve God and one's fellow man.

A holy restitution compels a man to give of himself without thought of reward or name or fame. This is the result of illumined knowledge, which is superior to the restitution of returning deed for deed or act for act.

— Ann Ree Colton

Until a person repents and makes restitution for his transgressions against Holy Laws, his sins remain alive to do their destructive work in his life and being.

Some sins are as mud, quickly washed from the soul with the tears of repentance and contrition and simple acts of penance and restitution. Longtime sins are as caked mud, requiring more effort to soften and remove. Still other sins are as dark stains on the soul's record; these sins require continuous scrubbing through sacrificial works of penance and restitution until they are completely cleansed.

It is sorrowful when the soul's scales become so imbalanced by one's wilful sinning that he attracts suffering and torment. Because he has hardened his heart toward God and humankind, he does not know the cause of his sorrow, nor does he recognize or acknowledge the need for repentance, confession, penance and restitution.

The man whose heart is without holiness, suffers torture only by undergoing penances in ignorance of their meaning.

— Mahabarata

A man is a faithful and prudent servant when he is quick to atone for all his offences, interiorly by contrition, exteriorly by confessing them and making reparation.

— Saint Francis of Assisi

It is the Recording Angel who keeps the equation balanced between penance, repentance and restitution.

The Recording Angels know exactly the time the de-mand is present to rectify. If one does not hear or heed, he remains laggard.

— Ann Ree Colton

Repentance may be with or without restitution. If a person steals money from someone, he may be repentant, but he may still keep the money. If he is *honorable*, his repentance will be accompanied by restitution — and he will return the money.

Many probationers on the Path repent of their sins, but only the honorable ones make restitution. God patiently waits for His children to repent *and* to make restitution for their transgressions; for, in so doing, they are proving honorable in His sight.

Repentance attains its crown when coupled with restitution.

When a penitent desires to make a full and honorable restitution for every sin-debt darkening his soul's record, he is blessed with the virtues of honorableness, character and integrity. God rewards honorableness with His choicest blessings through soul-gift quickenings and Grace-Inheritances so that a sincere aspirant may utilize these precious gifts and graces to make a more rapid restitution.

There is restitution without penance and restitution with penance. Restitution with penance proves that one is sincere in his contrition and sense of shame for wrongdoing.

A person can make restitution for a wrong committed and still feel no sense of shame or contrition. When one desires to prove to God the sincerity of his repentance, his restitution will be accompanied by acts of penance. In this way, he reveals a contrite heart and a right spirit.

Many persons sin, repent, make penance — and sin again. Such persons are yet in bondage to the spirit of insincerity. It is only when a truth-seeker on the Path *proves* his sincerity that his penance will produce the restoration of his integrity, honorableness and credibility in God's sight.

The longer one proves faithful to the Scriptural Commandments, the Law of Tithing and the Sermon-on-the-Mount Principles, the more credibility he has as a servant of God. Penance made by a devotee or initiate who has proven faithful in his vows to God for many years acts as a quickener of the Grace-Flow from God's Love and Mercy.

The keeping of vows to God determines one's credibility as an earnest, dependable steward of His Word and Altar. When a tried and proven guardian of the Dharma makes penance, it results in mighty blessings for the world.

To waver from the keeping of any Holy Law or Commandment decreases one's credibility; therefore, his acts of penance are hollow. When one proves his credibility in God's sight during many years of faith and devotion, even a small act of penance produces powerful results for good.

Obedience to one's Living Teacher, and doing all things asked of him as a probationer and student, establish his credibility as a future disciple of Jesus.

Grace-Inheritances come to those who prove trustworthy as devotees, initiates, Teachers and Apostles under Christ because of their credibility in the sight of God. Credibility reveals spiritual maturity. Those who qualify for the major Grace-Inheritances from God are the spiritually-mature ones who are attuned to His Word and Will.

The best of you is he who is the best at repaying.
— Muhammad

When we ask for Truth, the whole Truth and nothing but the Truth, we are asking for rectification.

— Ann Ree Colton

A wise parent teaches his children about restitution and penance. If a child breaks a neighbor's window, he should

be taught the importance of making restitution by working
to pay for a new window. He should also do some act of penance to show that he is sincerely sorry, such as mowing the
neighbor's yard for a period of time or washing the win-
dows. Too often, parents will pay for their child's damage to
the property of others rather than teach their child the importance of personal responsibility through restitution and
penance.

> *Restitution is a catalyst to Grace-attraction and
> Soul-satisfaction.*

Penance and restitution are powerful ways of establishing
one's honorableness in the sight of God and his fellow man.
An enlightened Teacher discloses to his students numerous
ways to make penance and restitution. This knowledge is
necessary before a penitent can unite with the blessings that
flow from deeper levels of Redemption Grace.

Many teachers, priests and ministers who teach the importance of repentance and confession do not teach the importance of penance and restitution. This omission is costly to
their flocks in the amounts of Grace unreceived.

There are no accidents in God's Holy Law of Attraction.
The Spirit of God is speaking through everyone and everything. Through self-honesty confessions humbly stated before
the Altar of God, one attains the Salvation that can manifest
only through a cleansed soul-record. Specific confessions, as
well as general confessions, hasten the day of his liberation
and enlightenment.

> *Confession without rectification is hypocrisy.*
> —Ann Ree Colton

Many aspirants on the Path continue to sin in ways that
they do not realize are offenses against the Great Laws and
Commandments of God. Also, numerous individuals who
repent expect a total pardon from God without making resti-

tution for all sins committed in their present lives and past lives. Repentance and confession *begin* the process of communing with the Forgiving and Merciful Love of God; however, a truly contrite heart *knows* that it must also perform humble acts of penance and make a full and honorable restitution for each and every sin of omission and commission.

Penance and restitution for cardinal sins against the Scriptural Commandments, the Body Temple and the Divine Image require a lifelong observance of humble tasks in service to God and one's fellow man. The permissive generation does not take major sins seriously. The honorable soul humbles himself before God and serves his Maker in the spirit of humility, contrition, penance and restitution for his own sins and for the sins of the world.

The *knowing* that one should make penance and restitution for his own sins and for the sins of the world is the first sign of spiritual maturity. Through penance and restitution, a holy glow begins to radiate from the Divine Image, the soul, the kundalini and the chakras, the nerves, the glands, the eyes and the pores of the skin — and one progresses toward the higher States of Grace.

In a *Dimensional Confession*, a devotee confesses the sins of his present life and past lives, the sins of his parents and ancestors and the sins of the world. The more *specific* his prayers of confession, the more he will experience the Christ-quickenings that will enable him to bless and heal miraculously and dimensionally.

> Heavenly Father, I confess my many sins of the present life and past lives; the sins of my parents and ancestors; the sins of the people of the state, the nation, the world; and the sins of persons in religious and spiritual ministries. I pray to do all things in the right spirit of penance and restitution. Please help me to reverence, love

and see Thy Image in all souls. In Jesus' Name.
Amen.

*"All thy works shall praise thee, O Lord; and thy saints
shall bless thee. They shall speak of the glory of thy kingdom,
and talk of thy power; To make known to the sons of men his
mighty acts, and the glorious majesty of his kingdom."*
(Psalm 145:10–12) The Saints are united with the majesty of
God's Kingdom because their every breath, prayer and action
is observed in the spirit of penance and restitution for the sins
of the world. Being pure in heart, the sins of the world touch
them not. Centered in the Virtues of Renunciation, Holy
Poverty, Selflessness and Love, they are immunized and insulated against the evils of greed, lust, pride, vanity and the
other snares of the Antichrist.

The Saints in Heaven and on earth work to overcome
darkness with Light in the world; this is their lifelong dedication to God. When a devotee of the Lord dedicates to overcome darkness with Light, he comes under the telepathic
tutelage of the Saints who teach him about the joys and
graces of penance and restitution.

The moment a seeker after truth proves sincere in his
repentance, honest in his confessions, humble in his penances
and honorable in his restitutions, his integrity will bring all
virtues into holy accord with the Commandment of Love —
and the Cycles of the Moon, the Sun and the Planets will
place priceless Treasures of Grace on the altar of his heart.
*"But as for me, I will walk in mine integrity: redeem me, and
be merciful unto me."* (Psalm 26:11)

> *If a soul were to do penance without discern-
> ment, that is, if her love were centered mainly on
> the penance she had undertaken, it would be a hin-
> drance to her perfection . . . She should be dis-
> cerning in her penance, with her love fixed more on
> virtue than on the penance. For penance ought to*

be undertaken as a means to growth in virtue, according to the measure of one's need as well as one's capability.

—Saint Catherine of Siena

If one does not have the spirit of humility with penance, it is an act of hypocrisy; it is non-virtuous.

— Ann Ree Colton

No amount of penance can help a person whose mind is not purified.

—Buddha

THE PARADOX OF PENANCE

The man hath penance done,
A penance more will do.

—Coleridge

Penance is another side of giving; it is giving up all the things that stand between one and God. By giving up, one makes restitution.

— Ann Ree Colton

When one makes penance in the spirit of gratitude to God for the great Principle of Redemption, his soul rejoices—and sends joy into his heart and mind. The heart and mind filled with the soul's joy through penance draw closer to God and His Dimensional Joys and Ecstasies that come through Spiritual Exaltation.

Penance is not a drudgery—it is a joy. This is the Paradox of Penance; for, through penance, one unites with the Mercy, Love and Joy of God.

Penance is potent and most holy. One simple, pure act of penance is worth many meditations; it releases great virtue and healing into the world.

Penance observed in the right spirit of humility, contrition and love is a powerful Sacrament through which a devotee *redeems* Past-Lives' Grace. As this Grace becomes part of his present-life dedication to God, the gifts of his soul used in previous lives will fortify and bless his efforts to serve his Lord and the human spirit.

To make penance for one's own sins is to unite with Soul Grace. To make penance for world-sins is to unite with World Grace.

> *Penance purges. Purgings purify. Purifications enlighten. Enlightenment produces Spiritual Gifts. Spiritual Gifts enable one to serve God with peace and power. Peace and power are charged with God's Holy Spirit.*

Many religiously-inclined persons cannot perform strenuous acts of penance; however, any physical act of contrition, regardless of its simplicity, finds great favor in the sight of God.

Every act of penance is followed by a test to see if one is truly repentant and contrite. After an act, prayer, fast or pilgrimage of penance, a devotee should be especially vigilant in his thoughts, emotions and actions, for *the Testing Principle* will reveal dark areas in his nature and temperament that require healing. Also, God's Law of Attraction will reveal the *Truth* about one's self through all who cross his path. The aspirant will attract persons and conditions, both negative and positive, that are exact projections of his soul's record.

Ministers, priests, teachers and preachers who do not teach their flocks the importance of penance and restitution and the knowledge of reincarnation are omitting three major truths from the puzzle of Eternal Life.

A true act of penance is filled with contrition, humility, and faith in God's Forgiveness, Mercy and Love. After each sincere act, offering, fast, prayer or pilgrimage of penance, one comes closer to God through a stronger union with His Spirit.

The Angels go before a devotee during each Pilgrimage of Penance when he observes all aspects of the pilgrimage in Jesus' Name and for the Glory of God. Any act of penance in Jesus' Exalted Name is rewarded with priceless blessings.

Life is a pilgrimage to the Divine Image. Each spiritual pilgrimage on earth prospers one's progress toward the Image of God within his soul.

When a devotee makes a spiritual pilgrimage in the spirit of penance and restitution for personal sins, ancestral and parental sins, and for world sins, the Grace of God will move upon him more profoundly in increasing measures. This will activate greater degrees of Grace through the Sacrament of Communion. Thereafter, more miracles of healing and reconciliation will occur; spiritual gifts will manifest more rapidly; and numerous other blessings of Redemption Grace will shower upon him.

The Divine-Image Consciousness utilizes dimensional blessing-powers through the knowledge of penance and restitution as sacred principles leading to Godhead Grace and Galaxy Grace.

Each time one fasts he is in the state of repentance. In making a penance and resolution, he overcomes "the second death." (Revelation 2:11)

The habit of making a penance with right resolution clears the Undersoul. When one sets up a system of penance—doing without certain things which have kept him bonded to his selfish nature—he overcomes the second death. Penance is a side of giving which means giving up or self-denial.

A continuity penance in the Name of Jesus and our Father frees one to undergo the ninety days of contrition after death with full cognizance and spirituality, blessing all.

—Ann Ree Colton

THE HOLY TITHE

The tenth shall be holy unto the Lord.
—Leviticus 27:32

Pay all tithes for which one might stand in arrears.

—Saint Francis of Assisi

To make penance and restitution for tithes withheld from God in one's present life and in previous lives accelerates the Flow of Providential Grace in all areas of his life. A heart open to God through a giving spirit heals selfishness, greed, penury and miserliness.

It may require numerous lifetimes through reincarnation before an individual is capable of giving God an *honest* tithe. It may require countless lives before he evolves the virtues that inspire him to make penance and restitution for tithes not given in his present life and in past lives. The desire to make penance and restitution for tithes not given by oneself, his parents, ancestors and others in the world denotes an enlightened comprehension attained through Virtue Clusters quickened by the Spirit of God.

Before a truth-seeker can fulfill with reverence, devotion and love the Holy Law of Tithing, the Sabbath-Day Commandment and all other Laws of God, he must have all Virtue Clusters quickened in his heart and consciousness mind. The masses of persons in religions who fail to give an honest tithe to God or to worship Him each Sabbath Day are missing important Virtue Clusters. Each Scriptural Law requires that correlating Virtue Clusters be quickened in order for it to be observed in the right spirit. A right spirit comes with the quickening of all Virtue Clusters through a wholehearted repentance. *"Create in me a clean heart, O God; and renew a right spirit within me."* (Psalm 51:10)

All Virtue Clusters can be quickened in the twinkling-of-an-eye through a sincere repentance, or they may require many lifetimes and ages before they become spiritually-quickened vortices of light within one's being. Repentance, confession, penance and restitution are important keys to the evolutionary process of Virtue-Cluster quickenings through the Image of God.

> *There is that maketh himself rich, yet hath nothing: there is that maketh himself poor, yet hath great riches.*
>
> —Proverbs 13:7

> *Charge them that are rich in this world, that they be not high-minded, nor trust in uncertain riches, but in the living God, who giveth us richly all things to enjoy.*
>
> —1 Timothy 6:17

The virtues of gracious giving, selflessness and compassion inspire one to place his life and its energies on God's Holy Altar in the spirit of penance and restitution. His Christlike attitudes of self-denial and love give birth to the Virtue of Holy Poverty through which he may serve God and his fellow man in the spirit of total dedication.

Total dedication inspires one to return to God all blessings, graces and inheritances received through His Holy Spirit. This beautiful expression of the Virtue of Holy Poverty keeps a devotee united with the Providence of God which provides for all of his needs in perfect timing. Total dedication through the Virtue of Holy Poverty is a major stride toward one's receiving the Divine-Image Consciousness.

A self-minded person prays only to receive blessings for

himself. Such persons receive a healing of their selfishness the moment they begin to pray that God send blessings to *all* of His children. When a pray-er is no longer limited in his consciousness mind by the enclosure of *self*, he will have expanded his consciousness mind's capacity to think with compassion toward the needs of all living souls. This necessary step from *self* to compassion for *all* may require numerous lifetimes of evolution through reincarnation or it can occur in one moment of time!

The desire to pray for all souls and to make penance and restitution for the sins of the world reveals a noble character and saintly compassion. God rewards these sacred attitudes with the blessings, quickenings and anointings of Holy Grace. The Soul's Grace-energies and the Divine-Image Grace-energies replace the ancestral sin-energies in the genes and the chromosomes and the past-lives' sin-energies in the soul's record. Thus, by thinking of the welfare, health and prosperity of *all* persons on earth, one becomes an enlightened world-server through the Divine-Image Consciousness.

A penitent who desires to make amends for tithes not given to God in his present life and in past lives may be inspired to give a *double tithe* or more in the spirit of penance and restitution. Redemption Grace is further prospered if his double tithe is offered in the spirit of penance and restitution for tithes not given by his parents, ancestors and others in the world.

Any tithe or offering placed on God's Altar beyond the holy tenth will reduce the darkness in the soul's record and will increase the Flow of Soul Grace and Divine Grace. It is extremely important that a penitent prove honorable in God's sight in his attitudes toward penance and restitution regarding *all* Holy Laws and Commandments.

Dear God, I place my Double Tithe and Offerings on Thy Holy Altar in the spirit of Penance

and Restitution for times past when I failed to fulfill Thy Holy Laws of Giving and Love.

O Lord, heal me of conscious and subconscious fears related to giving and sharing, that I may unite with Thy Providential Grace in this life and in all lives to come.

I pray that my Special Dedication may also be observed in the spirit of Penance and Restitution for Tithes not given by my parents, ancestors and others in the world.

May all Thy children learn of the joy and wisdom of giving for the preserving and prospering of Thy Holy Word. In Jesus' Name. Amen.

A tithe is the fulfilling of the Law. To give to God more than the tithe in the spirit of penance and restitution is to gradually restore one's integrity and honorableness in His sight. All monies spent during spiritual pilgrimages and other sacred dedications rendered in Jesus' Name should be offered in the spirit of penance and restitution. Any amount of money and time offered in service to God beyond the tithe produces a powerful cleansing action in the soul's record, thereby blessing one's present life and future lives — and also blessing his children as *gene-grace.*

"For the love of money is the root of all evil." (1 Timothy 6:10) Many wrong attitudes toward money may be inherited through the ancestral genes. The love of money or fears regarding the absence of supply must be healed before a devotee can gain freedom from negative ancestral attitudes regarding money and possessions. God provides bountifully when the Heart Chakra is a whirling-vortex of love energies, inspiring gracious giving, faith in Divine Providence, and a commitment to a life of selfless serving.

An aspirant's attitudes toward money and time are indicators of his ancestral gene-inheritance. Greed and procrastination may be passed on from one generation to another through ancestral genes. When resistances toward giving to God an honest tithe are inherited through the ancestral genes and through past lives, a probationer on the Path must exert superhuman effort to place his first honest tithe on God's Altar. The first honest tithe represents a major breakthrough in his awakening from the ancestral-gene hypnotic spell that causes many persons to worship money rather than God.

> *Ye cannot serve God and mammon.*
>
> —St. Matthew 6:24

PARDON: ABSOLUTION GRACE

> *For thy name's sake, O Lord, pardon mine iniquity; for it is great.*
>
> —Psalm 25:11

> *Thou art a God ready to pardon, gracious and merciful.*
>
> —Nehemiah 9:17

When a person who has committed many crimes is called before a judge, he can either lie by denying his guilt, or he can repent, confess his crimes, and throw himself on the mercy of the court. In the higher life, one must be willing to repent, confess his sins, and ask to make restitution. To such persons, God, the Judge, is merciful; and, witnessing their remorse, He places them on *probation*. Through this act of God's Mercy, a repentant sinner becomes a probationer on the Spiritual Path. If one has the wisdom to ask for God's help and guidance in his making a full and honorable restitution, he will pay his sin-debts while *out of prison*—that is, free from karmic bondages.

The increasing freedoms of the soul occur while one is making a willing restitution and is proving his sincere repent-

ance through works of penance. The Grace of God and the
Light of the Christ bless all earnest probationers with priceless Gifts and Realizations that hasten the day of their attaining Total Absolution — a Full Pardon!

*"This is my blood of the new testament, which is shed for
many for the remission of sins."* (St. Matthew 26:28) When
one is centered in the Flow of Redemption Grace through the
reverent observance of the Scriptural Commandments, his
receiving of the Sacrament of Communion keeps the sins
recorded in his soul's record in a state of *Remission*. While
one's sins are in a state of Remission, he is free to utilize each
day as an opportunity to make penance and restitution for
the sins recorded in his soul's record, the sins of his parents
and ancestors, and the sins of the world.

Through a spiritually-quickened consciousness, one feels
no separateness from any person on earth, for he knows that
all persons are being created in the Image of God. He serves
all persons through his prayers, meditations and attitudes of
love that constantly embrace the *world family*.

The attitude of ministering to all souls in the world through
one's reverencing the Image of God in them at all times is a
powerful way of making penance and restitution for the sins
yet recorded in the soul's record. Gradually, the Remission-
of-Sins Grace through the Sacrament of Communion will accomplish the cleansing of the dark side of the soul's record.
The freedoms, joys and blessings that open to him in increasing measure will be his assurance that the Mercy of God and
the Redemption Power of Jesus are rewarding him with *Absolution Grace*.

Through Absolution Grace, one may work with the more
powerful degrees or *Voltages* of God's Spirit within his heart
and mind. In this, he unites with the Greater Seals in the
Kingdom of God, thereby serving the Creator as an illumined
seer, prophet and revelator. Enlightened personages never
feel separate from the sins of the world, for their union with

God through the Divine-Image Consciousness makes them more empathetic and compassionate toward the suffering and misery in the world caused by the sins of men.

Jesus, while being scourged and crucified, was making Penance for the sins of the world. Through His suffering and His victory over death, Jesus freed many souls from the painful problems caused by their sins. Such is the nature of Penance. There is great freedom in all sacrificial acts observed in the spirit of Penance for world-sins.

The penance of a devotee links him with the Penance of Jesus on the Cross. The Cross led to Jesus' Resurrection. Penance leads the devotee to his own resurrection under the Mantle of Jesus.

Through the Penance of Jesus on the Cross, God gave a great Gift to all sincere penitents in every age and time — the Gift of Pardon, the Total Absolution of sins. The Disciples of Jesus, Mary Magdalene and others moved forward in service to God through the Pardon or Absolution of their sins, thereby accepting with gratitude the Mercy and Forgiveness of God through the suffering and Crucifixion of Jesus. Many persons rejected Jesus and the Gift of Pardon by lapsing back into lives of sinning.

The Penance-power of Jesus awaits all contrite souls in every century as a Perpetual Reservoir of Grace. Those who accept this Gift of Grace begin an entirely new way of life blessed by the Providence and Love of God.

The Mercy of God is great. The Mediation of the Christ is mighty. Blessed are the faithful and the meek who follow the Path of Pardon and Absolution to perfect oneness with the unceasing riches of God's Grace!

> Let the wicked forsake his way, and the unrighteous man his thoughts: and let him return unto the Lord, and he will have mercy upon him; and to our God, for he will abundantly pardon.
>
> —Isaiah 55:7

12

DIVINE-IMAGE VISUALIZATIONS

I will extoll thee, my God, O king; and I will bless thy name for ever and ever. Every day will I bless thee; and I will praise thy name for ever and ever.

— Psalm 145:1,2

He who is blessed of God has the Blessing Power.
— Ann Ree Colton

THE SPIRIT OF DIMENSIONAL BLESSINGS

Bless all souls being created in Thy Image and
　　Likeness, O Lord.
Bless all gifts, graces and talents being expressed
　　by Thy children.
Bless all animals and other living creatures.
Bless all trees, plants, flowers and other bounties
　　of Nature.
Bless the Cycles and Energies of the Moon, the
　　Sun, the Planets, the Stars and the Galaxies
　　in Thy Mighty Universe.

The key to the higher degrees of consciousness leading to the Divine-Image Consciousness is the attitude of *Blessing.* To bless the Lord as the Creator of the Universe, the Giver of the Gift of Eternal Life and the Abiding Intelligence in the

Core of every person's being is to bless dimensionally all Souls, the Stars and Galaxies.

The Divine-Image Consciousness inspires one to continually bless all persons at all times. Wherever the Spirit of God guides and directs him, he expresses the attitude of blessing.

To practice the art and science of Dimensional Blessing in one's home and in the world is to become an adept in the ethical and enlightened use of a powerful, supernatural, God-given energy—the spirit of Blessing. He who uses this energy perpetually in service to God makes mighty strides toward the Godhead, the Eternal Homeplace of the Divine Image.

Freedom comes through the spirit of Blessing. As one blesses God and all souls, so is he blessed by the Angels, the Saints and the Host of Heaven. When the attitude of blessing is observed as a spiritual discipline and dedication, a devotee has no time for thoughts of criticism, judging, depression or faultfinding; he transcends the earthbound levels of consciousness and begins to experience the freedoms, joys and inspirations of an enlightened consciousness.

As one receives the Grace and Love of God through the continuous attitude of blessing, his comprehension of the importance of blessing increases dramatically; also, the range and sphere of his blessing-power expand inwardly and outwardly.

All are one through the Image of God in them. All persons in all nations, races and religions are in one world-family through the Image of God in their souls. Whenever one prays with the deep and earnest desire that *all souls* in the world be blessed through the Image of God in them, he is rendering an invaluable service to his fellow man. Such persons have a heart's love that embraces all souls in the world with an unconditional love.

It is easy for the consciousness mind to develop habits of cursing others through negative thoughts such as hate, envy and jealousy. Judging and unforgiving thoughts also place curses upon others. Such thoughts fall far short of the attitude of blessing.

To continue to think negatively about one's self or others is a form of addiction. Unfortunately, many aspirants fail to reach their goal of union with God because of negative-thought patterns developed over many years and lifetimes.

One begins to change from cursing-thoughts to blessing-thoughts through the dedication to think, feel and act through the Commandment of Love. This dedication is the key to his progress toward union with God. As the cursing-consciousness becomes the blessing-consciousness, the energy-currents within his thoughts and emotions are filled increasingly with love. Through love, he communicates with the Love and Wisdom of God.

The blessing-consciousness is the love-consciousness. Gradually, through love-attitudes, one develops a consciousness mind that expresses the power of *Dimensional Blessings*.

When you love one another, you are reverencing the Image of God in each other.

A devotee's success on the Spiritual Path is dependent upon his reverencing the Image of God in *all* persons in his life and in the world. If he cannot bless the Image of God in any individual or group of individuals, this signifies that dark shadows still exist in his soul's record of the present life and former lives.

"For if ye forgive men their trespasses, your heavenly Father will also forgive you: But if you forgive not men their trespasses, neither will your Father forgive your trespasses." (St. Matthew 6:14,15) Love and forgiveness cleanse the dark shadows from the soul's record — and one is then free to bless, reverence and behold the Image of God in others.

"Love your enemies, bless them that curse you, do good to them that hate you, and pray for them which despitefully use

you, and persecute you. "(St. Matthew 5:44) The test of one's love is in his ability to love and bless his enemies and to see the Image of God in them. God continually tests His devotees to see who has a sincere gentleness and harmlessness and who is anger-prone and retaliative. How one reacts to these inevitable tests of his temperament determines his future usefulness to God as a guardian of the Dharma. If he fails the tests of temperament, he may require many lifetimes of lessons designed to inspire in him a holy equanimity, patience, reverence and love for the Image of God in *all* souls.

"Ye have heard that it hath been said, An eye for an eye, and a tooth for a tooth: But I say unto you, That ye resist not evil: but whosoever shall smite thee on thy right cheek, turn to him the other also." (St. Matthew 5:38,39) The desire to retaliate is a primitive eye-for-an-eye trait that must be healed either in one's present life or in a future life if he is to walk the Path of Harmless Love.

When one makes his way of life the seeing of the beauty of the Image of God in all persons in his life and in the world, he is *ministering* as a true servant of the Lord. The Omniscient Spirit of God knows who is reverencing His Image in others and who is prejudiced toward any race, religion, nation or the opposite sex. A devotee, priest or minister cannot be an effective and enlightened servant of God as long as the motes of prejudice blind his eyes to the Image of God in *all* persons, regardless of their religious, nonreligious or irreligious inclinations.

> *A servant of God is a servant of God's Image in others.*

"Oh how great is Thy goodness . . ." (Psalm 31:19) The Image of God is Pure Good. This Good manifests as miraculous healings, exorcisms, virtues and spiritual gifts. To bless the Image of God in a person is to bless the Source of All Good. To bless others is the key to attaining the exalted

degrees of Spiritual Ecstasy and Divine Bliss—the purest and finest essences of God's Good.

Divine-Image ministering awakens one from all hypnotic spells of the Antichrist and permits the Good of God to fill his being with the Essences and Elixirs of His Holy Image and Spirit. Through this mighty ministering come Transformation, Redemption and Illumination.

When one who teaches Scriptural Truths to others teaches to the Image of God in them, he is sealing sacred knowledge into the core of their eternal beings. He is not fooled by their personality masks, for he is reverencing them as everlasting creations of the Living God.

To behold the Divine Image in others while teaching them the Word of God enables one to see beyond the personalities of his listeners and to commune with their immortal souls. The personality of an individual is limited in its comprehension of Timeless Truths, but his soul and the Divine Image, being Timeless, respond with dimensional quickenings and versatile vitalities. Those who place these inner stirrings into outer actions experience the miraculous healings and transformations that lift them out of personality-karmas into soul-freedoms and Divine Grace.

> *The Spirit of Truth working through the downpouring of the Holy Esse seeks to return man to his state of pure Image. It seeks to remove him from the suggestible state of sin; the belief that he is destined to sin; or that he is by nature on the human plane born in sin and fated to sin.*
>
> —Ann Ree Colton

HEALING MIRACLES

> *God is the Creator. Our Father is the Maker. All Imaged in the likeness of the Father are makers.*

The spiritual power of Making is made possible by Imaging. The power of Imaging in man is visualization.

The mind is a visualizing and imaging vehicle or instrument. To visualize, one must literally see while in a spiritual state of God-awareness that which is the true Image or the Superior Vibration over a negative, limited vision in the lower vibration or the darkened side of polarity.

A hierarchy-nature healer always visualizes the opposite of a negativity, or only pictures for the one he would heal the opposite of its state. In this way, he visualizes and indents as a pictograph for the person to be healed the rightful balance in the polarity, and thus brings about the healing.

To visualize with the sattvic Imaging Power is to use hierarchy nature and to return as a pure divine soul to the God-Image fixed in the inner parts of his higher etheric nature. This Image cannot be sick, disturbed or distorted, or know sickness, disease, suffering or sorrow. This Image is whole. Its breath, its life and its light thrive upon the Will of God pictured as perfection within all persons, all things created.

— Ann Ree Colton

The Image of God is the most powerful healing energy in the Universe. The miraculous healings of individuals, marriages and families are the direct result of receiving the blessings of God through His Image.

Healing miracles occur when an afflicted person taps Image-of-God energies within his being — and he is instantly restored to health. Also, when a devotee or healing mediator touches Image-of-God energies within the one for whom he is praying, the person's suffering will cease — and he will be immediately restored to health. Such is the nature and power of God's Love and Mercy within His Image.

Jesus manifested healing miracles of diverse kinds through His Love, Compassion and Divine-Image Consciousness. All who minister, heal and serve in Jesus' Name are seeking to emulate their beloved Lord and His Healing-Miracle works. The miracles that occur through their love and compassion are due to their tapping the Image-of-God energies within themselves and within others.

Jesus healed miraculously in the twinkling-of-an-eye because of His knowledge of the Image of God. Sin is not part of the Image of God. This is why sin-laden persons can experience the immediate healing of diseased cells, afflicted organs and other distresses of the physical body, the emotions and the mind.

Jesus passed on to His Disciples the power of Healing Miracles, Exorcism and other spiritual powers. These manifestations of Divine Grace can occur only through a cognizant and reverent awareness of the Image of God as a reality. In each century, all enlightened Apostles of Jesus endowed with Healing-Miracle Powers work directly with the soul and the Image of God in themselves and in others.

When one heals and blesses in the spirit of Dimensional Blessings, he knows that the soul and the Divine Image are eternal, containing supernatural energies beyond Time and Space.

To be healed instantaneously and miraculously is proof of the power and closeness of the Image of God. Devotees in the process of earning the Divine-Image Consciousness experience from time to time the miraculous healing of others through their prayers, meditations and visualizations.

Through right visualization and mantra-suggestibility, the healer returns the one sick to his true Image or Divine Matrix. All healing is the return to one's Constant or the primordial Matrix where the Imaged or Archetypal Design of the one sick knows not sickness or death.

He who knows the sattvic and practices the sattvic
with his hierarchy nature is a healer of first magnitude,
a master over the tumults of separation and dysfunction.
— Ann Ree Colton

DIMENSIONAL-BLESSING PROCEDURE

I behold the Beauty of the Image of God in you.

The Divine Omnipresence is looking at one through the eyes of every person in the world. The friendships, reconciliations, inspirations and surprise blessings that manifest in his life are the results of his daily efforts to behold the beauty of the Image of God in others.

When an aspirant blesses every person in his life and in the world through his knowledge of the Divine Image, he becomes a true servant of God. Utilizing the spirit and power of Dimensional Blessings, he unites with deeper levels of the souls' records of others and activates a finer degree of charitableness and compassion within his own being.

"Bless the Lord, O my soul." (Psalm 103:1) To bless on *soul-levels* is to bless dimensionally and eternally the past, the present and the future. Thus, when a devotee visualizes and blesses the Image of God in a person, he is blessing *all* of the person's previous lives, present life and future lives. This practice opens the dimensional-blessing powers in his own soul and also seals *eternal blessings* into the soul of the one receiving his blessing. To seal eternal blessings into all persons through one's love is to utilize powerful energies of the soul and the Divine Image during his prayers, meditations and daily living.

The power of Dimensional Blessing can be extended and expanded in the following manner whenever one looks upon or prays for a fellow human being.

DIMENSIONAL-BLESSING PROCEDURE

1. Bless the person's past lives, present life and future lives, knowing that he is an eternal creation of God through the Divine Image in his soul. The blessing upon all previous lives will help to free him from the unconfessed crystallized sins in the subconscious causing problems and afflictions in his present life.

2. Bless the parents, ancestors and all other family members of the person, knowing that they, too, are being created in God's Image throughout their past, present and future lives.

3. Bless the person's birth sign (Aries, Taurus, etc.) and all other persons in the world born under the same Birth Sign. Bless the twelve Birth Signs through which the human spirit is expressing the Image of God.

4. If the person is male, bless all persons expressing the Masculine Polarity of the Image of God. Then bless all who are expressing the Feminine Polarity of the Divine Image. While blessing, one should *know* that he is blessing *all* men and women who have ever lived on earth, all who are living in the world today, and all men and women who will ever live in the future ages of the planet.

5. While blessing the Image of God in the person, know that the same Eternal Image resides in the souls of all persons. Thus, by blessing *one* of God's children, you are blessing all of His children *eternally*—past, present and future.

When the attitude of Dimensional Blessing becomes a natural way of life, all persons placed by God in the devotee's life receive powerful, eternal blessings. Also, his prayers, meditations and all other devotional, creative, teaching and healing services rendered as a disciple of Christ Jesus are rewarded bountifully through the Magnanimity of God's Love.

To know that one is blessing the Image of God in all persons, past, present and future when he blesses the Image of God in one person, is the key to freedom through blessing. Each time one utilizes the spirit of Dimensional Blessing in this manner, he reduces the darkness in his soul's record as well as the darkness in the souls' records of others.

To bless billions of souls *in the spirit of penance and restitution* with each act of blessing the Image of God in them is to experience *dramatic* reductions of the darkness in one's own soul-record. This miraculous lessening of burdens each day will brighten his spirit with the reality of his drawing closer to the Scriptural promises of Salvation, Redemption and Enlightenment.

> *Harmony in one's household is the beginning of his becoming a peacemaker in the world.*

If a devotee has offended marriage vows, moral principles and family ethics in the present life and in past lives, he will attract inharmonious relationships with one or more family members. Unpleasantness, problems and troubles with a marital partner and in family life will persist until the soul's record is cleansed — and the devotee has made a satisfactory restitution in God's sight. Harmony and love in the household denote that the Grace of God is blessing the husband, wife and children.

A husband and wife who say to one another each morning *"I behold the Beauty of the Image of God in you"* will invite the sweet blessings of God and His holy prosperings. The Love, Joy and Beauty that the Creator has *sealed* into His Image will begin to heal, enfold, inspire and spiritually quicken the married couple. If parents speak these words to their child or children at some time of the day, they will experience a new closeness through the ever-increasing blessings moving upon them from the Divine Image. Children should also be taught to say these words to their parents, brothers and sisters during the reverent time of family worship each morning or at some other time of the day.

When a husband and a wife practice each day the Dimensional Blessing of the Image of God in each other, their marriage will experience miraculous transformations through the expanding expressions of love, reverence and devotion to God and to one another. Children who are taught to bless the Image of God in their parents and in each other will experience the quickening of virtues, talents and soul-gifts that will enrich and ennoble their lifetimes.

When a devotee says to a person "Bless you," he should know that he is meaning "Bless the Eternal Image in you." A dimensional blessing such as this reaches into the Godhead Core of the person's everlasting being, activating ripples of good throughout Eternal Life.

The more one blesses all persons in his life and in the world through the Divine-Image visualizations, the more the Creator will send into his life individuals who will desire to bless *him*. This is God's perfect Law of Attraction at work through the Principles of Love and Grace. It is inevitable that one will be blessed if he continually blesses all persons in his life and in the world, for he emanates a spiritual love-energy that others trust.

> *When you practice the Divine-Image Blessings*
> *for every one you meet and see, no one is a stranger.*

Divine-Image visualizations increase one's reverence for life, reverence for the soul of every person, and reverence for all God-given energies. Reverent attitudes are holy attitudes, and holy attitudes lead to the Image-of-God Consciousness.

Spiritual joys are elusive only when one fails to express attitudes of reverence and love.

Jesus could forgive those who plotted against Him and carried out His Crucifixion because of His knowledge of the Image of God in the soul of each human being. When a follower of Jesus blesses the Divine Image in his adversaries, as well as in friends and loved ones, he is emulating the example of His Lord.

To *minister* to every person — friend or foe — through the Divine-Image visualizations is the high-calling ministry unceasing. It is the Path of the Saints, the Path of Jesus, the Path of Forgiveness and Reconciliation, the Path of Anointing and Illumination, the Path of Freedom and Resurrection.

The Saints' deep love for man as a sacred creation of God opened them to the dimensional wavelengths of the soul and its supernatural gifts. The enlightenment of the Saints and other anointed ones inspired them to bless and love their fellow men; even while being persecuted, slandered, imprisoned and martyred, they blessed their persecutors and tormentors. These holy attitudes inspired them to forgive their adversaries, thereby enabling them to retain a sacred oneness with their Beloved Lord

> *Precious in the sight of the Lord is the death of his saints.*
>
> —Psalm 116:15

To *think* of any person during meditation, in a dream, or at any other time of the day and the night is a nudge from the Angels to visualize the Image of God in the person. This Divine-Image visualization accompanied by the sending of love-blessings to the person will render an invaluable ministering service in Jesus' Name.

Apostleship is a twenty-four-hour-a-day ministering in the Name of the Lord of Love.

The Dimensional-Blessing Procedure requires but a few seconds of time; however, its positive rewards are everlasting. As one evolves the ability to utilize this profound act of Blessing at all times, his subconsciousness, consciousness and superconsciousness become blended in one harmonious blessing-instrument sanctified and anointed by the Holy Spirit.

The Creator is constantly blessing His children; when one constantly blesses all souls in the world, he becomes one with the Almighty through the spirit of Blessing. The blessings received from God increase to the degree that one blesses others selflessly and lovingly.

Heavenly Father, please help me to see Thy Image in every soul. In Jesus' Name. Amen.

Whenever a devotee sends a blessing to someone, he should begin the blessing in the Divine-Image Core within his own being and send it to the Divine-Image Core of the person. This dynamic practice of love-blessing from core to core is the key to the Gift of Healing Miracles.

When one speaks prayers and mantrams containing the word "I," he should visualize all souls in the world, present and future, receiving the blessing of his words. Through the Divine-Image visualizations first touching the core of his being and then moving outward toward the cores of all souls, he is rendering a world-healing service, for the love and compassion in his heart make of first-person prayers or any other prayers mighty healing energies for the good of all.

The amount of energy and time used to pray for the blessing of one's self is the same amount of energy and time that can be used to pray for the blessing of *all* persons; in this, the *billions* of persons in the world will receive the blessing-benefits of his prayer.

"If any man will come after me, let him deny himself, and take up his cross, and follow me." (St. Matthew 16:24) To pray *only* for one's self is to attract reprovings from the soul

and the Angels working with the soul's record; for, when one thinks solely of himself, he is *failing* to think of all other persons in the world who are in need of his prayers. A devotee who expresses the virtue of self-denial thinks only of the welfare of others rather than himself. When he applies the Divine-Image visualizations in his prayers, he is embracing *all souls* with his love and compassion; and, in so doing, he receives the choicest blessings from the Creator and His Host.

When a devotee prays for the healing of a negative trait or fault, he should know in his heart that he is praying for the healing of all persons with the same fault. Through the Image of God in him, he is ever at one with the Image of God in others. As long as his motives are pure and selfless, he will experience healings and blessings that will draw him closer to God, and his prayers will shower continuous blessings upon the human spirit.

Whenever one attends a worship service in the Sanctuary of the Lord on the Sabbath Day, Holy Days and at other times, he should send Dimensional Blessings to all worshippers and nonworshippers throughout the Earth, for all are children of the One God. He should feel a deep gratitude for all martyrs, saints and dedicated personages of the past who have made possible his religious freedoms; next, he should bless their souls — and the Dimensional Blessings through the Image of God will go directly and immediately to their souls, whether they are in Heaven or have returned to the Earth.

The presentation of tithes and offerings on God's Holy Altar is a timely opportunity to send Dimensional Blessings to the Image of God within all persons in the world. This blessing not only seals *eternal* blessings into the tithes and offerings, but it sends blessings into the souls of all persons in the world in the present age and in all future ages. During this prayer of blessing, one should know that all tithes and offerings given with love will help to provide spiritual freedoms,

Scriptural instruction and sanctuaries of worship for the faithful in all ages to come.

When one serves or receives the Sacrament of Communion, he may minister to all souls in the world through his knowledge of the Divine-Image Dimensional-Blessing Power. The Healing and Redeeming Grace of the Christ through the Bread and the Wine become magnified and multiplied when the heart's love is extended to all souls in all places and times.

Through the Divine-Image Consciousness, one receives the Sacrament of Communion for all persons in the world who are yet ignorant of the Power and Promises of the Lord Jesus; he does this on the level of the Image of God in them, visualizing their future good, well-being and enlightenment in God's timing for them.

To receive the Sacrament's blessings and to return these blessings into the world and into the Cosmos for God to use as He will, opens one's heart and mind to realizations and revelations of the Image of God as it relates to the Universe. When one receives the Sacramental Blood and Body of the Illumined Christ Jesus as the Cosmos Son of the Living God, knowing them to be filled with Image-of-God atom-energies, he begins his *communion* with higher levels of Soul Grace and Divine Grace.

To conduct a Wedding Ceremony through the Dimensional-Blessing Procedure is to seal eternal blessings into the bride and groom, and into all persons in the world who are reverencing their Marriage Vows. If the one conducting the Wedding visualizes blessings upon all individuals who will speak Marriage Vows in all future ages, he will contribute to their happiness and well-being.

When one blesses the future, he is blessed today; when he blesses today, he is blessing the future—for the power of blessing in the Name of the Christ unites him with the Timeless Dimensions of the Inner Kingdom.

All Spiritual Gifts are Dimensional Gifts. All Dimensional Gifts of the Soul come through using Dimensional-Blessing Powers in service to God.

The Christ has come to open to mankind the World of Dimensional Energies within the Soul and the Kingdom of God. The Soul-Gifts of Prophecy, Revelation and Miracles are Dimensional-Energy Gifts beyond Time and Space.

> *I will come to visions and revelations of the Lord.*
> —2 Corinthians 12:1

THE BREATH AND THE BLESSING OF FOOD

> *And as they were eating, Jesus took bread, and blessed it, and brake it, and gave it to the disciples, and said, Take, eat; this is my body.*
> —St. Matthew 26:26

> *And when he had said this, he breathed on them, and saith unto them, Receive ye the Holy Ghost.*
> —St. John 20:22

The blessing of food before each meal through the saying of *Grace* is an excellent time to employ the Dimensional-Blessing Procedure. As one speaks his words of blessing the food, he should visualize all persons in the world enjoying the Providence of God through tables filled with nutritious food. The Gratitude-Prayer before each meal will send Dimensional Blessings into the world through the *knowing* that one is blessing the Image of God in every man, woman and child in the present and in the future. Such prayers and visualizations will hasten the day when all persons in all ages will be blessed with an abundance of food and water, and the pain and misery of poverty, malnutrition and starvation will be healed forevermore.

1. Each time one says *Grace* before a meal, he should speak the words from the Divine Image in the Godhead Core of his being; he should feel a heartfelt gratitude for the food on the table and for all other blessings of God in his life.

2. Visualize the Image of God in all persons in the world in the present time and in all future ages. With compassion, desire for them to know the Providence of God in all areas of their lives and beings.

To expand and extend the Dimensional-Blessing Power during the saying of *Grace* before each meal, one should utilize the ancient mantra: **God is in the breath. Breath is God.** After the Prayer of Grace is spoken, he should speak aloud, softly or silently these words as he inhales: **God is in the breath.** He should then direct his inhalation breath toward the Godhead Core of his being. As he exhales slowly, he should say or think the words **Breath is God,** feeling deep gratitude for the food God has placed on his table and the loved ones seated at the table. Next, he should visualize the exhalation breath carrying the blessings of his love from the Image of God in the Core of his being into the Divine-Image Cores of those seated at his table. He should then send the Dimensional Blessing into the Divine-Image Cores of all individuals in the world and into the Cores of all Souls, Stars and Galaxies in the Cosmos. He should conclude by speaking or thinking the words: **Bless Thy Image in All Creation, in All Souls, O Lord. In Jesus' Name. Amen.**

The *breath* is an important part of the Power of Blessing, for the Spirit of God is blessing man with the gift of life through the breath. One should pray that God will use every inhalation and exhalation of his breath during his life to bless all Souls, Stars and Galaxies in the Universe, and all Dimensions in the Kingdom of God. When the *desire* to bless all souls and all seen and unseen worlds is within the *subconsciousness* as well as the consciousness, each breath becomes an eternal blessing for All Creation! As the attitude of Dimensional Blessing is expressed with each breath throughout one's life, he quickly attains the beautiful States of Grace promised by the Scriptures.

Inhalation Breath: Before speaking a prayer, mantram or mantra, a devotee should first move his heart's love and mind's light toward the Image of God within the Core of his being. *Exhalation Breath:* He should begin speaking the words of his prayer, mantram or mantra with great love and compassion, knowing that his words are blessing *all* Souls in the world through the Image of God in them, and also blessing all Creations in the Cosmos. This practice will assist in his becoming adept in utilizing the Divine-Image Consciousness at all times of the day and the night.

Dear God, thank Thee for Thy Gift of Breath. May each breath taken in the day and the night bless all Souls being created in Thy Image and all Creations in Thy Mighty Universe. In Jesus' Name. Amen.

RESTITUTION AND THE IMAGE OF GOD

Come, ye blessed of my Father, inherit the kingdom prepared for you from the foundation of the world.

—St. Matthew 25:34

Every person in one's life has been placed there by the Creator. When he (1) visualizes the Divine Image in each person in his life, (2) blesses the Image, and (3) ministers to the Image with love, he will move very quickly into the Grace of God through restitution. These three steps will transform all of his attitudes into kind and compassionate expressions of love.

To reverently and continuously bless all individuals, families, races, nations and religions—past, present and future—as a world-healing service in Jesus' Name is to make *Dimensional Restitution* for one's own sins of the present life and past lives. This Dimensional Restitution through the spirit of Image-of-God Eternal Blessings activates the superconscious energies of the soul and the Divine Image. The resultant healings, rewards, inspirations and freedoms reveal that a rapid cleansing of the soul's record is occurring through the Mercy of God and the Redeeming Power of Christ Jesus.

Thoughts about *any* person, living or dead, are opportunities to make restitution through Divine-Image blessings. Through restitution come Absolution and Redemption.

The *Remission-of-Sins* experienced through the Sacrament of Communion is the beginning of Redemption. Restitution enables one who receives the Sacrament to experience the *Absolution* degrees of Redemption. To continually bless the Image of God in all souls in the world—past, present and future—is to make a rapid restitution and to experience the miraculous Redemption Power of Christ Jesus as a daily reality.

A devotee should begin each prayer, meditation and fast by first uniting through love with the Image of God within the Godhead Core of his being. He should then send his love into the world as eternal blessings upon the Image of God in the souls of all persons. Next, he should send his love into the Universe of Stars and Galaxies. The Omnipresent Spirit of God will reciprocate his restitutive love with indescribable blessings of Grace, Truth and Forgiveness.

Dimensional Restitution made through blessing the Image of God in all souls in the world—past, present and future—removes the obstructions to the Love Core, the Soul Core, and, in time, the Divine-Image Core. The more love one places in his beholding the Image of God in others, the greater is the degree of his restitution and the faster his progress toward Spiritual Illumination.

> *But now being made free from sin, and become servants to God, ye have your fruit unto holiness, and the end everlasting life.*
> —Romans 6:22

It is important to remember:

> • To bless someone dimensionally is to bless all of his past lives, present life and future lives. This blessing takes only a moment, but it is extremely powerful *when observed in Jesus' Name.*
> • When you are ministering to the Divine Image in one person, you are ministering to the Divine Image in *all* persons, for the same Image of God is in all living souls.
> • When you minister to the Divine Image in *one* child, you are ministering to the Divine Image in *all* children.

The attitude of ministering is extended into a mighty Blessing-Power when one practices Divine-Image visualizations *throughout the day*, blessing in a profound way all persons in his life. As long as a devotee observes these beautiful visualizations *in the spirit of ministering*, he will make rapid restitution for unpaid sins of his present life and past lives.

Restitution through blessing the Divine Image in others is a powerful cleanser of the soul's record. The faster the soul-record is cleansed, the more freedoms and prosperings are attained. The Christ, the Door to freedom of the soul, inspires the heart and the mind to make restitution in numerous ways.

The inspirations and realizations that accompany and follow one's Divine-Image visualizations and blessings will confirm that he is doing a good and pleasing thing in the sight of God. Such confirmations are part of the joys of the higher life.

The cleansing of the soul's record through Divine-Image visualizations observed in the spirit of penance and restitution eventually leads to God's rewarding one NOW for the Grace the recipients of His blessings will receive *in coming lives*. This is why a sincere penitent practicing Divine-Image visualizations — blessing the past lives, present life and future lives of all persons in his life and in the world — can be miraculously healed, quickened and enlightened by the Christ. For God is rewarding him NOW for the good that will manifest in the future lives of those whom he is blessing with *Eternal Blessings*.

As more and more persons employ the Divine-Image visualizations of Eternal Blessings upon each person in their lives and in the world, the human spirit will experience healings and quickenings that will remove the veils between mankind and the Inner Kingdom and the Outer Universe.

> *He who seeth Me everywhere and seeth every-thing in Me, of him will I never lose hold, and he shall never lose hold of Me.*
> — Bhagavad Gita

> *Man is an image which comprises everything.*
> — Zohar

BLESSING THROUGH LOVE-TELEPATHY

> *Through love, God is creating the Universe. Through love, God is creating man in His Image and Likeness. Through love, man learns of God, His Image and His Universe.*

The speed of light is slow and cumbersome when compared to the speed of love. The speed of love produces *instantaneous* blessings any place on earth or in the Universe.

When one sends love-blessings to the farthest Star or Galaxy, the blessings are received instantaneously through the speed of love. Love is God's Gift to man that enables him to overcome Time and Space.

When one dedicates his life to the observance of the Commandments of Love, he learns to bless through the spiritual degrees of love-telepathy. The telepathic power of love can heal and bless at a distance as quickly as in one's immediate environment. Love-blessings sent telepathically to the farthest corners of the earth are received by the souls of those living there. During times of prayer and meditation, a devotee should visualize his love blessing all souls on earth. The Spirit of God will confirm that he is rendering a right and good service to his fellow man.

When one enfolds with his love the planet Earth, the Solar System and the Universe, he has expanded his consciousness awareness of the unanimity of all Celestial Creations in the Cosmos.

The soul and the Image of God are highly-sensitive telepathic senders and receivers. Men are presently learning the laws governing mental telepathy; they have yet to learn the laws governing soul-telepathy and Divine-Image telepathy. However, the laws and ethics related to soul-telepathy and Divine-Image telepathy are known to spiritually-enlightened personages. The most important of these laws is *Love*.

Heavenly Father, please help me to understand and to work with the speed of the Christ Light in its Healing and Exorcism Grace through the Image-of-God Consciousness.

Jesus came to open to mankind the Soul-Dimensions of the Godhead. The powerful Godhead-energies in the Third

Heaven within the core of man's being are gradated through the Second-Heaven and the First-Heaven degrees of light. As one progresses toward this Inner Kingdom of Godhead-energies, the Lord Jesus becomes his Shepherd and Teacher in the ethical use of these energies. The Commandment of Love Ye One Another is one's only protection when contacting the powerful Godhead-energies within the Inner Kingdom.

In the present age, the human spirit is being introduced to the world of atomic energies and the world of soul-energies. Even as atomic energies can be used for good or evil, so can soul-energies be used for blessing or for cursing. Man is being required by God to learn to live morally and ethically with the knowledge of atomic energies and soul-energies; he can no longer remain ignorant of their reality and their potentials.

Atomic energies and soul-energies used with love are opening new vistas to the tremendous powers the Creator is placing in the hands of His children. The constant practice of beholding the Beauty of the Image of God in one's fellow man is the beginning of his becoming adept in the miraculous telepathic-powers of love through the dimensional energies of the soul and the Image of God.

> Love is the key to all mysteries in Heaven and on Earth.

"Canst thou bind the sweet influences of the Pleiades." (Job 38:31) All Stars and Galaxies in the Universe are blessing each other with "sweet influences," for it is the nature of God to bless. Man is constantly receiving these Universal-Energy blessings. When he reciprocates by sending love-blessings telepathically to all celestial creations in the Cosmos, he becomes one with all Love-energies of God throughout the Universe.

"Draw nigh to God, and he will draw nigh to you." (James

4:8) The love one carries in his heart for the beautiful Universe and for the Sacred Image of God opens the *Seals of Grace* in the Three Heavens. The more he blesses God and the Heavenly Host in the Inner Kingdom and in the Outer Universe, the more he becomes receptive to the *Greater* Seals of Grace which shower upon him the blessings of insights and understandings regarding the Moon, the Sun, the Planets, the Stars and the Galaxies. This knowledge contributes to his attaining the Apostolic Crown of Enlightenment through the telepathic power of Dimensional Blessings.

> *Every Star and Galaxy has its secrets to reveal regarding the Image of God.*

God gives to each of His children the power to *anoint* others with blessings. Even as Jesus continuously blessed others during His life on earth, so do all who walk the Path of Love emulate their Beloved Lord by blessing others.

To anoint one's fellow man, near and far, through telepathic love-blessings is to receive blessings through the *Anointing Power* of the Heavenly Host. Each Angel, Saint, Archangel and Illumined Being in Heaven is a master of the telepathic power of love-blessings and other holy anointings.

Through the telepathic sending of love-blessings, one becomes an enlightened anointer; and, as he blesses, so is he blessed by the Anointing Spirit of God.

The receiving of the *Divine-Marriage Anointing* comes after one proves his love for God and His children throughout the many tests and trials of the probationary years on the Path. The love-blessings *sealed* into his being by the Telepathic Anointers in Heaven and on Earth prepare him for the time when God will place His Spirit upon him in the Divine Marriage. Thereafter, he will serve his Lord and Maker as an enlightened servant of His Altar and Word in the state of *Fulness Grace.*

Behold my servant, whom I uphold; mine elect, in whom my soul delighteth; I have put my spirit upon him.

—Isaiah 42:1

In infinite being, one is in a state of constant awareness within the Presence of God. In infinite wisdom, one is in a state of constant union and communion with the Mind of God. In infinite love, one is in a constant state of blessing, anointing, healing, manifesting. All men, one by one, must enter the door to the Blessed Infinite.

—Ann Ree Colton

13

THE ETERNAL NOW

You can be in the Eternal Now under the tute-lage of the Eternals when you have total belief in Life Everlasting.

— Ann Ree Colton

TIME AND TIMELESSNESS

Time was created as an image of eternity.

— Plato

Thy kingdom is an everlasting kingdom.

— Psalm 145:13

Time, Space and Light are revealing their secrets to the human spirit. The movement and Cycles of the Planets, the Stars and the Galaxies are disclosing key truths regarding the nature of the Universe.

The Solar System containing the life of man on Earth has billions of brother and sister Stars within the Milky Way Galaxy. The Milky Way, moving through Space over one million miles an hour, is a slow traveler compared to distant Galaxies traveling several hundred million miles an hour.

God makes the Earth's journey through the Cosmos so gentle that men do not sense the movement or rotation of their planet. Life on Earth proceeds at its own pace with no concern about the diversity of Time-Cycles and Velocity Variables of the myriad Galaxies, Stars, Planets and Moons.

"The gift of God is eternal life." (Romans 6:23) The Creator sends enlightened Teachers to the world from time to time to teach His children that Life is Eternal and that Love, Truth and the Soul of man are part of this Eternality.

Most persons on earth are not interested in the philosophical ramifications of Life Everlasting, nor do they desire to contemplate the innumerable Stars and Galaxies whirling and dancing throughout Outer Space. They are content to satisfy their senses with every pleasure available to them. The pleasures of the world are so enticing that the minds of most persons remain earthbound year after year, life after life, age after age.

Occasionally, a rare soul will exclaim, "I have seen a glimpse of the ineffable Glory of God. The Spirit of God is beyond Time and Space. The Love of God is Eternal, Timeless." This realization is profoundly true. It may occur during a reverent time of meditation, in a prayer, while reading a Scriptural verse, or at some other time. However, when one experiences this sublime truth, he will never be the same again, for he has begun to unite with the Omnipresent Spirit of God as the *Eternal Now*.

While Time, as man knows it, is based upon the Cycles of the Sun, the Moon and the Earth, Timelessness, as the soul knows it, is based upon the Eternal Spirit of Almighty God. The Eternal God is the Past, the Present and the Future as *One*. To bless and anoint in His Name is to unite with the Past, the Present and the Future through His Everlasting Image.

God desires for His children to be free *Now*. He desires for His children to be enlightened *Now*. He has sent His Beloved Son, Christ Jesus, to give them the formulas for freedom, lifting them from the darkness of unknowing and sin to the light of Knowing and Grace.

The Christ Light is blazing throughout the Universe. Men who sit in darkness are oblivious to the awesome power of His Omnipotent Light.

To *know* that one is in the Eternal Now through the Image of God is to begin his work as a son of light under Christ. The sense of the Eternal Now comes through the Anointings received through God's Holy Spirit beyond Time and Space. Each powerful Anointing by the Spirit of God awakens in His servant increasing measures of the Divine-Image Consciousness. *The Divine-Image Consciousness and the Eternal-Now Consciousness are one.*

To live in the Eternal Now at one with the Spirit of God is joy. There is no regretting the past or fearing the future, for one is living in the Eternal Now of God's Love-Presence and Joy-Presence.

Jesus of Nazareth lived in the Eternal-Now Consciousness, and He tried to teach its principles to others.

"Take therefore no thought for the morrow." (St. Matthew 6:34) Many persons suffer illness or death caused by their worries and fears about tomorrow. Prophets of gloom paint a fearful picture of the future; and their followers move through life crippled by the fear of prophesied earthquakes, tidal waves, or nuclear destruction.

Numerous individuals suffer unhappiness because their minds are guilt-ridden by sins committed in the past. Guilt-memories push out every other kind of thought, and they wallow in despair or depression day after day. Such persons not only corrode their own health and well-being, but they make miserable the lives of their loved ones.

"Perfect love casteth out fear." (1 John 4:18) One who is healed of fears of the future and guilt-burdens of the past — and loves God, Life and his fellow man — is free to live in the joy of the Eternal Now.

My doubts and fears are of a dying yesterday.
I shall trust and try, for the Now is my true
Eternity.

— Ann Ree Colton

A happy man is too contented with the present
to think about the future.

— Albert Einstein

Love is the key to a joy beyond the temporal joys in the world, a joy that springs forth from the Eternal Essences of God's Spirit within the soul and within His Image. *"In thy presence is fulness of joy."* (Psalm 16:11)

To serve the Image of God in others is the greatest joy in life.

Jesus had the type of consciousness that expressed with naturalness the Supernatural and Dimensional aspects of God's Eternal Love; therefore, He could prophesy with ease, heal miraculously all manners of afflictions, raise the dead, speak with a rare wisdom, and perform other mighty works and miracles.

The love that produces joy in the Eternal Now is filled with the divine energies and essences beyond Time and Space. Through a sense of oneness with the Eternality of God, one knows that there is *a Greater Reality* beyond the finite and the limited, a Reality of the Infinite and the Limitless.

Man is limitless creation in God. We are limitless
in God's Limitlessness.

— Ann Ree Colton

When one meditates, his mind is either cluttered with numerous anxieties, fears and guilts, or he meditates with faith, hope and joy in the Eternal Now. If there are anxieties regarding the lack of money or supply, these concerns will intrude on his meditation peace and communion with Omnipresence. Joy in the Eternal Now inspires a trust in the Providence of God to provide for all of one's needs, physically, emotionally, mentally and spiritually. The fear of lack of supply is healed when one's faith in God and love for His Commandments open the door to His Providence.

The abuse of money leads to the misery of poverty. The reverent use of money in service to God leads to the joys of Holy Poverty. Holy Poverty is an attitude of total relaxation based upon trust in God's Providence each moment of the day and the night. This attitude of trust over the years unites one with the harmony, effortless effort and the pure creations that bless all servants of God who are living in the joy of the Eternal Now.

All joys and blessings received from God should be immediately returned to Him in the spirit of Holy Poverty. In this, one will receive ever-increasing joys and blessings within the Holy Increase of God's Eternal Spirit. A devotee should visualize his placing all joys and blessings on the Altar of the Universe, that God may use their energies in His creating of all Stars and Galaxies and in His creating of Man in His Image. He should visualize his joys and blessings becoming part of the Light of the Christ as a brilliant Eternal Light illuminating all Celestial Creations in the Cosmos.

An aspirant on the Path may repent for his *known* sins; however, sins committed in past lives unknown to him may present themselves for payment in his present life. The only way to retain the joy in the Eternal Now during such times is to immediately confess to God his sins and transgressions of his previous lives as well as his present life. In this, he will continue to walk humbly and meekly with his Lord.

To live each day in the humility-spirit of penance and restitution for one's own sins and for the sins of the world enables the Christ to work more quickly to liberate him from the claims of unpaid sins, and to transenergize the dark sin-energies into the lighted energies of Redemption Grace. Thus, through the Redeeming Power of Christ Jesus, a devotee may remain constant in the joy of the Eternal Now.

Thinking overweightedly on the past produces senility for the aged. Thinking entirely on things for the future produces non-reality and non-reliability for the present. Thinking on things and caring only for the present produces emasculation or lack of refinement of the senses.

—Ann Ree Colton

Renounce the craving for the past,
renounce the craving for the future,
renounce the craving for what is between,
and cross to the opposite shore.

—Buddha

When one has a clear and peaceful conscience, he can experience the joy of the Eternal Now, crossing to the shore of Heaven's Light. Through a clear conscience, he may behold the Face of God smiling at him through each Holy Law and Commandment. A clear conscience combined with a steadfast faith and loyalty to one's vows enables him to see and to serve the Image of God in his fellow man. To be cognizant of the Divine Image as an Eternal Constant on earth and in the Cosmos is the key to the rewards and blessings received in the Now.

If one practices the Presence of God as the Eternal Now, he will experience His Presence of Love as an Eternal-Now Love; His Presence of Joy, as an Eternal-Now Joy. It is impossible to be unforgiving, impatient, irritated or angry if one is living in the joy of the Eternal Now.

Procrastination is a compressed energy caused by one's moving out of timing with the Grace of God manifesting through the Cycles of the Moon and the Sun. When the compressed energy of procrastination is activated by a hypersensitivity, it explodes into hatred, anger and other violent words, emotions and actions.

A procrastinator is a sleeping bomb due to the increasing compression of Time-energy. When one works in harmony with God's Energy-Laws through the Cycles of the Moon and the Sun, he remains in a state of Increasing Grace. The Holy Spirit blesses, anoints, quickens and enlightens all vigilant devotees who reverence the Gift of Time and the Cycles of Creation.

> *Procrastination is death to God's Increase.*
> *If you are a procrastinator, you are harming your own Image; you are harming life itself.*
> *Punctuality leads one right to the Now of service to God.*
>
> — Ann Ree Colton

The Antichrist tries to get one *out of timing* with God's Grace through unpunctuality and procrastination. The Christ tries to get one into timing with the clock of the world and the Clock of the Eternals. To be *in timing* with the Flow of God's Grace through punctuality and gratitude for the Sacred Gift of Time is a necessary step toward the attaining of the Eternal-Now Consciousness and its joy-centerings.

A clock has a central point from which two hands extend and move. The moving hands of the clock create the sense of Time; the central point of the clock remains the same. The central point symbolizes the *Central* Spirit of God creating the myriad Time-Cycles in the Universe.

To unite with God is to unite with His Godhead Point, which is the Eternal Center or Constant from which all Time-Systems are projected. All Stars and Galaxies have an ending; however, the Godhead is the Everlasting Center of all Celestial Creations throughout Eternal Life.

The Timeless Point of the Godhead is the Point in which the Image of God is sealed; from this Eternal Godhead Point is sent forth every energy-atom in the vast Universe. All Souls, Stars and Galaxies are contributing in great and glorious ways to the majestic symphony of the Image of God.

All Holy Beings and Presences in the Kingdom of God

dwell in the Eternal Godhead Light. Man on earth is being prepared for the time when he, too, will dwell in the Eternal Godhead Light. He is destined to become a Transcendental Being through the Image of God. Through Time-Cycles, he will attain the goal of Timelessness and Spacelessness.

> *The syllable OM is verily thine image. Through this syllable thou mayest be attained.*
>
> —Upanishads

The sounding of the OM is a powerful way of communing with the Godhead or *Jewel in the Lotus* wherein is sealed the Image of God. The outer and inner petals of the Lotus open in God's timing, revealing to the devotee an ever-increasing understanding of the Divine Image as it relates to Time, Timelessness, Virtues, Conscience, Logic, Love and other sacred Truths.

> *Om is the Name-Sound of God. OM is the Power Mantra Name for the Omnipotent Power of God. The OM, which is the sacred sound of the Word, is the mighty Mantra inviting God-Realization.*
>
> *The OM sound is both prayer and mantra. OM erases the negative past, explodes the present negatives, creates the future as perfect, as joy.*
>
> *We master the Time element of Space in this planet into Space-expansion through the sound of the mantra OM, that we may enter into the Hierarchy powers under the Christ. Christ is that One who opens the way to Timelessness and Space-liberation.*
>
> —Ann Ree Colton

The Eternal-Now Consciousness is the Greater Reality. It knows of the importance of all Time-Cycles, but is *beyond* the Time-Cycles.

God is saying to His children: *"You are Eternal. Your Soul*

*is Eternal. My Image in you is Eternal. My Spirit is beyond
Time and Space. Man, being created in My Image and Likeness, is, in his soul and spirit, beyond Time and Space. Learn
of the secrets and mysteries of Love, for through My Love,
Life is Eternal. And through My Love in you, you will know
the Eternal in the Now."*

The brain of man is experiencing evolutionary quickenings
that are opening new capacities in thinking and knowing.
The fusion of the left and right hemispheres of the brain will
require ages of Time-Cycles for those who resist the spiritual-
quickening process. Through sacramental meditation and
other worship disciplines, one experiences the quickening of
the mental-body atoms that accelerates the blending of both
hemispheres of the brain. Through these quickenings, his
sense of Time changes dramatically, for the influences of the
Eternal Atoms of his being become more prominent in his
feelings, thoughts and actions.

The left hemisphere of the brain senses Time as an orderly
linear progression that moves from the past through the present into the future. The right hemisphere of the brain is nonlineal; Time is perceived differently; the foreseeing of future
events is possible.

The brain's lineal and nonlineal relationships to Time —
past, present and future — become harmoniously blended
through reverent prayer, meditation, fasting, mantramic
speaking, creativity through music, dance, writing, art and
other spiritual dedications. These devotional and creative activities enable one to live naturally and comfortably in the
Time-Cycles of the Solar System while giving birth to the
prophetic capabilities of the mind and the soul.

The Memory, as an Eternal Treasure Trove, reveals its
glistening jewels of ageless wisdom as one proves worthy in
God's sight. In this, one need not stumble through life while
learning the difference between right and wrong; through the
Gift of Memory, he *knows* the difference between right and

wrong. The Memory of soul-wisdom earned during the journey of Eternal Life is his to use in service to God.

The Memory and the Conscience stand as sentinels to the Temple of the Soul. Through Memory, Conscience and Prophecy, one *knows* the Past, the Present and the Future as one in the Eternal Now.

> *That which hath been is now; and that which is to be hath already been.*
> —Ecclesiastes 3:15

> *Time is fulfilled when time is no more. He who in time has his heart established in eternity and in whom all temporal things are dead, in him is the fulness of time.*
> —Meister Eckhart

> *And the angel which I saw stand upon the sea and upon the earth lifted up his hand to heaven. And sware by him that liveth for ever and ever, who created heaven, and the things that therein are, and the earth, and the things that therein are, and the sea, and the things which are therein, that there should be time no longer.*
> —Revelation 10:5,6

PSYCHIC ENERGIES AND THE SOUL

> *All persons have psychical powers. As long as one remains irreverent toward the spiritual nuances within the Universe, he will continue to express the crude, electrical, psychical energies in his emotions and thoughts. The psychical power is similar to a current of raw electricity. It has the power to bring disquiet, to disturb the peace.*
> *As the mentality and the emotions of men come*

to balance, spiritual nature comes to birth. The
spiritual nature harnesses the psychical power and
keeps it under control.

—Ann Ree Colton

The *psyche* is the soul. Psychic energy is soul-energy. Psychic energy is a gift from God.

The senses have their energy domain in the physical world. The Creator, through His Image in man, is beginning to quicken *soul-energies*, which are mankind's first glimpses of the dimensional energies of the soul beyond Time and Space. Even as God has opened to His children the knowledge and use of atomic energy, so is He opening to them the knowledge and use of the soul's prophetic energies and other supernal energies.

When one is devoted to God and His Commandments, the psychic energies are spiritualized expressions of his love for God. However, when one is not observing the Commandments of God, he will exploit psychic energies for his own personal gain. Such abuses are reproved by the Laws of God.

Even as sexual energies can be used reverently or irreverently, so can psychic energies be used reverently or irreverently. A materialistically-inclined individual will try to benefit financially from prophetic abilities, or he will use his gifts to inflate his ego or to dominate others. Pure love and selfless motives protect one from misusing the energies of the soul that are introducing him to the world of prophecy and other sacred gifts.

Everything one experiences of a *prophetic* nature, such as intuition, apprehension, precognition, foreknowing, and prophetic visions and dreams contains soul-energies beyond Time. All persons experiencing these perceptions or visions of the future are uniting with the soul's eternal energy-essences.

Inspirational thoughts beyond mundane thoughts contain psychic or soul energy. Thoughts inspired by the Spirit of

God contain the sacred energies of the soul and the Kingdom of Heaven.

The energies of the soul are manifesting in increasing measures because man is beginning to be initiated in the ethical and noble use of these precious energies beyond Time and Space. The ethical stewardship of the soul's dimensional energies will involve mankind for many ages, for these energies represent his next stage of progression through the Timeless, Eternal Image of God. Even as many ages of time have been devoted to man's learning of the world of the senses, so is the human spirit now entering new levels of discoveries and expressions related to the world of the soul beyond Time and Space.

> *The higher psychic mind is jewel-like, centered in a mentality of flawless, selfless love.*
>
> *All persons having the pure, higher psychical powers inoffensive to others have earned them as holy-stigmata fresh springs of the soul.*
>
> *All persons having healthy, harmless, psychical presence are healers and anointers. Such initiates have certain knowledge of Timelessness.*
>
> *The higher psychical energy upholding the yeast of consciousness, when turned to God, gives illumination of the mind.*
>
> *The spiritual consciousness of man is not in bondage to Time.*
>
> —Ann Ree Colton

OMNIPRESENCE AND THE COINCIDING PRINCIPLE

> *Prove me now herewith, saith the Lord of hosts.*
> —Malachi 3:10

> *All great sages and all great seers know God, experience Him and prove Him through the Coinciding Principle.*

The Coinciding Principle proves God to man by im-
parting to him the Presence of God as the Intelligible
and Caring Constant.

Coinciding begins when one recognizes there is a
mathematical Law of Order caring for him.

The Coinciding Principle becomes refined, quick,
flawless, perfectly polarized through faith and trust.

He who has full expression of the Coinciding Princi-
ple has the power to prophesy.

To be in Omnipresence and to live through the Co-
inciding is freedom.

— Ann Ree Colton

Time is an energy that can be molded, expanded, compressed, quickened and transcended. All spiritual gifts and
soul-powers relate to the overcoming of Time and Space.

Union with God means union with His Omnipresence.
When a devotee begins to receive the Gift of Prophecy and
other soul-gifts, he is initiated through *the Coinciding Prin-*
ciple. Through this mighty Principle, God as Omnipresence
establishes a close communion with him.

The Coinciding Principle works through cyclic timings involving days, weeks, months, years, lifetimes and ages; it also
works through split-second timings and phenomenal coincidences that prove the Presence of God. It is an awesome and
wondrous experience each time God proves in a surprising
and unexpected way His Power to Create the Miraculous
Coincidings involving split-second timings.

When the Coinciding Principle is opened, the
true communion and communication begin, and
all of the vital interrelated strengths flow together
as an affirmative vehicle within the Will of God.

In the Coinciding within the Esse, God removes
space from Himself and proves Himself in one tril-

lionth second of time. Holy synchronization of the Coinciding assures one that he is and that God verily Is.

The Coinciding Principle by which God reveals Himself protects the good. The Coinciding Principle sets up the miracles to protect the good. These are the filigree-miracles.

— Ann Ree Colton

The important events and major blessings in one's life represent beautiful and sweet manifestations of God's Grace through the Coinciding Principle. A memorable miracle is an unmistakable sign of a dramatic Omnipresence-blessing through the Coinciding Principle.

Each holy inspiration, insight, realization, healing, prophecy, exorcism and revelation received after one dedicates his life to God gives evidence of the Coinciding Principle — for each blessing coincides with his spiritual progress.

Through the Coinciding Principle, a servant of God who has made the Vow of Holy Poverty may work with joy and effortless effort, for food, clothing, money, inspiration and all other physical and spiritual needs are provided by the Divine Omnipresence in perfect timings through the Coinciding Principle.

As one progresses on the Spiritual Path, he must reach the time when he *knows* with full certainty that God, as the Omnipresent Truth, is communicating with him each moment of the day and the night. Through the Coinciding Principle, each person in his life, and all that is occurring in his body, heart, mind, soul and being are revealing his soul's record and his soul's Covenant with God.

Every moment of the day, one lives in the Coinciding Principle.

There are no accidents in the Coinciding. Each Coinciding is the fulfillment of the Law.

When you live in the Coinciding, everything is God-sent.

Once you are in the Coinciding, you are no longer subjected to the gross compulsions of the Maya-grid system. Seeing through a glass darkly is seeing in the Maya world. Seeing clearly is seeing through the Coinciding in which one is aware of Omnipresence as being ever-present in all affairs human and otherwise.

— Ann Ree Colton

The soul's record is the strongest magnet in the world. The light in the soul's record *attracts* blessings, prosperings and joys. The darkness of unconfessed sins in the soul's record *attracts* reprovings, problems and sorrows.

A problem of any kind is caused by an unconfessed sin.

In the prodigal-son states of consciousness, persons express evil, violence, immorality, selfishness and other negative traits because of their resistances to Scriptural Laws, Commandments, Virtues and Ethics. The more highly-evolved a person is, the more quickly he is reproved for his sins of omission and commission. Each reproving is through the Omnipresence-timings within the Coinciding Principle. Many persons have soul-covenanted with God to experience reprovings for sin-offenses in longer spacings of Time; for example, an evil-doer may not experience reproofs for his sins until a coming life.

According to Cyclic Law, that which appears to be an accident is actually a *negative coincidence* caused by the accumulation of many minor and major infractions against the Scriptural Commandments. A serious life-changing or life-ending accident or illness may be the culmination of many negative cycles over numerous lifetimes.

As long as one remains in timing with the Cycles of Dedicated Observance of the Ten Commandments, the Tithe Law, the Love-Commandments and the Sermon-on-the-

Mount Principles of Jesus, he will remain in the Flow of God's Grace.

> *You are in the Coinciding when you know the Flow.*
> — Ann Ree Colton

A Teacher's task is to shepherd each student to the unceasing Flow of God's Grace. The more a student or devotee is in the Flow, the more the Coinciding Principle is recognized by his consciousness mind. After he becomes centered in the Flow, he *knows* that the Coinciding Principle is operative every moment of the day and the night through the Omnipresence of God.

The Cycle of each Planet and the Cycles of the Sun and the Moon are constantly activating Coinciding-provings of Omnipresence. These Coincidings not only relate to one's present life but also to his previous-lives' influences upon his present life.

All that will occur in one's present life, all persons in his life, all talents and abilities are exact coincidences set in motion in previous lives. Every person, place and event in his future lives will also fulfill the Coinciding Principle as related to his soul's Covenant and the Image of God.

As the soul's record is cleansed, the blessings increase in one's life. A State of Grace occurs when the magnet of the soul's record continually attracts manifold degrees of Divine Grace in perfect timing to his needs.

A prophet anointed by God's Spirit receives his knowledge of future events through his union with the Archetypal Kingdom and with the souls' Covenants and the souls' records of masses of persons as well as individuals.

Whatever an individual will be in his present life and in future lives is known in the Omniscient Mind of God. If it pleases the Creator to reveal to His servant knowledge of his coming life or lives, or the coming life or lives of others, He can do so at any time.

The closer one is to his soul's eternal knowing, the more he becomes prophetic. From the apex of the Holy Mountain of Illumination, he has a panoramic view of the Past, the Present and the Future.

Timing-confirmations of God's Omnipresent Love and Truth add joy after joy to the spiritual life. One also gains an increasing awareness of the Angels and their ability to mold and shape the energy of Time.

Each time one experiences a miraculous confirmation or remarkable coincidence, he should speak a prayer of thankfulness and praise. His gratitude to God and the Angels will strengthen his union with the miraculous manifestations of Divine Grace.

After every Coinciding experience in Esse, one should give thanks to God. In this, he Passes the blessing to all—thus, the Coinciding continues as an unceasing movement and quickening for all.

One lives in a Timeless state when he is working, living and thinking within the Coinciding Principle. One lives then within astonishments without astonishment.

Thinking in the Coinciding Principle within the Esse gives the interflow of the past, the present and the future as unity. From this comes the spiritualized intellect.

Time becomes one within the One.

—Ann Ree Colton

14

THE FACE OF GOD

When thou saidst, Seek ye my face; my heart said unto thee, Thy face, Lord, will I seek.
—Psalm 27:8

The Lord bless thee, and keep thee: The Lord make his face shine upon thee, and be gracious unto thee: the Lord Lift up his countenance upon thee, and give thee peace.
—Numbers 6:24–26

THE TRUE SELF AND THE FACE OF JESUS

For God, who commanded the light to shine out of darkness, hath shined in our hearts, to give the light of the knowledge of the glory of God in the face of Jesus Christ.
—2 Corinthians 4:6

To live from love is to dry Your Face. It's to obtain pardon for sinners.
—Saint Therese of Liseux

Even as Stars have different magnitudes of brightness, so do Souls have different magnitudes of brightness. The brightness in the Soul of Jesus and the Brightness of every other Soul in the Solar System produce a great *Light* in the Universe. This may be likened to the Stars of different sizes in the

Milky Way Galaxy radiating their *composite* light into the Cosmos. God works on Cosmos levels through the composite light of Souls He assigns to a Solar System and Galaxy.

To view the planet Earth with spiritual eyes from a distance in Space would reveal a most beautiful composite light of all Souls radiating together through the Image-of-God facets and attributes earned over the Eternals. The lessons men are learning individually and collectively on Earth are adding greater degrees of Light to their Souls, their True Selves and to the Universe.

The magnitude of brightness in a person's Soul has been earned throughout numerous existences and experiences in countless Stars and Galaxies. The *Self* that has learned all that God would have it learn thus far in Eternal Life is *the True Self*. The True Self is the Higher Self, the Everlasting Self.

Whatever one has earned and learned during Eternal Life are the assets with which he works in the present Solar System. Whatever he has not earned and learned is yet sealed within the Image of God. Each life on earth contributes to the earning and learning process. The lessons one fails to learn in his present life will repeat themselves in coming lives until they become permanent memories in his soul's record and True Self.

> *The True Self is the Real, Deathless, Eternal, Everlasting Self Imaged of God.*
>
> *All things having movement are energized processes through which the Face of God is seen, and the original Face of one's own True Self is made manifest. The True Self is Self-Luminous. The True Self is that which gives momentum to your Soul.*
>
> *The True Self has your answer to the lesser self, which is automated by conceptual absorption from past lives, from ancestors, from present karma. One should get into the Interflow of that True and Luminous Self seek-*

ing to come forward and show its Face to you, which is really the Face of God made Omnipresent in you.

—Ann Ree Colton

The True Self works with the higher energies of the Moon, the Sun and the Planets. The lower self works with the lower energies of the Moon, the Sun and the Planets. The face of Jesus is known and seen by those who follow Him to the *Promised Land*: the Grace-Atmospheres and Holy Electricities of the Higher Celestial Energies.

Nothing is wasted in God's Plan; every atom of energy — be it dark or light — contains important lessons for growth, evolvement and enlightenment to be sealed forevermore within the True or Higher Self. The True Self is beyond race, ancestry and family, for it dwells in the Eternal and Universal I Am that I Am. The True Self is the Divine-Image Self, the Self that knows God face to face.

Heavenly Father, may the Prodigal-Son Self be healed, and may the Divine-Image Self come forth in its Fulness of Grace. In Jesus' Name. Amen.

Persons who wear the mask of ego and express their lower natures are unable to see the Face of the True Self. When one lives within the virtues of his higher or divine nature, he may look into the Face of his True Self or *Beloved*. The Face of the True Self prepares him to look into the Face of Jesus and the Face of God.

Beyond the masks of countless egos experienced in former lives is the True Self, the Real, the One in the One. The opening to Holy Spirit is the Grace of God where one goes above and beyond the ego and sees the True Self motivating all.

The True Self is the Imaged Self as envisioned by our Father in Heaven and animated by the Elohim gods or Hierarchy.

The True Self is at home in God.

*All creation is in the mind. Mind, when free within
the hierarchy nature of the True Self, creates with God.*
— Ann Ree Colton

Each devotee on the Path must reach the time when he can look into the Face of Jesus through the Face of the True Self. While a person is still living a life of immorality and selfishness, he cannot look into the Face of Jesus. When one is sincerely repentant for his sins of omission and commission, he may begin to look into the Face of his Redeemer.

Prayer and meditation prosper in peace and grace only to the degree that a devotee can look into the Face of Jesus. If the heart loves another more than God, the eyes are looking elsewhere rather than into the Eyes of his Lord. If one loves himself more than God, his eyes are closed to the Holy Face.

Many students on the Path are never satisfied with the blessings that God pours into their lives. They always want *more*. This attitude reveals the spirit of greed that discolors their dedications to God.

Gratitude for each and every blessing received through God's Mercy inspires one to live each moment with peace, contentment and happiness. One who *trusts in God* is always content with whatever blessings he receives, knowing that when he is ready for more Grace, the Creator will provide according to His Wisdom and Perfect Timing. This knowing of God's Goodness, Bountifulness and Love is a soul-knowing born of many lives of serving Him. This knowing of God's Wisdom and *acceptance* of His Will is the basis for a happy communion with His Countenance.

If God graces an aspirant with an enlightened Teacher, the student should be attentive to instruction and apply its wisdom. His gratitude for sacred instruction through reverent application begins the quickening of his soul-gifts and spiritual powers. These priceless quickenings indicate that the Light of God's Countenance is revealing a glimpse of its Dimensional Beauty and Glory.

*A virtue can appear in the world as a Face of
God, for when one witnesses virtue, he has seen the
Presence of God.*
—Ann Ree Colton

*As for me, I will behold thy face in righteousness:
I shall be satisfied when I awake, with thy likeness.*
—Psalm 17:15

The Joy of God is a Universal Constant. Jesus promises
joy to those who follow Him, for joy is a natural state of being for those who love the Laws of God and see His Face
within all virtues. The Face of the True Self, the Face of Jesus
and the Face of God can be perceived only in the light of
holy virtues. This truth is experienced by all anointed Saints
and other sacred personages who have attained the Divine
Marriage.

*The Laws and Commandments of God, when
fulfilled with love and devotion, become the lens
through which one may behold the face of the
Lord.*

Jesus had love for all; however, His Covenant as Savior and
Messiah of the world required that He suffer persecution and
a painful crucifixion. There are times when one who serves
in Jesus' Name experiences persecution and, sometimes, martyrdom. At such times, he is being prepared for a closer look
at the Countenance of God through the Covenant of Suffering for righteousness' sake.

When the children of God shall truly behold His Face, all
curses will be changed into blessings; all sins, into grace.

*And there shall be no more curse: but the throne of
God and of the Lamb shall be in it; and his servants
shall serve him: And they shall see his face; and his
name shall be in their foreheads.*
—Revelation 22:3,4

Through Him (Jesus) we can look up to the highest heaven and see, as in a glass, the peerless perfection of the face of God. Through Him the eyes of our hearts are opened, and our dim and clouded understanding unfolds like a flower to the light; for through Him the Lord permits us to taste the wisdom of eternity.

—Clement of Rome

Beyond the Christ is the Father's Face shimmering in Light. Always he who seeth the Christ seeth the Face of the Father.

—Ann Ree Colton

THE SPIRITUAL BODY

Before the physical body ever existed in the earth, the incorruptible energy-body existed. It is the body one lives in before physical birth and after physical death.

To the seer in the physical world, this body, when seen, appears as a lightning flash of quickened vibration. When the seer extends his sight into the higher astral luminosities of the First Heaven, this body appears luminous, glorious in color, magnified in light. When the seer extends his sight into the Transcendental, this incorruptible body appears as a radiance-body, having etheric vibration, astral luminosity, and spiritual white light radiating from all dimensions into all dimensions.

—Ann Ree Colton

"There is a spiritual body." (1 Corinthians 15:44) The spiritual body is the incorruptible, everlasting body of man. The invisible body consists of Pure Spirit; the Real or True Self lives in this body of Eternal Light.

The deathless atoms within the spiritual body function at rates of quickening beyond Time. However, man also has atoms in his physical, emotional and mental bodies yet to at-

tain the greater rates of quickening that manifest only
through experiences in the Time-Cycles of planets such as the
Earth.

In the higher life, one asks to be quickened spiritually by
the Christ—and the atoms of his being respond accordingly.
Through these atom-quickenings, he is transformed and
enlightened.

Jesus, after His Crucifixion and Resurrection, appeared
physically to His Disciples. He could do this because of the
quickened atoms in His bodies that enabled Him to visit the
Time-system of the Earth and then return to the Timeless
Dimensions of the Kingdom of God. The ability to manifest
a physical body at will represents an advanced state of Image-
of-God progression attained by Illumined Beings such as
Jesus, Mary and other Great Souls in the Heaven Worlds.

Man is presently being initiated in the secrets of Time;
eventually, he will be initiated in the secrets and mysteries of
Timelessness. More and more seekers after truth are experiencing initiations in the Timeless Dimensions of the Inner
Kingdom. To unite with the Spirit of the Living God is to be
one with His *Eternal* Spirit *within* all Time-Cycles and *beyond* all Time-Cycles.

The Image of God is being fulfilled through all temporal
and eternal bodies of man. The physical body is a temporary
body for earth existence. The soul, inhabiting the physical
body for brief periods or lives on earth, remains an integral
and everlasting part of the spiritual body and the True Self.

In an Earth-system requiring physical bodies, the soul is
in a *visible* body; however, in Solar Systems not requiring
physical-body lessons, the soul functions solely through the
invisible spiritual body. The Image of God is *eternally* functioning in Solar Systems where there are physical-body expressions and in Solar Systems where only the spiritual or
everlasting body is creating with and for God.

The soul in its Covenant with God determines the *type* of

Solar System in which it will dwell, that it may manifest certain Divine-Image facets and attributes. The physical body, as a temporary learning-body, perishes; the soul, the spiritual body and the True Self never die.

The Image of God is the Eternal Constant in all bodies, lives, Stars, Galaxies. A man may be ignorant of the Divine Image in his physical body; he may be ignorant of his spiritual body and eternal life. Ignorance is a void yet to become energized by the Spirit of God. The overcoming of ignorance produces the fruits of Enlightenment. Enlightenment is an inspired awareness of the reality of the spiritual body, the soul, the True Self, the Image of God and Everlasting Life as Eternal Constants within the Cosmos Will and Universal Plan of God.

The Higher Self or Eternal Self is the Instructor of man. The Higher Self is at home in the Spiritual World.

The Light of the Higher Self may be experienced through prayer, contemplation and meditation.

The Higher Self contains the image of what man has perfected in other eternities or world systems.

The Higher Self is at one with the Image of the Father and with the Greater Host or Hierarchs who watch over the molding and shaping of men.

— Ann Ree Colton

THE DIVINE OMNIPRESENCE AND THE SOUL'S RECORD

Almighty God, pour down upon us Thy Grace that we may see Thy Face and know Thy Omnipresence in all souls, all situations.

— Ann Ree Colton

The Light radiating from the Face of God provides *guidance* for every step in one's life. The Omnipresent Creator proves His closeness to the devotee through countless coincidings, miracle-blessings and inspiration-creations.

Enlightened personages who receive the Glory of God's Fulness of Grace are able to look directly into the blazing Light of His Countenance. Before one can look into the Face of God, his eyes must be filled with love, compassion and kindness.

A devoted keeper of vows to God can look into the Face of the Lord with a clear conscience. The failure to keep one's vows to God creates a cloudy conscience that obscures His Face. The joys that come with a cleansed conscience are due to the radiant Light of God's Countenance smiling upon His faithful servant.

Moreover I call God for a record upon my soul.
—2 Corinthians 1:23

God, the Omnipresent Truth, is revealing the Truth about one's soul-record each moment of the day and the night. The light in the soul's record is the grace one has earned in the present life and in previous lives. The dark in his soul's record is the record of the unconfessed sins committed in his present life and in former lives. When one knows that *all* persons in his life have been placed there by the Hand of God according to his soul's record, he can work more closely with the Creator in healing and resolving the darkness in his soul's record and increasing the light and grace.

Sins and grace have electromagnetic qualities that work with the *Law of Attraction*. There are no accidents in the perfect mathematics of God's Law of Attraction. This Holy Law is perfect in its justice—and one receives into his life lessons and blessings in perfect timing to his need. A devotee who knows and accepts this verity is ready to commune with God as the Omnipresent Truth.

When one first steps on the Spiritual Path, the negative and positive deeds recorded in his soul's record are as a ball of twine with a tangled assortment of colors. There are numerous knots in this jumble of multi-colored threads.

The initiatory process requires that a probationer isolate each thread and untie each knot. In this, he can begin to identify and remove each unbeautiful thread and begin to weave his spiritual garment of dedication with the beautiful threads. The magnifications of Truth occurring through the Moon's Cycle each lunar month help him make these necessary identifications as quickly as possible.

The removal of the unsightly threads of wrong attitudes expressed in the present life and in past lives, and the untangling and untying of the knots of unpaid sin-debts give clarity to one's thoughts and emotions. As his soul's record becomes uncluttered and cleansed, his life becomes simplified — and the Light of God's Countenance may begin to communicate with him as the Omnipresent Truth.

The face of every person in one's life and in the world represents a Countenance of God. The Creator is speaking very clearly through the persons and conditions in his life; however, only *He* can provide the Grace that enables one to see His Face in all souls and all situations. Until an individual receives this Grace, he will remain totally unaware of the Countenance of the Divine Omnipresence.

Happy and unhappy relationships reveal the soul's record of untangled and tangled threads. Inharmony and unhappiness in personal associations and marriages always indicate snarled and knotted threads in the soul's record. The Hand of Jesus can quickly untangle these threads if one asks Him with reverence, faith and humility. Through the steadfast keeping of all Scriptural Laws, Principles and Virtues, the threads will *remain* untangled and new knots will not be created.

> *The untying of each karmic knot releases Grace. Through the untying of many karmic knots, one may begin to behold the Face of God within the Holy Increases of Grace.*

THE MOON: PROTOTYPES AND POLARITIES

> *This verily, is the door of the heavenly world—*
> *that is, the Moon. Whoever answers it, him it lets*
> *go further.*
>
> —Upanishads

The Countenance of God is within the Godhead Core in every living soul; it is also a Cosmos Countenance looking upon mankind from the Stars and the Galaxies. The Cosmos Countenance of God is first recognized through the twelve Zodiacal Constellations: Aries, Taurus, Gemini, Cancer, Leo, Virgo, Libra, Scorpio, Sagittarius, Capricorn, Aquarius and Pisces.

When one reverences the Moon as a beautiful creation of God, he has begun to expand his consciousness mind toward the mighty Universe of Cosmos Energies and Cycles. As long as one's consciousness is earthbound, he will remain unlearned regarding the dynamic Energies and Cycles of the Moon.

The Moon passes through all twelve Zodiacal-Constellation Signs during its Cycle of 29½ days. The magnification-light of God's Truth through the Lunar Cycle blesses each person with the knowledge of his soul's record of the present life and past lives. If one accepts with gratitude the Moon's revelations about his soul's record, he can work with the Creator and His Son to cleanse the darkness recorded therein and to increase the light.

> *The twelve faces in the twelve shewbread in Aaron's Lodge in the Tabernacle in the Wilderness represent the true Countenance of God, or His quickened Image which man is to become as a son of God.*
> *All faces represent the Countenance of God.*
>
> —Ann Ree Colton

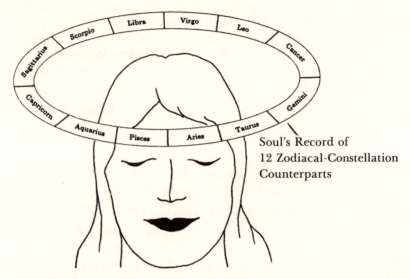

Soul's Record of
12 Zodiacal-Constellation
Counterparts

The twelve zodiacal types that God places in one's life are mathematically attracted through the just scales within His Law of Attraction. One attracts sweet blessings and loving associations through the good sent forth in past lives that returns in his present life. He attracts painful lessons and un-loving relationships through the sin-energies sent forth in previous lives that return on the lunar energy-tides in his present life.

Through the commitment to fulfill the Commandments of Love, one loves purely and reverently all twelve zodiacal types God places in his life. His dedication to bless the Image of God in *all* souls, when combined with love-inspired works of penance and restitution, accomplishes powerful cleansings of the darkness in the soul's record. In time, he will behold the Face of God smiling at him through the faces of the twelve zodiacal types of persons in his life. Also, the Moon will bless him with increasing *Tides* of Grace earned in previous lives.

The cleansing of the soul's record through the Cycles of the Moon produces *Prototypal Illuminations*. The cleansing of the soul's record through the Cycles of the Sun produces *Archetypal Illuminations*.

Within each person there is a masculine polarity and a feminine polarity. From life to life these two polarities seek to become one and blend. The feminine polarity represents the chaste, the reverent, the love. The masculine polarity represents the courageous, the orderly, the lucid. It is God's intent that these qualities fuse or blend. This is the Divine, Inner Marriage. Persons who attain this balance or androgynous blending become the advanced ones of humanity.

— Ann Ree Colton

Each aspirant on the Path must make his peace with the Heavenly Father working through the Masculine Principle and with the Divine Mother working through the Feminine Principle.

Gross egotism causes a person to believe that either male or female is superior to the other sex. Male and female are *equal* in God's sight, for they are *equal* in His Image.

In the illumined individual, the Image of God is polarized and harmonized through the perfect blending of the Masculine and the Feminine Polarities. It is the work of all true devotees of the Lord to attain the *marriage* of the Yin–Yang Polarities within their beings. This inner marriage produces the Spiritual Illuminations of the Divine-Image Consciousness.

The first time a man or a woman is unkind to the opposite sex, or does injury or harm to them in any way, manner, thought, word or action, he or she has begun to cause a breach between the Masculine and Feminine Polarities within his or her own being.

Prejudice toward the opposite sex, unfaithfulness in marriage, malicious and evil thoughts, feelings and actions toward male or female, and any other interaction with men and women in which love, reverence and respect are absent — all cause major imbalances in the Masculine and Feminine Polarities within one's own being. The moment one desires to rectify these imbalances, he has turned his face toward the beauty of the Image of God within his own soul and within the souls of *all* in the world—male and female.

The Magnification Cycle of the Moon each lunar month reveals with clarity the Masculine and Feminine imbalances remaining in the soul's record. *Any* unpleasant or unhappy experiences with the men and women in one's family or in other associations reveal unconfessed sins in the dark side of the soul's record. If these problems and difficulties relate to one sex more than the other, the Spirit of God through the Moon's Magnification Tides is revealing the Yin–Yang imbalances in one's nature.

To be disrespectful toward women for many lifetimes, to abuse them sexually, or to offend the Image of God in them in any way verbally, mentally, physically or emotionally is to invite tribulations and troubles through womankind in one's present life and in coming lives. Women who offend the Divine Image in men through word, thought, emotion or action will attract painful consequences, penalties and unhappiness through the men in their present life and in future lives.

The Law of God is perfect in its justice each moment of the day and the night. If one knows this to be true, he can begin to confess to God his offenses against the opposite sex in the present life and in previous lives. Such confessions and the works of penance and restitution that follow will manifest miraculous healings of the soul's record as well as restore the equilibrium between the Masculine and Feminine Polarities within his own being. The Lunar Cycle will disclose the inner balances and victories occurring within the devotee through the love, harmony, healings and reconciliations occurring in his outer life.

Dear God, I confess my sins and transgressions against the Blessed Polarities of Thy Image. Please forgive my offenses against men and women in my present life and in past lives. Help

me to reverence all persons as Thy sacred creations, and inspire me to love each and all with a
pure, selfless and unconditional love.

Heavenly Father, please restore the Polarities
of Thy Image within my being. I pray for the
harmonization and polarization of the Masculine
and Feminine expressions of Thy Image in *all*
persons in the world. In Jesus' Name. Amen.

Homosexuality is caused by unconfessed ancestral sins and
by several or more past lives in which the Masculine and
Feminine Polarities have been severely imbalanced by offending the Laws of Nature and the Laws of God. The harmonization and polarization of these two Polarities may occur
through the powerful formula of Repentance, Confession,
Contrition, Penance and Restitution.

The seed of man is filled with Image-of-God energies and
vitalities. To offend the Holy Laws governing the Procreation
Energies is to cause major ruptures and breaches in the Masculine and Feminine Polarities within one's being. For such
offenses, the karmic penalties are severe because the Procreation Energies relate to the Image of God as an Eternal Constant perpetuating human life on earth and in the Cosmos.

Instant polarization is through Jesus.
— Ann Ree Colton

If a person expressing abnormal sexual behavior fails to
turn to God in the spirit of contrition and repentance, he will
attract future lifetimes in which the Masculine and Feminine
Polarities must begin to be painfully restored. One can avoid
these coming lives of painful lessons and restrictions of freedom by applying each day the beautiful and powerful teachings of Jesus. The history of the world is filled with countless
testimonies of the Power of Jesus to heal all conditions of
polarity-imbalances within the body, heart, mind and soul.
"With God all things are possible." (St. Matthew 19:26)

Dear Lord, I confess my many offenses against Thy Image in my present life and in previous lives. May the Miracle Light of Thy Beloved Son, Christ Jesus, manifest the harmonization and polarization of the Masculine and Feminine Polarities within my being, that I might express Thy Will for me in this life and in all lives to come. In Jesus' Name. Amen.

PRAYERS OF CONFESSION

What is within us is also without. What is without is also within.

—Upanishads

God always sends to you outside what you are on the inside. Always realize this and you will be an honest disciple.

—Ann Ree Colton

Understand that thou thyself art even another little world, and hast within thee the sun and the moon, and also the stars.

—Origen

The Soul's Covenant with God before each lifetime determines one's sign of birth. Each birth sign has specific virtues for him to evolve through Image-of-God quickenings.

Over the ages, each individual has experienced numerous births under all twelve zodiacal signs. All persons in his present life are perfect reflections of the negative and positive aspects of his previous-lives' zodiacal birth-sign expressions.

The Moon, as the magnifier of the soul's record, reveals each moment of the day and the night the attitudes, traits and reflexes of the lower nature and the virtues, gifts and graces of the higher nature. If the Moon is in the sign of Taurus when blessings manifest, these good tidings indicate that the Taurus portion of the soul's record contains grace earned in previous lives. If negations occur during the Moon in Taurus, this denotes that the soul's record is yet darkened by the unconfessed sins of past lives when one was a Taurean, or when he sinned against a Taurean, or if he sinned while the Sun or the Moon was in the sign of Taurus.

Acts of good motivated by selfless love; prayers, meditations, fastings, tithings and other spiritual dedications observed sacramentally in service to God — all are recorded in the soul's record as Light and Grace. If the devotee expressing these worthy works is born a Virgo, he will be earning Virgo Grace, which will bless his future lives. Also, his blessings upon the persons in his life representing the twelve zodiacal signs are recorded in his soul's record and will return to him as blessings in his present life and in future lives. The *time* of each deed, thought and emotion inspired by love is recorded in the soul's record during the Cycles of the Moon and the Sun through the twelve signs of the zodiac. Thus, a life dedicated to good works, sacrifice and worship will produce its rewards through the Lunar and Solar Cycles in one's present life and in future lives. *"Cast thy bread upon the waters; for thou shalt find it after many days.."* (Ecclesiastes 11:1)

May the Image of God in thee shine forth the radiance of His Divine Countenance.

Grace is holy harmony. To be in a State of Grace is to be in harmony with all twelve zodiacal prototypes in one's life and to be receptive to the Grace-Flow of the Holy Spirit. From meditation to meditation, he is in a state of peace, prospering and love. This is God's Countenance shining upon him through the twelve zodiacal prototypes and the Inner Kingdom.

As the soul's record is cleansed, the Face of God begins to smile upon His servant through the Faces of the Moon, the

Sun, the Planets, the Stars and the Galaxies. This communion with the Countenance of the Creator is a Grace made possible through the Mediation of Christ Jesus: the Proclaimer of the New Covenant, the New-Era Dharma.

> *And he had in his right hand seven stars: and out of his mouth went a sharp two-edged sword: and his countenance was as the sun shineth in his strength.*
>
> —Revelation 1:16

During the probationary period of the spiritual life, the Lunar Cycles *magnify* the areas of one's lower nature where repentance is not wholehearted. If the devotee is unforgiving or unloving toward any person in his life, the Moon's Cycles will continue to magnify his erroneous attitudes until they are corrected.

If a probationer feels any animosity, jealousy, anger or unforgiveness toward any individual, loved one or co-disciple, he should immediately confess to God this offense against the Commandment of Love. Any unloving or unforgiving attitude reveals an unresolved dark area in the soul's record. The devotee should be *specific* in his prayers of confession regarding the birth sign of the one he cannot love or forgive. If a person born in the sign of Leo is offending, persecuting or irritating the devotee, the aspirant should confess to God his offenses against the Leo Prototype in the present life and in past lives.

Heavenly Father, I confess my offenses against the Leo Prototype and Thy other Sacred Prototypes in my present life and in previous lives. Please help me to love *all* of Thy children and to reverence Thy Image within them. "I can of mine own self do nothing."* I need Thy help in

---

*St. John 5:30.

this and in all things, O Lord. Let all victories
be Thine. In Jesus' Name. Amen.

To *confess* the Power of God to forgive sins and the Power
of Jesus to redeem the contrite in spirit manifests miraculous
healings, spiritual quickenings and sweet blessings of diverse
kinds.

> *We must be willing to face the other in ourselves
> —and not say 'Neti, neti, not me, not me: that's
> not me!'*
>
> —Ann Ree Colton

> *He that covereth his sins shall not prosper: but
> whoso confesseth and forsaketh them shall have
> mercy.*
>
> —Proverbs 28:13

If a devotee is the recipient of negative emotions, words or
actions directed toward him by a person born in the sign of
Gemini, he should speak a specific prayer of confession for
his offenses against the Gemini zodiacal prototype. This
prayer-formula relates to all other zodiacal prototypes who
direct any negativity toward him.

**Dear Lord, I confess my sins of the present
life and past lives against Thy Gemini Prototype
and all other Zodiacal Prototypes being created
in Thy Image and Likeness. With Thy help, I
pray to make a full and honorable restitution.
May all Scales of Thy Just Laws come into perfect balance, that I may love all and serve all in
the right spirit of Compassion, Selflessness and
Humility. In Jesus' Name. Amen.**

If a devotee experiences a negative encounter with a Pis-
cean woman, he should know that God is calling him to account for sins committed against His Pisces Countenance and

against the Feminine Principle. This applies to all negative experiences with the male and female individuals in his life.

> **Dear God, I confess my sins of the present life and past lives against Thy Pisces Countenance and the Feminine Principle and Polarity. I pray to love all souls with a pure and perfect love inspired by Thy Holy Spirit. In Jesus' Name. Amen.**

When God, the Omnipresent Truth, places in one's Path one or more persons expressing sinful or anti-virtue behavior toward him or others, *he should immediately confess the sin, fault or anti-virtue as his own, for God is revealing to him an area of unexpiated sin-darkness in his soul's record of the present life and past lives.* In time, a devotee will begin to perceive repetitive, negative patterns during the *same* positions of the Moon each Lunar Cycle; also, the *same* zodiacal prototypes, such as Aries, Taurus, etc., will direct angers, jealousies or other anti-virtue behavior toward him. If these negative traits and attitudes are confessed as his own in the spirit of self-honesty and humility, he will experience deeper levels of God's Mercy and Forgiving Love.

A devotee who encounters a person expressing the fiery energy of anger toward him at any time during the day should meet the anger with nonretaliative love, blessing the Image of God in his antagonist. Each time anger is directed against him, or he witnesses anger in others, he should confess the sin of anger and ask God's forgiveness for times when he expressed anger in his present life and in past lives. **In such instances, the devotee should confess to God the sin of anger in his soul's record and pray for its healing; confess the sin of anger in his adversary and pray for his healing; confess the sin of anger in his parental and ancestral lines through the genes and the chromosomes, and pray for their healing; and confess the sin of anger in all hate-**

filled, belligerent, hostile persons in the world and pray for their healing.

Prayers of specific confessions should be observed whenever one is faced with *any* negative encounter, or anti-virtue behavior of a loved one, friend, co-disciple, business associate or any other person whom God places in his life each day. These confessions and reverent prayers offered in the Name of Christ Jesus will manifest miraculous healings in his soul's record and in his genes. In this, he will decrease the darkness in his own being and in the world — and increase the Light. With continued practice, this formula for soul-freedom can be accomplished in a moment's *knowing* through a deep feeling of contrition, humility and faith in God's Forgiveness.

Any anti-virtue one encounters during the day through personal experience or through observation is direct guidance from God as the *Omnipresent Truth* revealing dark areas in his soul's record. Prayers of repentance and confession, compassionate works, and blessing the Image of God in others — when observed *in the spirit of penance and restitution* — are his keys to the increasing freedoms that come through the Redemption Power of Christ Jesus.

If one meets anger with anger, he is still in bondage to the *spirit* of anger darkening his soul's record and moving through his gene-reflexes. As long as one expresses anger, tantrums, and other uncontrollable emotions, the ages-old eye-for-an-eye attitudes are saturating his genes rather than the virtue-energies of love, compassion and harmlessness. Even though such persons may be in religious or spiritual teachings, they have not yet *repented*, for they are still in bondage to anti-virtue behavior through the genes and the soul's record.

God is always giving His children the *opportunity* to repent. However, as long as one does not desire to express virtues more than anti-virtues, he has not yet repented. Self-deception inspires one to think that he is virtuous when, in reality, he is expressing anger, lust, covetousness, prejudice, unforgiveness, critical-mindedness, pettiness and a host of other anti-virtues.

> **Heavenly Father, I confess the sin of _____.
> Bless those whom I have offended and sinned
> against in this life and in past lives. Please for-
> give me and help me to make a full and honor-
> able restitution.**
>
> **I pray for all souls in the world who are ex-
> pressing the sin of _____. May they be
> healed, that they may fulfill Thy Will for them
> as children of Thy Spirit. In Jesus' Name.
> Amen.**

Wherever God reveals a fault or sin-tendency in one's own nature, mate, child or any other person, the devotee should know that this is direct guidance from Omnipresence to pray confessional prayers for *all persons* in the world who are similarly afflicted. To be specific in such prayers reveals to God that one is discerning the difference between right and wrong and that he desires the greatest good for all souls in the world.

If one has a Capricorn mate, God's Face is seeking to reveal itself to him through his mate's face. How one's mate looks at him is how God is looking at him through the Capricorn *Countenance*. This same principle pertains to the birth signs of all other persons in his life.

If one's mate is expressing a fault or negative trait, he should immediately confess the fault or trait as his own. His honest recognition of God's Holy Law of Attraction in his marriage, when accompanied by specific confessions and Divine-Image blessings, will manifest miraculous healings and grace-anointings. The tendency to blame others is to close one's eyes to the Face of God as the Omnipresent Truth.

> **Heavenly Father, I confess my sins of the
> present life and past lives against Thy Sacred**

Prototypes. Please help me to love all souls with a love made pure and perfect through Thy Holy Spirit. I ask this in the Name of Thy beloved Son, Christ Jesus, Who said: "Be ye therefore perfect, even as your Father which is in Heaven is perfect."* Amen.

To work *with* the flowing Cycles of the Moon and the Sun is joy when one lives each day in the spirit of dedication to God and His mighty Laws and Principles of Creation. The unenlightened remain oblivious to the Cycles of the Moon, the Sun and the Planets. The enlightened perceive the Wisdom of God in these beautiful Cycles through which the Creator blesses and anoints with His Spirit.

If one is out of timing with the Cycles of the Moon and the Sun, he will be out of timing with the Cycles of his Soul and Spirit. Unpunctuality and procrastination reveal that one is out of timing with all Sacred Cycles.

To be in timing with God's Grace-Flow, one must be in timing with the Lunar, Solar, Soul and Divine-Image Cycles. To be in timing with these mighty Cycles is to experience enlightenment through God's Grace and Truth.

The key to Spiritual Illumination is the Cycles ordained by the Creator for the Earth, the Solar System, the Soul and the Universe.

Jesus, as co-atom to our Father, makes His homeplace within our Constant, where dwells the Father's Image within us. Through the Cycles and Rhythms, the Father establishes His Image-Making and His Timing-limit as to Imaging. Jesus determines how the Image functions through Manifestations.

—Ann Ree Colton

---

*St. Matthew 5:48.

GOD-REALIZATION   Divine   *Godhead Dynamo:*   GODLY
ARCHETYPES   Image   *The Jewel in the Lotus*   ELECTRICITIES

                                         CHRIST JESUS:
                      Electricity of the Divine Image   THE MEDIATOR
                      Electricity of the Cosmos   OF THE NEW
                                           COVENANT

SOUL-KNOWING

SOUL-WISDOM   Soul   *Dynamo of Dimensional Energies*

SOUL-GIFTS

                      Electricity of the Soul

                      Compassionate Thinking. Self-Honesty.
                      Humility. Reverence for all life.
                      Harmlessness. Christ Mind.

PROTÉGÉ OF THE SAINTS   *Love Core*
   Love makes all energies   *Love-Commandments: Love of God, Creator of the*
   sattvic.   *Universe; Love of Neighbor (World Family);*
                      Love of One Another (Discipleship and Apostleship)

STATE OF GRACE THROUGH
REDEMPTION-THINKING: ENLIGHTENMENT

Divine
Image

Soul

                      Dark curtain of unconfessed sins keeps the Holy
———————   *Electricities of the Soul and the Image of God*
                      from moving into the heart and the mind.

Pride. Egotism. Competitiveness.   *Critical-minded.*
Permissiveness. Pettiness.   *Judgmental.*
Fantasy-mindedness.   *Self-love.*
Stubbornness.   *Hypersensitivities.*
Disobedience.

UNENLIGHTENED STATES
OF HEART AND MIND

15

DEDICATION OF THE DAY

Heavenly Father, I dedicate this day unto Thee: my prayers, meditations, serving, study, creation and recreation. I pray to do each thing in right timing according to Thy Will and Plan and for Thy Glory. In Jesus' Name. Amen.

THE TONE OF COMPASSION

And Jesus went forth, and saw a great multitude, and was moved with compassion toward them, and he healed their sick.

—St. Matthew 14:14

Go forth . . . for the help of the many, for the well-being of the many, out of compassion for the world.

—Buddha

Be compassionate.

—Upanishads

Compassion is the key to every spiritual gift. When a love-inspired compassion fills one's feelings and thoughts throughout the day, he is able to behold with holy constancy the Image of God in his fellow man. Compassion sounds a *pure tone* at one with the music and harmony of all higher-energy Creation-processes in Heaven and on earth.

Compassion heals the desire for retaliation and revenge, thereby releasing Christ-Light healing tones and energies into one's genes, cells and soul's record. His attaining of the Divine-Image Consciousness is dependent upon the Christ-quickenings of the Compassion Cluster of Virtues and the other Virtue Clusters.

When compassion is the key tone sounding throughout one's days and nights in service to others, he is a true protégé of the Saints and an inspired servant of God. The compassion of the Saints places them in high degrees of communion with the Creator and His Son.

A devotee who dedicates each day to God through a morning prayer should know in his heart that all he will do throughout the day will be in the spirit of penance and restitution for his own sins of his present life and past lives, the sins of his parents and ancestors and for the sins of the world. This beautiful attitude born of a compassionate heart and mind attracts the Blessings of God that manifest as spiritual gifts and soul-powers. Through these sacred gifts and powers, one is prepared for communion with the Godhead-Dimensions of Grace and Truth: the Essences and Elixirs of Spiritual Exaltation and Illumination.

The compassion and humility expressed through the *attitude* of penance and restitution keep one in a State of Expanding Grace under the Merciful Love of God and the Redemption Power of Jesus. As long as one remains centered in the Commandments of God and the Principles of Jesus, he will express love and virtue throughout the day.

A devotee who begins each day with a Prayer of Dedication to God should also speak aloud the Ten Commandments, the Beatitudes and the Lord's Prayer. These powerful stanzas will add to his life and being the miraculous love-essences of the Divine Presence that will prosper his union with the higher-energy wavelengths of the Moon, the Sun and the Planets.

God is liberal with His Grace. However, if a devotee is not vigilant, he will squander God's Grace by thinking and speaking incessant criticisms of others. Thinking and speaking with compassion and love will keep him centered in the Flow of God's Manifold Grace.

Criticisms build barriers between the mind and the Image of God. Compassion clears the way for the mind to behold, serve and minister to the Image of God in all souls.

Criticism of others makes of one a devil's advocate. Compassion makes of him a disciple of the Lord.

The eyes are either eyes of criticism or eyes of compassion, eyes of judging or eyes of blessing, eyes of anger or eyes of love. The eyes of compassion, blessing and love grace a servant of God with the light of understanding and wisdom flowing from the dimensional wellsprings of the soul and the spirit.

Compassion, not criticism, is the way to God-Realization. Compassion lifts one above the critical-mind levels of thinking. Criticism is a misuse of precious mental energies. As long as the spirit of criticism controls the mind, one cannot visualize or bless the Image of God in others. Such persons not only remain spiritually unenlightened, but they invite constant reprovings from their souls for offending the Commandment of Love.

Self-control must be in the body, the emotions and the mind. When a devotee uses his mental energies to judge or criticize others, he has yet to express self-control in his thoughts. A devotee without self-control in his emotions is as a vehicle that can swerve out of control at any time; such persons endanger the health and well-being of themselves and their loved ones. A probationer without self-control cannot be trusted with the sacred task of preserving the Word and Altar of God.

A devotee who asks Jesus to quicken the Virtues of Self-Control and Compassion will experience a miraculous transformation in his attitudes and in his use of all energy-processes within his mind, emotions and body.

> *The compassion that you see in the kind-hearted is God's compassion: he has given it to them to protect the helpless.*
>
> — Ramakrishna

> *But whoso hath this world's good, and seeth his brother have need, and shutteth up his bowels of compassion from him, how dwelleth the love of God in him?*
>
> — 1 John 3:17

All spiritual gifts and soul-powers coming to birth through the Image of God are released in exact degree to one's expression of compassion from day to day, life to life. Compassion inspires one to heal others and to teach them the Word of God. Compassion compels him to be patient, kind, loving, forgiving. The *Brotherhood of the Image* consists of the compassionate ones whose lives are testimonies to the Mercy, Wisdom and Love of God.

> *And Jesus, when he came out, saw much people, and was moved with compassion toward them, because they were as sheep not having a shepherd: and he began to teach them many things.*
>
> — St. Mark 6:34

> *To be compassionate, one must act like Jesus.*
>
> — Ann Ree Colton

> *I see God in every human being. When I wash that leper's wounds, I am nursing the Lord Himself. Is it not a beautiful experience?*
>
> — Mother Teresa of Calcutta*

---

*Gratitude to Mother Teresa of Calcutta for permission to use her quotations.

When the hands of Compassion hold the Cup of the Sacrament and the lips of Compassion drink the Wine and receive the Bread, the Christ places His Light into the core of one's being—and he may thereafter serve his Beloved Lord with freedom and fulness of Grace.

Through the Sacrament, the Christ unites sincere penitents and devotees with the Grace of ancestors in the genes and the Grace of past lives in the soul's record. These and other degrees of Grace manifest through the Sacrament as long as one ministers to others in the spirit of penance and restitution for his own sins and for the sins of the world.

The more one desires to serve God each day in the spirit of penance and restitution, the more the Creator provides him with the Dimensional Gifts and Graces through which a rapid restitution may be accomplished by healing, blessing, ministering and creating in service to Him. This closeness to God through a compassionate love for all of His children activates the miracle-producing tones and energies of the soul and the Divine Image.

An anointed Apostle under Christ is endowed with the ability to free others from their bondages to ancestral-gene sin-tendencies and past-lives' negative traits. Through compassion, he works each day as an enlightened servant of God, Teacher of Truth, and Guardian of the Dharma.

TEACHER'S PRAYER

Heavenly Father, I confess the faults and sins of the students and the world as my own. With Thy help, I pray to make a full and honorable restitution for my many sins of this life and past lives. May I serve Thee and Thy children with compassion, humility, wisdom and love. In Jesus' Name. Amen.

VIGILANCE: REDEMPTION-THINKING

Be sober, be vigilant; because your adversary the devil, as a roaring lion, walketh about, seeking whom he may devour.

—1 Peter 5:8

Vigilant thinking is Redemption-thinking. To think through Jesus' Redemption Power is to be free from negative downpulls in thought and feeling.

Sincere penitents receive the *Mary-Magdalene Experience* of exorcism through the Mediation of Jesus. If a probationer is yet in bondage to negative thinking and feeling regarding past sins or present trials, he has *not* had the Mary-Magdalene Experience; he is yet floundering between dark and light.

To have a total Mary-Magdalene Experience, one must resolve, dedicate and covenant to never again think negatively or to express negative emotions. To sink into negation in feelings or thoughts is to sin, thereby negating Redemption Grace.

After repentance and confession, vigilance in thought and feeling is mandatory, or else one will remain subject to Satan's subtle attacks that place clouds of darkness between his mind and his soul. At such times, the aspirant is rendered useless as a servant of God—and his negative thinking and feeling become *curses* directed at himself and others.

To be centered in the Love-Commandments keeps one close to Jesus and His protection. Negative thoughts, feelings and memories are Satan's entry to draw one into despair, depression, self-pity and a sense of unworthiness or hopelessness.

Through His Redemption Power, the Christ heals the memory and the conscience of a sincere devotee, thereby enabling him to experience and express illuminative degrees of the memory and the conscience.

"We have the mind of Christ." (1 Corinthians 2:16) To be centered in the Love-Commandments is to give birth to the Christ Mind. The Christ Mind is the natural result of the Mary-Magdalene Experience and the Redemption Power of Jesus. The memory and the conscience, as great attributes of the Image of God, become scintillating dimensional energies in the Christ-Mind Initiate.

To think negatively about any human being is to sin. To feel negative emotions toward any human being is to sin. Vigilance in thinking and feeling protects one from committing these and other sins. Vigilance in thinking and feeling invites the *Holy Electricities* of the soul and the Divine Image into the heart and mind.

Negative thinking is *contraclockwise* thinking. *Clockwise* thinking is optimistic, cheerful, inspired, and perceives the Image of God in every person in one's life and in the world.

The Christ-Mind Initiate is always cognizant of the Image of God within himself and within others. Thus, he can serve with impartial and unconditional love all whom the Creator places in his life from day to day, from meditation to meditation.

> *The Antichrist works through guilts; the Christ works through Grace. The Antichrist works through fears; the Christ works through Faith.*

Satan *magnifies* negative thoughts and emotions in his victims. Christ *magnifies* inspired thoughts and love-filled emotions in His followers. To be nonvigilant is to place one's consciousness mind in the hands of Satan. To be vigilant in thinking is to remain in a State of Grace blessed by the Christ.

To minister as a servant of God requires extreme vigilance in thinking and feeling. As long as one retains negative mental grooves, he will think repetitive, harmful thoughts about himself and others. Satan expertly seeks to draw one's thoughts into these negative mental grooves, and to remove him from the spiraling action of creative-spiritual thoughts. Negative emotional grooves also invite the influences of the Antichrist to disturb one's peace of mind and to block his communion with God.

All negative mental and emotional grooves are healable when one realizes that they *need* to be healed. Obsessive thoughts and feelings are due to unhealed grooves caused by former sins or painful memories. Through these obsessions, Satan manipulates and directs one's thoughts, memories, feelings and lives. The result is great unhappiness with one's self and others.

The *subconscious* desire to punish oneself for past sins keeps him exposed to the Antichrist. Through Christ, freedom comes; however, one must *desire* spiritual freedom more than he enjoys self-punishment or self-pity.

If an aspirant has a traditional religious background or early-childhood training in a church that instilled a strong sense of guilt in its followers, it will be more difficult for him to forgive himself—and he will be inclined to punish himself repeatedly for the same sins. Such persons should pray to have a *personal* experience with the Redeemer, Christ Jesus. If they remain faithful to the Commandments of God, they will be blessed with the Mary-Magdalene Experience and will begin a new life free from guilt and fear.

To be liberated by the Christ is to be free from all negative thoughts, feelings and memories. Devotees who remain vigilant, optimistic and enthusiastic walk the earth as the redeemed of the Lord, and their works of light bless the world.

Heavenly Father, I pray to think only those thoughts that are good and pleasing in Thy sight. In Jesus' Name. Amen.

LEARNING FROM MISTAKES

> *Freedom is not worth having if it does not include the freedom to make mistakes.*
> —Mahatma Gandhi

> *Every person must learn—and he only learns from making mistakes.*
> —Ann Ree Colton

Mistakes are an invaluable source of learning. He who learns from his mistakes acquires wisdom. He who refuses to learn from his mistakes is unteachable.

The making of mistakes is a necessary part of learning the difference between right and wrong, good and evil. A cardinal sin is a major mistake that involves painful penalties. The penalties incurred through wilful sinning contain valuable lessons for the evolution of the consciousness.

The Prodigal-Son Consciousness may be divided into two categories: (1) wilful disobedience to Moral and Holy Laws; and (2) spiritual ignorance without malicious intent or evil motive. While spiritual ignorance may be passive or wilful, there are penalties exacted for all offenses against the basic Scriptural Statutes: the more malicious the crime, the more stringent the penalty. Violence against one's fellow men offends the Image of God in them and within one's self.

The more spiritually evolved the consciousness mind, the more quickly one experiences the *grace* of being reproved for his sins of omission and commission. In this, he will make payment for the sin-mistakes made in his present life; he will not have to face them in coming lives as unpaid soul-debts.

God is forgiving me.
Christ is redeeming me.

To come into timing with the cadence of all persons redeemed over the ages through the Mercy of God and the

Redemption Power of Christ Jesus is pure joy. Thereafter, a faithful devotee who has learned from his mistakes may work to attain the noble or enlightened expressions of the consciousness mind.

Attitudes toward mistakes differ with each level of consciousness-mind attainment. Before one becomes law-minded, he may think that his sins are unknown to God, and therefore he believes that he will not be held accountable. Many lifetimes in different cultures and religions may be necessary before such persons begin to evolve a recognition of the just Law of Sowing and Reaping. *"Whatsoever a man soweth, that shall he also reap."* (Galatians 6:7)

Until one assumes personal responsibility for his sin-mistakes, he will be unable to identify a Cardinal Truth: *the reproving action of the Soul works with the Image, Will and Law of God.*

God is extremely patient and merciful with all of His children; however, there is an appointed time in the Soul's Covenant with the Creator when the prodigal son must begin his ascent up the Holy Mountain, that he might receive his Birthright-Inheritances as a child of God.

> *If I were to say I was a perfect being, I would be the greatest of sinners. I always prepare my prayers and consecrations for Sacrament with: "Father, have mercy on me, for I am a sinner." But I do not feel myself unworthy or in a state of guilt, nor do I dwell on my errors. I look upon my errors as concealed blessings, for through them I have been taught to forgive others and also how to know that God is my Solution and True Teacher.*
>
> — Ann Ree Colton

> *Anger clouds the judgment; you can no longer learn from past mistakes.*
>
> — Bhagavad Gita

The mistakes committed *after* one steps foot on the Spiritual Path come under a different level of God's Patience and Mercy, for he has finally reached the time in Eternal Life when he is *trying* to unite with the Divine Omnipresence.

God-Realization *is* the Divine-Image Consciousness. The manner in which a devotee of the Lord receives reprovings for his mistakes determines his progress toward God-Realization.

A devotee who cannot forgive himself for his mistakes builds a heavy energy-mass of guilt that he carries with him. Persons weighed down by guilt have yet to unite with the Redeeming Power of the Lord Jesus. *"Come unto me, all ye that labour and are heavy laden, and I will give you rest."* (St. Matthew 11:28) As long as one carries the heavy burden of guilt, he will be unable to enter the higher atmospheres of Grace within the Love-Presence of God and Christ.

Some devotees flagellate themselves with the rod of self-loathing. Regardless of how small a mistake may be, they punish themselves unmercifully. Such a person is his own judge and jury. As long as one desires to flagellate or punish himself, he has not united with the understanding of the *sacredness* of the Body Temple and the Image of God dwelling therein.

Some devotees react to their making foolish mistakes by wallowing in self-pity. A probationer who expresses self-pity or depression for mistakes made may be likened to a soldier who leaves his battle station. He is betraying his Lord and his fellow disciples by removing Himself from active involvement in the Holy War against evil, immorality and corruption.

Some devotees continue to blame others for mistakes made by themselves. Such aspirants have yet to evolve the Virtue of Self-Honesty. As long as a devotee on the Path retains the tendency to sin, complain, or blame others, he has not united with the Redemption Power of Jesus.

Wise devotees know that mistakes are part of the Learning Process regarding their ascent up the Holy Mountain toward Spiritual Illumination. They are as runners in a marathon race who, upon tripping or falling, immediately recover and resume the race. Each mistake honestly and quickly confessed to God keeps one united with His Merciful Love and with the Redemption Power of Jesus.

> *Often, actually very often, God allows His greatest servants, those who are far advanced in grace, to make the most humiliating mistakes. This humbles them in their own eyes and in the eyes of their fellow men. It prevents them from seeing and taking pride in the graces God bestows on them or in the good deeds they do, so that, as the Holy Ghost declares: "No flesh should glory in the sight of God."*
>
> — de Montfort

> *It is important that we face ourselves; this is one part of Intentional Suffering. The energy that comes from facing oneself and being honest flows out as compassion for all others who make mistakes.*
>
> — Ann Ree Colton

PART IV

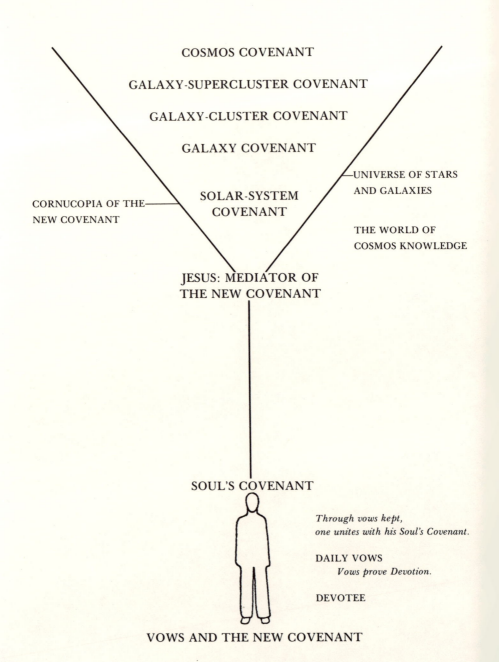

COSMOS COVENANT

GALAXY-SUPERCLUSTER COVENANT

GALAXY-CLUSTER COVENANT

GALAXY COVENANT

CORNUCOPIA OF THE——
NEW COVENANT

SOLAR-SYSTEM
COVENANT

——UNIVERSE OF STARS
AND GALAXIES

THE WORLD OF
COSMOS KNOWLEDGE

JESUS: MEDIATOR OF
THE NEW COVENANT

SOUL'S COVENANT

*Through vows kept,
one unites with his Soul's Covenant.*

DAILY VOWS
Vows prove Devotion.

DEVOTEE

VOWS AND THE NEW COVENANT

16

EVOLUTION THROUGH VOWS

*For thou, O God, hast heard my vows: thou hast
given me the heritage of those that fear thy name.
So will I sing praise unto thy name for ever, that I
may daily perform my vows.*

—Psalm 61:5,8

VOWS AND THE NEW COVENANT

*When men on earth make covenants, their
covenants ring mightily in the Heaven Worlds.
When they fulfill their covenants, they are of
Heaven.*

—Ann Ree Colton

Jesus, "the mediator of the New Covenant" (Hebrews 12:
24), has come to reveal new knowledge of the Image of God
as related to Man and the Cosmos. Through His New-Covenant action over the centuries, the Door will open wider and
wider to the Stars and the Galaxies. *The Principle of Vows
and Covenants* is the key to this Door of Cosmos Knowledge
and the understanding of the Plan of God for the Universe.

*"The secret of the Lord is with them that fear him; and he
will shew them his covenant."* (Psalm 25:14) God works
through *Covenants.* Every Star, Star Cluster, Galaxy, Galaxy

Cluster and Galaxy Supercluster has its Covenant with God. Every Soul on the planet earth has its Covenant with the Creator.

The Milky-Way Galaxy Covenant with God determines its placement in the Cosmos as a mighty vortex of Star-clustered energy. The Galaxy Covenant also determines the number of Stars and their creations within its 100,000 light-years diameter.

The Solar System in which mankind dwells has a Covenant with God which places it near the Orion Arm of the Milky Way Galaxy 33,000 light years from the brilliantly-lighted Galactic Core.

The Galaxy Covenant, the Solar-System Covenant and the Soul's Covenant work in unison in their covenanted expressions of the Image of God. As one unites with his Soul's Covenant through love and vows, Jesus as the World Teacher becomes his Teacher of Universal Truths regarding the Image of God, the Stars, the Galaxies and Eternal Life.

Through the Image of God and the Mediation of Jesus, man is destined to attain the mind in Christ: the *Galaxy Consciousness*. Presently, the minds of men are unable to grasp the full meaning and significance of the awesome Power of Jesus as the Mediator of the New Covenant — the Door to the Inner Kingdom and the Outer Universe.

> *The New Covenant means man is moving into a new era of consciousness and coming closer and closer to the Cosmos vision of Hierarchy and God as to the Plan and Will of God for man in earth.*
> — Ann Ree Colton

The New Covenant is seeking to pour its Grace-Treasures into the world as a mighty Cornucopia of Revelations and Illuminations.

When man becomes like Jesus (1 John 3:1-3), a whole new world of the Image of God will open to him. Through his consciousness mind and enlightened vows, he will work directly *with* the Hierarchy Host and their exalted devotion to God and His *Cosmos Covenant*. Individuals who attain this sublime state of Image-of-God progression will work with the more powerful energies of the Universe as Christed sons of the Living God.

The New-Covenant degrees of God's Image will open to man the wondrous reality of his hierarchy-like potential as a co-creator with God on Cosmos levels. The more one becomes like Jesus through the Image of God, the more he is graced with the vision and knowledge of the New Covenant, and the more the Universe of Stars and Galaxies is free to reveal its secrets and mysteries.

Through the Mediation of Jesus, the understanding of the Principle of Vows and Covenants will be expanded far beyond mankind's present comprehension. When a devotee of the Lord lovingly keeps his vows in unwavering service to the Creator, all barriers to his union with the mighty Power of Jesus will be removed—and God's Countenance will smile upon him through His Universal Image and Everlasting Covenant.

> *Now the God of peace, that brought again from the dead our Lord Jesus, that great shepherd of the sheep, through the blood of the everlasting covenant, Make you perfect in every good work to do his will, working in you that which is well pleasing in his sight, through Jesus Christ; to whom be glory forever and ever. Amen.*
> —Hebrews 13:20,21

THE SOUL'S COVENANT

> *From everlasting to everlasting, thou art God.*
> —Psalm 90:2

The Soul's Covenant with God and His Image is an *Eternal* Covenant involving countless Solar Systems and Galaxies.

The attributes of the Divine Image in the individual manifest in gradual stages over the ages and the eternities.

In man's present Solar-System existence, the Soul's Covenant is timed to the Cycles of the Solar System and the Milky Way Galaxy. In great intervals of Time correlating to each 250 million-year Cycle of the Milky Way Galaxy, the Soul's Covenant with God is fulfilling major accomplishments in all energy-processes through which one is learning and evolving from life to life on the planet Earth.

When the Solar System concludes its 9–10 billion year life-span, the Soul will have fulfilled its Covenant with God to the minutest degree. The Soul's Covenant, being an Everlasting Covenant through the Eternal Image, will continue in future Solar-System mansions within the Galaxies of God.

Each life one lives on earth is a jewel in the mighty mosaic of Life Everlasting. The Image of God works through the Soul's Covenant in each life to manifest important facets and attributes that contribute toward one's growth from age to age.

The Soul's Covenant with God determines before each birth one's placement in the world through race, nation, family and ancestral lines; the sex of the individual, male or female; the negative and positive inheritances through the genes and the chromosomes; his birth sign, skills, earning capacities, learning abilities, creative aptitudes, educational opportunities, religious and spiritual inclinations; the energies to be utilized in his physical, emotional and mental expressions; the lessons to be learned, the degree of volition; the time of birth and the time of death; the *timing* of reprovings and blessings; the sins of past lives to be expiated and the grace of previous lives to be received in cyclic stages; the virtues, conscience and logics to be quickened; and the level of vows to be experienced. The enlightenments and illuminations to be attained through closeness to God are also determined in the Soul's Covenant of those who prove faithful in the keeping of holy vows.

Each person is today that which he has earned through his Soul's Covenant with God in countless Solar Systems and Galaxies. All *disciplined* energies used by an individual represent victories for the soul and the Image of God attained through numerous lives in ages past. The energies yet to be disciplined constitute the areas of learning to be mastered either in the present or in the future. Through disciplined physical, emotional and mental energies, one is able to keep his vows to God. The vows, in turn, enable his consciousness mind to identify his Soul's Covenant with God for his present life on earth. This consciousness-mind identification with the Soul's Covenant is pure joy, for it is a necessary prelude to one's experiencing the realizations, revelations, gifts and graces of the Divine-Image Consciousness.

The inability of man to perceive life as an *Eternal* process through the Image of God is his major stumbling block to Spiritual Illumination. When the heart and the mind know with an inspired certainty that life is Eternal and that the Image of God is a reality, one has made his first major consciousness-mind identification with his Soul's Covenant with the Creator.

To be grateful for the Soul and its Covenant with God is to accept the Will of the Almighty. To desire to work *with* God in all energy-processes being provided by the Soul is the beginning of wisdom. Thereafter, one's vows to God kept each day with devotion and love draw him ever closer to the Godhead Core and the Mighty Image sealed therein.

A Vow is a beautiful Castle of Spirit.

IMAGE-OF-GOD QUICKENINGS AND THE SOUL'S COVENANT

Vows are the steps to the Throne of God.

The Soul's Covenant is one with the Covenant of God for all mankind and with the Covenant of God for all Stars and

Galaxies. All Covenants throughout the Cosmos represent different stages of Image-of-God quickenings.

The soul of each person on earth has *covenanted* with God to become like Jesus at some time in Eternal Life. This noble attainment is destined to occur during the duration of this Solar System or in a future Star-mansion. The various stages of the Soul's Covenant leading to one's becoming like Jesus involve numerous ages of progression and evolvement through Image-of-God quickenings.

In His prophecies, Jesus gave to the world a glimpse of man's future hierarch-like powers. Hierarch-like works will be accomplished by man when the Soul's Covenant, through Image-of-God quickenings, produces the higher spiritual-individuality degrees of consciousness.

The first stage of the Soul's Covenant produces for man the virtues of a *Tribal Consciousness*. When one expresses a Tribal Consciousness, his vows relate primarily to the preservation of his tribe. The second stage of the Soul's Covenant evolves the virtues of the *Family Consciousness*. The Family Consciousness inspires persons to make vows to preserve the family, the family name, and to protect their nation. The next stage of Image-of-God quickenings pertains to one's expression of the Soul's Covenant to attain the virtues of Individuality.

Numerous persons are faithful to their Marriage Vows; many others are irresponsible and unfaithful. Among those who vow to love and cherish their mates, a high percentage of husbands and wives commit adultery. In religious and spiritual ministries, the loyal servants of God are faithful in their vows; many others are emotionally, mentally and morally incapable of keeping holy vows.

Vows are an important part of the evolutionary process for the human spirit. As man evolves over the ages, the types of vows he speaks reflect his progress.

Non-spiritual individuals have no desire to speak vows to

God. Their primary ways of learning about the Principle of Vows relate to their speaking of Marriage Vows and to the tests and trials that challenge their keeping of these vows.

A vow or vendetta spoken for retaliation or destruction represents the beginning stage of an evolutionary energy-process. When a person vows to do harm to someone as an act of revenge, he has begun to unite with the *Principle* of Vows, even though it is in a negative way. Many lifetimes on the eye-for-an-eye level of vows may be required before he begins to express the positive or more spiritual level of vows.

The moment one desires to speak vows to God, he has made a monumental breakthrough in the evolutionary process related to the Image of God. Also, he has expanded his consciousness mind regarding the Principle of Vows and Covenants. When one vows to preserve the knowledge of the Scriptural Laws and Commandments, he begins a direct union with the Providence and Wisdom of God within the Cornucopia of the Covenant.

Reverent individuals on the Path of Devotion unite with the Covenant of God through vows spoken as protégés of the Saints; then, as Saints; and, in time, as protégés of the Hierarchs.

> *Men are imaged in the Father's likeness and in Elohim-Hierarchy's likeness. Everything that Hierarchy is and everything that the Father is, men will become in eternal time.*
>
> — Ann Ree Colton

The keeping of vows to God evolves a spiritualized individuality, for the pure essences of God's Spirit within the Covenant begin to permeate one's being. Through vows, one experiences the transformation of his total being through the Love-Presence of God within the Covenant. In this, he knows himself to be a child of God being created in His Likeness.

As the splendor of God's Wisdom within the Covenant

moves upon one who is faithful to his vows, eternal truths related to the Image of God are revealed to him. This is the beginning of the Divine-Image Consciousness.

Each stage of the Soul's Covenant through Image-of-God quickenings—from the tribal, family and individuality expressions of consciousness to the Divine-Image Consciousness —represents numerous lifetimes over many ages of time. Thus, man evolves from total ignorance of the Covenant of God to an enlightened awareness of the Covenant.

"I am the light of the world." (St. John 8:12) The Presence of the Christ Light in the world accelerated all learning processes for the human spirit through Image-of-God quickenings; it also accelerated the reprovings that come for failure to observe the Scriptural Commandments, Principles and Virtues. To embrace these Divine Edicts through holy vows enables one to come under the providential blessings of the Covenant and to inherit "the unsearchable riches of Christ." (Ephesians 3:8)

> *To serve God is to pledge one's loyalty and love to Him.*

VOWS IN RIGHT TIMING

> *To every thing there is a season, and a time to every purpose under the heaven.*
> —Ecclesiastes 3:1

Everything in God's Plan is based upon Laws of Timing. The Principle of Vows is also subject to these Timing-Laws. If one establishes a love-rapport with God, he will be spiritually guided and inspired regarding the perfect timing to speak vows and also the nature of the vows spoken.

"All the paths of the Lord are mercy and truth unto such as keep his covenant and his testimonies." (Psalm 25:10) The Old Testament and the New Testament contain the knowl-

edge of the Covenants between the Creator and His children on earth. A seeker after enlightenment unites with these Covenants through the promises and disciplines represented in his vows.

During Biblical times, the patriarch Jacob vowed to tithe to God. (Genesis 28:20-22) Through the Holy Law of Tithing as a Scriptural Covenant, God promises to provide abundantly for all of one's needs. When one vows to keep this powerful Covenant under any and all circumstances, he prospers on all levels of life and being.

It is one thing to tithe to God and another thing to *vow* to tithe. The *vow* strengthens one's closeness and communion with the Creator and His Providential Grace.

> *The vows you make to tithe support God's Word and make it into flesh, that men may believe and know. This is what your tithe means: that it is alive with the fervor of the Holy Spirit and blesses all and feeds the hungry, the hungry spiritually and the hungry physically.*
> — Ann Ree Colton

The *Ark of the Covenant* (Numbers 10:33) contains the Ten Commandments. When one *vows* to keep the Ten Commandments, he is fulfilling God's Will by keeping this Covenant. The Covenant is a Cornucopia of Bountiful Blessings that pours forth from the Heart of God to the heart of man.

The Fourth Commandment, relating to the Sabbath Day, is called in Scripture a "perpetual Covenant." (Exodus 31:16) The *vow* to keep the Sabbath Day each week makes one receptive to the precious blessings of God that come through this powerful Covenant. The vow to observe the Sabbath-Day Commandment also opens one to Sabbath Grace earned in past lives. This is true of all the other Commandments of God when they are observed as *holy vows*.

One of the joys of making vows in right timing is that one unites with the *Grace* of vows he made to God in previous lives. This Grace is activated increasingly as he proves faithful to his vows in his present life. As long as his vows are kept in the right spirit, they become arteries through which past-lives' *Vows-Grace* blesses, fortifies and inspires him.

The Vow of Tithing and the Vow to fulfill the Ten Commandments, when extended by the Vow to observe the Commandment of Love Ye One Another, move one into an accelerated flow of Grace through the Mediation of the Christ. It is always *right timing* to vow to fulfill with reverence and love the basic Commandments of the Old and New Testaments.

Thinking through the Ten Commandments and the Law of Tithing produces the *Covenant Consciousness*. Thinking through the Sermon-on-the-Mount Principles produces the *Christ Consciousness*. Thinking through the New-Covenant Mediation of Jesus as the Door to the Inner Kingdom and the Outer Universe produces the *Divine-Image Consciousness*.

> *The importance of vows grew upon me more clearly than ever before. I realized that a vow, far from closing the door to real freedom, opened it.*
> *Where therefore the desire is gone, a vow of renunciation is the natural and inevitable fruit.*
> —M. Gandhi

Until the *desire* is gone, a person will not be able to make a vow in right timing. This is especially true of the Vow of Celibacy, which is taken and then broken by many persons. The spirit of the vow can be offended by thinking lustful thoughts as well as engaging in sexual acts.

> *Celibacy stemming from intellectual decision or austerity vows taken in wrong timing, due to heavy regimented religious vows, manifests abnormalities in the mental, emotional and sexual life.*
> —Ann Ree Colton

Chastity is interpreted by many as celibacy. However, in the Householder Life, chastity means that husband and wife express reverence and pure love in their use of the sexual energies.

Chaste thoughts are as important as chaste acts. *"Ye have heard that it was said by them of old time, Thou shalt not commit adultery; But I say unto you, That whosoever looketh on a woman to lust after her hath committed adultery with her already in his heart."* (St. Matthew 5:27,28)

Samson took the Vow of the Nazarite, which required that he "shall separate himself from wine and strong drink . . ." and "shall let the locks of the hair of his head grow." (Numbers 6:1-3,5) Food, drink, clothing and the hair are often associated with vows taken in various religions in the world. Many persons vow to be vegetarians, or to refrain from eating specific foods or drinking various beverages. Some religious orders require the Vow of Silence, or the Vow to live a cloistered life. Many servants of God in the world have taken Vows of Chastity, Obedience, Poverty, Renunciation and other sacred vows.

The Vow of Holy Poverty made in right timing inspires one to know that he is a *steward* — and not the owner — of whatever monies, properties and other blessings God provides for him to use in his ministry. Individuals who crave personal fortunes cannot keep the Vow of Holy Poverty, for they desire the things that money can buy, rather than placing God first in all endeavors.

The Vow of Obedience made in right timing inspires one to be obedient to the Scriptural Commandments, the Principles of Jesus and his Living Teacher's instruction. The keeping of the Vow of Obedience establishes one's integrity as a trustworthy guardian of the Dharma. Persons with excessive pride, egotism, laziness, procrastination, forcefulness or self-will cannot fulfill the Vow of Obedience.

Vows made to God in right timing are a joy, not a burden.

When a man and a woman have a true and pure love for each other, the speaking and keeping of their Marriage Vows are a joy. So it is when a devotee has a true and pure love for God: his vows of commitment to the Creator and His Son are a joy.

Vows spoken out of timing become a burden and create karmic complications in the present life and in coming lives.

> *Better is it that thou shouldest not vow, than that thou shouldest vow and not pay.*
> —Ecclesiastes 5:5

> *Do not make a vow unless you mean it, because that vow is heard as thunder in Heaven.*
> — Ann Ree Colton

Vows kept build the body of spiritual insulation or "the whole armour of God." (Ephesians 6:11) Vows not kept betray the Martyrs, the Saints, the Lord Jesus, and the Word of God.

Many devotees make the vow to worship God each day through prayer and meditation. The Vow of Sacramental Fasting is a beautiful dedication, especially when observed with one's Teacher and co-disciples.

> *Every person, on entering the Path and making his first Vow of Dedication, is as a virgin. Thus, he opens himself to seduction trials on all levels.*
> — Ann Ree Colton

Vows involve a major area of testing in the spiritual life. Satan especially tries to cause probationary students of the higher life to break vows made before God's Holy Altar.

Vows, as links with God, may be strengthened over the years, or they may be shattered through fickleness, insincerity and nonvigilance. Where there is nonvigilance as to vows, there is no real sense of ministry, no secure foundation for the building of lasting works of good.

Probationers on the Path who love family, money, prestige or power more than they love God and the Truth make *vows-karma* by failing to keep their promises to protect the Word and Altar of God.

Tamasic and *rajasic* individuals are not likely to keep their vows to God. The tamasic ones are too lazy and procrastinating; and the rajasic ones are too busy with other interests to establish any degree of loyalty to God.

> *The younger brother of rajasic is tamas, which means lazy, inert, slow, not keeping promises, especially not fulfilling vows which are given to God on His Holy Altar.*
>
> —Ann Ree Colton

God perpetuates His Dharma from generation to generation, century to century, age to age through His faithful servants who keep their sacred vows with honor and integrity. Vows kept qualify an aspirant for the receiving of his Spiritual-Birthright Inheritance in cyclic continuity. In time, the Creator *anoints* with His Spirit those who keep their vows with love.

Vows spoken in right timing qualify a faithful devotee for the opening of the Sacred Seals of Grace. The priceless Archetypal Seals of Grace in the Third Heaven can be received only when one proves faithful in his vows to God over the years.

The knowledge of God's Scriptural Word has been preserved over the ages by those who have kept their vows to Him. Millions of unknown servants of God throughout the centuries have proved faithful to their vows. Each page of Scripture and each sanctuary of worship in the world is a testimony to their faithfulness and love.

Many persons who have spoken solemn vows to God have been persecuted, imprisoned, tortured and martyred. The history of the world is filled with the heroic examples of

Saints, Martyrs and other courageous souls whose vows kept them closely united with their Beloved Lord. God rewards with abundant gifts and graces all who suffer persecution and martyrdom while remaining faithful in their vows to Him.

Vows-Grace assures a Truth-seeker of being guided to an enlightened Teacher from life to life.

MARRIAGE VOWS AND MINISTRY VOWS

Vows are not between you and the church; they are between you and God.

— Ann Ree Colton

In modern times, many marriages end in divorce; in such instances, Marriage Vows were not spoken sincerely or in right timing. An increasing number of couples are living together without exchanging Marriage Vows. Even as there is a mass exodus from the Covenant of God's Commandments, so is there for many persons an exodus from the Principle of Vows.

Loyalty and other cardinal virtues earned through numerous lifetimes of keeping Marriage Vows are the same virtues necessary before a spiritual aspirant may qualify for the Divine-Marriage Anointing.

Numerous aspirants on the Path expect to enter into the marriage or union with God without speaking vows of any kind. These individuals may be likened to a man or a woman who prefers a live-together relationship in which one or the other can leave at any time. God places His Spirit only on devotees who are faithful in their vows to Him during the rugged trials of the probationary years.

When a man and woman marry, they are caught in a tug-of-war between ancestors who honored their Marriage Vows and ancestors who dishonored their Marriage Vows. How one reacts to this tug-of-war depends upon his own attitudes toward Marriage Vows—whether he leans toward the direction of betrayal or whether he proves honorable and sincere.

Marriage Vows, if kept, protect a husband and wife from becoming victimized by the unconfessed sins of parents and ancestors who offended Marriage Vows. Marriage Vows, if not kept, expose a husband and wife to these unexpiated ancestral sins and their devastating effects upon the marriage. Pettiness, hypersensitivities, angers, tempers and other anti-virtues expressed by a husband or wife are offenses against the Marriage Vow to Love and to Cherish. Such negative traits and immature attitudes are open doors to telepathic intrusions from parents and ancestors who also betrayed their Marriage Vows.

Unconfessed sins are passed on from one generation to another. Selfless love, a true devotion, and commitment to one's Marriage Vows are his only protection from the evil influences of parents and ancestors who betrayed their Marriage Vows.

Marriage Vows, if kept, unite the husband and wife with ancestors who also were faithful to their Marriage Vows. The virtues of these honorable and ethical ancestors become an invaluable strength, contributing to the harmony, happiness and prospering of the married couple.

Vows kept protect a devotee of the Lord from being drawn back into family and ancestral karma and past-lives' karma. Keeping one's vows to God is his only protection for remaining on the Path of Devotion. Vows not kept cause him to forfeit the Remission-of-Sins Grace offered by Jesus through the Sacrament of Communion.

A vow to God cannot be kept unless one does so by the Grace of the Holy Spirit. The Holy Spirit protects one during the inevitable testings of his Ministry Vows and Marriage Vows. During times of testing, a devotee should speak words such as: *"Dear Lord, I pray to keep my Marriage Vows* and*

---

*Single aspirants should omit the reference to Marriage Vows.

Ministry Vows as Thou wouldst have me fulfill them. In Jesus' Name. Amen." Instantaneous blessings and helps will follow the speaking of this prayer, for the Principle of Vows is a powerful Cosmos Principle, and to ask God's help in the keeping of all sacred vows is pleasing in His sight.

If a person fails to fulfill his Marriage Vows or Ministry Vows, he should remember that all vows not kept in the present life and in past lives may be rectified through repentance, confession, penance and restitution — and the Grace forfeited through the failure to keep vows may be redeemed. The redemption of Vows-Grace through the Great Redeemer, Christ Jesus, produces the spiritual-quickenings of virtues, conscience and understanding that enable one to henceforth fulfill his vows in the right spirit in the present and in the future.

> **Dear Lord, I pray to keep my Vows as Thou wouldst have me fulfill them. Please forgive me for times past when I have not fulfilled my Vows in the right spirit. Help me to make an honorable restitution for all offenses against Thy mighty Principle of Vows by myself and others in the world. In Jesus' Name. Amen.**

"Woe is unto me if I preach not the Gospel." (1 Corinthians 9:16) Persons whose souls have covenanted with God to preach the Gospel will continue to attract woes as long as they resist their calling. However, the moment they *vow* to fulfill their Soul's Covenant to teach God's Word, they will begin to experience the healing of their woes and the receiving of holy joys and soul-gifts.

Some students on the Path experience great conflict between the keeping of their Marriage Vows to a mate and their Ministry Vows to God. Peter and the other married disciples had spoken Marriage Vows before they met Jesus; nevertheless, their Apostolic calling required that they leave home and family and spend the remainder of their lives in service to God. Their Soul-Covenant to establish the Teachings of Jesus in the world required their faithfulness to their new responsibilities as anointed servants of the Living God.

To take the Vows of the Ministry and to be ordained as a Minister is more important than the Vow of Marriage.

— Ann Ree Colton

Ministry Vows are more demanding than Marriage Vows. In Marriage Vows, one vows to love and cherish one person. In Ministry Vows, he vows to love and cherish all persons being created in the Image of God.

And he said unto them, Go ye into the world, and preach the gospel to every creature.

— St. Mark 16:15

When a husband and a wife dedicate their marriage to God, they serve together as Apostles of the Lord Jesus. The joys of an Apostolic Marriage are the joys of vows kept to God and to one another. In this, Marriage Vows and Ministry Vows become one in service to God.

In a marriage where the husband and wife vow to see and to serve the Image of God in each other, there is the opportunity for rapid spiritual growth. This is a beautiful vow that brings the husband and wife closer to God each day. In the highest expression of such marriages, the marital partners encourage and assist each other to qualify for the Divine Marriage with their Lord.

When married couples begin their day by speaking together the words, **"I behold the Beauty of the Image of God in you,"** this powerful statement — spoken and fulfilled in the spirit of a vow — produces an atmosphere in which the Presence of God and His Angels will bless, heal and inspire. When a husband and wife behold the Beauty of the Image

of God in each other, each day is filled with dazzling jewels
of grace and love.

> *Having taken the inward vow, it is the task of the*
> *Teacher to remain constant where there is incon-*
> *stancy; to remain loving where there is unloving;*
> *and to remain chaste within his vow of selflessness,*
> *which is the integrity-armor of all true Teachers.*
> — Ann Ree Colton

Students who desire to become Teachers and Ministers of
God's Word should make the Vow of Selflessness and also the
Vow of Patience. A Teacher must be prepared to teach year
after year, with unending patience and unconditional love,
all whom God sends to him for sacred instruction. Regardless of how long a student resists Scriptural directives, the
Teacher must patiently continue to offer a "cup of cold
water" in Jesus' Name.

The *Bodhisattva Vow* is taken by illumined personages
who covenant with God "to continue to return to the earth
until every blade of grass is enlightened." This beautiful vow
requires an inspired patience based upon a deep love for
one's fellow man.

> *All Laws proceed from the Law of Love. All*
> *Vows proceed from the Vow to fulfill the Law of*
> *Love.*

17

THE TRANSCENDENTAL MARRIAGE

*A marriage on the level of Apostolic dedication
should keep first in mind always that the marriage
is entered into as an offering to God, whereby the
energy-processes and love-receptivity build the temple for the Omnipresence of God.*

—Ann Ree Colton

MARRIAGE AS A COSMOS PRINCIPLE

*The Christ is writing a new chapter on the pages
of history regarding marriage.
Through the Image of God, illuminative stages
of marriage are destined for the human spirit.*

In the present age, single and married individuals who are
experiencing pressures and stresses inwardly and outwardly
rarely understand what is occurring to them. Even as Cosmos
experiences the fiery-chaos births of new stars, so are the
births of new facets of God's Image in man accompanied by
periods of chaos and upheaval.

The appearance of Jesus of Nazareth as Savior and Messiah
of the world began a powerful impulse that is gathering mo-
mentum with each century, preparing all souls for the next
stages of Image-of-God quickenings. Through the increasing
Christ-Light, all tribal, family and religious customs that

stifle the soul-freedoms and the spiritual uniqueness of the individual are being challenged and will eventually disappear.

Traditions that hold persons in rigid limitations in thinking, feeling and acting are being uprooted by the powerful Plow of Christ Jesus, who is preparing the earth for mighty Transformations and Illuminations.

Marriage can be beautiful, productive and creative; it can be a spiritual adventure of service to God and apostleship under Christ. This is the High-Calling Marriage in which the Spirit of God is expressing and blessing through both the husband and the wife.

For thousands of years, *men* have played the dominant roles in religions, societies and families. Through the Christ-Spirit influences, the male-dominated marriages of Tribal-Genesis and Family-Genesis are changing to marriages in which husbands and wives express an equality as partners. This change in attitude represents a major victory for the Image of God and points the way to momentous advances in marriage and in family life.

In ages past, a Transcendental or Samadhi* Marriage was impossible because of the male-dominated marriages. However, in the present time, if husband and wife are so inclined, the sweet blending of the masculine and feminine polarities through the Synchronization Grace of the Christ and the Image of God makes possible a Transcendental or Samadhi Marriage anointed by the Holy Spirit.

The evolution of marriages in the Age of Self-Genesis and in future Ages will enable the Divine Image to reveal new facets of the Glory of God within the soul and within the Universe.

Marriage is a mighty *Cosmos Principle*; the Feminine Polarity and the Masculine Polarity play prominent roles in *all* of God's Creations throughout the Cosmos. Mankind stands on the threshold of comprehending the Image-of-God

---

*The term *Samadhi Marriage* was introduced by Ann Ree Colton.

Principle of Male and Female Polarities as related not only to human life on earth but to the life of Stars and Galaxies.

In the Lesser Self-Genesis Age, all partnerships in marriage or out of marriage are undergoing transition, for something is seeking to come to birth in a mighty polarity shifting. It is the divine intent that marriage shall come into a holy synthesis, and thereby establish a more ideal state of equal strengths and talents, thus producing a union of harmony and love.

In a synthesis-harmony in marriage, the bride and the bridegroom think upon one another as a fusing of the two into the one; they look to God to use their complementary attributes—loving emotional, creative mental.

All initiatory marriages are marriages of opposites in temperament. All Synthesis-Harmony Marriages are marriages between those of similar nature.

Until men reach Cosmos-Genesis, the Synthesis-Harmony Marriage will be a rarity. It is grace when one marries a similar, and thereby magnifies his own nature through the person he loves. When one is fortified by magnification of his own qualities through his mate, this is an Anointed Marriage.

— Ann Ree Colton

FOUR KINDS OF MARRIAGE

If a spiritualized love fails to be between two people who love, love is expressed on the human-race levels of karma. The expressions of human-race love are rivalry, jealousy and competition. In spiritualized love, there is union in marriage through which those who marry become vessels for God.

The mastery of the household is the first mastery of spiritual powers.

— Ann Ree Colton

In the present age, there are four kinds of marriage: the Karmic Marriage; the Grace Marriage; the Apostolic Marriage; and the Anointed Marriage. The Karmic Marriage is an unhappy marriage; the Grace Marriage is a happy marriage. A marriage dedicated to God and Christ is an Apostolic Marriage. The Apostolic Marriage prepares a married couple for the joys and blessings of an Anointed Marriage. The Anointed Marriage is a Transcendental Marriage in which the husband and the wife minister to others as enlightened servants of God.

Grace is an *Atmosphere* charged with the Presence of the Light of the Christ and the Love of God. In a Grace Marriage, the pure love-motives and selfless attitudes of the husband and wife elevate their hearts and minds to the Atmosphere of Divine Grace. Such marriages are *Grace* for the world, for they reveal the true purpose and nature of marriage as a Holy Sacrament and Celebration.

A marriage sanctified by God's Love and Grace is an ongoing Celebration, blessing the world through a man and a woman united harmoniously on all levels of body, heart, mind and soul. *"From the beginning of the creation God made them male and female. For this cause shall a man leave his father and mother, and cleave to his wife; And they twain shall be one flesh; so then they are no more twain, but one flesh. What therefore God hath joined together, let no man put asunder."* (St. Mark 10:6–9)

To retain the joyous feeling and knowing that marriage is a Celebration, a husband and wife should rededicate their Marriage Vows to God and to each other every morning. While kneeling before the Family Altar, they should speak words such as *"Father, we rededicate our Marriage Vows unto Thee and to one another. Please be with us. In Jesus' Name. Amen."*

When a husband and wife dedicate their marriage to God and Christ in the spirit of Celebration, they become true guardians of the Dharma and stewards of the mysteries of God; their marriage experiences the joys, rewards and inheritances of Enlightenment. Insulated by their love for God and for one another, they are immune to the subtle telepathies of the Antichrist and are centered in their Souls' Covenants with God. Such marriages represent the New-Era Apostolic and Transcendental Marriages that will inspire and lift other marriages in this and coming generations.

In an Apostolic Marriage, the husband is a gentle man; the wife, a gentle woman. Their gentleness, harmlessness and meekness place them under the protective blessings of the Lord Jesus. *"I am meek and lowly in heart."* (St. Matthew 11:29)

In a Transcendental Marriage, both husband and wife have earned the Divine-Marriage Anointing. Their Samadhi Marriage follows the course of pure creations inspired by the Holy Spirit; husband and wife work, create and worship together in a harmonious blending of the masculine and feminine polarities within their beings.

A marriage devoted to God is a spiritual pilgrimage in which the husband and the wife climb together the Holy Mountain of Illumination.

Often, newlyweds who have spoken Marriage Vows before God's Holy Altar will permit themselves to be swallowed up by the world; they will forget to worship God and to observe His Commandments. Self-infatuation becomes the predominant theme in many husbands and wives. Whenever a married couple displaces the love of God with the love of self, the marriage removes itself from the Grace of God and His Protection.

In a Karmic Marriage, there are constant bickerings, arguments and agitations. The anti-virtues of the husband and the wife invite the presence of Satan who seeks to demoralize and then to destroy the marriage. In marriages where Satan is successful, there is unhappiness, separation, divorce.

Anger in a home is like rottenness in fruit.
— Talmud

Anger expressed by a husband or wife is an offense against their Marriage Vows to Love and Cherish one another. Vigilance in keeping one's Marriage Vows prevents the adversary, Satan, from entering the marriage through the open door of anger. Through vigilance and the other beautiful virtues, the Vows of Marriage provide a solid wall of protection against the Antichrist — and the husband and wife can fulfill God's Will with peace, oneness and joy.

An anger-possessed bride or groom will turn their marriage into a Karmic Marriage. Tantrums used for the purpose of getting one's own way are karmic negativities inherited through the sins of ancestors, parents and past lives.

Any anti-virtue retained by the husband and wife will turn their marriage into a Karmic Marriage. The healing of *all* anti-virtues through the Exorcism and Reconciliation Powers of Jesus will transform an unhappy marriage into a Grace Marriage.

Father, may our home be free from arguments, dissensions, angers, resentments, bitterness. May we abide in the Peace-Presence of the Lord Jesus. We dedicate our marriage unto Thee, O Lord. Consecrate our Altar. Bless our kitchen, our bedroom, and all other rooms in our home—for we would live and serve as peacemakers in our home and in the world. In Jesus' Name. Amen.

In the spiritual life, one learns from the Scriptures the *higher degrees* of the cardinal virtues. If this knowledge is utilized in a marriage, the couple will experience a Grace Marriage, for the *Presence* of God abides in the higher degrees of the virtues. In a Grace Marriage, the husband and the wife live in the peace-atmospheres of the higher virtue-light blessed by the Love of God.

A Grace Marriage must be *earned*. It is earned by placing God first in the marriage; by keeping all vows made to one's mate and to God; by reverencing the Ten Commandments, the Law of Tithing and the Sermon on the Mount; and by expressing selflessness, kindness, politeness, patience, forgiveness, love and all other cardinal virtues. As every worthwhile thing in life must be earned, so must a Grace Marriage be earned. To *sustain* a Grace Marriage, both husband and wife must maintain Total Vigilance.

The Transcendental Life can occur only when a devotee of the Lord expresses the beautiful Clusters of Virtues that reflect the Image of Christ. These same virtues elevate a marriage to the Grace Atmospheres of Transcendence blessed by God and His Son.

Every virtue is a Christ-Light energy. Every anti-virtue is an Antichrist dark-energy. An Apostolic Marriage in a State of Divine Grace through Christ lifts the husband and wife *above* the turbulent sea of anti-virtue energies and unites them with the exalted wavelengths of Holy Telepathy blessed by God and His Host. Such marriages remain in a State of Providential Grace that provides for all their needs and enables them to serve with total freedom the Lord they worship and adore.

> *The miraculous and glorious blending of the husband and the wife through the masculine and feminine polarities within the Image of God is a monumental healing.*

A marriage based upon virtues and ethics has every opportunity of becoming an Apostolic Marriage; and, in time, an Anointed Marriage. When both husband and wife are virtue-minded, they worship, serve and love God as co-disciples under Christ. In this, their Apostleship will eventually qualify them for the Fulness-Anointing by the Holy Spirit.

When two persons truly love each other, they encourage, inspire and assist one another to attain union with God. In such marriages, the husband and the wife become *co-atom* to each other. A co-atom husband and wife are blended and harmonized physically, emotionally, mentally and spiritually. Their working together in holy harmony seals many victories into their souls' records, thereby blessing their future lives.

A husband and wife who remain steadfastly dedicated to the dynamic stanzas of the Beatitudes of Jesus escape the countless snares of the Antichrist; also, they become centered in the mighty Flows of Divine Grace.

In an Apostolic Marriage and an Anointed Marriage, extra efforts to express vigilance and the other sacred virtues are necessary so that the marriage will remain blessed with miraculous healing powers and soul-gifts.

> **Bless all households, O Lord. May Thy Presence brighten each home with joy. Please exorcise all dark spirits that would snuff out the joy and happiness in a household; and fill the hearts of those who dwell therein with love for Thee and for one another. In Jesus' Name. Amen.**

THE GOLDEN RULE: VOLITION AND DETACHMENT

The desire for liberation, freedom, and detachment is innate in all men.

Detachment is the ultimate goal and gift of purification.

Volition in you is automatically responsive to the Will of God. Volition puts you into a God-situation, where you must serve God. It is a spontaneity fully-clothed in Godly incentive and attributes.

Men are always seeking enough voltage to reach

Heaven. Through volition, the voltage of Heaven reaches you.

                           —Ann Ree Colton

Single or married devotees who would qualify to receive the Anointing that will transform them into enlightened Teachers must first be initiated in the importance of *Volition* and *Detachment*.

Volition is a gift from God. Volition can be withdrawn by the Creator or it can be increased on many levels. A criminal loses the gift of volition when he is incarcerated. A Saint expresses the wise use of volition in service to God.

Sins create karmic enclosures that decrease or remove the gift of volition through restrictions, afflictions or energy-losses. To sin is to place oneself in a prison of his own making.

Any time one meddles, dominates, manipulates, criticizes, judges, or makes decisions for another adult, he is offending their right of volition; and by so doing he is offending the Golden Rule: *Do unto others as you would have them do unto you.*

It is extremely important that a devotee extend to everyone in his life the right of volition. If he does this in the spirit of the Golden Rule, he will attract persons who will respect his right of volition.

Therefore all things whatsoever ye would that men should do to you, do ye even so to them: for this is the law and the prophets.

                           —St. Matthew 7:12

What you do not want done to yourself, do not do to others.

                           —Confucius

Since, for each one of us, our own self is the most important, respect the self of your fellow man as you respect your own.

                           —Buddha

Do unto all men as you would wish them to have done unto you.

— Muhammad

What you do not want done to you, do not do to anyone else.

— Apocrypha

May I do to others as I would that they should do unto me.

— Plato

In the spiritual life, one must be vigilant regarding his God-given gift of volition. The moment he intrudes on the volition of another person, he enters into their karmic enclosures and sacrifices his own freedom.

A Teacher of the higher life is constantly seeking to win for each student the *expanding* of God's gift of volition: unwary students *lose* volition; vigilant students gain more volition.

Detachment protects one from usurping the volition of others. A love-filled detachment enables him to *mediate* for others while remaining free from their sin-debt enclosures. All spiritual freedoms increase in the lives of those who practice detachment and love, understanding the *sacredness* of their own volition and the volition of others.

The sage is detached, thus at one with all. Through selfless action, he attains fulfillment.

— Lao Tzu

He who would be serene and pure needs but one thing, detachment. List ye, good people all: there is none happier than he who stands in uttermost detachment.

— Meister Eckhart

In marriage, one should respect the volition of his or her mate. Often, one or both marriage partners will try to make their mate into their own image, rather than inspire each other to fulfill the Image of God. Whenever a husband or wife continually resorts to petty criticisms, wilful bossing, and impatience with their mate, they are trying to make their mate into their own image, thereby failing to reverence the Image of God in their mate and also failing to respect the volition of another.

A devotee who fails the tests of volition in his marriage cannot serve God as a teacher of truth because he would not respect the volition of students. A teacher who does not respect the volition of his students is inevitably drawn into their karmas; he thereafter forfeits his right to represent the Christ in their lives.

To respect the volition of *all* persons in one's life is necessary before a devotee can progress spiritually and work to earn the Divine-Marriage Anointing.

Persons who seriously offend the volition of others will reincarnate in countries where tyrants or dictators will limit or remove their volition.

Detachment *without* love produces a cold mate. Detachment *with* love produces a warm, caring mate who does not intrude on the volition of his or her beloved. He who learns the wisdom of detachment with love will taste the sweet nectars of God's Love.

Ancestral-gene karma cannot do its destructive work in a home or marriage when the husband and wife respect the volition of each other.

Ancestral-gene karma tries to inspire one to live in the image of his ancestors and to force his mate and children to live in the ancestral image. The ancestral image is *not* the Image of God. The ancestral image has been developed by unenlightened opinions and possessive desires of one's ancestors. The ancestral image tries to hold one in soul-thwarting enclosures. Until recent times, parents chose the mate for their son or daughter. There was no volition in a child's choosing

his or her own mate, for *all* was ancestrally determined —
from marriage to work to family life. Everything one did was
under the scrutiny of his parents and ancestors. This total
subservience to ancestors for *millions* of years developed an
ancestral image. Today, many persons still feel compelled to
conform to the ancestral image.

The coming of the Christ began man's detachment from
the ancestral image and the awareness of one's Spiritual Identity and Cosmos Destiny through the Image of God. Presently, each person is undergoing a transition from the ances-
tral-image consciousness to the Image-of-God Consciousness.

A devotee cannot experience the Redemption Grace of
the Lord Jesus as long as he is the victim of ancestral-gene
karma. Ancestral-gene karma manifests in many negative
ways through offenses against volition and detachment.

Ancestral-inherited angers; the tendency toward tantrums
and rages; lustful attitudes and actions; these and other temperament problems are passed from one generation to another through the genes. He who comes to the Christ comes
to peace — a peace made possible only by his detachment
from the influence of unrighteous ancestors.

Through the Redemption Grace of the Lord Jesus, one becomes detached from the *negative* ancestral-gene influences
and retains the *positive* ancestral-gene traits. This blessing is
earned when one respects the volition of mate, family members, co-disciples, and all other persons in his life.

> *There are times when one must call upon Ances-*
> *tral Grace, Ego Grace and Divine Grace. When*
> *these are as one, one is a vehicle for Holy Spirit. A*
> *functional ego can be turned free in soul for the*
> *Esse when these three points of Grace unite. In the*
> *spontaneity flashes of this union, one becomes an*
> *illumined seer, prophet and server for God.*
> — Ann Ree Colton

Ancestral-inherited attitudes often relate to money, sex and pride. Fears about money, selfish traits regarding sex, and motives based on pride may be inherited through ancestral-gene karma. To become a disciple of the Lord Jesus, one must attain detachment from fears about money, selfish attitudes in sex, and family, racial, intellectual and religious pride. Trust in God and His Providence, purity and reverence in sex, and the expression of humility enable one to attain detachment from these three major hindrances to Divine Grace and Spiritual Illumination.

> *The ills of the temperament are displayed in selfishness, in impatience, in irritations, in dissatisfaction.*
>
> —Ann Ree Colton

To become angry or irritated with others because their clothing tastes and food choices differ from one's own is to offend the Principle of Volition. If a devotee truly practices the Golden Rule, he would not want to intrude his own thoughts and wishes on others, even as he would not want them to intrude their wills on his freedom of choice.

A disciple of Jesus may be called upon to visit homes, families and nations where the clothing and food customs are different from his own culture and standards. Any feeling or thought of criticism of others will be felt by them, and the devotee's representation of the Lord Christ will be minimized or nullified in their eyes.

"Judge not, that ye be not judged." (St. Matthew 7:1) A non-judging attitude should be applied in one's home, in his workplace, in the sanctuary and in the world. In this, he will not allow personal attitudes to offend the volition of others.

Many marriages end in divorce due to petty irritations regarding the living habits of one's mate. To see one's mate through the eyes of love and the Golden Rule avoids the problems and troubles resulting from petty irritations related to eating, wearing apparel, bathroom traits, and other aspects of marriage.

When a family says "Grace" before a meal, they should realize that they have invited the Lord of Grace, Christ Jesus, to be present at the table. The saying of "Grace" invites the blessings of God. A family member can block these beautiful blessings if he turns the mealtime into a time for quarrels and criticisms.

The Presence of Jesus will bless each family and marriage when the husband, wife and children remain reverently grateful to God for the provision of food and for the joy of being together. Each meal eaten sacramentally will bring marriage partners and family members closer together. Petty irritations, criticisms and quarrels negate the sacramental nature of mealtime and give entry to satanic spirits that thrive upon the dark energies within pettiness.

> *Pettiness snuffs out the joy and enthusiasm in a marriage.*

The spirit of pettiness afflicts many marriages, families and households. Petty annoyances and irritations cause many husbands and wives to withdraw their love from one another. If the Antichrist can induce a husband and wife to become constantly irritated by petty annoyances, he will drive wedge after wedge into their marriage, first destroying their happiness and love for each other and then moving them toward separation or divorce. When Marriage Vows are forgotten and love ceases, Satan rejoices.

Bickerings over trivial matters reveal that satanic forces have begun to influence the thoughts, feelings and tongues of the husband and wife. An unyielding pettiness expressed by a husband or a wife will eventually affect all aspects of their marriage. Petty wives and husbands place burdens on their mates that often lead to extramarital affairs.

Possessive deceased ancestors find telepathic or etheric

penetration into a marriage and family through the pettiness of their offspring. The ancestral dead and the living remain linked through their mutual pettiness.

When the spirit of pettiness is continuously directed toward a devotee by a mate, it will try to distract his mind from thinking on the Eternal Plan of God and his ministering to others in need. If he becomes the victim of the spirit of pettiness possessing his mate, he, too, will become petty, thereby causing him to lose his footing on the Spiritual Path.

> *Respect the Volition of others if you would have them respect your Volition.*

Pettiness vanishes in households where there is detachment and respect of volition. The petty irritations that cause inharmony and unhappiness in a marriage miraculously disappear through the practice of detachment and respect for the volition of one's mate. When a husband and wife both understand the importance of volition, detachment, love and the Golden Rule, their marriage will be blessed by the virtues, providences and soul-gifts proceeding from the Image of God in each other.

> **Heavenly Father, I pray to fulfill my Marriage Vows as Thou wouldst have me fulfill them. Please heal me of all petty irritations stemming from ancestral-gene karma and past-lives' influences, that I might come into perfect timing with my Soul's Covenant with Thee. I pray to become a co-creator with Thee through the hierarchy nature and the Divine Image. In Jesus' Name. Amen.**

SEVEN-YEAR CYCLES

> *Every seven years a draught of remembrance relating to past lives is drawn into certain levels of*

*one's consciousness beneath the surface layer of
consciousness. This draught of remembrance adds
something which is beyond that gathered from the
daily experience in life.*

— Ann Ree Colton

A marriage may be harmonious until the husband or the
wife experiences a draught of remembrance from past lives
that produces subtle or extreme changes in personality, nature and temperament. If the husband and the wife understand the reality of reincarnation and the seven-year cycles,
they can fortify themselves and each other whenever the soul
presents unpaid sin-debts for payment. During these inevitable cycles in a marriage, their dedication to God and their
Marriage Vows may be severely tested. At such times, the
couple should turn more to prayer, compassion, forgiveness,
patience and love, or else the marriage will begin a downward spiral. It is extremely important to remain near God
and Christ in one's heart and mind in order to meet each
seven-year cycle of both the husband and the wife.

Helping each other to change soul-record darkness into
Light through the Mediation of Christ Jesus is a great victory
for a married couple dedicated to Holy Apostleship.

Grace earned in previous lives also moves forth from the
soul's record in seven-year cycles. A life of prayer, meditation, fasting and selfless serving prospers the Flow of this
beautiful Grace earned in former existences.

In marriage, one is married to the past-lives' Grace and
debts of his or her mate. If a husband and wife accept this
truth, they can work together to pay the unpaid sin-debts as
quickly as possible and become more firmly centered in the
increasing Flow of past-lives' Grace.

The Law of Attraction that inspires a man and a woman
to marry is *perfect*. The soul-record of the husband and the
soul-record of the wife are mathematically related through

the perfect Law of God. Therefore, the faults of one's mate are projections of his own faults either in his present life or in past lives. If he recognizes this truth, he will realize that God's Just Law is enabling him to make restitution for previous times in which he expressed the same faults as his mate.

The moment one sees a fault in his mate, he should *pray* for his mate and hold his mate in the Christ Light. In his prayers, he should humbly confess the fault as his own, knowing that God's Omnipresent Truth is revealing the fault as an unresolved sin-shadow in the soul's record of *both* husband and wife. One may not be expressing the same fault as his mate, but he can be assured that he has expressed the same fault in the present life or in a past life. If he judges or criticizes his mate, he will add fuel to Satan's fire seeking to destroy the marriage. However, if he prays to God for the healing of his mate, he will be serving God and Christ as a Mediative Healer. Also, his humility and self-honesty will enable him to make restitution through his prayer-mediation, forgiveness, kindness, gentleness and love. Healing through restitution will occur more rapidly if he includes prayers for the healing of *all persons* in the world who are expressing the same fault or faults as his mate.

If one works with God in the right spirit of love, humility, confession and restitution, his own faults and his mate's faults will be healed by the Miracle Light of the Christ. However, as long as he judges, criticizes or condemns his mate's faults, he will fail to make restitution for lives past when he expressed the same faults — and the faults of both husband and wife will become increasing sources of irritation, sensitivity and unhappiness.

A person who thinks he is perfect and that his mate is the only one in the marriage with faults is expressing immature attitudes that will prevent the marriage from receiving the Healing Love of God and the Redemption Grace of Christ Jesus.

Heavenly Father, I confess my mate's faults as my own. I pray, with Thy merciful Help, to make a full and honorable restitution for all sins committed in this life and in past lives. May our marriage be blessed with constancy in love, forgiveness, non-judging, compassion and meekness. And may we serve as Apostles of Jesus in the spirit of love and joy. In His Holy Name. Amen.

THE FAMILY ALTAR

Love one another, and worship and serve God together—this is the key to a happy and grace-filled marriage.

When two devotees of the Lord marry, the Antichrist will try to *divide* them, that he might limit or end their service to God and Jesus in the Holy War.

"Salute one another with an holy kiss." (Romans 16:16) To preserve the integrity of a marriage dedicated to God, the husband and wife should begin each day with a holy kiss and hug. As two disciples of the Lord going forth in Apostolic service, they should embrace reverently and lovingly before the Family Altar, speaking to each other words such as: *"Beloved co-disciple in the Christ, I love thee."* This will begin their day of service to God and His Son *in the right spirit* of sacred discipleship. They also should extend to each other a holy kiss and hug the last thing at night with words of love and affection.

If a husband and wife cannot extend to each other a holy kiss and hug as Apostles in Christ, this is a certain sign that satanic spirits have entered their household and have begun their work of separation and division. At such times, the husband and wife should confess the unresolved sins of ancestors, parents, past lives and the present life that have caused this breakdown in communication with each other. The enemy has infiltrated their household because they have failed to be vigilant in the keeping of their Marriage Vow to Love and Cherish each other.

Hugs are healing. Hugs observed throughout the day with a reverent love are *holy*. To lovingly hug one's mate and children each day is to maintain a sweet love-presence within the marriage and family life. Sincere expressions of love and gratitude for one another invite the Angels of God to bless the home. Such households are happy, disciplined, reverent, peaceful.

A holy hug and a holy kiss are devoid of physical passion; they are an expression of love for the *soul* of one's mate, child, friend, or co-disciple. They also are an expression of love for the *Image of God* in the recipient of the warm embrace.

> *Love is the greatest exorciser.*
> — Ann Ree Colton

To reverence the soul and Image of God in another through a prem, hug or kiss is a powerful healer and exorciser. To love one another in faithful obedience to the Commandment of Love is to remain a disciple of Jesus.

A mundane marriage has no spiritual goals; it is based upon materiality, self-interests and the pleasure principle. In an Apostolic Marriage, the husband and the wife are active disciples of Christ Jesus. Their marriage is based upon a mutual love for God and a joint-dedication to perpetuate the Dharma.

A true disciple of Jesus is blessed with a *dignity* that comes through his or her covenant to minister in His Name. In an Apostolic Marriage, both husband and wife radiate this dignity in the world. During a holy kiss and hug, one is recognizing and honoring the *dignity* of his or her mate as a dedicated disciple of Jesus and guardian of the Dharma.

It is beautiful in God's sight when a husband and wife confirm their Marriage Vows throughout the day by sharing words of kindness, encouragement, love-touches and timely hugs and kisses. When husband and wife are inspired through God's Holy Spirit, each *knows* exactly when the other needs a tender word, a loving glance, an assurance of their friendship, trust and respect.

I pray to become a Love-Presence in my home.

An Apostolic Marriage especially requires a Love-Insulation so that a continuous service to God and the Lord Jesus may be maintained. In this, the love of the husband and wife increases within the Holy Increase of God—and the Creator uses their love to manifest blessings and healings in the world.

In an Apostolic Marriage, the respect and love a devoted husband and wife express toward each other enable them to transcend the turbulent sea of destructive energies plaguing the world and destroying numerous marriages. This respectful and loving attitude enables them to remain at one with the Wisdom, Grace and Love of God. Centered in the Love-Commandment of Jesus and in their unwavering faithfulness to the Vow to Love and Cherish one another, they experience the joys and miracles of dedicated discipleship under Christ.

Marriage is a Gift of God. An Apostolic Marriage is a perpetual source of Divine Blessings flowing to the world through the love of husband and wife.

The Family Altar in the home is the place where many virtues and soul-gifts come to birth in the parents and in their children. If the Family Altar is missing from the home, the parents are poor examples to their children.

The Creator opens the love between a man and a woman so that He can accomplish something very beautiful for the world. This love increases each time a husband and wife reverence the Family Altar. Their lighting of the candle on the Family Altar is a daily testimony of their faith in God and desire to do His Will.

When the schedules of a husband and wife do not permit them to worship together at the Family Altar through prayer and meditation, the differences in their schedules reveal that they have yet to attain synchronicity in soul-record timings and in their masculine and feminine polarities. Prayers by husband and wife to come into timing with God's Will for them will manifest changes in attitudes and work-responsibilities that will bring their polarities into harmony with all worship-rhythms.

Polarities-harmonization and timing-synchronization will enable the husband and the wife to fulfill their Marriage Vows, their Souls' Covenants and Worship-Dedications within God's Perfect Flow of Grace. The miracles occurring in and through their marriage will reveal the sacred reasons why God brought them together as husband and wife and as devotees on the Path of Enlightenment.

In marriage and family life, in associations with co-disciples and a Living Teacher, a probationer, devotee or initiate is held accountable for each and every word that proceeds from his lips. When a loved mate or the Teacher passes from the world, the first thing one will think is: "Did I say or do anything to harm this beloved one?" At this time, many persons feel sorrow and guilt. Blessed is the devotee who searches his heart — and his heart reports that he has not said one word to hurt or harm his beloved mate or Teacher.

In every marriage, there should be grace-praise, grace-gratitude, grace-appreciation. This keeps the Polarizing effects within superconsciousness.

Very often a chela or student, feeling that he might appear hypocritical, avoids open praise of a mate, thinking that it may be used against him to advantage as to the state of place and the state of face-saving in the marriage.

If one has retained any form of pleasure through seeing the humiliation of the mate caused by the cutting down of pride by initiation, he must hasten to rectify this with honest praise built upon the manifested virtues of his mate. By this he will keep constant to his Promises and Vows as a life shoulder-sharer in walking the Path as Initiates.

—Ann Ree Colton

18

THE HEALING OF PETTINESS

If we liberate our souls from our petty selves, wish no ill to others, and become clear as a crystal diamond reflecting the light of truth, what a radiant picture will appear in us mirroring things as they are without the admixture of burning desires, without the distortion of erroneous illusion, without the agitation of sinful unrest.
— Buddha

A humble devotee is lacking in vanity and pettiness.
— Paramahansa Yogananda*

Pettiness never purchased a spiritual mantle.
— Ann Ree Colton

ETERNAL ATOMS

There is a natural body, and there is a spiritual body.
— 1 Corinthians 15:44

The dedicated practices of the higher life enable the disciple to free his spiritual atoms, which are the permanent portions of Life, Image and Light.

---

*Gratitude to the Self-Realization Fellowship for permission to use quotations by Paramahansa Yogananda.

They are atoms of the pure stream of the Eternals
and consist wholly of Light and of the Body of God.
                — Ann Ree Colton

The continuity of Everlasting Life is made possible for man through the Eternal Atoms within his being. Through these Eternal Atoms of the Soul and the Image of God, each person lives from life to life, age to age, and eternity to eternity in spiraling states of progression.

The Eternal Atoms of the Divine Image are more powerful than the ancestral genes. This is why any person can be spiritually transformed when he escapes the influences of negative gene-traits and becomes his Real or True Self as imaged of God. When the Eternal Atoms of the Divine Image and his wholesome ancestral genes direct his destiny, he lives and creates as an enlightened personage in the gravity world.

All healthy ancestral genes and the Divine-Image Eternal Atoms are harmonized and synchronized by the Lord Christ. Thereafter, one may receive the rewards and inheritances of Spiritual Illumination.

See the Diamond, not the dross.

A devotee of the Lord should see in each person the Diamond-like Image of God; he should not be deceived by the dross covering the Diamond. The dross is not the True Self. The Image-of-God Self is the True Self, Eternal, Everlasting. As the dross is removed, the radiance of the Image-of-God Diamond moves forth in increasing splendor.

To create through the Diamond of the Divine Image is to work with the *Archetypes* of this Solar System; and in so doing, one is working and creating in harmony with the Archetypes of *all* Solar Systems in their respective Galaxies.

A petty person sees only the dross and not the Diamond. A person free from pettiness sees the Diamond and not the dross. He knows the dross of unresolved sins will disappear in time, but the Diamond of God's Image will remain forevermore scintillating in resplendent Light.

To see the Beauty of the Image of God in another is to help the other to come closer to the time of his birth to his Divine-Image Diamond. To see only the dross in others through the eyes of pettiness and criticism seals them more into the burden of their sins.

"The light of the body is the eye: if therefore thine eye be single, thy whole body shall be full of light." (St. Matthew 6:22) The eye single is the eye eternal. To see through the eye single is to see the Eternal Plan of God as a reality and the Diamond of the Divine Image manifesting its infinite facets throughout Life Everlasting. Persons in bondage to the spirit of pettiness cannot see through the eye single, the eye eternal. Trivialities and meaningless repetitions keep their eyes fixed on self and self-desires, thereby preventing their seeing beyond the personal into the Eternal.

Pettiness keeps the mind earthbound. Petty obsessions with earth-related matters, concerns and objects blind the eyes to the beautiful Universe and its secrets and truths. These priceless Cosmos wonders are pressing to be discovered by receptive minds and hearts freed from the stranglehold of pettiness.

> *Elevate us, O Lord Jesus, above the pettiness in the world, that we may abide in the Eternal of God.*

STRAINING AT GNATS

I am one with the Universe through love.
I am one with the Image of God through love.
I am a mortal seeking to be immortal.
I am a soul seeking to be illumined by the Spirit of God.

"Ye blind guides, which strain at a gnat, and swallow a camel . . ." (St. Matthew 23:24) Throughout the world, individuals who strain at gnats and swallow camels are those who become extremely upset about trivial matters, yet feel no remorse while unashamedly offending the major Commandments of God.

In modern times, it is very difficult for a religious or spiritual ministry to maintain the integrity and high standards of the Scriptures because of the spirit of pettiness that afflicts so many aspirants and leaders. Petty jealousies, rivalries, prejudices, and other expressions of the lower nature keep the Christ Light from entering their hearts, minds and souls. Unfortunately, students, devotees and ministers afflicted by the spirit of pettiness place stumbling blocks in the paths of others as well as themselves.

Individuals on the Path who remain neurotically attached to their own petty standards may become physically ill if anyone disagrees with them. This unwholesome condition is more than a surface sickness. Deep healings and exorcisms by the Christ Light are required to free them from this unholy prison of neurotic pettiness, self-will, and disrespect for the feelings and thoughts of others.

Many persons who pray and meditate each day remain unenlightened because of their habitual pettiness.

Pettiness eats away at the vital virtues of hope, good cheer and optimism. It corrupts the soul, blinds the eyes, corrodes the intellect, and demoralizes enthusiasm. The Grand and Glorious Universe remains a mystery to hearts and minds crippled by pettiness in thought, desire and action.

Pettiness inspires many probationers to become critics of others rather than disciples of Jesus. Such persons forget that they are on *trial* to see if they are worthy to represent Jesus as Apostles. Love, forgiveness, kindness and compassion are qualities that protect aspirants from falling into the pit of pettiness.

"If I cast out devils by the Spirit of God, then the kingdom of God is come unto you." (St. Matthew 12:28) Jesus must "cast out" or *exorcise* the devils or evil spirits in the heart and mind before one can be free to receive the Kingdom-of-God anointings and quickenings.

Pettiness, a rampant evil in the world, is a subtle and insidious spirit used by the Antichrist to keep numerous persons in bondage. The satanic spirit of pettiness especially delights in keeping truth-seekers in religious and spiritual ministries from earning the Divine-Marriage Anointing.

Petty obsessions and fixations are not easily identified when they are interwoven into the fabric of one's nature. When the spirit of pettiness becomes an integral part of one's feelings and thoughts, it directs the course of his life into labyrinths of difficulties and sorrows.

Few devotees on the Path repent of pettiness *because they do not know they are its victim*. It requires courage, self-honesty and humility before one can begin to recognize the areas of pettiness preventing him from receiving the blessings and inheritances of the Kingdom of God.

While the spirit of pettiness is one of the most difficult to identify in one's self, it is one of the most easily healed when the aspirant works directly with the Christ. When the spirit of pettiness is identified, healed and overcome, a devotee can begin to be his True Self.

The healing of pettiness enables one to experience many ages of spiritual evolvement in one moment of time through the Exorcism Power of Christ Jesus!

Pettiness denotes spiritual immaturity. The healing of pettiness leads to spiritual maturity. Before one can become an enlightened spiritual leader, minister or teacher, he must overcome all tendencies toward pettiness.

The spirit of pettiness manifests as petty complaints and

faultfindings, petty thoughts and criticisms, petty fears and obsessions, petty jealousies and rivalries, petty likes and dislikes, petty irritations and prejudices. The more pettiness a person expresses, the more he is locked into ancestral-gene karma.

When pettiness is an ancestrally-inherited trait through the genes, it permeates the pores of the skin, the nerve endings, the glands, the cells, and influences the emotions, thoughts and words. Therefore, if a devotee would qualify for the Divine Marriage with his Beloved Lord, he should pray to be healed and exorcised of the unholy and unrighteous spirit of pettiness. The Door to the Godhead opens not as long as one expresses pettiness.

Numerous modern-day students of the higher life have inherited the spirit of pettiness *and* the spirit of anger through their ancestral genes and through their souls' records of previous lives. These deadly samskaras* cause a student to express widely-fluctuating moods and abnormal behavior patterns. The chronic pettiness of such students triggers their frequent angers, rages and tantrums.

Some aspirants on the Path have brilliant minds able to appreciate and understand Scriptural truths; they also are blessed with Agape-hearts that desire to help others through knowledge shared and service rendered. However, these positive attributes may be contested by the periodic intrusions of the spirit of anger married to the spirit of pettiness. *This combination of positive and negative samskaras can be healed only through a Constancy in Love and Equanimity made possible by the Light of the Christ.*

When a devotee desires union with the fulness of God's Grace, he should pray to be healed of all expressions of pettiness. The healing of pettiness will enable him to behold, love and serve the Image of God in others. Thereafter, the Spirit

---

*In Sanskrit, the word *samskara* means *tendency*.

of God will bless his efforts to move closer to the Inner Kingdom. The healing of pettiness begins one's union with the
grandeur of the soul and with the Glory of God within His
Image.

*Pettiness delivers incessant, punishing blows to
loved ones. The sin of pettiness has destroyed countless marriages.*

The God-given gift of mental and emotional energies is
misused through petty criticisms of others. Many husbands
and wives destroy their marriages and their mates through
unceasing pettiness in criticisms, faultfindings, complaints
and irritations.

Petty obsessions by a marriage partner lead to arguments
and estrangements. Pettiness is an especially destructive spirit
because it causes a married couple to forget their Marriage
Vows to one another. It causes devotees on the Path to forget the Commandment of Love Ye One Another. Pettiness
exposes one to the army of the Antichrist and removes him
from the protection of the sheepfold of the Christ.

*"For by thy words thou shalt be justified, and by thy words
thou shalt be condemned."* (St. Matthew 12:37) Even as petty
thoughts are an offense against the use of mind-energies,
petty chatter and petty lies are offenses against speech-ener-
gies. The laws of energy in thought and in speech are violated
by pettiness. The Christ teaches purity in thought, word and
motive, for through purity one is protected from the snares
of the Antichrist.

When Satan begins to move toward devotees of the Lord,
he tries to make them look at their fellow disciples or their
Teacher through the eyes of pettiness. Petty faultfinding with
others causes them to forget that they have dedicated their
lives to serving the Lord of Love in the world.

The pettiness of Judas closed his eyes, ears and heart to the
miracles and wisdom of Jesus. Petty students of an Anointed

Teacher cannot see the mission and ministry of their Teacher as an Apostle of Christ. A petty student sees only the dirt on the Teacher's shoes; he does not see the long Path to Illumination trod by the feet in the shoes.

The petty attitudes of Judas prevented him from understanding the broad and deep wisdom within the promises and prophecies of Jesus—and Judas fell from grace. Petty desires prevent many disciples of the Lord from comprehending the noble truths and principles that lead to Spiritual Illumination. Such persons, like Judas, fall from grace.

The same energy in thought one uses to think a petty thought can be used to think a compassionate thought. God provides the energy for thought. A person in bondage to the spirit of pettiness uses the God-given thought-energy to think thoughts of petty hates, fears and covetings. An enlightened individual uses God-given thought-energies to think spiritual thoughts regarding the Image of God, Christ Principles and Cosmos Creation.

> *God in me is healing my fears.*
> *God in me is inspiring me to create beautiful works.*
> *God in me is Perfect Love, Universal Truth and Versatile Creations.*

A person in bondage to the spirit of pettiness does not have self-control or emotional discipline. His emotions thrash wildly about, like a stallion resisting the rider. The Christ becomes the rider who guides a devotee to his spiritual destination only when the aspirant has a sense of discipline and a desire to follow His Lord in life and in death.

A person in bondage to the spirit of pettiness has strong likes and dislikes. He has little or no flexibility in feelings and thoughts. He believes that his desires and likes should be everyone else's desires and likes.

Petty likes and dislikes lock one into a prison of karma. To be freed from this self-made prison, he should practice *detachment* from petty likes and dislikes, and keep his mind and heart centered on serving God and seeing His Image in his fellow man. Self-denial and detachment free one from bondage to the spirit of pettiness and from other unholy spirits.

Petty obsessions have deep roots in the lower subconscious. To be healed of petty obsessions requires delicate surgery by the Christ Light, for His Light must probe deeply into the stagnant core of the lower subconscious. All petty obsessions originate in the Anti-Virtue Core and then move upward into the consciousness mind. Prayers of repentance and confession assist the Christ to do His perfect healing work and to replace the spirit of pettiness with the spirit of freedom and joy.

"For it is written, As I live, saith the Lord, every knee shall bow to me, and every tongue shall confess to God." (Romans 14:11) The Christ uses the energy of self-honesty in one's prayers of repentance and confession to heal the *causes* of his negative traits and tendencies. The Healing Light of the Christ heals errant behavior patterns; heals the immune system, assuring health and vitality; heals the nervous system, inspiring peace, equanimity and constancy in love; and heals all other mental and emotional reflex and sensitivity systems.

Love heals pettiness. Love endears, ennobles, enlightens. When the Love of God and Christ are in one's heart, he loves *unconditionally*. Where love is *not*, the heart and the mind remain caught in the enclosure-fixities of pettiness. As love decreases, pettiness increases. As love increases, pettiness decreases.

The healing of pettiness opens a devotee to the Mind of Christ through love. Love and the Mind of Christ are one.

God is gracious, magnanimous, kind. When one draws nigh to God, his pettiness falls away, and he expresses graciousness, magnanimity, kindness and other beautiful virtues.

Dear Lord, please heal me of all manner of pettiness, that I may unite with the Greatness and Grandeur, the Secrets and Mysteries, of Thy Mighty Universe. In Jesus' Name. Amen.

TESTINGS

My child, if you come to serve the Lord, Prepare yourself to be tried. Set your heart right and be firm, and do not be hasty when things go against you; Hold fast to him, and do not forsake him, So that you may be honored when your life ends. Accept whatever happens to you, And be patient in humiliating vicissitudes. For gold is tested with fire, And men who are approved must be tested in the furnace of humiliation. Have faith in him, and he will help you; Make your ways straight, and put your hope in him.

— Apocrypha

An enlightened Teacher seeks to prepare each student for the testings that occur during the probationary period on the Path of Devotion. Many students fail in these preliminary testings because they stubbornly refuse to relinquish their chronic pettiness.

Each devotee on the Path must prove to God that he knows the difference between right and wrong regarding every Scriptural Commandment, Virtue and Ethic. There are repeated testings in the areas where he is uncertain or hesitant about the knowing of right from wrong.

In the areas of life where one has a positive knowing of the difference between right from wrong, he experiences the Forgiveness of God. Many tests of different kinds will continue to occur in areas of attitudes and behavior patterns in which he is yet uncertain about the difference between right and wrong, good and evil.

Even as a space capsule must be carefully prepared for its flight into space, so must each devotee be prepared for his ascent into the Higher Worlds. Each part of a space capsule must be properly tested to insure a safe journey; each virtue of a devotee must be thoroughly tested to insure his journey into the higher atmospheres of the soul and the spirit. The work of the tester is to test each virtue of the aspirant on the Path. The higher one travels into the Three Heavens, the more his virtues are tested.

"Then was Jesus led up of the spirit into the wilderness to be tempted of the devil." (St. Matthew 4:1) Jesus experienced the testing of His virtues by Satan before He began His world-changing Ministry. So do all who serve the Living God experience repeated testings of their virtues until they prove ready for world-serving as a full-fledged disciple and apostle of Jesus.

Father, I pray to serve the Holy Cause of the Lord Christ through virtues, love and ethics. Let my thoughts be kind, not critical; let my words be pure, not petty. With Thy help, I pray to make a full and honorable restitution for all offenses against Thy Image in the present life and in past lives. May all Scales of Thy Justice come into balance and harmony, that my heart, mind and soul may become chalices for Thy Cosmos-Eternal Spirit. In Jesus' Name. Amen.

FAULTFINDING

Don't find fault with anyone, not even with an insect. As you pray to God for devotion, so also pray that you may not find fault with anyone.
— Ramakrishna

When a man sees defects in others, his mind first gets polluted. What does he gain by finding faults

in others? He hurts himself by that. From my child-
hood I could not find faults in others. That one
thing I have never learnt in life.

— Sarada Devi

To constantly behold the Image of God in a loved one is to see their manifested virtues as beautiful, sacred energies. In this, the spiritual aspirant becomes a virtue-beholder rather than a faultfinder.

A person thinking through the lower mind is always trying to see the faults of others, that he might judge and criticize them. When one thinks through the higher mind, he does not look for the faults of others; he seeks to perceive their virtues and their good. He recognizes, honors and salutes their many lifetimes of struggle to earn their luminous virtues. Through higher-mind thinking, one knows that God, in His perfect timing, will heal the faults of each of His children and will quicken their virtues either in their present lifetimes or in future lives.

"Judge not, that ye be not judged." (St. Matthew 7:1) The critical mind, the faultfinder mind, the egotistical and self-centered mind are lower-mind expressions that keep one from thinking through the higher-mind levels of the Divine-Image Consciousness.

The visualization of the Image of God in others acts as a quickener of their virtues, conscience and other attributes of their souls. One who beholds God's Image in others becomes a non-judging, mediative healer. Divine-Image visualizations, through love and faith in God's Law of Timing, manifest miracles of healing and spiritual quickening for others.

When one is quickened by the Christ, he begins to overcome all tendencies to judge, criticize and find fault with others — and he becomes more selfless, patient, compassionate and love-filled. This transformation through quickened virtues also produces more enlightened attitudes toward Time, Timing and Timelessness.

"The Son quickeneth whom He will." (St. John 5:21) To work *with* the Christ through Divine-Image visualizations is to serve as His disciple on the highest level of apostolic service, for the healings and quickenings of others release Image-of-God *eternal* energies and blessings into their lives and beings. God rewards bountifully those who render service to Him and His children through love-inspired Divine-Image visualizations.

The chronic faultfinder has a compelling need to feel superior to others; and, by constantly looking for and criticizing their faults, he feeds an insatiable egotism.

Faultfinders have their own concepts about how every one else should live their lives, worship, dress, eat, think and behave. In this, the faultfinder delights in playing God, and tries to make persons over into his or her own image rather than inspiring them to fulfill the Divine Image.

Faultfinding for the sake of puffing up one's own ego is a negative spirit used by Satan to create unhappiness, disharmony and separation. *Petty* faultfinding is a combination of the spirit of pettiness and the spirit of faultfinding.

When one teaches God's Word to others, the Word of God becomes the revealer, healer and corrector of the faults of those who desire to be healed. The Word of God is the true judge of all faults and the healer of all faults.

When an unenlightened individual judges others, he does so on the personality levels of karma. He is not looking at another person as an evolving child of God being created in His Image through the energy-processes of Eternal Life.

A faultfinder assumes that he alone is perfect and knows better than God or any human being how life should be lived. Rarely do faultfinder persons observe the basic Commandments of God; rarely do they have self-control; rarely do they fulfill the Commandment of Love. Such is the nature of the faultfinder who is successfully deceiving himself while egotistically judging others.

The exorcism of the spirit of faultfinding is a major victory in the soul's record. When one can look upon the sins and faults of others and know that he, too, has committed the same sins and has expressed the same faults in his present life or in past lives, he is overcoming feelings and thoughts of superiority and separateness; and he is giving birth to the Virtues of Humility and Self-Honesty. By confessing the sins and faults of others as his own, he unites with the Forgiveness, Mercy and Compassion of God that produce healings, quickenings and exorcisms through the Christ. Such prayers of Dimensional Confession manifest great blessings in his own life and in the lives of others.

The egotism of thinking one's self to be superior to any person is callous self-deception, for in the soul's record of past lives one is guilty of all sins and faults common to the human spirit. To commune with the Image of God in his fellow man, a devotee cannot feel separate from any living soul. Separateness builds barriers between races, nations and religions; Divine-Image visualizations and blessings remove the barriers built through the sin of separateness.

When one confesses as his own the sins and faults of every person whom God places in his life from day to day — and humbly makes penance and restitution through selfless works and Divine-Image visualizations — his eyes are healed of the motes of faultfinding critical-mindedness, judging, self-deception, impatience, pride, separateness and other traits detrimental to spiritual progress. With the healing of these motes through the Father's Mercy and the Mediation of Christ Jesus, the devotee is able to visualize, bless and minister to the Divine Image in others. This is the beginning of his true union with the Wisdom, Glory and Love of God within His Image.

Heavenly Father, please heal me of the spirit of faultfinding and other motes in my eyes preventing me from beholding the Image Divine in

my fellow man. Let all be to Thy Glory, O Lord.
In Jesus' Name. Amen.

THE HIERARCHY NATURE

*Image in Man is perfect. God is the Power and
the Imager. Man's hierarchy nature contains the
Likeness of God and the Image of God. Whatever
man reproduces through his hierarchy nature is
destined to be in the Likeness of God.*

— Ann Ree Colton

THE HEAVEN WORLDS

*The higher energies of the Moon, the
Sun and the Planets.*

GRACE-STATES OF ENLIGHTENMENT.
THE HIERARCHY NATURE.

EQUANIMITY   DETACHMENT

THE PETTINESS BARRIER

THE WORLD OF SENSE-DISTRACTIONS

*The lower energies of the Moon, the
Sun and the Planets.*

PRODIGAL-SON ATTITUDES AND ENCLOSURES

When a devotee reverences the Image of God in each person in his life, he has begun to work with his hierarchy nature; he has transcended the Pettiness Barrier between the earth and Heaven. Free from the spirit of pettiness, he may think broad, noble and deep thoughts inspired by God's Holy Spirit.

The Omniscient Spirit of God *knows* when one is reverencing the Divine Image in his fellow man. Thus, the moment a devotee is exorcised and healed of the spirit of pettiness, his thoughts about the Image of God will expand into priceless insights and realizations.

To reverence the Image of God in every living soul is the one and only key to the Kingdom-of-God blessings of the hierarchy nature. As long as a devotee does not succumb to the tester's efforts to draw him downward to the low levels of pettiness, he will remain in a transcendent State of Grace.

The Pettiness Barrier challenges every devotee who desires to attain the Grace-States of Spiritual Enlightenment.

Pettiness is a state of consciousness. Compassion and detachment are a state of consciousness. A person in bondage to the spirit of pettiness has neither compassion nor detachment. Pettiness reveals a smallness of soul. Compassion reveals a greatness of soul.

> *There are few mighty mortal men. God gives authority to those who love, and who know the true authority to be the Law of God and the Will of God. He who names himself as an authority walks toward brambles and pitfalls, for he has a mind filled with fantasies and a will centered in self-delights. Earn thine authority by first cleansing away the small petty things, as thou wouldst sweep away the small fragments which make unsightly thy house. Believe on the greatness of thy soul so that thou might unite thyself with the greatness in the souls of immortal men.*
>
> — Ann Ree Colton

Every devotee of the Lord is weighed on the scales of the Sermon on the Mount. His worth to God is determined by his meekness and peacemaking ability. As long as he remains harmless, gentle, humble and cognizant of the Image of God in every living soul, he will express hierarchy-nature powers in service to God and the human spirit.

Love heals the emotions and the nervous system, and trans-energizes petty irritations into kindness, compassion and detachment. Detachment from all petty irritations enables one to remain centered in the Beatitudes and the Love-Commandment. Only when a servant of God is centered in the Ethics of Jesus can he express the hierarchy nature; and it is only through the hierarchy nature that he can utilize Divine-Image energies.

Christ Jesus makes possible one's communion with the Image of God within himself and within the ones for whom he is offering healing prayers. Even as the Son of God utilized His knowledge of the Image of God in his miraculous healings and exorcisms, so do those who heal in His Name draw upon the powerful energies of God's Image to manifest miracles of healing and exorcism.

Heavenly Father, I pray to fulfill my Vows as Thou wouldst have me fulfill them. Bless those whom I have offended through pettiness in thought, feeling, word and action. May I serve my fellow man with a right spirit of love, compassion and detachment. May Thy Light abide in me, that I may become a co-creator with Thee through the hierarchy nature and the Divine-Image Consciousness. In Jesus' Name. Amen.

Spiritual genius stems from the Divine Image. A devotee in harmony with the Celestial Cycles and energies is free to express his spiritual genius, individuality and uniqueness as a son of God. In this state of Transcendental life and being, he may express his hierarchy nature in communion with the *Flow* of Archetypal Knowledge from the Third Heaven.

Each zodiacal sign being expressed by the human spirit consists of lower and higher energies. As long as a person expresses the lower energies of his birth sign, he will express the negative sensitivities and pettiness common to his birth sign. The moment he begins to express the higher energies of his birth sign, Soul Grace and Divine Grace are free to move into his heart, mind and life through the higher-energy tides of the Moon, the Sun and the Planets.

When one utilizes the higher energies of the celestial bodies within the Solar System, he has begun to express his hierarchy nature. In time, the refining processes of the spiritual life will prepare him to receive the higher energies of the Stars and the Galaxies. This will produce the Galaxy Consciousness of the hierarchy nature. The Christ has come to grace each child of God with the Galaxy Consciousness.

The Galaxy Consciousness and the Divine-Image Consciousness are one.

Mercury, the planet closest to the Sun, is the smallest planet in the Solar System. Persons under the influence of the *lower* energies of Mercury are inclined to be absorbed with petty thoughts, judgings, criticisms and faultfindings. This is due to the contraclockwise energies in their lower chakras that draw upon the lower energies of the Moon, the Sun and the Planets. As a devotee overcomes the pettiness in his thoughts, he begins to unite with the *higher* energies of Mercury; and, in time, he will attain the Christ Mind.

Individuals born in the signs of Gemini and Virgo are especially vulnerable to the expression of pettiness when they respond to the lower energies of their governing planet, Mercury. However, through the Redemption Power of Jesus, sincere penitents and vigilant devotees born in Gemini and Virgo may accomplish a rapid union with the higher-energy wavelengths of Mercury; in this, they will begin to think sacred thoughts inspired by the Light of the Christ.

The Virgo gross-atom type of person falls in the category of the adversary-tester. The Gemini, when negative, also falls in the category of the adversary-tester. Both Virgo and Gemini being ruled by Mercury, the planet of the mind and the intelligences, when negative, become cruel assailants of the trusting side of the Heart Initiate.

— Ann Ree Colton

All twelve zodiacal prototypes are under Mercury's influences in varying degrees. While many persons are being initiated through the lower-energy wavelengths of Mercury, there are others who are responding to the higher-energy wavelengths of this powerful planet.

One who is united with the Christ as a faithful disciple and apostle is receptive to the higher energies of the Moon, the Sun and the Planets through the synchronized, clockwise energy-currents of his chakras.

All life revolves around the Image of God. The Image of God contains all that man will ever be in Eternal Life. When man on earth expresses the hierarchy nature, he will begin to understand the mighty Hierarchs working with the Stars and the Galaxies. Each Hierarch in the Universe is expressing a high degree of the Image of God that man also will express at some time in Life Everlasting.

The Christ came to enable man to be a full hierarch or son-of-God being.

— Ann Ree Colton

ETERNAL PATIENCE

In your patience possess ye your souls.

— St. Luke 21:19

The disciple should relate to the Eternals and work with Eternal Patience.

— Ann Ree Colton

"Love . . . is not easily provoked." (1 Corinthians 13:5)
The Commandment of Love inspires patience, kindness, and
a desire that all persons prosper physically, emotionally, mentally and spiritually. A love-filled patience is compassionate,
charitable, not easily offended or angered. Impatience is
quick to be offended and to express anger.

When one knows that every person is being created in the
Eternal Image of God, he expresses an enlightened patience
toward all souls in his life and in the world.

The patience of a true Teacher inspires him to be as loving the millionth time he teaches a key truth to resisting students as he was loving the first time he taught them the same
truth.

A teacher without love is without patience. A parent without love is without patience. An impatient teacher, minister,
priest or parent is not a good example to those under their
care.

> *I will not yield to irritations; for I know that irri-
> tation is the forerunner of anger, and that anger
> opens the door to the adversary.*
>
> — Ann Ree Colton

Petty irritations leading to impatience and explosive angers
denote that one has not earned spiritual insulation through
the energies of the Love-Commandment.

There are two kinds of worshippers: one desires to receive
whatever he can from God; the other seeks to give to God his
love, his life, his being. One who expresses the attitude of giving to God, rather than taking from Him, devotes his energies to patiently serving his fellow man. Such persons are well
on the way to receiving the Divine-Image Consciousness.

Those who desire to receive from God only for themselves
become impatient with Him; such persons have yet to unite
with the wisdom of Jesus within the words, *"It is more blessed
to give than to receive."* (Acts 20:35) The taker experiences

the diminishing of blessings; the giver who expresses patience experiences the expanding of blessings through God's Holy Increase. Persons who desire only to receive from God rather than to give to Him must evolve the spirit of giving in coming lives.

A devotee must be healed of *the spirit of irritation* before he can serve all types of persons in the world as an apostle of Jesus. Patience, equanimity, kindness, love and the abiding Presence of God and Christ within his being will bless others with healings, exorcisms and soul-grace quickenings.

As long as an aspirant is a victim to the spirit of petty irritations, he will continue to stumble on the Path. Increasing irritations with others remove many aspirants from the Path.

The spirit of petty irritations can work only through persons who are impatient. Petty irritations prevent the eyes from seeing the Image of God in others. When one is freed from the spirit of petty irritations through a love-inspired patience, he will be free to see the Image of God in his mate, children, co-disciples, friends and all other persons in the world.

> *O true and sweet Patience, thou art the virtue which is never conquered, but dost always conquer! Thou alone dost show whether the soul loves its Creator or no. Thou dost give us hope of Grace: thou art the solvent of hatred and rancour in the heart; thou dost free us from dislike of man; thou dost take all pain out of the soul; through thee the great burdens of many trials become light and through thee bitterness becomes sweet: in thee, Patience, queenly virtue, acquired with the memory of the Blood of Christ crucified, we find life.*
>
> *O Patience, how pleasing thou art! Oh Patience, what hope thou dost give to those who possess thee! . . . Thy vestment is embroidered with the different stars of all the virtues; because patience cannot*

be in the soul without the stars of all the virtues,
shining in the night of self-knowledge.

—Saint Catherine of Siena

Let patience have her perfect work, that ye may
be perfect and entire, wanting nothing.

—James 1:4

Because thou hast kept the word of my patience,
I also will keep thee from the hour of temptation.

—Revelation 3:10

19

RAPE OF THE ALTAR

Test everything. Lay hold upon that which is good. Similarly, do not treat with contempt the Image of God. Moreover, keep diligently thy youth with all care, in order that thou mayest be able to keep diligently thine old age with all care, lest thou be put to shame.

—Coptic Apocrypha

ONENESS THROUGH ENLIGHTENMENT

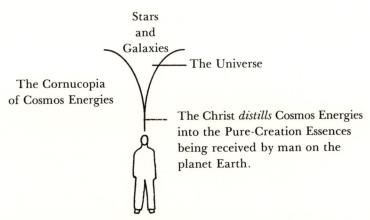

Stars
and
Galaxies

The Universe

The Cornucopia
of Cosmos Energies

The Christ *distills* Cosmos Energies into the Pure-Creation Essences being received by man on the planet Earth.

All Stars and Galaxies are in each healing on Earth. All Stars and Galaxies are in each inspiration received by the mind of man.

All Celestial Creations in the vast Universe are one through the Image of God. The energies within all Stars and Galaxies are working together in one accord. The Christ gathers the powerful Energies of the Cosmos and distills them into sacred essences of healing and inspiration on the planet Earth. When one thanks God for a healing or for a holy inspiration, he is thanking the entire Universe of Stars and Galaxies, for God is the Totality of Universal Creation!

The Spirit of God is the Omnipresent Intelligence creating all worlds. The Image of God is the One Blueprint for all past, present and future creations in the Universe.

The Christ came to remove the barriers between races, nations and religions through His teaching of the Eternal Commandment of Love. He also came to remove the veils between men on Earth and the Cosmos.

Through the Divine-Image Consciousness, there is no sense of separation from any soul on Earth or any Star and Galaxy in the Universe. All life is one within the One Spirit and Image of God.

"God is a Spirit." (St. John 4:24) God is the *Spirit* within all seen and unseen Creations in the Universe; the Christ, His Beloved Son, is the *Light* within all seen and unseen Creations in the Universe. *"I am the light of the world."* (St. John 8:12)

All Cosmos Energies and Degrees of Light are *one* in God. Man is one with the entire Universe through the Spirit and Light within his being. The Christ is awakening man to the reality of his oneness with the Cosmos.

> *Those who are outgoing and are charged with holy magnetism know no separateness.*
> — Ann Ree Colton

Separateness is nonexistent in the Spirit of God and the Light of the Christ. Separateness exists only in the minds of unenlightened men. Feelings and thoughts of separateness promote prejudice, bigotry and narrow-mindedness. The closer the heart and the mind come to God and Christ, the more one overcomes separateness in thinking and feeling, and the more he attains the enlightened state of *oneness* with All Creation.

Separateness is enclosure-thinking. As long as a person feels separate from any Soul on Earth or any Star in the Universe, he is in an enclosure. Each enclosure is an energy-field of Learning. Each anti-virtue represents an enclosure energy-field containing important lessons regarding Scriptural Laws and Holy Virtues. Races, nations and religions represent the larger enclosure energy-fields of Learning. Families and groups represent the smaller enclosure energy-fields of Learning.

Religions in which men and women do not worship side by side have enclosures within enclosures. They not only feel separate from other religions, but the men and women in their midst are separated from each other in their sanctuaries of worship.

For thousands of years, religions, nations, races and families have believed that men are superior to women. In the present time, this attitude of male-superiority is locked in the ancestral genes of many persons. The result is separateness.

Through union with the Image of God, separateness energy-enclosures disappear, for the heart and the mind know that male and female are *equal* in importance within the process of Universal Creation.

Separateness-thinking is spiritual ignorance. Oneness-thinking is the beginning of Enlightenment. Thoughts of superiority of one sex over the other is Anti-Image. Even as male and female are equally joined during the act of procreation, so are they equally joined in the quest for Spiritual Illumination.

The healing of gene-caused attitudes of separateness moves one to higher plateaus of understanding from which he can behold the Masculine and Feminine Principles and Polarities of God's Image as Eternal Constants present in all Cosmos Creations.

The union of the Masculine and the Feminine Polarities within one's being produces a Bliss-Communion with the Godhead. The closer one comes to this cardinal truth of Enlightenment, the more the mote of separateness is removed from his eyes. With the healing of separateness come new freedoms in heart and mind that give a clearer vision of the Image of God in earth and in the starry heavens.

During the past 2,000 years, the Christ has been accomplishing His Messianic task of overcoming separateness in the world. Doors closed for centuries between races, nations and religions are beginning to open; the knowledge of the Cosmos is increasing in each decade. Separateness is being overcome; with the total healing of separateness will come an enlightened consciousness aware of the oneness between all Souls and all Stars.

> *Now it came to pass that man lacked a help-mate that was his equal. God created this help-mate in the form of a woman—a mirror image of all that was latent in the male sex. In this way, man and woman are so intimately related that one is the work of the other. Man can not be called man without the woman. The woman is the labor of the man. The man is an aspect of comfort for the woman. One does not have the capacity of living without the other. Man is an allusion to the divinity of the Godhead; woman is a reference to the humanity of the Son of God.*
>
> —Hildegard of Bingen

Masters of Separation

The greatest sin in the world is separation.
Separateness in religion is an outrage against God.
— Ann Ree Colton

The Altar in sanctuaries and in homes gives testimony of man's faith in God. From century to century, the Altar has remained the most cherished reminder of the Power of the Almighty. Many lives have been spent in serving the Altar. Many lives have been lost while protecting the Altar.

To reverence the Altar of God in one's home or in a sanctuary of worship is to reverence the Creator of Life on Earth and in the Star-filled Heavens.

The history of religions in the world is stained with the sins of murders, tortures, atrocities, assassinations and wars commissioned by religious leaders. *Each sin committed by a religious leader against his fellow man is a rape of the Altar, a betrayal of the Image of God.*

In modern times, priests addicted to alcohol and tobacco; child-molesters in ministries; adulterous ministers; greed-motivated exploiters of God's Word; and many other offenders of Holy Laws, Virtues and the Body Temple in the religions of the world are betraying the Image of God. Their crimes are crimes against their souls and against the Altar of God that they have covenanted to serve.

The chronic pettiness of many religious leaders makes of them masters of separation rather than masters of enlightenment. Petty differences in doctrine keep religious ministries separated from each other, and therefore separated from the Image of God in each other.

Religious leaders in bondage to the spirit of pettiness are betraying the souls of persons in their charge and are perpetuating petty rivalries between churches and religions rather than fostering the spirit of brotherhood, friendship and love.

Pettiness and prejudice are sicknesses corrupting the soul of religion.

> *A creedless soul strives for an atmosphere free of bigotry, prejudice and dogma.*
> *Prejudice and separateness are time-consuming and corroding.*
> *To be creedless is to love all men as souls imaged in the likeness of God.*
>
> —Ann Ree Colton

"Father, forgive them, for they know not what they do." (St. Luke 23:24) In the drama of Jesus' Crucifixion, the Roman soldiers did what their ancestors had been doing for thousands of years—kill their enemies. The Hebrew priests did what their ancestors had been doing for centuries—kill the prophets, the anointed. When people are responding to the reflexes established in their genes by their ancestors, "they know not what they do"; they become automatons expressing the same hates, the same prejudices, the same compulsions to kill as did their ancestors.

Judas was filled with race-pride; he wanted to free his race from the cruel hand of Rome. Judas was the disciple of Jesus most strongly influenced by the ancestral genes of his race; therefore, he was the one who betrayed Jesus and caused His Crucifixion and Martyrdom. The petty hates of Judas saturating his ancestral genes caused his fall from grace.

Ancestral-gene karma reproduces the anti-virtue reflexes and sensitivities of one's ancestors and parents in his own responses to life. If his ancestors and parents were prejudiced toward a particular race or religion, he will be inclined to express the same prejudices. Thus, century after century, the sin of prejudice continues to be passed on through the genes of millions of persons. The wars and separateness caused by racial, national and religious prejudices are as old as history and are part of modern times. These wars based upon the

gene root-compulsions of prejudice, hatred, anger and covetousness will continue from generation to generation until
men realize that they are merely repeating the same sins as
their ancestors and parents.

There is no greater tyranny than *gene-tyranny*. Ancestors
steeped in sin, prejudice and covetousness for ages of time are
tyrannizing their offspring through the genes. The evils being perpetuated in modern times in the name of religion are
manifesting through persons unaware that their gene-inherited traits are compelling them to sin through inhumanity,
immorality, prejudice and separateness.

The desire to do good is also in the genes inherited from
ancestors who expressed virtues rather than a warrior or hostile spirit. In the spiritual life, one must identify the negative
and positive inheritances in his genes. His success on the Path
is determined by his becoming detached from all negative
ancestral-gene compulsions, attitudes, sensitivities and reflexes. This detachment can occur only through the Miracle-
Grace of the Lord Jesus and His command over all energy-
processes affecting the human spirit.

All persons who are lying, cheating, stealing, committing
adultery, hurting one another, warring in nations, races,
religions, families and marriages are victims of the same sin-
offenses committed by ancestors and parents. There is *no*
difference between their sins and their ancestors' sins, for all
are linked together through the genes and the chromosomes.

Male priests and ministers with strong prejudices toward
other religions, nations or the opposite sex are victims of
prejudices inherited through their ancestral genes and past
lives. A priest or minister who expresses prejudice toward
other races, religions or individuals is failing to reverence the
Image of God in his fellow man.

Male priests and ministers who express any degree of prejudice toward women becoming ordained Altar-servers are offending the Image of God. Until their prejudices are healed,

they will remain unenlightened regarding the Holy Image. Also, they subject themselves to coming lives when, as women, they will invite prejudices from others.

Prejudice toward the opposite sex is a major offense against the Image of God in oneself as well as in others. To limit or prevent any person's spiritual, creative or educational growth because of his or her race, religion or sex is a cardinal offense against the Image of God.

Father, may the leaders of nations and religions be inspired by Thy Love, Compassion and Wisdom. In Jesus' Name. Amen.

Prejudice in thought becomes a destructive, laser-like energy when directed toward any person, race, nation or religion. Thus, when a priest, minister or other servant of God holds prejudice in his thoughts and feelings, his prayers and meditations contain a destructive cursing-energy rather than a creative love-energy stemming from a reverence for the Image of God in every living soul.

Prejudice is an offense against the Commandment of Love as well as the Image of God; a number of cardinal virtues are also violated. Therefore, any priest, minister or other religious server who retains any shadow of prejudice is failing to express an unconditional, sweet, pure, holy love toward all souls being created in God's Image and Likeness. Such prejudiced persons in religious ministries and spiritual teachings have yet to evolve the clean hands and pure hearts necessary to unite with the Kingdom of God.

A prejudiced priest or minister who inspires others to express his prejudices is rendering a disservice to God. Prejudices create separateness. Love overcomes separateness. Love for the Image of God in all souls and in all Solar Systems opens wide the Door to Heaven's Light and Grace.

Prejudice and pettiness are two major reasons why many

priests and ministers and others in religious ministries fail to qualify for the Divine-Marriage Anointing.

Prejudice keeps one from seeing the Image of God in others. Pettiness keeps him from serving the Image of God in others.

Pettiness and anger form a deadly combination of dark energies, for if one's petty desires are not realized, he will express temper tantrums and anger tirades. If he is a religious leader with many followers, he can inspire them to do great harm to others.

Saul of Tarsus was responding to his ancestral-gene compulsion to kill worshippers in another faith; thus, he joined his fellow Hebrews in the persecution and murder of the first followers of Jesus. On the road to Damascus, the blazing light of Christ Jesus flooded the entire being of Saul. All of his ancestral genes and chromosomes became totally healed and transformed in a moment's encounter with the Christ Light, thereby making of him an illumined Christian. Such is the nature and power of the mighty Light of the Christ!

The past lives recorded in the soul of Saint Paul saved him from continuing as a persecutor of others through ancestral-gene compulsions and opened him to the Christ Light. The conversion of Saul the slayer to Paul the Apostle of Jesus, occurring in the twinkling of an eye, gives testimony to the Miraculous Power of the Christ to transform the genes and the chromosomes from ancestral sin-expressions to Soul-Grace memories and Divine-Image energies.

Heavenly Father, may the Lord Christ cleanse my genes and chromosomes of all impurities and wrong tendencies, that I might serve Thee with clean hands and a pure heart. In Jesus' Name. Amen.

Part V

20

IMAGE-OF-GOD GENETICS

The marriage between the scientific and the spiritual will give birth to a science of genetic understanding that will unite man with all Stars and Galaxies in their Songs of Creation.

THE CODE OF COSMOS

The student-disciple undergoeth the disciplines, that he may speak the Image-language of the Inner Worlds.

—Ann Ree Colton

The Creator is beginning to teach His children about His Eternal Plan through *Image-of-God Genetics.* Throughout many ages, men and women have struggled to reach this present era of scientific brilliance; they now stand on the threshold of major breakthroughs in comprehending the chromosomes and their relationship to the Cosmos. The threadlike chromosomes are microscopic representations of the threadlike formations of Stars and Galaxies strung on invisible energy-lines throughout the vast Universe.

The science of genetic engineering is leading to knowledge of profound significance. As scientists explore and discover the secrets and mysteries of the genetic code, the world is being prepared for the time when men will decipher the Divine-Image Code. *The Divine-Image Code and the Code of Cosmos are one.*

The Divine-Image Code relates to the sanctification of the genes and the chromosomes that produces illumined sons and daughters of the Living God. When the genes and the chromosomes are anointed by the Holy Spirit, they are free to express their higher levels of Divine-Image potential, thereby producing the hierarchy-like or son-of-God nature of man.

The genes and the chromosomes function most naturally when fulfilling their Divine-Image design. No longer burdened by sin-residue, they are free to transmit and receive telepathies on dimensional wavelengths of light and love under command of the Christ. Through Image-of-God Genetics, man is destined for greatness of soul through which he will become a co-creator with God on a Cosmos level; he will be a prophet and revelator utilizing the same Principles of Holy Telepathy that unite all Illumined Beings and Presences throughout the Universe.

The genes, the chromosomes, the nervous system and the soul — when centered in Scriptural Laws and Virtues — become powerful senders and receivers of the spiritual wavelengths of telepathy beyond Time and Space. Illuminative secrets of the Godhead and the Galaxies are revealed through the mighty telepathic capabilities of the genes, the chromosomes, the nervous system and the soul working in harmony with the Image of God.

The Christ, the Son of the Living God, is preparing the human spirit to comprehend the energy-dynamics and Cycles of the Soul, the Divine Image, the Solar System and the Universe. A continuous flow of inspiring realizations and revelations of Cosmic and Cosmos knowledge will manifest through His *Redemption Grace*.

Redemption must take place in the cells, the chromosomes, the genes and the DNA before a truth-seeker can become totally new in body, heart, mind, soul and spirit. Redemption born of repentance and contrition leads to soul-freedoms and archetypal revelations through the Christ Mind.

Redemption Grace provides the insulation from the forces in the world that seek to corrupt the genes and the chromosomes. To be redeemed through the Mercy of God and the Dimensional Power of the Christ is to experience the priceless rewards and inheritances of Spiritual Illumination.

Through repentance and contrition, the soul and the Divine Image energize the genes and the chromosomes with sacred energies, providing the DNA molecules with *eternal memories* and virtue-reflexes blessed by the Spirit of God. The Divine-Image Code regarding Eternal Life and Cosmos Creation begins to be deciphered through Holy-Spirit symbols, energies and memories. This is the high State of Grace being opened to the human spirit by the Great Redeemer, Christ Jesus.

The teachings of Jesus are the most powerful healers of the genes and the chromosomes. Devotees who experience the healing energies within His words and within the Sacrament of Communion are utilizing the dynamic principles of Image-of-God Genetics.

> *Man is more than the result of biological passion. He is more than the influence of a gene.*
>
> *Personality is a cloak put on in each life. God-divinity in man must be recognized as the true-identity countenance expressed in each life through the soul. This Image Divine desires to come forth, to manifest, to express. Man gives it freedom through love of God as his true Parent, Imager, Maker, Creator.*
>
> —Ann Ree Colton

CONTRITION

For thus saith the high and lofty One that inhabiteth eternity, whose name is Holy; I dwell in the high and holy place, with him also that is of a contrite and humble spirit, to revive the spirit of the humble, and to revive the heart of the contrite ones.

—Isaiah 57:15

What dost Thou chiefly require of a guilty and wretched sinner, but that he heartily repent, and humble himself for his sins. In true contrition and humility of heart is brought forth hope of forgiveness: a troubled conscience is reconciled; grace that was lost is recovered; a man is secured from the wrath to come, and God meets the penitent soul in the holy kiss of peace.

—Saint Thomas a Kempis

All prodigal-son tribulations and troubles are stern lessons that are seeking to inspire attitudes of repentance and contrition. Through repentance, contrition, confession and works of penance and restitution, the Christ becomes one's Teacher and restores his genes and chromosomes to their Image-of-God sacred purposes.

Contrition makes of one's repentance a whole and pure offering to God. As long as contrition is in the heart, a penitent will experience the cleansings and quickenings within the genes and the chromosomes that will free the gifts and powers of his soul.

The Path leading from the prodigal-son states of consciousness to Spiritual Enlightenment may require countless lifetimes or one lifetime—depending upon one's contrition and his faith in the Mercy of God and the Redemption Power of His Son. *"According to your faith be it unto you."* (St. Matthew 9:29)

There are seven stages that lead a prodigal son to Spiritual

Insulation and Illumination. Each progressive stage represents a profound transformation on the level of the genes and the chromosomes.

1. *Non-Identification.*   Persons express negative genetic traits without conscience.

2. *Identification.*   One begins to have a conscience when he expresses a negative genetic trait.

3. *Desire.*   There is the desire to be healed of negative genetic traits.

4. *Repentance, Contrition and Confession.*   Through reverent prayer, a wholehearted repentance and a contrite heart, the negative gene-traits are confessed to God.

5. *Penance and Restitution.*   There is the desire to make penance and restitution for all times one expressed negative genetic traits.

6. *Love and Compassion.*   One expresses love and compassion toward those placed in his life who are expressing the same negative genetic traits for which he is making penance and restitution.

7. *Spiritual Insulation and Enlightenment.*   The seventh stage produces the Spiritual Insulation through which a devotee-initiate may minister to those afflicted by negative gene-traits without judging them or feeling superior to them. In this, he becomes an enlightened servant of God and apostle of Christ Jesus. The seventh stage represents a major breakthrough to the understanding of the genes and the chromosomes as revealers of the Divine-Image Code and the Code of Cosmos.

Man reaches Jesus through contrition, confession and admission of wrongdoing, and thus frees his conscience. The most heavy sinner condemned by his own sense of guilt, when contrite—calling upon the Saints for redemption—has begun his own pilgrimage toward becoming a Saint.

A whole and right contrition is the emptying out of non-virtue. The emptiness gained from a whole contrition is refilled with a right and true Apostolic virtue in which the grace of the gifts supplants the load of sin, changing sin into powers for the Holy Spirit.

—Ann Ree Colton

THE HOLY WAR

And fear not them which kill the body, but are not able to kill the soul: but rather fear him which is able to destroy both body and soul in hell.
—St. Matthew 10:28

The Holy War between the Christ and the Antichrist is raging every moment of the day and the night. This battle for the souls of men is occurring on the level of the genes and the chromosomes.

God graces each of His children with the Gift of Volition. Through volition, one may choose to destroy his own life or the lives of others, or he may choose to reverence life and to create beauty in the world. Through volition, he has the free will to choose the Christ as his Teacher or the Antichrist as his teacher.

When men turn away from God, they turn toward the Antichrist who uses the energies of sin to teach lessons of pain, misery and sorrow.

Satan is a skillful genetic engineer. If he is successful in enticing a person into repetitive sins, each sin produces memory and reflex responses in the DNA that continue to reproduce sinful behavior as a way of life. In this, one becomes a sin-clone responding to the genetic conditioning by the Antichrist. Such persons place tremendous burdens upon their offspring for generations and also burden their own coming lives.

Evil men, addicts, cruel men, alcoholics, violent men, prejudiced men, perverted men — all have undergone engineering of their genes by the Antichrist. They are reacting to life and their fellow man exactly as Satan has programmed them.

All victims of the Antichrist genetic-engineering are compelled to destroy either themselves or others. Christ-blessed individuals who are expressing the pure tones of the Image of God are endowed with the desire to create beauty, harmony and peace in the world.

All transgressions against human decency and morality reveal the destructive influences of the Antichrist. The Evil One seeks to draw unwary individuals lower and lower on the ladder of reincarnation. Satan uses his knowledge of reincarnation to alter a sin-prone person's genes from life to life. In this way, he adds to his army of clone-like puppets who eagerly embrace life after life of crime, violence, immorality, perversion and addiction.

The Christ came to free all souls from bondage to the Antichrist. However, a person must *desire* to be free before his genes and chromosomes can be restored to their Image-of-God beauty, virtue and potential.

> *To tamper with or disarrange the genes through physical means is a sin against the Holy Ghost. The human race is in danger of becoming degenerated when men seek to exploit or to manipulate the forces controlling birth and death. This is the work of God and the Holy Ghost.*
>
> — Ann Ree Colton

A national leader, such as Adolph Hitler, would not hesitate to use scientific knowledge of genetic engineering to make human beings into an image of his choosing. This is the danger in genetic engineering by scientists and political leaders whose concepts of good and evil fall far short of the teachings of Jesus of Nazareth.

Holocausts on the genetic-engineering level will be an increasing danger in the world, endangering entire races and cultures. Unless the Ethics of Jesus are accepted by the world family of nations, gene-tampering by unethical scientists and others will produce calamities of monumental proportions.

God has mighty Laws that protect His Image and His Evolutionary Process. The sooner mankind familiarizes itself with Image-of-God Genetics, the more quickly will the human spirit become enlightened in the Ethics and Principles of Universal Creation as related to life on the planet Earth and life in the Cosmos.

The Christ has come to the world to seal into the human spirit the importance of Ethics. These Ethics are based upon ageless Scriptural values.

Through the Christ, the Image of God sounds its powerful-sweet Tones of Healing and Pure Creation through all genes and chromosomes. One who responds to these Image-of-God Tones expresses a newborn spiritual individuality and uniqueness through which he may begin his communion with the Three Heavens and with the Cosmos wavelengths of Revelatory Telepathy.

Gene-gravity holds one to the lower nature and the Ancestral-Sin Core. *Gene-freedom* occurs when the Christ Light transforms the genes and the chromosomes, thereby filling one's emotions and thoughts with the transcendental energies of the Love Core, the Soul Core and the Divine-Image Core.

**Heavenly Father, may Thy Image sound forth
its Sacred Tones of Holy Creation.**

CHRIST CYCLES

> *The Angels are the guardians of the genes, and the Hierarchs are the guardians of the chromosomes.*
> *The Sun is the energy used by Hierarchy to stabilize the chromosomes and balance them. Hierarchy works with the chromosomes. The planets, the Moon and the Angels work with the genes.*
> — Ann Ree Colton

The Solar-System Cycles play prominent roles in Image-of-God Genetics. The understanding of these Sacred Cycles enables one to work with the Spirit of God blessing the earth and its inhabitants through the rhythmic energy-influences of the Moon, the Sun and the Planets. All Solar-System Cycles, Seasonal Cycles and Holy-Day Cycles affecting the genes and the chromosomes are *Christ Cycles.* When the cycles of one's life move in perfect harmony with the Christ Cycles, he is one with the Creation-Energies of the Will and Word of God.

Holy vows build the Spiritual Insulation through which one becomes an enlightened servant of God at one with all Christ Cycles. Vows-Insulation protects every cell, chromosome and gene in the Body Temple, thereby enabling him to express his Divine-Image versatilities with joy and effortless effort.

To remain in a State of Grace requires utmost vigilance. The moment one permits negative thoughts or emotions to control his speech and actions, he invites intrusion through unwholesome genetic-tendencies. These intrusions indicate that he has yet to build a protective Insulation through holy vows kept in service to God.

To Vows-Insulated souls, the Christ removes the Veil to the Cosmos; one by one, the secrets and mysteries of God's Universe are revealed in their simplicity and splendor.

Telepathy may be on the level of the soul, the mind or the

genes. Gene-telepathy may be harmful or helpful, depending upon the lawfulness or unlawfulness of one's parents and ancestors living and deceased. Telepathic intrusion from negative ancestors is a commonplace occurrence, as such ancestors seek to control one's thoughts, marriage, family and life through gene-telepathy. Gene-telepathy blessings are also a reality through honorable, ethical and noble ancestors on earth and in Heaven.

A husband and wife giving birth to their Divine-Image natures are free from ancestral intrusions through the genes. The Image of God, as a Great Diamond, begins to radiate its beauteous facets through the married couple. In a spiritual-creative marriage, the masculine and feminine polarities within the husband and the wife are harmoniously blended and polarized.

As many persons grow older, they revert more and more to negative ancestral tendencies toward complaining, bitterness and meanness. Individuals who have made their peace with God express increasing degrees of Soul Grace, Higher-Self Grace and Divine-Image Grace as they grow older; such persons become sweeter, wiser, and more virtuous in their latter years.

The *ancestral image* is the foe of spiritual individuality. Spiritual individuality blossoms through the sanctified energies of the Image of God. The Image of God is *pure-creation* energies. Through spiritual individuality, one expresses pure-creation energies in service to God and man.

The Image of God is in the core of every cell; therefore, when a seeker after truth prays to be healed and redeemed, the powerful energies of the Divine Image are activated within every atom of his being. In this, he is healed and cleansed of ancestrally-inherited memories feeding and fueling negative behavior patterns, reflexes, grooves and molds.

The inner cleansing and healing of the DNA molecules, genes, chromosomes and cells through the Image of God are synchronized to the outer-world energy-dynamics and Cycles of the Moon, the Sun, the Planets, the Stars and the Galaxies. Thus, a true spiritual transformation involves inner and outer energy-processes that contribute increasingly to one's communion with the Spirit of God within the Soul, the Higher Self and the Divine Image.

The more one loves all persons with a holy love, the closer he is to the Image of God. Holy love enables a devotee to unite with the Illumination-Grace Flows from the Greater Archetypes within the Third Heaven. These majestic Archetypes link this Solar System with the Archetypes and the Heavens of all other Solar Systems in the Universe.

All treasures of knowledge, wisdom and grace-gifts are available to man through the Image of God. Over the ages and the eternals, every living soul will continue to reincarnate until he becomes like Jesus; in time, the Jesus-Man Prototype levels of expression and creation through the Image of God will be fulfilled in the world. More and more will the meek and the pure in heart inherit stewardship of the energies of the Earth and work consciously with the creation-energies of the Cosmos. When this occurs, new wonders and dimensional capabilities will manifest through the Image of God, illuminating the Jesus-like souls on the exalted levels of life, being and consciousness.

The Image of God is the Key to comprehending the Cosmos.

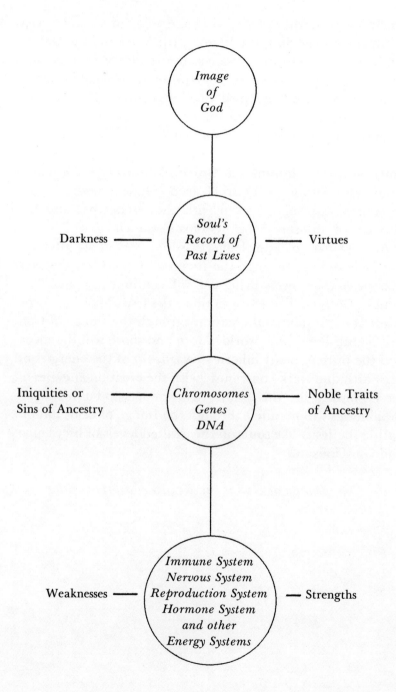

21

HEREDITY AND REINCARNATION

Personalities that are negative as a result of the working of the law of reincarnation and heredity can be changed by proper methods of concentration, spiritual discipline, and continuous mental and physical effort.

— Paramahansa Yogananda

The ancestral memory is seeking to immortalize itself at all times in its offspring or progeny. One must open the grace of ancestry and die to the ancestral forebearers' negative inclinations and compulsions.

The seer as a prophet crosses the bridge of the lower subconscious, which relates to gene-memory and the reincarnation soul-processes of the past. Having mastered these, he walks beyond the abyss into the Bridge of Light where he makes union with his hierarchy nature and becomes an imager-creator for God.

— Ann Ree Colton

Lawful and Unlawful Ancestors

The law of the Lord is perfect.

— Psalm 19:7

God's perfect Law of Attraction determines the strengths and weaknesses one inherits through his genes and chromosomes at the time of conception. Whether he is born in a family heavy-laden with ancestral sins or blessed with beautiful ancestral grace is determined by his soul's record of previous lives.

In every person's ancestral background, there have been lawful and unlawful ancestors. The attitudes and actions of these lawful and unlawful ancestors are passed on to their offspring as *tendencies* through the genes and the chromosomes.

Each time one reincarnates in the world, his past lives determine the genes that will influence his present life. If his previous lives were selfish and unlawful, he will function through a gene-mathematics linking him with the attitudes and reflexes of unlawful ancestors. If his former lives were selfless and lawful, he will express gene-traits similar to lawful ancestors.

Through God's Gift of Volition, each person has the free will to determine whether or not he will live according to the Commandments of God. If he chooses to ignore these Scriptural Statutes, he is responding to the strong influences of unlawful ancestors; his genes and chromosomes *compel* him to think, feel and act in manners contrary to the Commandments of God. However, if he uses the Gift of Volition to fulfill all Holy Laws and Commandments, he is blessed with the gene-tendencies of reverent, lawful ancestors.

When a person *desires* to unite with God in the Divine Marriage, the moment he steps foot on the Spiritual Path he becomes involved in a fierce tug-of-war occurring in his genes—a war between his unlawful and lawful ancestors. If his unlawful and unrighteous ancestors prevail, he will leave the Path; if his lawful and righteous ancestors are victorious, he will continue on the Path. The powerful genetic influences of unlawful ancestors account for the great number of probationers who forsake the Path and choose to live mundane, materialistic lives with little or no thought upon God and His Laws.

> *The record in the Undersoul inevitably calls for payment of karmic debts incurred by one's ancestors and ego in former times. One must battle the memory flowing from the attitudes and prejudices of ancestors.*
>
> *All initiates have the power to break the inherent genetic karmic chains; however, if untrained or faulty sentiment is present, one is subjected to intermittent genetic, karmic, possessive intrusion from the ancestral dead and from the living.*
>
> — Ann Ree Colton

Individuals who survive the tenacious tug-of-war occurring in the genes between unlawful and lawful ancestral tendencies do so because of a saving grace through their own past lives of reverence, faith and devotion to God.

Through the fulfillment of Scriptural Laws coupled with a constancy in love, renunciation, detachment, selflessness and other holy virtues, a devotee of the Lord remains *free* from the negative gene-influences of his unlawful ancestors.

If an aspirant wavers in his attitudes toward Sacred Laws, he will waver in his vows to God. His vacillations reveal that he is still subject to the influences of his unlawful ancestors affecting him through gene-reflexes.

Lust, greed, anger, pride, jealousy, prejudice, covetousness and all other anti-virtues reveal one's allegiance with unlawful ancestors. Such persons pass on these negative gene-reflexes to their offspring as heavy sin-burdens.

Every individual experiences seven-year cycles of absorption of past-lives' negative and positive memories; his cells also undergo cyclic changes in seven-year intervals. During a seven-year cycle, he may revert to immature, immoral or egotistical tendencies inherited from previous lives and gene-tendencies, or he may be the recipient of virtues, talents and soul-gifts. Thus, there are new energies, both positive and negative, coming forth through his genes and soul's record that must be identified, purified and harmonized if he is to remain in a State of Grace.

Any hypersensitivity resulting in irritability, moods, angers, tantrums, depressions and pettiness keeps one united with every ancestor who ever expressed these dark energies. The healing of insensitivities and hypersensitivities by Christ Jesus is one's first freedom from ancestral-gene karma and past-lives' karma, and his beginning to unite with Redemption Grace as a liberated soul blessed with virtue and love.

An insensitive student on the Path has not been quickened spiritually. A hypersensitive student is being quickened but has yet to make a full linking with the Redemption Grace of the Christ through the Love Commandment. A student with holy sensitivities is blessed with the peace, love and gifts that come through the Supernatural Presence of the Christ within Redemption Grace.

Even as millenniums were necessary for man to evolve his five senses to their present state of perception, so will future ages witness the evolution of his higher or holy sensitivities manifesting through the Image of God. To understand *the science of sensitivities* is of utmost importance to all who would become students and teachers of Image-of-God Genetics.

The ability to fulfill Marriage Vows and Ministry Vows relates directly to one's ancestral-gene reflexes and past-lives' attitudes. As long as a husband and wife are exposed to ancestral-sin energies permeating their genes and chromosomes, they will be unable to express a constancy in love toward God or one another. Their Marriage Vows will be forgotten as they succumb to ancestrally-inherited traits of pettiness, jealousy, quarrelsomeness and unforgiveness.

Marriage immediately exposes one to the genetic tendencies of his mate. If a newlywed expresses selfishness, is a money tyrant or is plagued with temperament problems, he or she has reverted to negative ancestral-gene tendencies. Selflessness, generosity and self-control are blessings inherited through ancestral-gene virtue-strengths and past-lives' noble traits.

"And ye shall hear of wars and rumours of wars." (St. Matthew 24:6) Persons in nations, races and religions inclined toward warrior tendencies, covetousness and prejudice have inherited ancestral genes that sound these predominant anti-virtue tones. The lessons being experienced through wars between nations are seeking to teach mankind *basic* virtues that would avoid the pain, misery and death caused by the mass destruction of human life.

Warlike tendencies passed on through the chromosomes and the genes make of certain nations, races and religions militant aggressors whose main desire is to dominate and manipulate other nations, races and religions. This warrior tendency passed on through the genes is as old as life on Earth. There is no genetic difference between the first person who ever killed another human being in a war and individuals in modern times who are still killing each other through wars. Evolution through the chromosomes and the genes is a very slow process. Killing through wars; individuals committing murder; immorality and all other negative behavior expressions reveal ancestral-gene influences and soul-record tendencies yet steeped in anti-virtue darkness.

The rare soul who turns toward God in any age or time must experience the healing of all negative ancestral-gene tendencies to sin and all past-lives' tendencies to sin recorded in the soul's record. The fact that these powerful dark-energy influences can be healed is a most beautiful miracle of God's Love, Mercy and Forgiveness. However, before this healing can occur within the cells, the chromosomes, the genes and the soul's record, one must make a clean break with darkness and embrace light. Many persons vacillate between darkness and light. Others think through gray-zones of consciousness; the difference between good and evil, virtue and vice, is unclear to them. Before the spiritual transformation process may occur in one's present lifetime, he must develop a keen sense of knowing the difference between right and wrong.

The Wisdom of God revealed through the Lord Jesus, the Prophets and the Saints gives a crystal-clear comprehension of the difference between lawful and unlawful behavior. As one lives according to Scriptural Laws and Virtues, he moves quickly from anti-virtue darkness to the light of oneness with the *Presence* of God within Truth, Wisdom, Love and Joy. For him, the spiritual life with its wonders and miracles has begun.

In each life one expresses a prototypal identity in which he has companion egos infusing their imaging upon him as an identity.. One must be free of imposed identity images. He must stand forth as divinely conceived and imaged by God, the Infinite Imager of all.

Persons related to man by blood seek to imprint or impress upon the mind and emotions of each one ancestral identities *rather than* divine identity.

The higher-genesis mind does not discard his ancestral strengths, nor his own reincarnation strengths from past lives. With open sight he sees and assesses the weaknesses and the strengths. He chooses the positive rather than the negatives of his physical and karmic heritages. Through the high suggestibles, he builds upon the divine strengths in his own divinity under God. He does not reject ancestry, but he refuses to live within the restrictions of negative impressionability, and thus opens himself to the Voice of God reminding him of his true nature and being.

In Great-Soul birth, one is a sun outshining the candle of gene and chromosome memory, overwhelming the instinctual of the race, of the genesis. Beyond genes, *they come, enlarged by the Eternals, one destiny, one goal, functioning within the manifold of Dimensional Consciousness. They are of the first Living Waters or Breath of the Purusha.**

—Ann Ree Colton

GENETIC TENDENCIES

Bald people are descended from bald people, people with blue eyes from people with blue eyes, and squinting persons from squinting persons . . . at least in the majority of cases.

—Hippocrates

All in God's Image are blameless and innocent. Man cannot be free to become a whole person radiating the total soul-light until he becomes one with God through the Commandment of "Love Ye One Another."

When one dedicates to love God with all his heart, his mind, and his soul, love will reorient him to a world of perfect relationships. The ancestral memory cells of the body will respond to the curative and exhilarating elixir of love. If there be ancestral memory of non-loving and abuse, perfect love will cleanse away the mirrored offences registered and mirrored in each cell of blood-memory.

The sins of the fathers are overcome through spiritual transenergization processes.

—Ann Ree Colton

Powerful Laws of the Universe govern the genes and the chromosomes. The moral, ethical and spiritual lessons being taught by these Laws may be temporarily avoided; however, the longer they are ignored, the more painful are the lessons

---

*Purusha is a Sanskrit word meaning *Soul Wisdom, Union, the Father Principle as Soul-Consciousness.*

that inevitably return either in the present life or in future lives.

The Commandment of Love Ye One Another is for *all* persons. From the cradle to the grave, one is required by the Creator to reverence, honor and fulfill the Commandment of Love, for Love is the Primary Law of the Universe.

Love is the Energy and Essence of God creating the Cosmos.

An Ocean of Love is within each person — the Ocean of God's Love deep within his being. When this Love is blocked by ancestral-sin boulders, only a microscopic trickle of love can find its way into outer expression. To work with the Creator and His Son in the removal of these huge boulders is to experience and to express increasing degrees of Divine Love.

Love, as an Eternal Law, is the most powerful cleanser of the soul's record and the cellular system. Love insulates a devotee and prospers his progress toward the attaining of the Image-of-God Consciousness.

The race-genes inherited from one's ancestors determine the color of his hair, his eyes and the pigmentation of his skin. Race-genes also contain tendencies toward laziness, procrastination and prejudice or tendencies toward virtues such as industriousness, thrift, loyalty and a sense of humor.

Certain ancestral lines pass on peace-loving dispositions to their offspring, while other ancestral lines are aggressive warriors from generation to generation.

Anger is a widespread ancestral-gene tendency that provokes violence, murder, mate abuse, child abuse, tantrums and other primitive behavior patterns.

Anger is a genetic storm. Genetic storms are as real and as destructive as any hurricane or tornado. Many lives and marriages do not survive the genetic storms caused by atavistic compulsions and reflexes yet prominent in the DNA memory.

Agnosticism, atheism, adultery, alcoholism, addiction,

depression, and the tendency to commit suicide may be traced for generations in certain family lines.

"Ye cannot be partakers of the Lord's table, and of the table of devils." (1 Corinthians 10:21) Demons and devils attach themselves to ancestral lines contaminated with numerous unconfessed sins. Lust-demons, sadism-demons, anger-demons and other evil spirits are passed on from one generation of a family to the next. In certain instances, exorcism of these ancestral demons occurs through a child who covenants in his soul to suffer a major affliction as a scapegoat for the many unconfessed sins of his parents and ancestors. Such children may be born with serious chromosomal or genetic problems. *"And as Jesus passed by, he saw a man which was blind from his birth. And his disciples asked him, saying, Master, who did sin, this man, or his parents, that he was born blind?"* (St. John 9:1,2)

If a person worshipped God and reverenced His Image in previous lives, his virtues become his protection and insulation from the sins or iniquities of his parents and ancestors. Such persons have learned the difference between right and wrong, good and evil, and therefore do not yield to negative genetic tendencies to which others in the family may fall victim.

A devotee with past-lives' virtue-grace born into ancestral lines heavy-laden with cardinal sins will remain centered on the Path while many other probationers succumb to sin-tendencies affecting them through the genes and the soul's record. Throughout the religions of the world, numerous aspirants continue to remain the hapless victims of their ancestors' sins and past-lives' sins.

Judas, more than the eleven other disciples, responded to his negative ancestral race-gene tendencies and betrayed Jesus after three years. The first three years on the Spiritual Path are an intense struggle on the level of the chromosomes, the genes and the soul's record. During this period, a probationer who succumbs to ancestral tendencies toward pride, ambition and disloyalty will become a Judas-like betrayer of the Jesus Ethic.

One of the most commonplace genetic inheritances through the ancestral lines is the attitude of an eye for an eye. Entire families, races and religions are keeping alive this primitive, tribal trait through their compulsive retaliations. Jesus, in His teachings of love and nonretaliation, gave to mankind the key to freedom from bondage to ancestrally-inherited negative gene-tendencies.

When one unites with the wisdom within the words of Jesus, he experiences changes of attitudes and reflexes that make of him a gentle man. There are few gentle men and gentle women in religions and nations where the eye for an eye philosophy still reigns supreme through the genes and the chromosomes.

The stronger the retaliation reflex, the more one is afflicted by negative ancestral genes.

A person who yields to negative ancestral-gene tendencies may be likened to a caterpillar; in this stage of existence, he remains earthbound in his desires and thoughts. The initiatory process during which the virtues of the soul and the Divine Image manifest in one's being correlates to the chrysalis stage and the miraculous transformation of the caterpillar into a butterfly. The birth of one's spiritual identity and uniqueness through the Image of God is symbolized by the beauty and freedom of the butterfly; thereafter, his heart and mind may soar into the higher atmospheres of Heaven's Light and Grace.

No ancestral pattern in the cell of man can compare, challenge or make void the record of a past life. The record of former lives holds the preponderant or superior place over any ancestral inheritance. What man has been in other lives determines what he will do with his

gene and ancestral inheritance, how he will relate him-
self to them. If he has more soul-memory of eternal in-
heritance, his auric light and auric vehicle will begin its
blessing on the first breath of his living. However, if he
brings to this world a record of violence, hate, hostility,
he will unite with all of the negatives of his gene-inheri-
tance, and he will scourge the earth rather than bless it.

— Ann Ree Colton

CONFESSION OF ANCESTRAL SINS

All sins of mankind caused by offense against the
chromosome system and the gene system must be trans-
versed or mastered by the infinite processes of unfold-
ment through the self.

The soul cannot establish its light in earth misery,
suffering. In this present time, men must return to their
consciences. This can happen only when they confess for
the sins of their ancestors, for the sins of their nation, for
the sins of all persons, inclusive of themselves.

When you make confession for the sins of your ances-
tors, you are blessed by the downpouring of grace from
the ancestors—and those not yet born and those born
will all benefit from the grace. This is a great service.
Confession for our ancestors is an everyday situation in
the Family Atom. One should confess every day for his
ancestors.

— Ann Ree Colton

When the unconfessed sins or iniquities of the ancestral
lines afflict or weaken the immune system, the nervous system, or other bodily processes of their progeny, their children
experience health problems that are payments for ancestral
sins. The misery and suffering caused by unconfessed sins are
taking a terrible toll in modern times.

Through the Christ, one who repents, confesses his sins
and embraces the Laws of God and the Ethics of Jesus is

granted the remission of his own sins and also the remission of the debilitating and destructive effects of unpaid parental and ancestral sins. When the Gift of Remission of Sins is combined with one's daily worship of God, devotion to Scriptural Commandments, and serving others selflessly in the spirit of penance and restitution, there is a strengthening of his immune system, nervous system and all other bodily processes.

The soul's Covenant to serve God and the Christ as Their ambassador is the "high calling." (Philippians 3:14) In order to become an effective minister and apostle in Jesus' Name, one must be centered in the powerful protective energies of the Love-Commandments and prove faithful in his vows to God. In this way, he becomes spiritually insulated and protected from the disastrous effects of unconfessed ancestral sins and past-lives' sins.

> *Ancestral sins are stronger and more confining than iron bars.*

The only way one can avoid negative ancestral-gene influences is to assert his volition in the direction of Scriptural Laws and the Redemption Power of Jesus. This step toward righteousness and lawfulness immediately begins his disconnection from atheistic, agnostic, adulterous and selfish ancestors.

The Laws of God are Godhead-energies creating the Cosmos. The moment one begins to fulfill Scriptural Statutes, these powerful energies combine with the Christ Light to begin a cleansing of all atoms of his being, that he may gain freedom from the sin-tendencies and anti-virtue reflexes of unlawful ancestors. This may be likened to a strong medicine instantly destroying all harmful bacteria—and a total healing occurs.

A penitent who confesses his own sins and the sins of his ancestors remains safely protected from the influences of unlawful ancestors as long as he reverences the Laws and Com-

mandments of God. To stray from any Holy Law is to expose oneself once again to the sin-burdens of unlawful ancestors.

An attitude of humility and the desire to make restitution for all offenses and transgressions of the present life and previous lives hasten the day of a *full pardon* by the Lord of Love. Absolution and Redemption occur when the Christ heals all genes and chromosomes in one's being. This healing is the key to his attaining a State of Grace blessed by his lawful, reverent ancestors and by the Host of Heaven. Henceforth, he may use the Gift of Volition to glorify God through the Divine-Image Consciousness—liberating souls in bondage to the sin-burdens of ancestors and past lives.

> *It is the unknowing that makes one sin, but when there is deliberate, grievous harm by a parent to a child, this sin remains in the samskara action within the genes. Those born to such ancestral lines must make restitution for their ancestry as well as for their own past karmas which attracted them to such parents.*
>
> *To truly be free in the Family Atom, one must forgive, confess and make restitution, if necessary, for his ancestral inheritance of sin and of his own karmas.*
>
> —Ann Ree Colton

ABORTION

> *Those who reject their children—whether by abortion or by birth itself—are self-destruct in their own life-force and destruct in the life-chain of gene regeneration.*
>
> —Ann Ree Colton

The minds and hearts of many persons in nations and religions are conscienceless regarding the taking of life. To destroy is unholy—and to be the destroyer of life is to be possessed by unholy spirits.

Persons and leaders in nations and religions who condone

or encourage abortions are blind to the Image of God in the babe-to-be. Reverence for life in the womb and life in the world is the beginning of a humane attitude toward the Sacred Gift of Life and an enlightened attitude toward the Immortal Soul and the Eternal Image.

Abortion is a tragic reminder of how far the human spirit has moved away from the Image of God.

Women who consent to abortion have been programmed in their genes through immoral and unethical behavior patterns caused by the unconfessed sins of ancestors and past lives. The millions of abortions occurring in the world each year are sealing this destructive attitude more deeply into the genes and DNA memories of those who are consenting to, or are performing, these grievous offenses against the Image of God.

Women and men with a strong sense of morality and conscience earned in previous lives understand the importance of reverence for life as represented by the babe in the womb. Such women and men are spiritually protected from the karmic complications and long-range problems that follow conscienceless abortions.

In each future generation, individuals inheriting ancestral-genes contaminated with the abortion-compulsion will be more and more inclined to abort the life in their own wombs. Such persons will move farther and farther away from the Image-of-God Consciousness. Individuals born with a conscience inspired by a reverence for life will continue to sound tones of love, goodness and harmlessness that will perpetuate moral, ethical and spiritual principles regarding Birth, Life and Creation.

Satan utilizes the abortion-compulsion inherited by women and men through the genes to involve them in complex karmic problems in their present lives and in future lives. When individuals identify with the Commandment *Thou shalt not kill* on all levels of life and being, they will begin to break free from the coils of misery and suffering created by the satanic demons that inspire in receptive minds the desire to destroy life in the womb and in the world.

The demons and devils of the Antichrist work through the sin-darkness in the soul's record and the sin-tendencies in the ancestral genes. The widespread abortions in the world will cause many conscienceless individuals to become possessed by the satanic spirits that delight in destruction and in placing heavy burdens on their victims from life to life.

> *The greatest gift of God to the world is a child. An unborn child is a clear image of God Himself, and in destroying an unborn child, we destroy love, we are destroying the image of God in the world.*
>
> *Even that child in the street who has nothing, who is rejected by everybody, that one, too, is the image of God.*
>
> —Mother Teresa of Calcutta

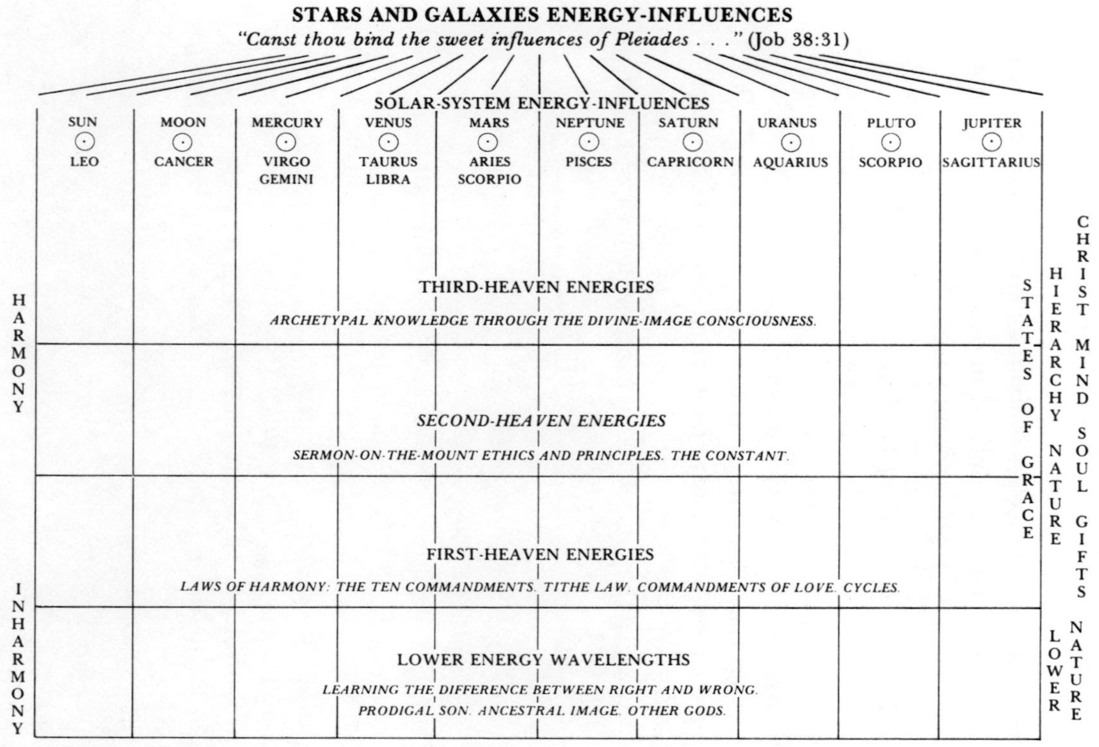

STARS AND GALAXIES ENERGY-INFLUENCES

"Canst thou bind the sweet influences of Pleiades . . ." (Job 38:31)

SOLAR-SYSTEM ENERGY-INFLUENCES

SUN / LEO	MOON / CANCER	MERCURY / VIRGO GEMINI	VENUS / TAURUS LIBRA	MARS / ARIES SCORPIO	NEPTUNE / PISCES	SATURN / CAPRICORN	URANUS / AQUARIUS	PLUTO / SCORPIO	JUPITER / SAGITTARIUS

THIRD-HEAVEN ENERGIES — *ARCHETYPAL KNOWLEDGE THROUGH THE DIVINE-IMAGE CONSCIOUSNESS.*

SECOND-HEAVEN ENERGIES — *SERMON-ON-THE-MOUNT ETHICS AND PRINCIPLES. THE CONSTANT.*

FIRST-HEAVEN ENERGIES — *LAWS OF HARMONY: THE TEN COMMANDMENTS. TITHE LAW. COMMANDMENTS OF LOVE. CYCLES*

LOWER ENERGY WAVELENGTHS — *LEARNING THE DIFFERENCE BETWEEN RIGHT AND WRONG. PRODIGAL SON. ANCESTRAL IMAGE. OTHER GODS.*

Left margin (vertical): HARMONY · INHARMONY

Right margin (vertical): CHRIST MINISTERS AND TEACHERS OF SOUL NATURAL GIFTS · LOWER NATURE

ENERGY-SPECTRUM OF THE CELESTIAL BODIES

22

HARMONY

. . . the morning stars sang together, and all the sons of God shouted for joy.

—Job 38:7

HARMONY AND THE CELESTIAL ENERGIES

Love and harmony are one.
In no other way is spirituality expressed except through the harmony of love which exceeds all negation.

— Ann Ree Colton

The Commandments of God are Laws of Harmony. When one is faithful to the Scriptural Commandments, he is in a state of harmony with God and with himself. His life is in harmony with the Laws of the Creator governing the Universe. He lives, breathes and radiates harmony—and he blesses others with his harmony.

Harmony reigns supreme throughout the Universe. The Commandments of God are man's first link with the harmony of the Moon, the Sun, the Planets, the Stars and the Galaxies.

One's use of volition determines his degree of communion with the lower or the higher energy-wavelengths of the celestial bodies. The lower energy-wavelengths of the Moon, the Sun and the Planets represent important stages of the initia-

367

tory process. On these lower levels of celestial energies, persons are learning the difference between right and wrong. *These are the only energy-levels in the entire Solar System where inharmonies exist. This slim band of initiatory energies makes possible the trial-and-error evolutionary struggles of the human spirit.*

> *From the first breath in life, man in the Earth as a consciousness being is in an incessant state of Initiation stemming from the energies of the Planets, the Sun, the Moon and the Earth.*
>
> *Mankind is presently moving out of a prodigal-son cycle and moving toward the interim time of the beginning of the scientific-spiritual tools extending dimensional consciousness.*
>
> —Ann Ree Colton

The higher energy-wavelengths of the Moon, the Sun and the Planets introduce reverent and righteous servants of God to the harmony of the Universe. The enlightened heart and mind function on the higher energy-wavelengths of the celestial bodies.

A State of Grace is attained and sustained only when one is in harmony with the Wisdom and Love of God within the higher energy-flows of the Moon, the Sun and the Planets. These exalted energy-flows are preparing devoted servants of God for communion with the harmony of God's Love and Wisdom within the Stars and the Galaxies. To attain this high degree of communion with the Living God is to receive the Christ-Mind Gift of the Galaxy Consciousness.

The genes of each individual sound tones either in harmony or out of harmony with the Tones of God's Word creating the Cosmos. His *gene-tones* determine whether he unites with the lower or higher planetary tones. The more his gene-tones are influenced by the soul's tones and the Divine-Image tones, the more he unites with the higher planetary tones and their cyclic blessings and Grace-Inheritances.

All degrees of Illumination Grace are experienced within the higher energies of the celestial bodies in the Solar System. The purity within one's heart enables him to think through the finer frequencies of light moving upon the planet Earth.

The higher energies of Mercury produce the Christ-Mind Initiate. The higher energies of Saturn produce the durable, disciplined servant of God. When the higher energies of Mercury and Saturn are blended with the higher energies of the Moon, the Sun and the other Planets, one may serve God within the Illumination-Grace Flow of His Holy Spirit.

A probationer remains receptive to the lower energies of the Moon, the Sun and the Planets as long as he expresses nonspiritual attitudes and prodigal-son tendencies. The lower energies of Mercury combined with the lower energies of Mars make of one an aggressive, anger-prone, retaliative individual. The lower energies of the Moon combined with the lower energies of Saturn cause one to express undisciplined emotions.

Individuals on the Path who continue to vacillate between the lower and higher energies of the Moon, the Sun and the Planets have yet to attain constancy in love and virtue.

Enlightenment comes when one remains in a State of Grace through the higher celestial energies while transenergizing the heavy energies of the earth into energies of light through the Christ. All persons are exposed to the same energies of the Moon, the Sun and the Planets; however, enlightened personages have a love for God and the Truth that enables them to constantly change all lower energies into the light of *Pure Creation*.

The union with the higher energies of the Moon, the Sun and the Planets prepares a sincere devotee-initiate for union with the higher energies of the Stars and Galaxies. Each major stride forward on the Path of Devotion lifts one to a higher level of energy-influences blessing the world from the Cosmos. *"Canst thou bind the sweet influences of Pleiades . . ."* (Job 31:38)

The higher energies of the Moon, the Sun and the Planets are under command of the Christ. This Higher-Energy World is filled with the Love-Presence of God, thereby linking the Solar System with the Divine Harmonics of all Stars and Galaxies in the Universe.

The lower energies of the Moon, the Sun and the Planets are used by the Antichrist. On this level of energy-action, men are irreverent, materialistic and pleasure-seeking; religiously-inclined individuals responding to the lower energies of the Solar System are fickle, hypocritical and self-deceived.

All initiatory trials of the spiritual life are seeking to lift a devotee's thoughts and emotions to the higher wavelengths of the Sun, the Moon and the Planets. When he becomes centered in the higher wavelengths of the celestial bodies, he has earned the first States of Grace within the Harmony-Flow of God's Holy Spirit.

The Christ has come to open the Door to the Cosmos-energies and their illuminative splendor. To follow Him to the higher energies of the Moon, the Sun and the Planets is to become a *Cosmos Disciple* at one with the energy-processes of God's Holy Spirit. This high State of Grace represents a true and complete union with God as the Spirit of Creation within the Total Universe.

> *To be in the Flow of the Holy Spirit is to be in harmony with All Creation.*
>
> *Harmony is Joy. Harmony is Pure Creation. Harmony is oneness with the Divine Omnipresence. Harmony is discipleship under the Lord of Harmony, Christ Jesus.*
>
> *The Spirit of God is Harmony. The Spirit of Christ is Harmony. He who is united with God and Christ is blessed with Their Harmony, which becomes his Spiritual Birthright.*

TONES AND THE CELLS

> *The Universe is Music.*
> *Man is Energized Music.*
> *Everything is harmony according to the Divine.*
>   —Ann Ree Colton

The Stars and the Galaxies are Pure Music. All Celestial Bodies are contributing to the Symphony of the Universe. The Image of God is the Central Theme in this mighty Symphony.

The Laws of God are great Musical Tones. When one fulfills the Laws of God, he is at one with the Tones of God's Laws creating the Universe — and he adds his own pure tones of love and devotion to the Symphony of Universal Creation.

The soul is pure music and tone. Meditation, when filled with love for God and His Son, is pure music, uniting one with the music of the Soul and the Divine Image.

Mantrams and mantras are music; psalms and chants are music. The *Sound Current* in the Three Heavens is music.

The Cycles of the Sun, the Moon and the Planets are great Tonal-Symphonies that blend in perfect harmony with the Tonal-Symphonies of the Stars and the Galaxies.

Man is presently learning of the Tones in Virtues. Virtue-tones will unite him with the tones of his soul. The tones of his soul will unite him with the tones of the Universe.

God's Word is Music, Tone, Harmony. The cells in the body are sounding tones either in harmony or out of harmony with the Music of God's Word and ordered Plan.

Wholesome attitudes toward Scriptural Laws and Commandments sound pure tones from each cell, chromosome and gene. These tones keep one united with God's Creation of the Universe.

A devotee evolves on the Spiritual Path only to the degree that he opens himself to the Music of God's Love and the

Christ-Light Tones in their benefic cleansings, purifications and sanctifications of his entire being. When his sin-laden cells, chromosomes and genes are miraculously healed through the Music of God's Love and the Christ-Light Tones, his freedom from ancestral-gene compulsions to sin enables him to serve the Living God in the state of Redemption Grace.

The will is the conductor of the orchestra of cell tones. If the will is selfish, the cells send forth the energy-tones of selfishness — and selfishness exudes from the pores of the skin. When one *asks* the Lord Jesus to heal his selfishness that he might express the Virtue of Self-Denial in service to God, the Christ answers his request by sweetening the cells with the Peace-Tones of His Love. Each cell then changes its tones from selfishness to selflessness — and the pores of the skin exude a sweetness and gentleness of the soul.

Sickness, afflictions and unhappiness denote cells that are sounding tones out of harmony with God's Holy Universe.

Each anti-virtue sounds a tone of discordance and dissonance that affects the tones of the cells in the body. The repetitive soundings of anti-virtue dissonance-tones cause the cells to become disorganized — and sicknesses or afflictions result.

All faults and anti-virtues placed on God's Altar for healing experience the Transformation Power of the Christ. The Music of the Christ Peace-Tones moves upon the atoms and cells in one's being, thereby changing the tones of discord and disharmony within the cells into the tones and essences of the Soul and the Image of God.

The sweet tone of pure and selfless love brings peace to the tones of the cells through the *Presence* of God and Christ *within* love. This divinely-blessed love carries healing-energy tones to each cell, chromosome and gene in the body — and healing miracles occur.

Sins cause inharmonies. Grace creates harmony.

All chromosomes and genes have a pure and original Divine-Image state within each cell. Sins create energy-crystalizations that distort the harmonious functions of the chromosomes and the genes. These energy-crystallizations cause the genetic problems and tendencies to sin passed on from generation to generation. The chromosomes and the genes are cleansed by the Christ Light and Tone through repentance, confession, penance and restitution. Thereafter, one may express his *True Self*, adorned with the garment of Soul Grace and Divine-Image Grace.

The Christ heals supernaturally through His powerful laser-like Light and penetrating Tone. His Light and Tone reach deeply into the core of one's being through the Virtue of Faith. Such healings are permanent healings; for, through one's faith, the Christ Light and Tone have penetrated to the Image-of-God Core in his being. In this, the sin-encrustations on the genes and the chromosomes within each cell are removed, thereby freeing him from the burdens of unconfessed ancestral sins and past-lives' sins and also the *tendencies* to sin. All who receive this Miracle of Healing through the Christ are the redeemed, the liberated, the enlightened.

> **Lord Christ Jesus, anoint me with the Music of Thy Light and Tone. Wash clean each cell in my being, that I may be free from all ancestral sin-compulsions. Bathe my genes and chromosomes in the pristine Light of Thy sweet Love-Presence and Dimensional Grace, that I may express the Image of God with peace, harmony and joy. Amen.**

The Divine Image is the key to man's comprehending the Plan of God for the Creation of the Universe. When the chromosomes and the genes are cleansed and sanctified by the Light, Tone, Music and Peace of the Christ, they combine with the nervous system and the soul to receive and to transmit the Cosmos-Eternal Essence and Energies of the Image of God.

The Christ utilizes wavelengths of Light and frequencies of Sound and Tone unknown by mankind in the present age and time.

Jesus emphasized the importance of love because of the healing power of love's energies. Love, being of God's Holy Spirit, uses Light, Sound and Tone to manifest miracles.

Love *processes* all energies into Light and Grace: the energies of the genes and the chromosomes, the energies of the cells, the energies of the nervous system, and the energies of past lives. All become synchronized and harmonized through the Supernatural Christ working through one's faith and love.

Nothing is lost in God's Plan. The darkest sins represent unlearned lessons. When sin-darkness is changed into Light through the Christ, the Light brings virtues and conscience to birth in the heart and the mind.

The *tones* of repentance and confession expressed by a sincere devotee united with the Christ Light and Tone produce a chemical change throughout the chromosomes, the genes, the cells and the soul's record. The Christ Light and Tone utilize a devotee's prayers of repentance and confession and works of penance and restitution to cleanse, heal and quicken his entire being. This holy cleansing, healing and quickening gives one a fresh new start in Eternal Life. The ancestral-gene tendencies and past-lives' tendencies that once drew him into the darkness of sin can no longer influence his feelings, thoughts and actions; in this, he is free to express his spiritual identity as a son of God.

One must work with the Christ each moment of the day and the night in order to remain in a State of Grace. Any lapse of virtue indicates the need for a deeper repentance and more honest confessions to God. Humility and gratitude must be in every breath in the day and the night. Humility remains a viable virtue-energy through the perpetual attitude of penance and restitution.

Even as Jesus' suffering atoned for the sins of the world, so does a disciple of Jesus emulate His Lord by working each day in the spirit of atonement for the sins of the world. This enlightened attitude holds the key to his remaining in the exalted States of Grace through the Christ, for he is working directly with the Son of God to change the darkness in the world into light. This major accomplishment on the Ladder of Eternal Life is the beginning of his attaining the son-of-God degrees of the Divine Image. *"Beloved, now are we the sons of God . . ."* (1 John 3:2)

> *In the beginning of this eternity, the Christ Spirit, the Son of God, played His Light-Tones upon man-to-be, that man might have a quickened soul, and eventually an illumined mind; and that man would, in time, thirst for the greater ideas of truth—thereby receiving direct wisdom from the Archetypes.*
>
> *As the Light-Tones of the Christ continue to move upon men, men will become more and more noble in their thoughts, and their minds will become vortices of creation.*
>
> —Ann Ree Colton

ROBBER-GENES AND PESKY SPIRITS

> *Beloved, believe not every spirit, but try the spirits whether they are of God.*
>
> —1 John 4:1

There are *robber-genes* that try to rob one of his virtue. The robber-genes are the negative tendencies inherited from unlawful and unethical ancestors.

The Antichrist, the Great Thief, works through the robber-genes in one's cells to try to penetrate his Spiritual Insulation. If successful, Satan steals one's virtue and, therefore, his grace.

Petty irritations are caused by robber-genes. *Pesky spirits*, as harassing spirits under the Antichrist, work through the petty irritations of a person to rob him of peace and harmony. A husband and a wife become the victims of pesky spirits in their household when they express petty irritations with one another. Until an individual or a married couple is exorcised by the Christ, they will continue to lose Virtue, Grace, Peace and Harmony.

All single and married persons on the Path must gain the Gift of *Discerning of Spirits*.* This Gift of the Soul enables them to be protected from the destructive influences of the pesky spirits and other satanic forces.

Through the Healing Power of Christ Jesus, petty irritations are healed on the gene and the chromosome level. With the healing of the robber-genes, the pesky spirits are exorcised, and one's *Armor-of-God Insulation* is strengthened. The protection earned through Insulation is maintained through vigilance, faith and love.

When the Mercy of God blesses a sincere penitent, the Virtue and Grace stolen from him by the Antichrist are redeemed by the Christ! The return of Virtue and Grace establishes for him a firm union with the Harmony of God and His Holy Increase.

"Thou shalt have no other gods before me." (Genesis 20:3) *All* of the offerings of Time and Energies of the present life and past lives placed before the anti-virtue altars of "other gods" can be redeemed by a penitent through Christ Jesus. As the Great Redeemer, He recovers all of one's misdirected offerings to false gods and places them before the Altar of the Living God. In this way, one experiences the Redemption of Time and Energies that become *Grace* for him to use in his service to God in his present life and in future lives.

---

*1 Corinthians 12:10.

VISUALIZATION:

Feel deep repentance and contrition for all sins in the soul's record — and place yourself in the Merciful Love of God. Visualize the Christ retrieving all the energies you have placed before the altars of the gods of lust, anger, greed, pride, pettiness, etc. in this life and in all previous lives; then visualize His purifying this mass of energy and placing it before the Altar of the One God. In your heart, ask for this Miracle of His Redemption Power. Express an enthusiastic gratitude to God for the wondrous Miracle of Redemption Grace through His Beloved Son!

Visualize all persons in the world experiencing Redemption in God's timing for them.

As long as one remains faithful to the Living God and His Commandments, his State of Grace will continue to increase through the higher energies of the Moon, the Sun and the Planets. Redeemed Grace increases one's faith and all other virtues. Spiritual transformations and miraculous healings occur through Redeemed Grace. When a penitent no longer scatters his energies before the altars of many anti-virtue gods, his soul opens the door to the dimensional energies of his Spiritual-Birthright Inheritance. The Bridegroom appears and calls him to the Divine Marriage.

"Then saith Jesus unto him, Get thee hence, Satan: for it is written, Thou shalt worship the Lord thy God, and him only shalt thou serve." (St. Matthew 4:10) Satan tried to steal the Virtue and Grace of Jesus after Jesus fasted for 40 days and nights. So does the tempter try to steal the Virtue and Grace of all persons, especially those who are servants of God, for servants of God have more Virtue and Grace for him to steal.

The Antichrist tries to rob a devotee of the Lord of his Spiritual-Birthright Inheritance. The more a devotee inherits Holy Grace through his worship-dedications, the more desirous Satan is to steal this precious Grace.

Nonvigilant aspirants who permit Satan to steal their Virtue and Grace either forsake the Spiritual Path or become laggards. Such persons are unaware of Satan's subtle cunning and hand their hard-earned Virtue and Grace to him like naive victims of a skillful swindler. In time, nonvigilant probationers learn that they are spiritually bankrupt, for the tester has stolen all the Grace of their Inheritance. The loss of Grace is the loss of Virtue, the loss of Enthusiasm, the loss of Harmony, the loss of Volition and other losses that lead to unhappiness and spiritual impoverishment.

When one is in the Harmony-Flow of God's Holy Spirit, he experiences steady increases of Grace through the Inheritance. He works daily with the Lord Jesus to strengthen his Armor-of-God Insulation through the healing of his genes and the exorcism of unholy spirits. To work with Jesus is to increase in Virtue and Vigilance. The earning of the Gift of Discerning of Spirits and other spiritual gifts brings the protection and insulation necessary to remain in an increasing State of Grace.

While many aspirants on the Path are being swindled by Satan, there are those who are increasing in Grace. To increase in Grace is to increase in Virtue, Joy, Enthusiasm, Harmony and in Spiritual Gifts.

". . . *hold fast that which is good.*" (1 Thessalonians 5:21) If one does not "hold fast" to the good, it will be stolen from him by the Antichrist. To hold fast to the good is to be a wise and alert steward of Good, Virtue, Grace and Soul-Gifts.

The Christ-Jewel of Redemption is a valuable prize of precious Grace. The moment a devotee on the Path begins to receive the Christ-Jewel of Redemption Grace, he becomes a target for the Antichrist. Redemption Grace is highly-charged energy; if Satan can steal this energy, he can use it for mass destruction.

Vigilant devotees who protect the Christ-Jewel of Redemption bless the masses with the powerful energies within this Holy-Spirit Grace.

A devotee who strays from the harmony of the Commandment of Love Ye One Another has begun the process of falling from Grace. Satan has been successful in enticing him into petty irritations with others, angers through loss of self-control, stubborn refusal to work with his Teacher, or procrastination tendencies.

Married disciples of the Lord who fall into Satan's trap of petty irritations with each other have forgotten their vows to love and cherish one another and their vows to God to observe His Commandments of Love. The Antichrist uses their negligence and betrayal of their vows to steal from them the Christ-Jewel of Redemption. Such marriages are loveless, for the husband and the wife have become combatants in the arena of petty irritations.

It requires eternal vigilance for a single or married servant of God to hold fast to the Christ-Jewel of Redemption!

Behold, I come quickly: hold that fast which thou hast, that no man take thy crown.
— Revelation 3:11

23

SYNCHRONIZATION AND CELEBRATION

Through love, life becomes a Celebration of the Image of God. Through love, healings manifest; soul-gifts are quickened; and the Holy Ghost draws nigh.

Love is an Eternal Celebration.

THE MIRACLE OF SYNCHRONIZATION

Heavenly Father, thank Thee for the Miracle Powers of Thy Beloved Son, Christ Jesus. If it is Thy Will, I pray to come under the Blessings of His Synchronization Grace, that I might better serve Thee.

May the Lord of Supernatural Love bring into synchronization my emotional, mental, physical and etheric bodies; my cells, nerves and all other bodily processes and polarities. May He synchronize all genes and chromosomes with the higher purposes of my Soul's Covenant and Thy Sacred Image.

May the Lord Jesus bring into synchronization all Chakras and their energies, blending my emotions, thoughts, soul and spirit in holy harmony and creative peace. May He synchronize my soul's record of past lives with my present life, that I may serve Thee in the State of Fulness Grace.

Dear Lord, may Christ Jesus synchronize all events and associations in my dedication to Thee. May He synchronize all Cycles in my life and being with the Cycles of the Commandments, the Solar System, the Milky Way Galaxy and the Universe.

Blessed art Thou, O Lord; and blessed is Thy Son, Christ Jesus, the Great Synchronizer. Through Him, Thy children are redeemed, healed, quickened and enlightened. Through Him, Time and Space are overcome; Love produces its priceless blessings; and Thy Grace-Inheritances are received in increasing measure. Thank Thee, Father. Amen.

To come into Total Synchronization through the Lord Jesus is to be in perfect harmony with all energies and cycles in the Solar System and in the Universe. This Messianic Blessing of Synchronization must occur before one can serve his Lord with freedom and understanding.

Synchronization Grace, Polarization Grace, Providential Grace and Redemption Grace are but a few of the many Gifts of God received through the Mediation of His Beloved Son. The attaining of these Gifts constitutes major aspects of the State of Fulness Grace.

After a penitent turns to God through a sincere contrition, all energy-processes within his life and being begin their healing and blending through the Synchronization Power of Jesus. In this, he experiences the increasing synchronization of his physical, emotional, mental and physical bodies; his cells, genes and chromosomes; his nerves, glands and organs; the kundalini and all chakras; his present life and past lives; all events, associations and relationships; and all personal cycles, Commandment Cycles and Celestial Cycles.

The synchronization of all chakra-energies through the Christ places a devotee of the Lord in a State of Holy Grace. The State of Grace is further prospered through the loyal observance of the Scriptural Commandments. The reverent fulfilling of each Sacred Statute places the aspirant in synchronized timing with the Cycles of the Moon, the Sun and the Planets, thereby beginning his communion with God as the Creator of the Universe of Stars and Galaxies.

Synchronization of the chakras' clockwise energies with the Commandment Cycles results in the harmonious blending of the emotions, the thoughts, the soul and the spirit. The synchronization of the chakras with the emotional, mental, physical and etheric bodies is accompanied by increasing quickenings of gifts, powers, skills and talents proceeding from the soul's record and the Image of God.

The synchronization of the cells insulates one from negative ancestral, primitive desires, compulsions and reflexes, and infuses the cells with the Peace-energies of the Christ. In this, one attains the higher States of Grace through chromosomes, genes and cells in harmony with the Laws of the Universe.

When the nerves are anointed and sanctified by the Creator and His Son, the nervous system is synchronized with all other energy-systems within the Body Temple and the Soul, thereby becoming a spiritually-sensitive antenna for sacred truths received telepathically from the Inner Kingdom.

All Lunar, Solar, Planet, Star and Galaxy energies and tones are being utilized by the Living God to create man in His Image. The more receptive one becomes to these powerful energies and tones through love, the more he is free to express Divine-Image capabilities and versatilities with freedom, naturalness and joy. To experience the glorious harmony and synchronicity between the cells and the Stars, the nerves and the Kingdom of Heaven, is to shout with joy the good tidings of the coming of the Christ!

> *The mastery of the tones of the planets gives the power of synchronization.*
> — Ann Ree Colton

To receive the Gift of Synchronization Grace through the Lord Jesus is a time of Celebration in Heaven and on Earth. Each Cycle of the Moon, the Sun and the Planets is part of this Celebration.

Jesus utilizes the Solar-System Cycles and energies in His shepherding of devotees to the Kingdom of God. All dimensional gifts and Apostolic powers coming to birth through the soul and the Image of God manifest through His mighty Power of Synchronization.

The marriage of the heart and the mind is occurring through the Cycles of the Moon and the Sun. The Moon works with man's emotional energies; the Sun works with his mental energies. The Cycles of the Planets also play important roles in the energy-drama through which the lower nature of man is transformed into his higher or divine nature blessed with soul-gifts and spiritual powers.

The Cycles of the Stars and the Galaxies are in harmony with all Lunar, Solar and Planetary Cycles affecting man on Earth. One who experiences the Synchronization Grace of Jesus knows no separation from any expression of God's Omnipresence throughout the Universe.

Through love, one is always under the blessings of the Stars and the Galaxies.

When a devotee of the higher life knows that all Celestial Cycles are contributing to the creation of man in the Image of God, he may express an inspired gratitude for the contributions of each Celestial Body—from the Moon to the most distant Galaxy. His gratitude will keep him receptive to the higher degrees of their benefic blessings.

The Love of God is present in every atom of Creation throughout the Universe. Thus, when one loves, he is receptive to wavelengths of blessings from the Love of God within the Cosmos. Through the Moon's influences, a servant of

God becomes a love-presence on the planet Earth and a love-presence within the Universe itself. Thereafter, all of his prayers, meditations, ministerings and creations are blessing the Universe as well as his fellow man on earth.

Uninitiated man is yet involved in self-love, love of money, love of fame, love of success, love of power. Through the initiatory energies of the Moon, each person is given the opportunity to expand his range of love from love of self to love of others on earth; the next stages of love-quickenings through the Lunar energy-tides and the Divine Image will produce the ability to love *all* creations of God within the Universe.

> *To be guided by the Spirit of God to an enlightened Teacher one has known, trusted and loved in previous lives is a time of Soul-Celebration and the happy anticipation of receiving illumined instruction in the present life.*

When an earnest aspirant on the Path meets his Living Teacher, the Synchronization Power of Jesus brings his life into timing with his Teacher's dedication to God. The vows to God made by the student and the Teacher enable them to work together in the spirit of Celebration while perpetuating the Word and Altar of God. The Teacher's work is to inspire the student to come directly under the Mantle of Jesus. This close association with the Great Synchronizer, Christ Jesus, is the key to one's becoming an Apostle anointed, sealed and quickened by God's Holy Spirit.

Through the reverent application of the Teacher's instruction, an obedient student experiences the synchronization of his dream world with the initiatory occurrences in his waking world. This synchronization supervised by the Angels of his soul's record brings him into increasing alignment with his Teacher's instruction.

> *The dedication of a spiritual personage is synchronized with the need of the world and the wisdom within the*

Higher Worlds so that men of the earth may receive
spiritual instruction in ripe timing.

Every Teacher must stand in the Synchronized Man-
tles of Great Souls who have preceded him.

The students of the West, when synchronizing the
Dharma of the East with the Christian Ethic as stated by
Jesus in the Sermon on the Mount, find their clues to
harmonizing the Jesus Ethic with the Eastern illumina-
tive procedures for the spiritual life.

— Ann Ree Colton

The Lord Jesus synchronizes the ancient Dharma of the East with the New-Era Dharma of the West. If a follower of Jesus is prejudiced toward the Scriptures of the East, he short-circuits this synchronization action. A truth-seeker who reverences the sacred truths of the East and the West is not the victim of prejudice, bigotry and narrow-mindedness; therefore, the Synchronization Power of the Christ is able to *ignite* the Wisdom-essences of the East-West Dharma in his heart and mind. The synchronization of the East-West Dharma through the Christ is essential for attaining a sacred oneness with God as the Divine Omnipresence within *all* souls in the world.

Through the Synchronization Power of Christ Jesus, all events, relationships and associations in one's life are harmoniously blended with the Archetypal Flow of Grace from the Three Heavens. This State of Grace enables the servant of God to do all things with effortless effort. Prospered by the Providential Grace of God, he works, creates and ministers in synchronized harmony with all inner and outer energy-processes.

The pure in heart are one with God and His Holy Universe through the Gift of Synchronization. Endowed with priceless Inheritances of Grace, their works produce unceasing testimonies of the Miraculous Mediation of the Living Christ.

During union with the Synchronization Power of Christ Jesus, the devotee-initiate experiences the synchronization of

Past, Present and Future; he unites with the Timeless and Spaceless Dimensions of his soul and the Kingdom of Heaven. In this, he becomes a prophet blessed with the ability to perceive the Past and the Future.

> *And as we have borne the image of the earthy,*
> *we shall also bear the image of the heavenly.*
> — 1 Corinthians 15:49

PURGINGS AND THE GREAT PHYSICIAN

> *How much more shall the blood of Christ, who*
> *through the eternal spirit offered himself without*
> *spot to God, purge your conscience from dead*
> *works to serve the living God?*
> — Hebrews 9:14

The lower energies of the Moon, the Sun and the Planets work through the Purification, Purging and Reproving Principles. The higher energies of the Moon, the Sun and the Planets work through the Blessing, Anointing and Inheritance Principles.

Through progressive Christ-Light purgings and quickenings, a truth-seeker begins to receive his *Eternal Inheritance.* (Hebrews 9:15) Each manifestation of his Inheritance is a Celebration timed by the Lunar, Solar and Planetary Cycles. The Moon, the Sun and each Planet bless sincere servants of God with priceless treasures of Grace through their ordained Cycles.

Major purgings by the Great Physician occur in the timings of the Lunar Cycles and the Seasonal Cycles, especially before the Holy Days of Christmas and Easter. The Christ-Light purgings between the Autumnal-Equinox time of Atonement until the days before Christmas prepare the devotee for the Birth of the Christ Child within his being. Each year, this Birth increases as a cyclic Celebration of Soul Grace and Divine-Image Grace, enabling him to become more Christlike in his virtues, attitudes, reflexes and sensitivities.

> *The Image of the Lord Jesus, His Perfect Proto-type, is reflected in our hearts and stirs with a holy vibrancy at Christmas.*
>
> —Ann Ree Colton

The timings of each New Moon, Full Moon, Perigee* and Apogee are especially utilized by the Christ in His purgings, cleansings, blessings, quickenings and soul-gift Inheritances. Through a cleansed soul-record, each New Moon and Full Moon becomes a time of Celebration blessed by priceless increases of Holy Grace.

Each *fiery trial* experienced on the Spiritual Path is an extended purging in preparation for a closer communion with the Kingdom of God. *"Beloved, think it not strange concerning the fiery trial which is to try you, as though some strange thing happened unto you: But rejoice, inasmuch as ye are partakers of Christ's sufferings; that, when his glory shall be revealed, ye may be glad also with exceeding joy."* (1 Peter 4:12,13)

To resist or denounce the purgings of the Great Physician is to die to the spiritual life. The Principle of Purging is a mighty Gift of God. He who receives this Gift with gratitude is blessed by the Synchronization Grace of Christ Jesus.

The exorcism of satanic spirits requires powerful purgings. The healing of selfish and egotistical attitudes requires strong purgings. Wherever there is darkness in the soul, the intense pressures of negation and evil must be purged or else persons would become totally immobilized by evil, sin and darkness.

A nation or a religion may be purged by the Christ Light.

Perigee is the closest distance between the Moon and the planet Earth during each lunar month; *Apogee* is the farthest distance each lunar month.

Each purging of masses of people is a time of decreasing sin-poisons and anti-virtue toxins from the World Soul.

A sincere follower of Jesus prays that the Great Physician will purge all darkness from his lower subconscious, emotions, thoughts, feelings, memories and soul-record. These purgings by the Christ occur through His *Light*, which enters into the core of one's being. If a contrite devotee knowingly works with the Christ Light in its purging action, healings and exorcisms occur more quickly.

No servant of God is exempt from Christ-Light purgings. All must be kept in a cleansed state of being if they are to serve their Lord with *"clean hands and a pure heart."* (Psalm 24:4) Divine Wisdom determines the intensity and duration of each purging.

Intense purgings sometimes occur during or after days of sacramental fasting, for on a fasting day the Light of the Christ penetrates the lower subconscious and loosens sin-residue. The released residue rises to the surface of one's consciousness where it may be *identified* and then confessed to God. Through contrition and confession, the dark energies of sin are transenergized into the lighted energies of virtues and grace-creations.

A probationer's progress on the Path is determined by his working with the Christ during the lesser and greater purgings. Following each purging, the Light of the Christ and the Spirit of God may abide more fully within his being. The aspirant must thereafter remain vigilant in his expression of love, virtues and ethics or else the poisons and toxins of anti-virtues will build up once again and require additional purgings.

The devotee experiencing a Christ-Light purging of his interior darkness can assist the Great Physician by speaking prayers of confession, gratitude and acceptance. Rapid healings are possible if he retains a childlike faith in God and an earnest desire to be purified and made whole.

Self-honesty enables the Christ Light to work more quickly and effectively toward permanent healings. Self-justification for one's sins defeats the purging action, for one resists the Light which is seeking to cleanse, heal and free him.

> *Let me look upon all new beginnings*
> *As holy opportunities for discovery.*
> *May I touch the wellspring*
> *Of the Great Physician*
> *And heal my wounds,*
> *That I may heal others.*
> — Ann Ree Colton

MEDITATION AND THE SYNCHRONIZATION OF PAST LIVES

> *It is absolutely necessary that the soul should be healed and purified, and if this does not take place during its life on earth, it must be accomplished in future lives.*
> — Saint Gregory of Nyssa

> *In thy samskaras thou wilt continue to live and thou wilt reap in future existences the harvest sown now and in the past.*
> — Buddha

Meditation is a divine art and science only as long as a devotee observes the Ten Commandments, the Law of Tithing, the Commandments of Love and the Sermon-on-the-Mount Principles. Through these mighty Statutes and Precepts, the Christ synchronizes the past lives of the meditator with his present life. Without this blessing of Synchronization, a meditator will have no defense against the more powerful surges of darkness from his soul's record.

The Christ works through Holy Law and through devotees who are reverencing Holy Law. The Christ Light, as Pure

Virtue, moves through those who are expressing pure virtues in service to God.

In an age of lawless behavior, many egotistical and self-deceived persons believe that God will reward them for their meditations. Such persons have yet to learn that God and His Son work only through the law-minded, the faithful, the humble, the pure in heart.

The darkness in the soul's record is a powerful energy. Many lives are destroyed when an accumulation of sin-debts incurred in previous lives is presented for payment in the present life. At such times, numerous persons respond to their unpaid sin-debts of former lives by sinking into periods of depression; others lash out at others, thereby adding to the darkness in their souls' records.

Many meditators fail to confess to God their sins, wrong desires and temperament problems. Such persons remain subject to the tidal-wave action of past-lives' darkness that inflames their present-life's anti-virtues.

The Christ requires that one *repent, confess, sin no more,* and *embrace Scriptural Laws* before His great Power of Synchronization will produce peace, order and harmony in their lives. While others are undergoing the pain and turbulence of past-lives' unconfessed sins, the devotee-mediator blessed with the Synchronization Grace of the Christ remains in a state of Holy Equanimity.

A devotee cannot serve God with harmony, poise and effortless effort until he experiences the Synchronization of his past lives with his present life. When he understands the importance of remaining constant in love and non-retaliative throughout all tests and trials, he enables the Christ to heal all previous-lives' sin-offenses so that he might serve God with undeviating loyalty in his present life.

The Christ has come. He will work with any one who is truly desirous of becoming spiritually liberated through law and virtue. Prayer and meditation without the blessing of the

Synchronization of Past Lives through the Christ lead to disastrous consequences. Prayer and meditation with His blessing of Synchronization lead to the receiving of the Holy Ghost. *"He that turneth his ear from hearing the law, even his prayer shall be abomination."* (Proverbs 28:9)

The more a devotee is centered in the Commandments of Love and the Christ Principles, the more he expresses his True Self through constancy in love and virtue. Until a probationer is constant in love and virtue, he will express several different personalities due to past-lives' influences. Some of these personalities of previous lives may be religiously inclined while others may be lustful, quick-tempered, selfish, greedy, lazy.

The diverse conglomeration of former-lives' attitudes, reflexes, sensitivities, virtues and anti-virtues creates an ambivalence that can be explained in no other way save through the reality of reincarnation. Even as one's words justify or condemn him, so do his past lives justify or condemn him.

The only way a devotee on the Path can remain stabilized amidst the conflicting pressures of past-lives' influences is through the Synchronization Power of Christ Jesus.

The more one is devoted to sacramental meditation, the more he will be subject to the tidal waves of past-lives' unconfessed sins; he will also be the recipient of previous-lives' talents and grace. Each cyclic releasement of former-lives' sin-darkness into one's present life is cast forth by the soul so that the Christ may transform the darkness into *Light* through humility-prayers, repentance-confessions, and penance-restitutions.

There are many subtle ways that previous lives can intrude upon one's present-life dedication to God. When the Christ synchronizes all past-lives' virtues and soul-powers and trans-energizes the dark energies of sins into light, a devotee experiences the profound transformation that leads to Redemption and Enlightenment.

Father, I pray to come under the Synchronization Grace of the Lord Jesus. May all energies and polarities in my life and being be synchronized through a love-harmony blessed by Thee and Thy Beloved Son.

A wise devotee praying in Jesus' Name *asks* God for the Synchronization of all past lives with his present life. Humility, faith, and the certain knowledge of reincarnation as a Holy Law inspire him to ask God for this essential Synchronization Blessing through the Christ.

The monumental Blessing of Synchronization holds the key to one's future progress on the Path in the State of Fulness Grace without the intrusion of past-lives' negative sensitivities, attitudes, reflexes, moods, cravings, habits and compulsions. Synchronization also brings harmony with all persons in his present life so that he may serve God with peace of mind in atmospheres of love and prospering.

> *Through the draughts of remembrance, the records of former lives seep upward from the darkened depths of the subconscious into the actions, emotions and thoughts at regular cyclic intervals.*
>
> —Ann Ree Colton

Persons who believe in reincarnation rarely recognize when their previous-lives' sins are intruding on their present life. These sins increase in one's present life if he does not recognize them and confess them to God. Many persons in religious philosophies continue to express egotism, pride, fickleness, self-deception, temperament problems and other unspiritual attitudes without realizing that these negative traits are inherited from previous lives.

When a man and a woman meet and marry, their first flush of romance may be followed by years of regret, sorrow or problems caused by negative traits that surface from their

past lives — traits such as anger, jealousy, selfishness, unforgiveness, and other anti-virtues. Unless these are corrected
and healed, the marriage is doomed to unhappiness and division. The same pattern occurs when a person desires to
enter a religious or spiritual teaching. After his first flush of
excitement, his negative traits from previous lives will surface
and intrude on his spiritual aspirations unless they are identified and corrected.

Certain negative tendencies and attitudes retained from
past lives are impossible for most students to detect without
a Teacher's help. The survivors of the initiatory process are
those who listen to their Teacher's suggestions and corrections. Those who fail to listen to their Teacher become the
victims of their past-lives' wrong attitudes and anti-virtues.
Their failure to repent and to change their negative traits will
increase the dark energies in their souls' records, which they
will take as hindrances into their coming lives.

The influences of one's previous lives will either bless or
curse his present-life's efforts to unite with God. The unconfessed sins of past lives remain as black energy-masses in the
soul's record until they are confessed to God and restitution
is made.

Each time one sins, he places a curse upon himself. If the
sin is not confessed to God, this self-curse is carried over into
his coming life on earth. A number of unconfessed sins will
produce a host of problems. Sins create inharmonious energies within one's being. These self-curse energies produce
wrong attitudes; uncertainties; negative sensitivities; and the
strong tendencies to sin again through immorality, addiction,
selfishness and other abnormal behavior. Many persons in the
world today are expressing these tragic results of their past-
lives' sins.

The dark energies of voluminous sins of omission and commission recorded in the soul's record become oppressive burdens carried from life to life. When a follower of Jesus

understands the relationship between his previous lives, the purging process and the Lunar Cycle, he may work with the Christ in the healing of the complexities in his present life caused by past-lives' sins. This Mighty Miracle of Healing enables a sincere penitent and devotee to experience *"the simplicity that is in Christ."* (2 Corinthians 11:3)

The simplicity life resulting from the Healing Power of the Great Physician awakens a devotee-meditator to his spiritual individuality. Thereafter, the Image-of-God energies are free to flow forth into his life and being through a cleansed soul-record.

> *In character, in manners, in style, in all things, the supreme excellence is simplicity.*
>
> — Longfellow

> *Blissful are the simple, for they shall have much peace.*
>
> — Thomas a Kempis

The sweet simplicity that comes through the Synchronization Grace of Christ Jesus lifts a meditator above the turbulences and complexities of the lower nature into the holy harmony of the sattvic nature at one with God.

> *A marriage anointed by the Spirit of God becomes a Celebration of love through the Polarization and Synchronization Power of Jesus.*

An Apostolic Marriage in which husband, wife and children are devoted to God without wavering can occur only when the family members are blessed by the Synchronization Power of Jesus blending and harmonizing their former lives with their present lives.

> *Meditation unites the yin and yang polarities, enabling the unitive Sattvic-Bliss to manifest, whereby one can see, know and hear within the extended synchroniz-*

ing states of consciousness. When meditation is practiced with regularity, the result shakes the little mind and shocks the ego. Reality comes; synchronization comes; joy begins in the now as a realized state in Grace.

— Ann Ree Colton

Distillation and Reconciliation

When Jesus reconciles one's present life with previous lives of grace and wisdom, there is a joyful Celebration that resounds throughout all dimensions of the soul and the spirit.

The unpaid debts of past lives come forth in cyclic tides. How one meets these tides determines whether or not he will qualify for the Divine Marriage.

A devotee with *soul-knowing* earned in past existences recognizes whenever dark energies from previous lives are beginning to intrude upon his present life's dedication to God. Through soul-knowing, he *knows* that he should humbly confess his sins of former lives as well as his present-life transgressions. The combination of love, humility and self-honesty expressed by an aspirant enables the Christ to take the dark sin-energies of many past lives and *distill* them into the purest elixirs and essences of virtues and love. The devotee who responds to the Distillation Power of Christ Jesus experiences dramatic transformations in his attitudes, thoughts and actions.

The Christ can take a heavy mass of dark sin-energies in the soul's record and the subconscious mind and distill them into one powerful drop of pure virtue. This highly-concentrated virtue then permeates one's being and adds its golden, luminous light to his emotions and thoughts. After times of honest confession, beautiful inspirations and realizations may flow into his heart and mind as precious proofs that the

Christ is purifying and distilling the dark energies of many sins into light, grace and creation.

Mary Magdalene, Saint Paul and all others in the world blessed with healings and quickenings by the Lord Jesus have experienced His Miracle Powers of Transformation through Synchronization and Distillation.

Many individuals *covenant* in their souls to work with God and Christ over a period of years to attain Enlightenment rather than experience it in one moment of Total Transformation. In such instances, the dark energies of unpaid sin-debts of previous lives present themselves in cyclic timings determined by the Moon and the Sun. If a devotee is vigilant, he will recognize these inevitable confrontations with the dark or anti-virtue energies expressed in past lives. Through repentance combined with humility, self-honesty and contrition, his confessions will invite the Power of God and Christ to keep him centered on the Path while the dark energies are transenergized into light, virtue and love.

To experience the Miracle Powers of the Christ in the purification and distillation of dark energies of past lives is to know a rapturous oneness with Redemption Grace. Each time the dark energies of former lives are changed into light, grace and creation, the devotee experiences deeper, broader and higher ranges of Redemption. In time, the cyclic purgings and purifications of the soul's record will lead to his receiving the Fulness-Anointing by the Holy Ghost.

Each Law of God becomes a mighty Cornucopia
of Grace through the Redemption Power of Jesus.

God places an enlightened Teacher in one's life to prepare him for the Fulness-Anointing by the Holy Ghost. Love is the only way an aspirant will qualify for this mighty Anointing through which the Laws of God pour forth their wisdom-essences.

As the Christ quickens one's past-lives' virtues and distills the dark energies of previous-lives' sins into pure essences of light, grace and creation, one learns of God's Goodness, Mercy and Love. This is the true Redemption that follows a sincere repentance and a close working with Christ Jesus as one's Savior and Messiah. Henceforth, the penitent may give testimony to the Compassionate Love of God and the Miraculous Powers of His Son.

All enlightened servants of God have experienced the Total-Transformation Grace of the Christ through His Powers of Distillation, Reconciliation, Synchronization, Polarization, Redemption and Illumination. Through the Light and Image of Christ, they know the Eternal Love of God as the Creative Essence of the Universe.

> *For I am persuaded, that neither death, nor life, nor angels, nor principalities, nor powers, nor things present, nor things to come, Nor height, nor depth, nor any other creature, shall be able to separate us from the love of God, which is in Christ Jesus our Lord.*
>
> —Romans 8:38,39

> *Christ is inside of you. Christ is inside of all. To have union with Christ Spirit, you must go inside and receive this spirit of Light and become Enlightened.*
>
> —Ann Ree Colton

HUMILITY AS A CONSTANT

> *Whosoever exalteth himself shall be abased; and he that humbleth himself shall be exalted.*
>
> —St. Luke 14:11

> *Service without humility is selfishness and egotism.*
>
> —M. Gandhi

Past-lives' attitudes of pride and egotism may surface at any time in one's present life. If he is a devotee of the Lord, he will retain his footing on the Spiritual Path only if he remembers to express humility.

Humility must be expressed as a *Constant* if one is to pass the many initiatory tests on the Path and remain united with the Synchronization Power of Jesus. Through the Holy Constant of Humility, all negative influences stemming from previous lives, ancestral genes and the world are immediately transenergized into light, love and creation. All Saints and Great Teachers emphasize the importance of humility because this mighty virtue is the *only* way one can remain at one with the Grace of God. *"God resisteth the proud, but giveth grace to the humble."* (James 4:6)

A seeker after Enlightenment should pray that God will bless him with the ability to express Humility as a Constant. Such prayers will produce miraculous changes in his attitudes and temperament.

> **Dear Lord, I ask for the Virtue of Humility and all other Virtues that will better enable me to serve Thee and Thy children through a steadfast faith and devotion. May I inspire others to express Humility as a Holy Constant, that they may transcend the lower nature and abide in the divine nature at one with Thy Image and Likeness. Let all be for Thy Everlasting Glory. I ask these things in the Name of Christ Jesus, the Light of the World and the Door to Thy Kingdom. Amen.**

"Ask, and it shall be given you." (St. Matthew 7:7) If one has earned the Virtue of Humility in past lives, his prayer for humility will return this beautiful Virtue-Diamond to him through the Christ-Quickening Power activated through *Asking*. If a devotee has not earned the Virtue of Humility in

previous lives, his asking God in the Name of the Christ will activate the Divine-Image releasement of the sweet energies of humility and all other virtues for which he prays. The Divine-Image energies of cardinal virtues and soul-gifts will move forth into his heart and mind as natural expressions that will bless, fortify and inspire his worship-devotions and daily ministering as a servant of God.

"*. . . the Son quickeneth whom He will.*" (St. John 5:21) Jesus has the power to quicken any virtue for which a sincere devotee asks. As an aspirant *identifies* the need for one or more virtues in his service to God, his prayer-asking for the virtue or virtues will enable Jesus to either reunite him with the virtues earned in former lives; or, if those virtues have not yet been earned, Jesus will quicken in him the Divine-Image virtue-energies. In this, the devotee will not have to reincarnate hundreds or thousands of lifetimes in order to evolve the same virtues through trial-and-error struggles, for the Quickening and Synchronization Powers of Jesus will miraculously provide these priceless virtues through the Divine Image in the Godhead Core of his being.

If a probationer does not have self-honesty, he will not ask Jesus for virtues, for he will not admit to himself or to God that any virtues are missing in his nature. Self-honesty enables one to see clearly the virtues that are weak or missing. Faith inspires him to trust in God to provide for all his needs; and, asking in Jesus' Name, will manifest the miraculous appearance of the virtues that will prosper communion with his Beloved Lord.

> *And whatsoever we ask, we receive of him, because we keep his commandments, and do those things that are pleasing in his sight.*
> —1 John 3:22

> *And this is the confidence that we have in him, that, if we ask any thing according to his will, he*

heareth us: And if we know that he hear us, what-soever we ask, we know that we have the petitions that we desire of him.

—1 John 5:14,15

Egotism is a commonplace expression in many persons today. The moment an aspirant on the Path yields to any thoughts or feelings of egotism, pride or sense of superiority, he jeopardizes the receiving of his Spiritual-Birthright Inheritance.

Humility is the solid foundation of all the virtues.
—Confucius

Do not believe that thou hast made any advance in perfection unless thou considerest thyself worst of all.

—Saint Teresa of Avila

Egotism inspires an aspirant on the Path to think that he is exempt from repentance, confession, penance and restitution. An egotistically-inclined probationer never expects to be presented with the bill for unpaid sin-debts of the present life and previous lives. He lives in a fantasy world of self-deception.

Egotism is more dangerous than any virulent disease, for it not only corrupts the soul in one's present life but it increases its dark energies in coming lives. The Christ Light is the Perfect Antidote for the healing of egotism and all other unholy energies.

It is easy to recognize past-lives' attitudes in little children. If they expressed egotism in previous lives, they will be self-ish and difficult to discipline; also, they will be takers, rather than givers. Such children should be taught the importance of modesty, humility, and the joy of sharing with others.

If genius talents used in past lives appear at an early age in the present life, a child may become insufferably egotistical. This is especially harmful when encouraged by parents inclined toward egotism, family pride or intellectual pride.

Children and teenagers who become addicted to alcohol and drugs are re-living past-lives' sins. Adulterous persons in marriage are re-living past-lives' sins.

Family pride, intellectual pride, talent pride, body-beauty pride, racial pride, national pride, religious pride and spiritual pride represent some of the pride-plateaus in the world. A person can remain on a pride-plateau for many lifetimes.

An individual with religious pride or spiritual pride is a victim of *the spirit of pride*. Such persons may think they are progressing on the Path of Virtue; however, they are merely living on the same pride-plateaus year after year. Humility is one's only escape from the pride-plateau existence and a direct communion with the Manifold Grace of God.

Genius expressed in past lives may come forth after one begins the daily practice of prayer and meditation. At such times, it is especially important for a devotee to remain constant in humility, for genius talents and skills are often accompanied by egotism and pride. Nonvigilant probationers who succumb to the egotism-sensitivities accompanying genius abilities inherited from former lives have permitted Satan to divert them from the Path of Humility. Through constancy in humility, one receives the genius gifts from previous lives and utilizes them in selfless service to God in his present life. These creative gifts and talents become priceless assets in his Apostolic ministering in Jesus' Name.

All spiritual practices observed through the Divine-Image Consciousness are filled with love, humility, compassion and the spirit of world-serving. In this, one is protected from the ever-present pitfalls of egotism, pride and selfishness.

When a servant of God meditates through the Divine-Image Consciousness, he is meditating for all souls, past, present and future; his love becomes a world-healing service that produces eternal blessings. Prayers spoken through the

Divine-Image Consciousness serve all persons in the world, for he is communing with the Image of God in himself and in all souls on earth.

When one takes the Sacrament of Communion through the Divine-Image Consciousness, he knows that he is taking the Sacrament for all persons in the world — blessing them eternally. When he is fasting, he is fasting for all persons as an act of love and compassion. The Constant of Humility keeps all spiritual practices under the choicest blessings of Love and Grace within the Holy Increase of God.

> *Lay aside ego and reach to Universe.*
>
> *True humility is to know that one is an Image of God and is therefore devoid of any ruthless, passionate excelling over any other human being. Humility, by nature, is unburdened, free of the cares oppressing the ego-involved. Humility provides an unchallenged authority which is experienced for the good of humanity in timing to the need to remember that God has given to every man the essence of goodness, of rightness.*
>
> — Ann Ree Colton

THE CELEBRATION CONSCIOUSNESS

> *The enlightened consciousness expresses each moment of the day and the night as a Celebration of the Creation of Man in the Image of God.*

For a saintly soul, life is a Celebration of the Image of God in himself and in all other persons. To walk the Path of Jesus and the Saints is a Celebration of communion with Heavenly Beings and Presences.

Saintly personages feel deep compassion for their fellow men. All who willingly carry the cross of suffering in the spirit of penance and restitution for the sins of the world are inspired by their love for the Image of God in the soul of every living being. It is this deep and abiding love that makes of each day a Celebration and a testimony of faith, devotion, and trust in God and His Eternal Plan. *"Gather my saints together unto me; those that have made a covenant with me by sacrifice."* (Psalm 50:5)

Each Sacramental Meditation is a Celebration of the closeness of God through the Mediation of His Beloved Son.

Each Sabbath Day is a Celebration of God's Creation of the Heavens and the Earth; it is a Celebration of the Resurrection of Jesus and His victory over death. Through the Sabbath Cycle, each day of the week becomes a Celebration of service to God.

Each Christmas, Epiphany, Easter and Pentecost is a Celebration of profound significance in the history of the world and in the soul's Eternal Covenant with God.

Each Sacrament of Communion is a Celebration of the mighty powers of Liberation, Redemption and Illumination blessing the world through Christ Jesus.

Each time one says *Grace* before a meal, he is *celebrating* the Love and Providence of God. The Lord's Presence grows increasingly stronger in households and in ministries where family members and co-disciples break bread together in the spirit of Celebration.

The birth of a virtue or a soul-gift is a monumental time of Celebration in the Soul's Eternal Record.

Each birthday of a sincere devotee is a time of Celebration on the level of the Soul in its Covenant with God.

Each anniversary experienced by a married couple faithful in their vows to one another over the years is a time of Celebration when sweet blessings come from the Heavenly Father and the Divine Mother.

A devotee faithful in his vows to God experiences profound increases of Grace each anniversary of his walk on the Path.

The opening of a Seal of Grace in the First, Second or Third Heaven is timed to the energy-processes and Cycles of the Moon, the Sun and the Planets. Each time a Grace-Seal is opened to a servant of God, there is joy and celebration on the soul-level. Each Seal of Grace that opens is part of his Spiritual-Birthright Inheritance.

When a devoted servant of the Lord passes from the world, his death becomes a time of Celebration in Heaven, especially if he has served the Cause of Christ with honor and integrity. Reunited with cherished friends, loved ones and co-workers on the Path who also dwell in the afterlife, he reaps the rewards of the just and the righteous. The Angels, the Saints and other Heavenly Beings and Presences under whom he has served welcome and bless him with great joy, healing music and love-anointings.

A devotee who responds to his Teacher's instruction becomes as a bride ready for the Bridegroom. His soul's radiance breaking through the clouds of pride, unknowing and sin creates a happy time of Celebration in the Eternals. When his humility, compassion and selfless love qualify him for the Divine-Marriage Anointing, this is a major event of Cosmos significance and Celebration in the Eternals.

The Divine Marriage is a Celebration of pure motives, Christlike attitudes, and faithfulness to Holy Vows; it is also a Celebration of virtues quickened, conscience cleansed, and the yin–yang polarities' harmonious blending.

Through the Divine-Marriage Celebration, one becomes part of the Celebration of the Saints and the Angels who are always proclaiming the Glory of God. The Divine-Marriage Celebration also makes him a part of the Celebration of the Stars and the Galaxies in their joyous dance of creation within the Cosmos Will and Plan of God.

The Moon, the Sun and each Planet add their special Jewels to the Crown of Illumination in Celebration of one's earning the Divine-Marriage Anointing.

"Blessed are ye when men shall revile you, and persecute you, and shall say all manner of evil against you falsely, for my sake. Rejoice, and be exceeding glad; for great is your reward in heaven: for so persecuted they the prophets which were before you." (St. Matthew 5:11,12) To "rejoice and be exceeding glad" during the most difficult and dangerous situations in discipleship is the spirit of Celebration. Over the centuries, the courageous martyrs, Saints and other followers of Christ Jesus who have been persecuted and martyred for righteousness' sake retained the spirit of Celebration throughout all adversities, trials and challenges.

A true Christian has the Celebration Consciousness. The Celebration Consciousness is the Bliss Consciousness, the Eternal-Now Consciousness, the Divine-Image Consciousness.

Heavenly Father, may mankind always know the Celebration of Life, Love and Creation. May each of Thy children discover his Divine Heritage as an Eternal Creation through Thy Holy Image. In Jesus' Name. Amen.

PART VI

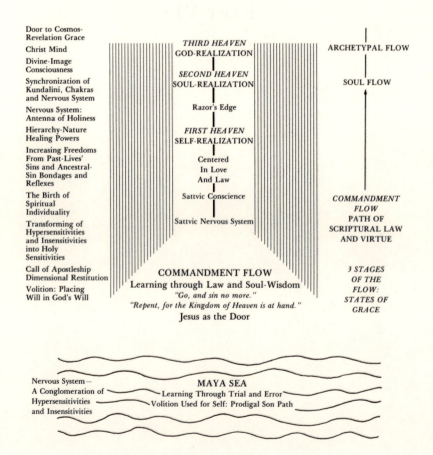

Door to Cosmos-
Revelation Grace

Christ Mind

Divine-Image
Consciousness

Synchronization of
Kundalini, Chakras
and Nervous System

Nervous System:
Antenna of Holiness

Hierarchy-Nature
Healing Powers

Increasing Freedoms
From Past-Lives'
Sins and Ancestral-
Sin Bondages and
Reflexes

The Birth of
Spiritual
Individuality

Transforming of
Hypersensitivities
and Insensitivities
into Holy
Sensitivities

Call of Apostleship
Dimensional Restitution

Volition: Placing
Will in God's Will

THIRD HEAVEN
GOD-REALIZATION

SECOND HEAVEN
SOUL-REALIZATION

Razor's Edge

FIRST HEAVEN
SELF-REALIZATION

Centered
In Love
And Law

Sattvic Conscience

Sattvic Nervous System

ARCHETYPAL FLOW

SOUL FLOW

*COMMANDMENT
FLOW*
PATH OF
SCRIPTURAL LAW
AND VIRTUE

*3 STAGES
OF THE
FLOW:
STATES OF
GRACE*

COMMANDMENT FLOW
Learning through Law and Soul-Wisdom
"Go, and sin no more."
"Repent, for the Kingdom of Heaven is at hand."
Jesus as the Door

Nervous System —
A Conglomeration of
Hypersensitivities
and Insensitivities

MAYA SEA
Learning Through Trial and Error
Volition Used for Self: Prodigal Son Path

VOLITION AND THE NERVOUS SYSTEM

24

THE SATTVIC NERVOUS SYSTEM

The will and the nerves are twin systems through which the soul may raise man to a higher degree of consciousness.

Within the nervous system there lieth the greatest system of telepathy man may ever conceive.

— Ann Ree Colton

THE PEACE OF CHRIST

Peace I leave with you, my peace I give unto you: not as the world giveth, give I unto you. Let not your heart be troubled, neither let it be afraid.

—St. John 14:27

The nervous system holds the key to the Process of Initiation and Illumination. When the nervous system is blessed with the Peace of Christ, it becomes a *sattvic** nervous system sensitively attuned to the Word and Will of God.

"Blessed are the peacemakers: for they shall be called the children of God." (St. Matthew 5:19) A peaceful nervous system is the result of union with God through love, law and virtue. Sattvic servants of God are inspired peacemakers whose

---

*In Sanskrit, *sattva* or *sattvic* means peace, purity, virtue, goodness, harmony and rhythm.

nervous systems, as antennas of holiness, receive sanctified telepathies from the Heaven Worlds.

The nervous system of a Saint is bathed in the energies of love and virtue. Therefore, a true Saint is not subject to the painful lessons and karmic involvements caused by a nervous system plagued by unholy sensitivities and petty irritations.

A sattvic nervous system may require ages to attain; or, through the Christ, the nervous system may be healed miraculously through His Supernatural Peace. *"These things I have spoken unto you, that in me ye might have peace."* (St. John 16:33)

Man is being gloriously and wondrously created in the Image of God. The kundalini and chakras, the nervous system, and all other energy currents within his body are potential dynamos of greatness and grace. When all energy-currents in the body, emotions, mind and soul are in perfect attunement with the energies of the Solar System and the Cosmos, one becomes an enlightened participant in the energy-processes of Universal Creation.

The Peace of Christ is charged with the sacred electricities of wisdom, joy and pure creation. The receiving of the Supernatural Peace of Christ represents a major attainment on the Path of Illumination, for it places all Body-Temple energies directly under the Grace of God radiating from His Image. A faithful devotee filled with the Peace of Christ is blessed with a sattvic nervous system, a strong immune system, a polarized hormone system and the harmonious synchronization of all other energy functions in the Body Temple.

> *The nerves, which relate man to the Spiritual Worlds through the kundalini or spinal structure, give to man the future hint of that prepared for him. His nervous system will become a great dispenser of mind, of spreading Light—a luminous Light.*
>
> —Ann Ree Colton

The calmer we are and the less disturbed our nerves, the more shall we love and the better will our work be.

—Vivekananda

A probationer on the Path cannot become a trustworthy spiritual leader until he attains a sattvic nervous system, for he must be able to express a peaceful composure and calm under any and all circumstances. The healing of the nervous system by the Christ enables him to minister to others without becoming irritated by their resistances, criticisms and ingratitude. If a devotee of the Lord permits himself to become irritated with others, he will become bitter or cynical. A sattvic nervous system enables one to see the Divine Image in all persons and to remain receptive to the telepathies of the Kingdom of God guiding and enlightening him.

A powerful gene-telepathy and nervous-system telepathy through the Image of God keep an enlightened Teacher linked with the Godhead Telepathic Flow that produces Christ-Mind Illumination Grace.

THE SOUL AND THE SENSES

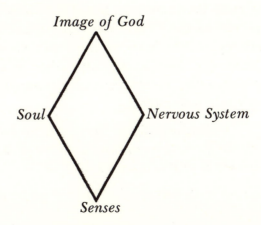

The Image of God in the Godhead sends forth its powerful energies to man through the soul. The soul, utilizing the *Principle of Gradation*, is the mediator between the Image-of-God energies and life on the earth-plane of existence.

The soul sends the energies of life into the body, the breath, the blood. All mental, emotional and physical energies are provided by the soul. The energies utilized by the senses are provided by the soul. The senses are the trial-and-error perceivers of life's lessons. Everything one learns on earth through the senses is indelibly recorded in the soul's eternal record.

The soul, working with the Image of God, determines the allotment of energies for each moment of one's life. When the soul withdraws the energies for life on earth, death comes, and one experiences the afterlife. The afterlife exposes him to other degrees of soul-energies and Image-of-God energies.

The nervous system links the soul with the senses. As the senses become disciplined perceivers of wisdom and knowledge, the soul opens its treasury of dimensional energies. This stage of progress represents a higher and finer state of energization through the Image of God.

The nervous-system energies determine one's placement on the Path of Eternal Life, for the nervous system relates directly to the Creation-processes of God working through His Image, the soul and the senses. Through spiritual-initiation procedures and purifications, the senses, the soul and the Divine Image become *one*; thereafter, the Spirit-of-God Image-energies may flow directly through a cleansed soul-record and a sattvic nervous system.

> *To minister in Jesus' Name as a mediator for His Healing-Miracle powers is to be a peacemaker twenty-four hours a day.*

SELF-CONTROL

> *The first requirement for the spiritual disciple is self-control.*
>
> *The Spiritual Worlds offer immense power. Spiritual practices assure one of power. Lack of self-control is a misuse of power, producing malignancies, suffering, separations, disasters.*
>
> —Ann Ree Colton

> *And if a man loves uprightness, Her labors are virtues; for she teaches self-control and understanding. Uprightness and courage; Nothing in life is more useful to men than these.*
>
> —Apocrypha

Self-Control is the first step on the Ladder of the Spiritual Life. He who attains self-control is a true devotee of the Lord ready to serve His Maker with constancy in love and emotional stability. The dignity of the Divine Image shines forth through emotional stability.

During his first years on the Path, a probationer must establish his integrity in the sight of God. His degree of devotion and self-control determines if and when he earns the Devotee's Anointing; next, the Initiate's Anointing; and, finally, the Teacher's Anointing. Many students desire to become Anointed Teachers, but few are willing to earn this Benediction through the initiations, disciplines, dedications and vows requiring self-control.

Regardless of how much spiritual training an aspirant receives, if he does not have self-control he will fall victim to Satan, and he is in danger of causing others to fall with him; this will add new sin-burdens to his soul's record. The Teacher who teaches the importance of self-control is seeking to keep this tragedy from occurring in the soul-records of his students—a tragedy carried over into coming lives.

It is impossible to be a servant of God without the insulation provided by the virtue of self-control and the other virtues emphasized throughout the Scriptures of the East and the West. A wise devotee listens attentively to his Teacher who is seeking to help him earn the Divine-Marriage Anointing.

Many probationers on the Path try to appear gentle in public, but their lack of self-control makes of them tyrants in their homes, expressing neurotic and selfish behavior. Such persons forget that God knows that they are leading double lives and are far from the constancy in love necessary for true devotees of the higher life.

It is brash and deceitful egotism to think one's self ready to become a teacher or minister of God's Word before he has attained self-control. The problems and troubles in ministries are caused by priests, ministers and members in their congregations who do not have self-control.

> *There has never been, and cannot be, a good life without self-control; apart from self-control, no good life is imaginable. The attainment of goodness must begin with that.*
>
> — Tolstoy

> *From every power that holds the world in chains, man frees himself when self-control he gains.*
>
> — Goethe

ANGER AND TANTRUMS

> *There is no sin or wrong that gives a man such a foretaste of Hell in this life as anger and impatience.*
>
> — Saint Catherine of Siena

> *Each time one boils over in temper, he adds to the tension and irritation within his own karma.*

Every time you are angry, you deplete the adrenal gland.
Every time you are angry without cause, you are damaging the brain.
Anger is conquered by its antidote—love.
— Ann Ree Colton

Meditation and prayer should make the nervous system more *peaceful*. However, if a meditator is *not* centered in Love and Law, he will become extremely hypersensitive and express irritations, angers and other unloving attitudes.

Anger is a rape of the Commandment of Love; it is a destructive energy that injures one's self as well as other persons. Anger, hate, prejudice, jealousy, impatience and covetousness blind the eyes to the Image of God in others.

The thief of anger steals grace. Each anti-virtue
is a thief that steals grace.

Individuals with hypersensitive emotions and nerves have hair-trigger tempers that the Antichrist can use at any time. Tantrum-prone students on the Path are revealing their arrested emotional development. Their immature behavior may be due to childhood traumas, parental neglect of discipline, or they may be expressing the gene-reflex tendencies of parents and ancestors with volatile tempers. Through the Abiding Presence of Christ, one is healed of the tantrum-consciousness, and thereafter becomes a stable and trustworthy servant of the Lord. The Gift of Peace divinely bestowed by God and Christ transforms the temperament, bringing an indefinable peace to the emotions and the nerves.

The more a devotee is filled with the Love of God and the Peace of Christ, the more he is a peacemaker centered in emotional stability, poise and equanimity. The Love of God and the Peace of Christ contain *Ageless Wisdom, Holy Vir-*

tues and *Pure-Creation Essences* that miraculously transform his emotions, thoughts, life and being.

> **Heavenly Father, I pray to be filled with the Love of God and the Peace of Christ, that I may be endowed with the Timeless, Ageless Wisdom of Love and the Harmony and Joy of Holy Peace. In Jesus' Name. Amen.**

An infant or child has a tantrum because he *wants* something. An adult of any age may continue to express childish tantrums whenever he or she *wants* something. A selfless devotee of the Lord does not *want* things, powers or pleasures of the world; he does not want control over the wills of others. All he desires is to *give* his love to God and to give his love to all whom God places in his life.

Givers do not have tantrums because they do not want anything or expect anything from others. Takers are prone to tantrums because they feel frustrated when thwarted in their desire to receive things, powers and pleasures.

The virtues of self-control, holy poverty, detachment and giving are a devotee's greatest protections in his expressing mature emotions, pure motives and sacred sensitivities.

Numerous persons who are meditating and praying continue sinning. They sin each time they express the critical mind, the judging mind, pettiness, prejudice, anger, jealousy, complaining and blaming.

"Go, and sin no more." (St. John 5:14) To sin no more is to bless God and to be blessed by Him. The Holy Increase of God's Mercy and Truth is a daily reality to those who sin no more in thought, emotion, word and deed. Beholding the Lord face to face, they delight in His abundance of Grace.

> *Even a sinful person, if he worships me with unswerving devotion, must be regarded as righteous,*

for he has formed the right resolution. He soon be-
comes righteous and attains eternal peace.
                                    —Bhagavad Gita

From the death of each sin, a soul power or gift
is made manifest.
                                    —Ann Ree Colton

THE SPIRIT OF INDULGENCE

Let your moderation be known unto all men.
                                    —Philippians 4:5

The sage avoids extremes, excesses, and com-
placency.
                                    —Lao Tzu

Satan works through *the spirit of indulgence* to take many captives in the Holy War. Some aspirants on the Path are the spirit of indulgence incarnate; their love of comforts, pleasures and self is far greater than their love for God and the Truth.

The indulgence of the senses keeps one linked to the Ancestral-Sin Core and the dark side of the soul's record.

The spirit of indulgence is expressed when one indulges in gluttonous eating and excessive television-watching. To indulge in depression and self-pity also denotes bondage to the spirit of indulgence under the Antichrist.

Depression, as an indulgence, is a cardinal sin.
Eating indulgently after a fast leads to fantasy.
Former-life habits remain imprinted upon the
etheric body. The etheric body is a chameleon-like
servant obeying and reproducing habit patterns
from former-life indulgence.
                                    —Ann Ree Colton

To indulge one's sensual appetites through the overeating of ice cream, cakes, candy, chocolate or the habitual drinking of soft drinks, coffee and alcohol offends the Body Temple and the Virtue of Moderation. The spirit of indulgence is especially destructive when related to addictive drugs and sexual excesses.

To indulge in lustful activities; to indulge in moods; to indulge in pessimistic attitudes, lying and unkind speaking — these take one farther away from the Kingdom of God.

One of the most common forms of indulgence for devotees on the Path is the attitude of likes and dislikes. They *like* some co-disciples and *dislike* others. This deadly indulgence removes them from the Grace of God, for they are not expressing the Commandment of Love Ye One Another. When one does not love all souls with an unconditional love, he forfeits the Holy Grace that comes only through a pure and selfless love for all.

To honestly face and confess to God one's physical, emotional and mental indulgences is necessary if he is desirous of uniting with the Healing and Redeeming Power of Jesus. Redemption brings freedom from bondage to the spirit of indulgence and other satanic spirits.

When the senses are no longer enslaved by the spirit of indulgence, the soul is liberated — and one may begin his true walk on the Path of Virtue in service to God and Christ.

Through the Redemption Power of Jesus, the five senses become expressions of *soul-energies*. The dimensional energies of the soul seek to make of one a prophet and revelator for God.

Satan approaches those who are receiving soul-energies and seeks to distract them from keeping their vows to God by playing upon the five senses. Any tendency toward sense-distractions and sense-indulgences will keep the senses from becoming flowing outlets for soul-energies. One's only protection during these testing times of his senses and nervous system is to keep his mind "stayed" on God. (Isaiah 26:3)

As one proves faithful in his vows to God, he experiences the Redemption Power of Jesus through soul-energies that transform his thoughts, emotions and actions. Soul-energies flow through his five senses, making him a co-creator with God through his Spiritual-Birthright Inheritance.

There are numerous casualties during the initiatory testing times of the senses and the nerves, for Satan skillfully entices unwary individuals into all manner of sense-distractions and sense-indulgences that negate the receiving of the soul's energies through the Redemption Power of Jesus.

Heavenly Father, I pray to be a good steward of all sense-energies and not squander them through selfish indulgences. May all sense-energies become soul-energies to be used in service to Thee. In Jesus' Name. Amen.

Schoolteachers who indulge their students; priests and ministers who indulge their flocks; husbands and wives who indulge their mates — all are victims of the spirit of indulgence.

To indulge in hurt feelings renders a probationer on the Path incapable of serving his Lord with emotional stability. The degree of one's hurt feelings reveals the size of his ego. The bigger the ego, the more he suffers hurt feelings. The absense of hurt feelings denotes the absence of ego — and the beginning of one's walk on the Spiritual Path.

Priests and ministers *indulge* their congregations when they fail to emphasize the importance of the Ten Commandments, the Law of Tithing and the Ethics, Principles and Disciplines taught by Jesus. These lax attitudes by individuals in positions of religious authority reveal that they have become the tragic victims of the spirit of indulgence.

Modern-day fathers and mothers often indulge their children's every desire even when their offspring show little or no gratitude or obedience. Parents who sanction their unmarried adolescent sons and daughters engaging in sexual affairs as long as they use birth control are reaching new lows in parental indulgence. Such parents are inviting misery and unhappiness into their children's lives through sexually-transmitted viruses and other painful diseases, as well as mental, emotional and psychological difficulties.

The world is undergoing an acceleration regarding the learning of the difference between right and wrong, morality and immorality. He who opens his ears to the Commandments of God and the Ethics of Jesus has begun his ascent up the Mountain of Illumination. As he is exorcised of the spirit of indulgence and other dark spirits, he will experience increasing measures of his Spiritual-Birthright Inheritance as a child of the Living God.

> *I am no longer a habit slave by choice. I am aware that bad habits will be the flaws in my next-life character. I am aware that good habits in this life will make life easier now and in the tomorrows to come.*
>
> —Ann Ree Colton

> *You are holy, Lord, the only God, and your deeds are wonderful . . . You are justice and moderation.*
> —Saint Francis of Assisi

SINS AND THE BODY TEMPLE

> *When parenthood begins as the natural result of love in the sexual life, giving begins. When one thwarts the giving side of parenthood through selfish desire—using the sexual force sensuously and selfishly—he closes the door on the pure and grace side of the genetic flow seeking to be manifested in the world.*
>
> —Ann Ree Colton

The ability to handle stress requires a healthy nervous system. The inability to handle even the slightest stresses denotes a nervous system overloaded with unconfessed sins. Such persons are easily irritated, upset and angered by trivialities. *The sins of ancestry are adversely affecting the lives of their children and children's children through easily-irritated, explosive nervous systems. This is one of the many ways that the unpaid sins of one's ancestors and past lives create havoc in his present life.*

The unconfessed sins of one's ancestors and previous lives not only impair the delicate circuitry of the nervous system, but they also weaken the immune system. A weakened immune system offers little or no protection against debilitating illnesses, diseases and afflictions.

Man cannot escape the checks and balances on God's Holy Laws and Commandments. He damages his own nervous system and immune system through his wilful transgressions, and he passes his unconfessed sins onto coming generations through the highly sensitive recording abilities of the genes and the chromosomes.

Nervous-system inharmonies, immune-system weaknesses, reproduction-system disorders and hormone-system imbalances relate to the unconfessed sins of past lives, parents and ancestors. Even as drug-taking, smoking and alcohol consumption adversely affect the fetus in the womb, so are the sins of parents and ancestors passed on to their offspring as defective energy-systems within the cells, the nerves and the glands.

Extreme temperament problems experienced by many women in timings related to the menstrual cycle reveal the presence of unconfessed sins. A woman without emotional self-control is especially vulnerable to the negative effects of the menstrual cycle. The bodily stress of the cycle cannot be contained by an already hypersensitive nervous-system — and the results are moods, angers, tantrums, depressions and other emotional abnormalities. The husbands of such women are exposed to the problems caused by their wives' difficulties because of the numerous unconfessed sins in their own souls' records.

> *There are the lunar moods women experience before and during menstrual periods. These may be either excessively loving or excessively negative. A balanced woman watches these moods and controls them creatively.*
>
> *The high side of the Menstrual Cycle is Shakti. The low side of the Menstrual Cycle is the Kali side of the Menstrual Cycle.*
>
> *Cycles of Aversion for each other in marriage come from the Undersoul and the ancestral-gene memory-reflexes working through the glandular system. When one is spiritually intuitive, he can be a blessing and a grace-companion during the Aversion Periods.*
>
> — Ann Ree Colton

A man's sexual sins; wrong attitudes toward sex; a lustful, sensual nature; and selfish or forceful behavior in sex — will aggravate the stress experienced by a woman heavy-laden with unresolved sexual sins in her soul's record. Both are caught in the cyclic tides of unresolved karma related to the reproduction system and the procreation energies. The unconfessed ancestral and parental sins regarding the procreation function compound the problems and unhappiness of the married couple, especially during the timing of the menstrual cycle.

Sexual sin-debts of ancestors, increasing from generation to generation, afflict the reproduction and procreation systems of their offspring. The same sexual sins being committed by their offspring in the present generation will place even heavier burdens on coming generations.

Even as Jesus healed the woman with the longtime problem

of the "issue of blood" (St. Matthew 9:20–22), so can He heal all disorders of the bodily processes for women and men who repent of their procreation-energy sins and other cardinal sins.

Repentance, confession, self-control, reverence in sex, asking for Jesus' supernatural help — all contribute to the healing of the hypersensitive nervous systems of husband and wife. A vigilant self-control will enable the couple to remain centered in harmony, peace and love.

As a woman-initiate becomes detached from the influences of ancestral, parental and past-lives' sins, the menstrual cycle and all other glandular cycles come under the blessings of the Synchronization Power of Christ Jesus.

Confession of one's own sexual sins, the sexual sins of his parents and ancestors and the sexual sins of the world begins the healing process. The supernatural help of the Christ *strengthens* the nervous system, thereby producing emotional self-control and other blessings. The result is a miraculous healing of the individual and the marriage — and a new life of harmony and fulfillment.

Procreation, the reproduction system, the immune system and the nervous system are sacred, for they are integral parts of the Body Temple, the Soul's energy-processes and the Image of God.

The irreverence for life through abortions; the irreverence toward Marriage Vows through adultery; the irreverence toward God's Image through perversions; the irreverence for the bodies and the souls of others through unlawful sex — all involve attitudes that must be changed to reverent attitudes before permanent healings can occur through the Mediation of Jesus.

Men are presently living in the dark age of immorality. Their only hope is a morality based upon Scriptural values and standards.

Life is beautiful when love is pure, Divine Laws are cherished, and the Body Temple, the Soul and the Image of God are reverenced. The reproduction system has much to teach men and women about the creation of the individual in the Image of God. This knowledge begins to open through reverence for life, reverence for morality, and reverence for the innate divinity of the human spirit.

Jesus heals the *whole person* by healing the nervous system, the immune system, the reproduction system and all other energy-systems of the physical body, the emotions, the mind and the soul. A soul cleansed of darkness is a soul liberated from the oppressive burden of unconfessed sins. To work *with* the Great Physician is to experience His Miracle Grace through the Mercy of God.

"With the mouth confession is made unto salvation." (Romans 10:10) It is not enough to confess one's own sins, for these cause only a portion of his problems and difficulties. He should also confess the sins of his parents and ancestors that are causing insidious and destructive influences upon his Body-Temple energy-processes.

> *The hormone system supports the pranic-energy life of the breath; this is the system most affected by Cyclic Law.*
>
> —Ann Ree Colton

The hormones play important roles in the determination of masculine and feminine tendencies. When the genes and the soul's record are heavy laden with unconfessed sins, one may experience major hormone-system imbalances.

All nerves, glands and organs are affected by the genes and the chromosomes. Masculine women and feminine men have major hormone imbalances. The great number of homosexuals in the world gives testimony to the procreation-energy sins of ancestors, parents and past lives. To be born with any sexual abnormality is a direct result of unconfessed sins that have accumulated in the genes, the chromosomes and the soul's record.

Homosexuals who have accepted their condition as being unhealable have little or no faith in the miraculous Mercy of God and the Healing Power of Christ Jesus. To unburden the soul through confession, repentance, penance and restitution helps to normalize the interrelated energy-systems between the Image of God and the present-life self.

To *know* that one is the victim of others' sins as well as his own sins is the beginning of his being healed, liberated and normalized through the Christ. His belief in reincarnation assists the Christ to heal the soul's record of past-lives' sins. If one does not confess the sins of previous lives, he limits the Healing Power of the Christ.

> *Seek with all thy heart to gain the sattvic peace.*
>
> *There can be little meaning in a life of hatred founded upon the preservation of envy, jealousy, covetousness, and revenge. The sattvic peace once gained assures health, intelligence, freedom.*
>
> *Every cell of the body is aggressive. When absent from the sattvic principle of love, there is sickness to the body. When one has finally reached the state of true self-awareness, his body functions in a dimension of health, unity and harmony.*
>
> *A sattvic nature supports the harmonies of the Universe.*
>
> —Ann Ree Colton

Sin is not of the Image of God; therefore, the sins of ancestors passed on through the genes can be easily healed by the Christ. The Sattvic Tones of His Peace are mighty cleansers of the genes, washing away the sin-residue of ancestral and past-lives' transgressions. Through the Holy Peace of Christ Jesus, a devotee of the Lord is freed from ancestral sin-reflexes and is blessed with a sattvic nervous system. As his emotions and nerves are restored to their Image-of-God influences, he may represent the Lord Jesus as an appointed apostle.

The *Ancestral Grace* registered in the genes remains as a priceless inheritance from ancestors who loved God and lived according to His Commandments. Ancestral Grace is part of the Image of God in the cells — therefore, it remains as virtue-strengths, talents and skills.

Many persons have little or no *soul* qualities of spiritual individuality; they are a conglomeration of forces and energies duplicating the sins of their ancestors. Unrighteous, immoral persons *are* the sins of their ancestors incarnate. They think like their ancestors, behave like their ancestors, sin like their ancestors. There is no difference between them and their ancestors' moods, depressions, hypersensitivities. If their ancestors were tyrants, they are tyrants. Tyranny through forceful wills, tyranny through angers and tantrums, tyranny through pettiness and all other tyrannies are ancestral abominations passed onto their *"children, and upon the children's children, unto the third and to the fourth generation."* (Exodus 34:7)

When does this robot-like sin-inherited behavior end? It ends with Christ Jesus! When the Light of the Christ is in one's heart, mind, soul and life, he is free to be his True Self at one with God and His Kingdom.

Sins cannot live in the Light of the Christ. Therefore, O devotee, embrace Christ; invite His Light to abide in thee. Face God; confess your sins and your ancestors' sins. He will forgive you, and His Son will redeem you. Be your True Self as imaged by Almighty God.

Let the Word of God be free in you through love. Let the Kingdom of God pour its bountiful Treasures upon you through faith. You are a child of God's Spirit, not an endless reproducer of ancestral sins afflicting your own children and their children. Resolve to stop this terrible sin-syndrome NOW.

Determine to be free. Pray to be free—free to be that Self which responds only to the Will and Love of God.

IN THE NAME OF THE CHRIST, BE FREE.

If the Son therefore shall make you free, ye shall be free indeed.

—St. John 8:36

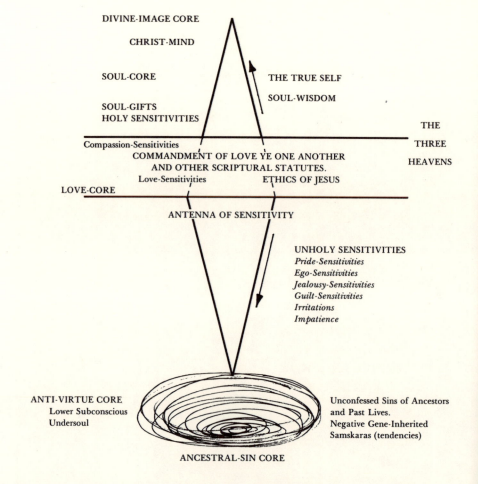

DIVINE-IMAGE CORE

CHRIST-MIND

SOUL-CORE   THE TRUE SELF

                                   SOUL-WISDOM

SOUL-GIFTS
HOLY SENSITIVITIES
                                                    THE

Compassion-Sensitivities   THREE
        COMMANDMENT OF LOVE YE ONE ANOTHER
          AND OTHER SCRIPTURAL STATUTES.   HEAVENS
        Love-Sensitivities   ETHICS OF JESUS

LOVE-CORE

              ANTENNA OF SENSITIVITY

                                    UNHOLY SENSITIVITIES
                                    Pride-Sensitivities
                                    Ego-Sensitivities
                                    Jealousy-Sensitivities
                                    Guilt-Sensitivities
                                    Irritations
                                    Impatience

ANTI-VIRTUE CORE   Unconfessed Sins of Ancestors
Lower Subconscious   and Past Lives.
Undersoul   Negative Gene-Inherited
                                             Samskaras (tendencies)

              ANCESTRAL-SIN CORE

SENSITIVITIES AND THE FOUR CORES

25

THE SCIENCE OF SENSITIVITIES

In troubles and afflictions from without as well as from within, grant me the grace, my God, to pluck out the evil root of 'touchiness.'
— Saint Bernadette Soubirous

I was really unbearable because of my extreme touchiness . . . God would have to work a miracle to make me grow up in an instant, and this miracle He performed on that unforgettable Christmas Day.
— Saint Therese of Lisieux

Man revealeth himself as sensitive, becoming healed, and thus becoming a healer.
— Ann Ree Colton

THE ANTENNA OF SENSITIVITY

In the present era, the downpouring of Archetypal spiritual wisdom is flowing into the souls of the initiated and the sensitive.

Spiritually-sensitive souls are aware of the Holy-Ghost action, and respond according to their spiritual aptitudes. Negative persons respond with irritation, dissolution, rebellion.

The more sensitive one is as to what God is, the more he will be Godlike.
— Ann Ree Colton

During the initiatory cycles of the higher life, the nervous system undergoes dramatic changes. This may be likened to a serpent shedding its skin and becoming extremely sensitive. Some devotees become so hypersensitive during these initiatory transformation-cycles that they either leave the Spiritual Path or they lead retreatist lives.

Each sensitivity-initiation crossroad on the Path claims many casualties. Devotees who survive these sensitivity-trials become enlightened initiates and teachers knowledgeable in the relationship between the nervous system, the genes, the emotions, the soul and the Image of God.

Sensitivity acts as an antenna that points either upward or downward. When the antenna of sensitivity points upward, one expresses love-sensitivities, compassion-sensitivities and other holy sensitivities in service to God and his fellow man. His sensitivities are inspired by the radiance of his soul, the Peace of Christ and the Grace of the Divine Image.

When the antenna of sensitivity points downward, one remains linked with the sins of his ancestors and past lives that produce pride-sensitivities and other unholy sensitivities. The miracles of the spiritual life begin the moment a penitent soul reverses the antenna of sensitivity from its downward position and directs it toward the Light of Heaven.

The unconfessed sins of one's ancestors and past lives create a vortex of dark energies within the Anti-Virtue Core that produces insensitivities and hypersensitivities. Through love and self-control, virtues become stabilized energy-expressions that radiate the sacred sensitivities of the soul and the Divine Image into the heart, mind and body.

Until a devotee becomes centered in love and self-control, his antenna of sensitivity will fluctuate back and forth from the upward position to the downward position. From time to time, such persons receive beautiful inspirations from Heaven's Light; however, when their unstable emotions swing the antenna of sensitivity toward the lower subconscious and the

Ancestral-Sin Core, they express erratic and unloving behavior patterns.

Sensitivities born of love and virtue make one sensitive to right and wrong. This holy sensitivity protects him from the many pitfalls that claim the unrighteous and the unlawful.

> *Good men and bad men differ from each other in their natures. Bad men do not recognize a sinful act as sinful; if its sinfulness is brought to their attention, they do not cease doing it and do not like to have anyone inform them of their sinful acts. Wise men are sensitive to right and wrong; they cease doing anything as soon as they see that it is wrong; they are grateful to anyone who calls their attention to such acts.*
>
> *— Buddha*

Every devotee who directs his sensitivity-antenna away from the Anti-Virtue Core toward the Higher Worlds learns of his spiritual uniqueness as a child of God. Herein begins his communion with the joys, ecstasies and bliss-visitations of God's Holy Spirit that produce Enlightenment and Illumination.

One can love his parents and ancestors more purely and see the Divine Image in them more clearly when he detaches himself from their negative tendencies and sensitivities. This detachment is necessary before he can express his spiritual individuality in service to God.

> *The Christ is the matchmaker between sensitivity and virtue. The Antichrist is the matchmaker between sensitivity and anti-virtue.*

When sensitivity is married to love, a devotee increases in holy sensitivities from prayer to prayer, meditation to meditation. When sensitivity is married to egotism, pride or guilt, he increases in unholy sensitivities from prayer to prayer, meditation to meditation. As long as an aspirant retains egotism, pride or guilt, he will express ego-sensitivities, pride-sensitivities and guilt-sensitivities rather than evolve the spiritual sensitivities necessary for a sustained telepathic communion with the Three Heavens.

Sensitivity minus love equals hypersensitivity or touchiness. Sensitivity plus love equals enlightenment and patience.

Hypersensitivities and insensitivities are Satan's domain. Spiritual sensitivities denote the Presence of God and Christ.

Egotism and pride fuel hypersensitivity; stubbornness and non-acceptance of sacred instruction increase insensitivity. A probationer who expresses both hypersensitivity in temperament and insensitivity toward study is in need of healings and exorcisms by the Christ.

A devotee with ego-sensitivities and pride-sensitivities is being insensitive to the Commandment of Love. Union with the energies of God's Spirit and the Christ Light within the Commandment of Love brings an instantaneous healing of hypersensitivity and insensitivity — and the aspirant is blessed with the holy increase of love-sensitivities.

> **Father, I pray for the healing of insensitivities and hypersensitivities. Please heal me, that I might serve Thee with holy sensitivities, emotional stability, and constancy in love. In Jesus' Name. Amen.**

Insensitivity is *tamasic*. Hypersensitivity is *rajasic*. Sacred sensitivities are *sattvic*. The transenergization of insensitivity and hypersensitivity into sattvic sensitivities blesses the devotee with spiritual-creative gifts. The Path of the Higher Life is the Path of Spiritualizing Sensitivities through the Holy Ghost and other Heavenly Mediators under the Christ.

The more the Holy Ghost abides in a servant of God, the more he has the magnification of Pure Truth. These increasing magnifications of Truth make him more sensitively attuned to the *Omnipresence* of God speaking to him through everyone and everything.

A devotee's volition in the use of physical, emotional and mental energies determines his rate of progress on the Path. Many probationers use volition to express more resistance toward Scriptural Wisdom. Their *insensitivity* toward the Word of God renders them incapable of rendering any meaningful service to their fellow man.

Many students on the Path remain insensitive to the wisdom of the Scriptures and hypersensitive to their Teacher's admonitions. Others are sensitively attuned to Scriptural wisdom and are grateful for their Teacher's suggestions and corrections. When one comprehends *the science of sensitivities*, he may better discern and confess areas of his nature and temperament that require healing through the Redemption Power of Jesus.

Probationers who remain insensitive to Scriptural instruction regarding love, law and virtues fail to experience the Christ-quickenings that would free them from karmic enclosures.

Insensitivity is not spiritual detachment. Insensitivity denotes an apathetic nature in bondage to laziness, procrastination, stubbornness, non-complying and selfishness. Spiritual detachment denotes love, empathy, compassion, and the desire to minister to others regardless of the cost or the consequences.

When a devotee expresses the love-sensitivities of the higher nature through all tests and trials, he is ready to represent Jesus in the world with a constancy in virtue and righteousness. His spiritual sensitivities at one with Scriptural wisdom and soul-wisdom enable him to serve His Lord with holy rejoicing regardless of adversities and persecutions.

Sensitivities clothed in the Love-Commandments become the Telepathic Sensitivity that unites one with the

Glory of God within the Three Heavens. This high degree of Redemption Grace through the Inheritance transforms a devotee into an enlightened Teacher anointed by God's Holy Spirit.

GUILT AND CONSCIENCE

The more one evolves, the more sensitive he becomes—and the more is he a valuable prize to the forces of darkness, that they may cast him down.
—Ann Ree Colton

Satan claims many victims at each stage of sensitivity-initiation. Until a devotee places his insensitivities and hypersensitivities on God's Holy Altar for healing, the Antichrist will continue to wreak havoc in his life and ministry. The healing of unholy sensitivities and the attaining of sacred sensitivities represent a major victory in one's quest for union with God.

Satan *knows* that every aspirant on the Spiritual Path will develop highly-sensitive emotions and nervous systems through prayer, meditation and fasting. He waits with his army of demons and devils to *ambush* nonvigilant aspirants who fail to unite with the teachings of Jesus regarding Love, Law, Ethics, Humility, Compassion, Patience, Self-Denial and Self-Control.

To be ambushed and captured by Satan in the Holy War through negative sensitivities is to fall from Grace. The closer a devotee is to his Teacher, the more he becomes a prized target of the Antichrist. Judas fell from a high level of Grace as a disciple of Jesus because of his nonvigilance and hypersensitivities. All devotees who do not express vigilance, loyalty and pure love are following the example of Judas. It is only a matter of time before Satan will take control of their vulnerable hypersensitivities and cause them to betray their souls, their Teacher, co-disciples, the Lord Jesus and Almighty

God. Few probationers are *chosen* for the Divine Marriage because the majority of aspirants are not vigilant during the testing times of their sensitivities.

The tempter works through jealousy-sensitivities to create distrust, fears, dissensions, worries and divisions in ministries, marriages, families, friendships and other associations. The healing of jealousy-sensitivities by the Christ inspires trust, love and holy detachment. Holy detachment brings peace to the mind and the emotions and establishes harmonious relationships.

When *guilt* for sins committed by one's self and his ancestors permeates the nervous system and the subconscious mind, his hypersensitivities may develop into neurotic or psychoneurotic difficulties. Destroying happiness at every turn, such persons remain shut away from Heaven's Grace and cause misery and sorrow in the lives of loved ones and others.

> *Persons filled with guilt are hypersensitive telepathic receivers of subtle earthbound-dead telepathy. Their heart stations of receptivity have no barricades against subtle minds seeking to penetrate their minds and wills.*
>
> — Ann Ree Colton

"Come unto me, all ye that labour and are heavy laden, and I will give you rest." (St. Matthew 11:28) All who are heavy laden with a guilt-saturated subconsciousness and a hypersensitive nervous system may find perfect peace through Christ Jesus, and thus begin their walk on the Path of Love toward Enlightenment.

Beloved Lord, please heal me of all sensitivities and guilts delaying my union with Thy Forgiving Love and Redeeming Grace. May Thy Light abide in me, that I may serve Thee and love Thee with a whole heart, mind and soul. In Jesus' Name. Amen.

A retarded conscience keeps one in a state of insensitivity to spiritual laws, morals and ethics. A fiery conscience inflames one's feelings of guilt and shame for sins, transgressions and betrayals. A sattvic conscience is expressed by one who has made his peace with God and His Scriptural ordinances.

Conscience-sensitivities combined with an unrepentant spirit cause a host of psychosomatic and psychological problems and afflictions. A peaceful conscience enables the emotions, the nerves and the subconscious to work in harmony with one another, the soul and the Image of God.

> *Emotional maturity can be achieved through (1) right responsibilities, (2) self-control, (3) receiving with praisegiving, with detachment, (4) love for all life, creatures, persons, (5) continued love phrasings and speaking, (6) love demonstrativeness, (7) love of God and of His Creation.*
>
> —Ann Ree Colton

MOODS AND CRAVINGS

> *Look upon the countenance of a man who is at one moment angry, at the next sad, a short while afterward joyful, then troubled again, and then contented . . . See how he who thinks himself one is not one, but seems to have as many personalities as he has moods, as also the Scripture says: 'A fool is changed as the moon.' (Ecclesiasticus 27:11) God, therefore, is unchangeable, and is called one for the reason that he changes not. Thus also the true imitator of God, who is made after God's Image, is called one and the selfsame when he comes to perfection, for he also, when he is fixed on the summit of virtue, is not changed, but remains always one. For every man, while he is in wickedness, is divided among*

many things and torn in many directions; and while he
is in many kinds of evil he cannot be called one.

—Origen

Water flows continually into the ocean
But the ocean is never disturbed:
Desire flows into the mind of the seer
But he is never disturbed.
The seer knows peace:
The man who stirs up his own lusts
Can never know peace.
He knows peace who has forgotten desire.
He lives without craving:
Free from ego, free from pride.

—Bhagavad Gita

The foes of the spiritual life are dark moods, obsessive cravings, wrong attitudes, temperament problems, and other physical, emotional and mental inharmonies. Angry moods, slothful moods, depression moods, self-pity moods, lust moods and all other destructive moods must be healed before an aspirant may experience a continuous oneness with the Love of God.

During the Process of Initiation, the Christ must help each devotee become free from ages-old accumulations of sin-residue in the subconscious mind. He must detach him from all attachments that delay spiritual progress; also, He must teach him the sacred truths that will liberate his heart, mind and soul to their divine capacities and expressions.

Negative sensitivities produce unwholesome moods and cravings.

A moody individual uses the same intensity of energy in an anger-tirade as he does in a mood of self-pity. He merely swings the pendulum-like action of his emotions from one extreme to another. Satan takes one's moods of depression and

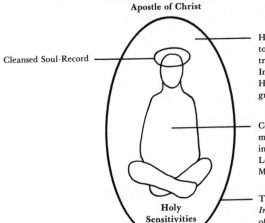

Whole-Armour-of-God Insulation
Apostle of Christ

Cleansed Soul-Record

Holy sensitivities enable one to receive the lighted Electricities of the Soul, the Image of God and the Three Heavens that produce progressive States of Grace.

Centered in the Ten Commandments, the Law of Tithing, the Commandments of Love and the Sermon-on-the-Mount Principles and Ethics.

The *Whole-Armour-of-God Insulation* is an energy-field of love, virtues and sacred vows.

Holy Sensitivities

Put on the whole armour of God.
—Ephesians 6:11

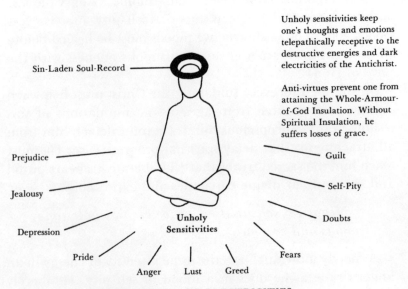

Unholy sensitivities keep one's thoughts and emotions telepathically receptive to the destructive energies and dark electricities of the Antichrist.

Anti-virtues prevent one from attaining the Whole-Armour-of-God Insulation. Without Spiritual Insulation, he suffers losses of grace.

Sin-Laden Soul-Record

Prejudice

Jealousy

Depression

Pride

Anger

Lust

Greed

Fears

Doubts

Self-Pity

Guilt

Unholy Sensitivities

SENSITIVITIES AND ELECTRICITIES

self-pity and uses them to divert him from service to God and Christ in the Holy War.

A probationer subject to expressions of fiery angers, deep depressions and self-pity should pray to come under the Healing and Quickening Power of the Christ. The wide swing of the Pendulum of Moods can be healed through one's faith in the Power of the Christ to *quicken* the Virtues of Equanimity, Self-Control and Constancy in Love.

One display of anger in public can ruin one's credibility as a disciple of the Lord.

Satan and his angels are always trying to drag a person down into despair and hopelessness. The Christ and His Angels are always trying to lift one up to the transcendental heights of Grace and Joy.

Depression and all other dark moods are extremely destructive and cast shadows between the heart and the soul, the mind and the Divine Image. The Christ, in healing the emotions, heals one of dangerous moods. A radiant, peace-blessed devotee is a true representative of the Lord of Light.

A moody marriage partner is vulnerable to Satan's evil influences. A husband or wife subject to a spectrum of negative moods becomes the instrument used by the Antichrist to disturb or to destroy marital happiness and family harmony. The healing of moods brings stability to the family, joy to one's mate, and builds an insulation against the tempter. Thereafter, one may be free to experience the Spectrum of Holy Love through God's Mercy and Angelic Intercession.

The emotional body is strengthened through pure love, forgiveness, faith and a commitment to fulfill the Beatitudes as a daily dedication. The healing of the emotional-body weaknesses and excesses is miraculous through the Quickening Power of the Christ.

The overcoming of any anti-virtue, negative sensitivity, dark mood or obsessive craving is a time of Celebration in the soul, for the Eternal Light of the Christ has begun to abide in one's being.

> *Undersoul soiled-darkness must be cast out that it may become a cleansed and pure companion for the Most High Soul which contains the original Seed or pure Image of God. The Most High Soul is a superconscious energy-vehicle of movement.*
>
> *The adversary lives and thrives on one's craving or desire energy. To relax tensity in desire is to make ineffective the adversary challenges.*
>
> *A feast day of fasting is to make union with all life by standing away from appetite, standing away from craving, standing away from false desiring, and seeing the true desiring.*
>
> *Blessed are the saintly, holy frugalities. He who comes under these neither craves nor wants.*
>
> —Ann Ree Colton

The healing of craving brings peace. Craving denotes the absence of self-control. As one attains the Virtue of Self-Control through the Quickening Power of the Christ, he may know the joys of freedom in body, heart, mind and soul.

O Lord Christ Jesus, please heal me of the spirit of craving, that I may desire only that which is good and pleasing in God's sight.

The craving nature keeps one bound to the Prodigal-Son Consciousness. Emotional, mental and physical cravings may become major obsessions. These intense moods of craving attract satanic demons and devils.

Unnatural cravings indicate the presence of intruding spirits or demons. The obsessive craving for food attracts the dark spirit of gluttony. The craving for sleep attracts the spirit of indolence, laziness. The craving for money attracts the demon of greed. The craving for attention, prominence or power attracts the demons of pride and egotism. The unwanton craving for sex attracts lust-demons that corrupt the soul through immoral, unlawful and abnormal sexual desires.

"What thing is this? what new doctrine is this? for with authority commandeth he even the unclean spirits, and they do obey him." (St. Mark 1:29) When one responds to the Healing Power of the Christ, he is *exorcised* of the intruding demons and devils of the Antichrist. As he experiences liberation from subservience to the senses and satanic spirits, he expresses a sweet submission to the Grace and Peace of God.

Craving is the opposite of Detachment. Detachment is the key to the freedoms that prepare one for Illumination.

"Deliver us from evil." (St. Matthew 6:13) *Deliver us from craving.*

> **Heavenly Father, may I serve the Lord Jesus as His disciple free from pride, free from competitiveness, free from the craving for power and authority. May I serve humbly, meekly, modestly and selflessly in the spirit of Holy Apostleship. May I see the Image of God in my fellow man. In Jesus' Name. Amen.**

THE THOROUGHBRED AND THE CHRIST

> *The horse is prepared against the day of battle: but safety is of the Lord.*
> —Proverbs 21:31

Some students who come to a Teacher of the higher life may be compared to powerful, undisciplined thoroughbreds. A thoroughbred accustomed to running free is extremely hypersensitive, rearing, kicking, running away from anyone who approaches with a saddle. As long as a student retains extreme hypersensitivities, he will remain undisciplined or *wild* in his emotions and thoughts — and therefore the Christ cannot be his rider.

God places in the Teacher's hands the responsibility for preparing each hypersensitive student for the Christ. Some students respond to sacred instruction, while many others do not.

During the first years of trying to instill a sense of discipline in an angry, disrespectful *thoroughbred* student, the Teacher may be kicked many times by the high-flying hooves. This necessary part of the training of a hypersensitive student exposes the Teacher to the violent refusal of the thoroughbred to accept any rider. Nevertheless, the Teacher always remembers that God has asked him to prepare the new student for the Christ as the rider.

If the thoroughbred responds to the gradual training and encouragements of the Teacher, he must be prepared for further training. This training requires that he become gentle, harmless and meek under any and all circumstances or else he will rear up suddenly at the slightest sound and throw the rider, the Christ. Only when the powerful, swift thoroughbred is gentle, harmless and meek — reacting to all distractions and dangers with equanimity — will the Christ climb upon his back and direct him to his spiritual destiny.

As long as the thoroughbred retains any hypersensitive reaction to stress, crisis or unexpected dangers, he will not be a constant, faithful carrier of the Christ. This may be likened to the sound of a gunshot frightening a horse — and causing the alarmed animal to immediately run for safety. In the Holy War, many gun shots are being discharged and bombs are exploding during surprise attacks as well as other times of open confrontation with the enemy.

Horses used to carry cavalry riders must be trained to not panic at the sound of guns firing or bombs exploding; other-

wise they would run away, carrying their riders with them—
and the battle would be lost. Before a student can become a
spiritual leader, teacher or minister, he must be as carefully
trained as a cavalry horse to remain obedient to the rider, the
Christ, under any and all adverse conditions. Those who express gentleness, harmlessness and meekness will become the
chosen ones in the Holy War, carrying their Lord to His Victory over the Adversary.

The student who progresses from a wild, dangerous stallion to a disciplined, courageous, obedient thoroughbred is
ready for the Lord of Love to become his rider. When the
Christ sees that the time has come to mount the gentle steed,
the Teacher wipes a tear of joy from his eyes, for his work
with the God-sent student has been accomplished—and the
New-Era Dharma will be preserved for another generation!

A devotee on the Path should expect the unexpected. He
should not permit any thing or any one to take him from the
course his soul has chosen. If he is "wise as a serpent," he will
know how to meet each and every crisis or surprise with
equanimity and wisdom; and if he is "harmless as a dove,"
his gentleness and love will keep him in direct communion
with the Guiding Spirit.

Whenever a crisis comes or a stressful situation presents itself, a devotee of the Lord should immediately enter into the
same attitude expressed during the peace and quiet of Sacramental Meditation. God will speak to him through the Still-
ness and provide him with the necessary guidance, wisdom
and inspiration. If he forgets this communion with the Inner
Silence during crisis times, his hundreds or thousands of
meditations in the past would have been for naught.

*To any crisis, react with love; react with wisdom;
react with calm; react with faith in God—and you
will be a true disciple of Jesus. When they stone*

you, you will not cry. When they persecute you, you will not complain. And when they crucify you, you will accept with the same meekness and forgiveness of Jesus of Nazareth.

If you would walk the Path of Jesus, emulate the example of His courage—and you will remain always at one with the Omnipresent Spirit of the Living God.

MAJOR TESTING TIMES: SUMMATION

Each test, when passed, unites a devotee with an increase of Redemption Grace through his Spiritual-Birthright Inheritance.

The Christ and the Antichrist are fighting for the soul of each person on the Path. The Christ is seeking to bless the student with the Grace-Gifts of the Soul through the Inheritance. The Antichrist is seeking to corrupt the soul of the aspirant and to block his receiving of the Inheritance.

I. APPLICATION. The first test on the Path is passed when one applies the knowledge of Scriptural Commandments, Principles and Ethics; he also applies the instruction received from his Living Teacher. Satan, the tester, is successful if he is able to close a student's ears to sacred instruction and to harden his heart toward the Principle of Vows.

II. SELF-HONESTY AND THE CONSCIENCE. The birth of Self-Honesty and the Conscience is an extremely painful period if one has committed numerous transgressions against the Ten Commandments, the Law of Tithing and the Ethics of Jesus. At this time, Satan will seek to bury the penitent in the avalanche of his exposed sin-debts; the choicest victims of the Antichrist are those who continue to wallow in their guilts. Devotees who are alert to this testing time of their faith, place themselves *totally* in the Mercy of God and the Redemption Power of Christ Jesus. The high State of Inheritance Grace attained through the birth of Self-Honesty and the Conscience increases through the Cycles of the Moon, the Sun and the Planets as long as one remembers to "sin no more." (St. John 5:14)

III. GENIUS GRACE. Devotees who survive the birth of Self-Honesty and Conscience receive the Genius Grace earned in previous lives. This portion of the Inheritance through the Redemption Power of Jesus should be used to glorify God; however, if Genius Grace is accompanied by egotism and pride, Satan will have an easy time removing him from the Path. Such persons will be unable to work with their co-disciples or their Teacher because of the egotism, pride and feelings of superiority that discolor their Genius Grace *redeemed* from past lives.

Humility, modesty, selflessness and love are one's only protections from falling into Satan's snares. These beautiful virtues keep him in the Harmony Flow of Soul Grace and Divine Grace received through the Inheritance.

Patience, compassion, empathy and pure love protect one from judging and criticizing his fellow disciples who are experiencing the first stages of breaking free from ancestral-sin debts and past-lives' sin-debts. The moment one forgets to be patient, merciful and loving, he has opened the door for Satan to begin to drive him from the Path.

IV. SENSE-DISTRACTIONS AND SENSE-INDULGENCES. The senses become soul-faculties through the purgings and virtue-quickenings of the Great Physician. The illumination of the heart and the mind begins with the purification of the senses. Satan is constantly seeking to take control of one's will through sense-distractions and sense-indulgences. The lives of many aspirants do not revolve around their love for God; their love revolves around their houses, possessions, pleasures and comforts. Through these and other sense-indulgences, they are blocked by the Antichrist from receiving their Spiritual-Birthright Inheritance.

V. TELEPATHIC SENSITIVITY. Telepathic Sensitivity results from the transenergization of insensitivities and hypersensitivities into love and compassion. Through Telepathic Sensitivity, one becomes a spiritual leader authorized by Heaven, for he is ever receptive to Divine Guidance and Sacred Realizations through the Holy Spirit. Telepathic Sensitivity makes of one an appointed disciple of Jesus blessed with Apostolic Gifts and the Christ-Mind Crown of Illumination Grace. This precious Grace manifesting through the Redemption Power of Jesus opens high degrees of the Inheritance.

Many devotees yield to Satan due to their hypersensitivities that are *not* clothed in the energies of the Love-Commandments. Without the Insulation of Love, their sensitivities gained through prayer, meditation and fasting become their downfall, for Satan cunningly transforms their hypersensitivities into hurt feelings and the inability to work harmoniously with co-disciples and their Living Teacher. Their fall from Grace assured, the tester looks for other nonvigilant devotees who are failing to clothe their sensitivities in the protective energies of the Love-Commandments.

VI. PURE MOTIVES. Once the Soul-Gifts and other Dimensional Gifts open to a devotee through the Inheritance, he is constantly tested in his ethical, selfless and honorable use of these Gifts in service to God and his fellow man.

Satan tried to entice Jesus into misusing His Miracle Gifts. When Jesus refused to change stones into bread or to become an all-powerful king through obeisance to Satan, He gave the example for all true initiates to follow. Pure motives are one's only protection during each subtle and quick trial by the tester. With each test passed, his Inheritance from God increases through the Redemption Power of Jesus.

Those who misuse or exploit their Soul-Gifts and Spiritual Powers experience the greatest falls from Grace. To the pure in heart, the Spirit of God keeps open the door to the Three Heavens.

Blessed are the pure in heart, for they are the few who become the anointed servants of the Living God.

26

THE ANOINTED TEACHER

It is a true Teacher who holds forth the Image of God to the disciple as a blueprint for the spiritual life.

— Ann Ree Colton

THE PERPETUATION OF THE DHARMA

Blessed is he that cometh in the name of the Lord.

— Psalm 118:26

Approach a teacher with humility and with a desire to serve.

— Upanishads

In Sanskrit, the word *Dharma* means Truth, Religion, Law, Virtue. A Teacher *anointed* by God's Spirit is dedicated to the perpetuation of the wisdom-treasures of the Dharma. The Teacher has earned the Anointing because he has proved his loyalty to God as a faithful devotee on the Path of Devotion. *"But the anointing which ye have received of him abideth in you, and ye need not that any man teach you: but as the same anointing teacheth you of all things, and is truth, and is no lie, and even as it hath taught you, ye shall abide in him.* (1 John 2:27)

The Dharma relates to all pure religious principles and

448

sacred truths sealed into the world by enlightened Teachers and Saints of the East and the West.

All true religions represent the Dharma. All persons who worship God through prayer, meditation, fasting and alms-giving are keeping alive these ages-old devotional disciplines, as well as preserving the moral values, ethics, and knowl-edge of Holy Laws inherited from former generations of worshippers.

An Anointed Teacher synthesizes and synchronizes the Im-mortal and Eternal Wisdom-Truths of the East and the West. A pure spiritual teaching in modern times is a distil-lation of all sacred Scriptural Truths of the Past and an in-troduction to new Archetypal Truths gracing the world through the Mediation of the Lord Jesus.

"Give, and it shall be given unto you; good measure, pressed down, and shaken together and running over, shall men give into your bosom." (St. Luke 6:38) God provides bountiful provisions for individuals and marriages dedicated to the perpetuation of the Dharma. In preserving the Dharma, one becomes a co-creator with God.

When one works each day to preserve the Dharma, he draws forth his supply from the greatest Source of Provision in the Universe — the Providence of God. The Providence of God, providing the energies for all Stars and Galaxies, is a never-ending Source of Provision. To be supported by the Providence of God is to be in a perpetual state of Divine Grace.

"Thou shalt love the Lord thy God with all thy heart, and with all thy soul, and with all thy mind." (St. Matthew 22:37) Meditation and prayer are prospered when the heart, mind and soul love God and are devoted to the perpetuation of His Word.

"And every one that hath forsaken houses, or brethren, or sisters, or father, or mother, or wife, or children, or lands, for my name's sake, shall receive an hundredfold, and shall inherit everlasting life." (St. Matthew 10:39) When the Dhar-

ma is more important to a devotee than his life, possessions and family, he is ready to serve God and Jesus with a whole-hearted, fearless love. His loyalty and devotion to the Will of God will earn for him the priceless gift of the *Anointing*.

When a servant of God covenants to perpetuate the Dharma in the world, his "daily bread" and all other physical, emotional, mental and spiritual needs are provided by the Providence of God. The more one serves God's Altar in the spirit of love, faith and sacrifice, the more all of his needs are met. *"Your Father knoweth what things ye have need of, before ye ask him."* (St. Matthew 6:8)

The greatest joy is to preserve the wisdom of the Sages, Saints and Great Teachers of the East and the West. This wisdom within the Dharma lives from generation to generation through the efforts of those who love God and His Creation.

The Dharma is wherever the Spirit of God is.

The Dharma is the Eternal Truth. It is the Word of God— the Word sounding throughout all seen and unseen Universes and Kingdoms.

The Dharma is pure and perfect Religion. All Scriptures contain sacred knowledge that lifts man from darkness to divinity.

The Dharma is Virtue. Wherever Virtue is revered, Treasures of Grace pour forth from the Godhead.

The Dharma is Law. All Decrees, Statutes, Directives, Laws and Commandments manifesting through the Mind and Will of God are man's bridge to Liberation and Illumination.

The Dharma is a Diamond-Light filling the Universe. He who serves the Spirit of God is rich with the priceless energies of the Diamond of the Dharma.

Who can understand the Miraculous Law of Provision? Only he who serves the Living God and His Holy Dharma.

I pray to flow with the Mighty Tide of the New-Era Dharma under Christ. God provides bountifully for those who love Him and perpetuate the Sacred Truths of the East and the West.

The preservation of the Dharma is a twenty-four-hours-a-day vigil for the Teacher. Students who retain the dangerous traits of egotism, ambition, temperament problems, unforgiveness and hypersensitivities pose a continuous threat to the perpetuation of the Dharma, for they are behaving in ways diametrically opposed to Jesus' teachings of humility, meekness, forgiveness, selflessness and love.

A Teacher of the Dharma may be likened to the conductor of an orchestra; his students are as the musicians. In modern times, many students often absent themselves from classes of instruction and do not comply with the basic Scriptural Commandments. A number of students are chronically unpunctual, and therefore out of timing with the Cyclic Flows of Divine Grace. Some students are fighting and arguing with each other, expressing angers and tantrums. From this grouping of permissive, disobedient, unpunctual, inattentive, lazy and temperamental "students," the Teacher is being asked by God to create a disciplined orchestra able to play the sweet melodies and soaring symphonies of Devotion.

All students experience a probationary period of grace. Those faithful few who prove worthy in God's sight are selected by the Christ to play in His mighty Orchestra of Disciplined Apostles. *"Many be called, but few chosen."* (St. Matthew 20:16)

When the pupil is ready, the Guardian Angel sends a Teacher representing the Christ.
The greatest enemies or foes against receiving one's Teacher are intellect, egotism, inertia.
—Ann Ree Colton

If you have deep love for the Lord of Love,
And for your Teacher,
The light of this teaching
Will shine in your heart.
It will shine indeed!

— Upanishads

Students who represent the greatest dangers to the Dharma are the immoral, the procrastinators, the unpunctual and the anger-prone. The immoral will turn any ministry into a sexually-permissive environment. The Teacher protects against Satan destroying the integrity of a ministry through immoral persons when he continues to teach the Morality Commandments as God's Will and Way.

Procrastinators will not work with the Timing-Flows of the Christ through a ministry dedicated to Him. Such students cannot keep pace with the other students, nor can they be depended upon to fulfill important assignments or tasks, thereby jeopardizing the Dharma. Procrastinators are in energy-jails of their own making and draw others into these jails with them if given the opportunity. Procrastinators have no sense of honor and no desire to comply with God or a Living Teacher.

The unpunctual are out of timing and would draw others out of timing. To be out of timing is a sin. To cause others to be out of timing is a greater sin.

Anger-prone students are extremely dangerous in a ministry, for their lack of self-control exposes them to Satan's commands.

Students who express anger, egotism, pride, jealousy and selfishness are Judas-like betrayers in their ministries. The sheep and the lambs—the meek and the selfless—are the builders and the preservers of the Dharma.

Sincere students are healed of their negative traits when they apply the sound doctrine of Jesus' Teachings and continually ask for His supernatural help. The Miracles of Jesus have been, are, and always shall be. To be healed by Jesus is to become His spokesman in a world filled with immoral persons, procrastinators, the unpunctual and the anger-prone.

> *Behold, I send you forth as sheep in the midst of wolves: be ye therefore wise as serpents, and harmless as doves.*
>
> —St. Matthew 10:16

> *Defective persons are born from having defected from God's processes of Law. They are soul defectives and must be re-envisioned by a Teacher who beholds the Image of God behind the screen or mask of defection.*
>
> —Ann Ree Colton

It is extremely difficult for any student to remain near a Teacher of the Dharma. This is due to the powerful Light and Truth of God and Christ that fill an Anointed Teacher. The Holy Light and Truth working through a Teacher constantly expose a student's faults, wrong attitudes and self-deceptions. The Truth is a Sacred Fire that burns the unrighteous and illuminates the righteous.

A Teacher of Truth is as a midwife helping sincere devotees give birth to virtues, conscience and spiritual gifts. Students who qualify for the receiving of the Divine-Marriage Anointing become the guardians of the ancient and new Dharma.

God knows the hearts of His anointed ones and keeps them filled with His Holy Spirit. In this, the Dharma is not only protected and preserved by His elect servants, but it is prospered by the Revelation Grace received through their communion with His Kingdom.

> *Christlike Teachers are often unheard and unseen by the spiritually ignorant; and even in the presence of the*

calloused beginner on the Path the signals, signs and tokens of what makes or represents a Teacher are ignored or obscured. Teachers of the Path in Heaven are many; Teachers in Earth on the Path as lamps for the ready are few. "The harvest truly is plenteous, but the labourers are few." (St. Matthew 9:37)

All Teachers are fortified against the stone-throwing of treacherous would-be disciples. They are insulated, for they are God-related directly to the Guidance of God.

— Ann Ree Colton

The Holy War is not a frivolous game; it is a dangerous encounter with evil. The moment a devotee removes his hand from the Hand of Jesus, he exposes himself to the Antichrist, who is seeking *"to destroy both body and soul in hell."* (St. Matthew 10:28) The only way one keeps his hand in the Hand of Jesus is through love, devotion and the diligent application of Scriptural Ethics and Principles.

The Inquisition has never stopped. From the time of Jesus' persecution and martyrdom, millions of His followers have continued to experience persecution and martyrdom at the hands of Judas-like persons in bondage to the inquisitorial spirit and its judging, criticizing and condemning of the righteous.

Some students come to a Teacher with a pink rose in one hand and a cup in the other. The pink rose is one's devotion to God; the cup symbolizes his teachableness — and the Teacher fills his cup with sacred instruction. Some students deliberately turn their cup over and refuse to receive instruction.

Beware of the unteachable ones.

— Ann Ree Colton

Other students come with a cup in one hand and a dagger in the other hand. The dagger symbolizes the critical mind. Such students continually stab their Teacher with the poisoned dagger of incessant criticisms. In this, they are crucifying the Teacher and the One in whose Name he teaches, Christ Jesus. Even while he is being stabbed by the sharp criticisms of disrespectful students, the Teacher continues to lovingly fill their cups with the sacred elixirs of holy instruction. *"Father, forgive them; for they know not what they do."* (St. Luke 23:34)

A probationer who continues to express anger, hate, jealousy, unforgiveness, covetousness, critical-mindedness, fault-finding, meanness or malice is adding darkness to his soul's record rather than increasing the light of virtues.

Individuals who persecuted the Saints and other righteous souls in past lives may be tempted to express the same inquisitorial attitudes in their present lives. If they are in a religious or spiritual teaching, persons with soul-records of persecuting the Saints and the righteous are extremely dangerous to the well-being and the life of their Teacher, for they may yield to the compulsion to judge, criticize and persecute the Teacher rather than receive him as an anointed servant of God.

Students who become the antagonists of their Teacher are in bondage to *the spirit of inquisition*. The more the Teacher is criticized and persecuted by students with the inquisitor-consciousness, the more God places His Spirit upon the Teacher. Each time the Teacher turns "the other cheek" after being attacked verbally by a student or any other person, he is rewarded bountifully with precious realizations and soul-powers.

> *Jesus was sent in Judas an artist with the artistry of the black master. Satan uses those having the subtle, insinuative, innuendo cultures. These innuendo cultures are satanic samskara-tendencies which are used by the arts of inquisition: to torture, to humiliate, and to distort by lies and insinuations the truth of the prophets.*
> — Ann Ree Colton

A student who constantly questions the integrity of an Anointed Teacher is an inquisitor who is seeking to cast down the Teacher from his hard-earned position of oneness with God. The inquisitor-student is a protégé of Judas.

Inquisitor-students are offending great Laws of the Dharma, for their destructive thoughts, feelings and emotions are used by satanic spirits in their attacks against the Teacher. If these attacks prove harmful to the health and well-being of the Teacher, or fatal, the inquisitor-students will have been used by Satan to shorten the life or to end the life of a servant of God dedicated to the perpetuation of the Dharma. Such students stain their souls' records with blood guilt, as did the inquisitors of old.

Saul, who later became Saint Paul, was an inquisitor before he experienced his conversion through the visitation of Jesus on the road to Damascus. *"Saul, Saul, why persecutest thou me?"* (Acts 9:4) Certain students follow the course of Paul by first persecuting their Teacher, then repenting and becoming true disciples of Jesus.

Anger crucifies. If an aspirant of the higher life expresses anger toward his mate, child or co-disciple, he is crucifying Jesus and he is crucifying his Teacher.

If an adolescent with moral parents lives a wild life filled with alcohol, drugs and immorality, he crucifies his parents. So does a devotee crucify his Teacher and Jesus whenever he expresses anger, immorality and selfishness. Jealousy, pettiness, procrastination and stubbornness expressed by students also contain dark-spirit energies that crucify one's Teacher and the Lord Christ Jesus in whose Name the Teacher teaches. *"Inasmuch as ye have done it unto one of the least of these my brethren, ye have done it unto me."* (St. Matthew 25:40)

Heavenly Father, I pray for all Enlightened and Anointed Teachers in the world who are being judged, criticized, persecuted and crucified by the lower natures of their students. May the

Christ place His Miraculous Light in all ministries devoted to the preservation of Thy Word
and Altar. In Jesus' Name. Amen.

WHERE ARE THE SHEEP?

*My sheep hear my voice, and I know them, and
they follow me.*
— St. John 10:27

Where are the sheep? Where are the lambs? Among the
modern-day followers of Jesus are numerous goats, wolves
and snakes. But where are the sheep, the lambs, the harmless ones?

The goat-followers are in bondage to laziness, stubbornness, procrastination, and refuse to comply with sacred instruction.

The wolves are the anger-prone with the tantrum-consciousness, the egotistical, the prideful.

The snakes are ever-ready to place their poisonous fangs
into their Teacher, fellow disciples and loved ones with each
easily-triggered sensitivity.

Where are Thy sheep, Jesus? Where are Thy lambs, Thy
doves?

Where are the pure in heart, the harmless, the forgiving,
the selfless, the loving, the giving of their all to God?

*That which leads the sheep must be harmless, in
a state of Ahimsa; never varying in love of God;
seeing God in all persons.*
— Ann Ree Colton

INDEX

Inclusive of Quotation References

A

abortion(s)   4, 363–365, 423

absolution   149, 151, 157, 182–184, 203, 363

acceptance   53, 59, 388

addiction(s)   4, 51, 94, 139, 140, 187, 345, 358, 393, 401

adultery   47, 138, 166, 333, 358, 362, 401, 423

Agape   45, 310

agnosticism   143, 358, 362

alcohol(ism)   331, 345, 358, 401, 418, 421, 456

Altar, Family (See *Family Altar*)

Altar(s) of God   125, 145, 168, 171, 172, 179, 180, 182, 198, 208, 253, 277, 287, 331, 372, 376, 377, 384, 434, 450, 457

ancestors   6, 22, 46, 137, 166, 178, 181, 193, 278, 288, 294, 296, 297, 300, 332, 333, 348, 350, 353, 356, 358–365, 373, 375, 382, 408, 421, 422, 425–431, 435

ancestral genes   166, 180–182, 293–297, 306, 310, 329, 332, 333, 335, 354, 355, 358, 398, 422

Ancestral Grace   110, 157, 159, 352, 426

Ancestral Image   146, 293, 294, 348

Ancestral-Sin Core   48, 417, 428, 431

Angels   29, 56, 57, 86, 140, 156, 169, 170, 177, 186, 196, 198, 208, 226, 281, 301, 347, 384, 404, 439

Cherubim   89, 90, 92

anger(s)   19, 20, 23, 34, 38, 46, 50–53, 143, 154, 166, 188, 215, 246, 247, 253, 260, 279, 288, 294, 295, 310, 324, 333, 335, 353, 354, 358, 359, 369, 377, 379, 393, 414–416, 422, 426, 436–438, 452, 453, 455, 456

animals   56, 57

459

OTHER BOOKS BY JONATHAN MURRO

THE PATH OF VIRTUE
A comprehensive book that describes the classic route to union with God traveled by all Great Souls of the East and the West.

GOD-REALIZATION JOURNAL
A book opening a new world of understanding related to the Presence of God. *God-Realization Journal* also describes the author's initiatory transition from a devotee to a teacher of the higher life.

BOOKS CO-AUTHORED
BY ANN REE COLTON AND JONATHAN MURRO

PROPHET FOR THE ARCHANGELS
The Life Story of Ann Ree Colton.

THE PELICAN AND THE CHELA
The Teacher-Student relationship in the spiritual life.

GALAXY GATE I: THE HOLY UNIVERSE
A remarkable book of spiritual revelations about Man, the Solar System and the Cosmos.

GALAXY GATE II: THE ANGEL KINGDOM
A book filled with enlightening insights into the World of Holy Mediators between God and mankind.

OWE NO MAN
Scriptural Principles of Good Stewardship and Divine Providence.

THE ANOINTED
Sacred Keys to Healing, Exorcism and the Divine Marriage.

BOOKS BY ANN REE COLTON

THE ARCHETYPAL KINGDOM
The dawning of a new Era of Understanding and Creation.

THE THIRD MUSIC
A powerful book describing the energy-worlds of the Mind, the Soul and the Universe.

KUNDALINI WEST
Knowledge of the Kundalini and the Chakras for the Western initiate.

477

WATCH YOUR DREAMS
An invaluable and necessary book revealing the soul-codes in dreams and their symbols.

ETHICAL ESP
An important book defining the difference between lower and higher ESP.

THE JESUS STORY
A miracle book in timing to the need for miracles.

THE HUMAN SPIRIT
A scientific, spiritual, and healing book on the creation, purpose and destiny of man.

THE SOUL AND THE ETHIC
A profound book on the soul and on the ethical use of soul-power.

THE KING
From the personal, hieroglyphic journal of Ann Ree Colton.

DRAUGHTS OF REMEMBRANCE
An extraordinary book on the subject of reincarnation.

MEN IN WHITE APPAREL
A book of vital revelations about death and the life after death.

THE VENERABLE ONE
An initiatory book for those who love Nature and who would unveil Nature's secrets.

VISION FOR THE FUTURE
A prophetic book to comfort men in a perilous time.

THE LIVELY ORACLES
A prophetic book on world events.

ISLANDS OF LIGHT
A book of initiation with an underlying prophetic theme.

PRECEPTS FOR THE YOUNG
Appreciated by the adult . . . inspiring to the child . . . beneficial to the family.

ANN REE COLTON FOUNDATION

Post Office Box 2057   Glendale, California 91209